ON THE SOCIAL ORIGINS
OF MEDIEVAL INSTITUTIONS

THE
MEDIEVAL MEDITERRANEAN

PEOPLES, ECONOMIES AND CULTURES, 400-1453

EDITORS

MICHAEL WHITBY (Warwick)
PAUL MAGDALINO, HUGH KENNEDY (St. Andrews)
DAVID ABULAFIA (Cambridge)
BENJAMIN ARBEL (Tel Aviv)
MARK MEYERSON (Notre Dame)

VOLUME 19

Joseph F. O'Callaghan

ON THE SOCIAL ORIGINS
OF MEDIEVAL INSTITUTIONS

Essays in Honor of Joseph F. O'Callaghan

EDITED BY

DONALD J. KAGAY

AND

THERESA M. VANN

BRILL
LEIDEN · BOSTON · KÖLN
1998

This book is printed on acid-free paper.

Library of Congress Cataloging-in-Publication Data

On the social origins of medieval institutions : essays in honor of
Joseph F. O'Callaghan / edited by Donald J. Kagay and Theresa M.
Vann.
    p.   cm. — (The medieval Mediterranean, ISSN 0928–5520 ; v.
19)
    Includes bibliographical references and index.
    ISBN 9004110968 (cloth : alk. paper)
    1. Spain—History—711-1516.   I. O'Callaghan, Joseph F.
II. Kagay, Donald J.   III. Vann, Theresa M.   IV. Series.
DP99.06   1998
946'.02—dc21   98–35744
                                                                          CIP

Die Deutsche Bibliothek – CIP-Einheitsaufnahme

On the social origins of medieval institutions : essays in honor
of Joseph F. O'Callaghan / ed. by Donald J. Kagay and Theresa M.
Vann – Leiden ; Boston ; Köln : Brill, 1998
    (The medieval Mediterranean : Vol. 19)
    ISBN 90–04–11096–8

ISSN   0928-5520
ISBN   90 04 11096 8

PRINTED IN THE NETHERLANDS

CONTENTS

The Relationship Between Government and War

LIST OF ILLUSTRATIONS

Figures

Frontispiece: Joseph F. O'Callaghan

Illustrations 1–11 can be found between pages 200 and 201 in the essay "The Hybrid Trebuchet: The Halfway Step to the Counterweight Trebuchet" by Paul E. Chevedden.

1. The city of Naples, defended by Richard, count of Acerra, is besieged by King Henry VI of Germany in 1191. Henry's army bombards the city with stone-shot launched from a pole-framed traction trebuchet. The machine is operated by a pulling-crew of eight knights and a "shooter" holding the sling. The defenders prepare to launch stone-shot from a similar machine mounted on a tower. Peter of Eboli, *Liber ad honorem Augusti*. Bern, Burgerbibliothek, MS 120, fol. 109r.

2. A hinged counterweight trebuchet from *Bellifortis*, a treatise by Conrad Kyeser of Eichstät, which was left incomplete at his death in 1405. The main beam, counterweight box, sling, projectile, windlass and framework are all clearly visible. The machine has some of its dimensions numbered; the long arm of the beam is forty-six feet, and the short arm eight. The prong at the end of the long arm, which is essential for the release of the sling, is not depicted. Instead, both cords of the sling are incorrectly shown as attached to a ring at the extremity of the long arm. This massive machine used a simple peg-and-hole catch-and-trigger device to retain and release the beam. A hole is drilled in the base of one of the machine's triangular trestles, shown in the foreground, for the insertion of the peg. A restraining rope, attached to the base of the other triangular trestle, is drawn over the long arm of the beam at a point just above the windlass and is looped over the bottom end of the peg. When the peg is lifted out of its socket, the looped end is released, and the beam flies free. Trebuchet beams were often banded circumferentially with iron (as shown in the illustration), or lashed with rope, to help withstand splitting. This type of machine was identified in Arabic historical

sources as the Western Islamic trebuchet (*manjanīq maghribī*). Göttingen, Niedersächsische Staats- und Universtätsbibliothek, Cod. MS philos. 63, fol. 30r.

3. A pole-framed hybrid trebuchet with a fixed counterweight bombarding a fortification. It is operated by a single man. From *Avis aus Roys*, an anonymous manual of instruction for kings and princes written and illuminated in France (probably Paris) about the middle of the fourteenth century. New York, The Pierpont Morgan Library, MS M. 456, fol. 127r.

4. Muslim siege of Constantinople as depicted in the *Cantigas de Santa Maria* (c. 1280).
Figures 4 and 5 form a narrative sequence. This illustration shows a trebuchet (foreground L.) in the process of assembly. Its rotating beam with a fixed counterweight is being mounted on the trestle frame of the machine. The chief engineer is guiding the axle bearings of the rotating beam onto the journal blocks surmounting the two trestles. Behind the counterweight trebuchet is a "hand-trebuchet" operated by a single man. This traction machine consists of a forked beam, pivoted on a horizontal axis that is supported by a single-pole frame. The pulling rope, attached to the frame of the machine, passes around a pulley affixed to the forked end of the beam, giving the puller a mechanical advantage. *Cantigas de Santa Maria*, 28c. Escorial, MS T.I.1, fol. 43r.

5. Muslim siege of Constantinople as depicted in the *Cantigas de Santa Maria* (c. 1280). A trestle-framed counterweight trebuchet (foreground L.) is being prepared for discharge while massed crossbowmen are about to unleash a barrage of bolts to clear the battlements of defenders. Under a mantlet, sappers, wearing close-fitting *cervellières* and scale cuirasses, dislodge stones from the city wall. The tent encampment (shown above the trebuchet as a form of perspective) has "behind" it heavy armored cavalry in European-style equipment, led by two Muslim commanders in turbans. Mary intervenes in the siege and uses her mantle, held by two saints and two angels, to protect the city from bombardment. Protective screens, suspended from the battlements of city walls and castles, were widely used in the pre-gunpowder era throughout Eurasia and North Africa to shield fortifications from bombardment. *Cantigas de Santa Maria*, 28d. Escorial, MS T.I.1, fol. 43r.

6. A trestle-framed counterweight trebuchet having a fixed and a hinged counterweight. In front of the trebuchet is a cat-castle (*chat-chastel*), a combination of "cat" or mantlet (here equipped with a ram) and a "castle" or mobile siege-tower. From Paolo Santini's *Tractatus*, 1470–1475. Paris, Bibliothèque Nationale, Codex Latinus 7239, fol. 109r.

7. *Center*: The Chinese pole-framed trebuchet called a "Whirlwind" (*hsüan-kêng*) machine because it could be turned to face any direction. According to the Chinese military treatise *Wu Ching Tsung Yao* ("Collection of the Most Important Military Techniques"), completed in 1044, this trebuchet had a beam of 5.5 m in length mounted on top of a pole-frame that stood 5.2 m in height. Attached to the butt-end of the beam were forty pulling ropes hauled down by a crew of fifty men. The machine could throw a stone-shot weighing 1.8 kg a distance of more than 77 m. *Left*: The Chinese "hand-trebuchet," operated by a single man. A pole, fixed in the ground, carried a pin at its topmost extremity that acted as a fulcrum for the arm of the machine. Tsêng Kung-Liang, ed., *Wu Ching Tsung Yao* (*Chhien Chi*), ch. 12, p. 50a.

8. The Chinese "four-footed," or trestle-framed, trebuchet with a composite beam of 8.6 m made up of seven wooden (or perhaps bamboo) spars lashed together with rope or bound with metal bands. The beam was mounted on a trestle frame that rose to a height of 6.5 m. The butt-end of the beam had 125 pulling ropes attached to it that a crew of 250 men hauled down. This machine could throw a stone-shot weighing between 53.7 and 59.7 kg a distance of more than 77 m. Tsêng Kung-Liang, ed., *Wu Ching Tsung Yao* (*Chhien Chi*), ch. 12, p. 48a.

9. The single pole-framed traction trebuchet (*manjanīq ʿarrādah*), illustrated in Ibn Urunbughā al-Zaradkāsh's *Kitāb anīq fī al-manājanīq* (867/1462–1463). A small counterweight is fixed to the butt-end of the rotating beam of this machine to enhance its power. Istanbul, Topkapı Sarayı Müzesi Kütüphanesi, Ahmet III Collection, MS 3469/1, *Kitāb anīq fī al-manājanīq*, fol. 44r.

10. Detail of a stone fragment with a relief carving on its outer face depicting a siege. This fragment, mounted on a wall in the Church of Saint-Nazaire in Carcassonne, France, dates from the early thirteenth

century. Some scholars believe it depicts the siege of Toulouse in 1218 during which a stone-shot hurled from a trestle-framed treb-uchet killed Simon de Montfort. The relief carving shows a trestle-framed traction machine being prepared for discharge. Pulling ropes are attached to six rings affixed to the butt-end of the beam, and a six-member pulling-crew is set to launch a rounded stone-shot that the operator of the machine is placing in the pouch of the sling. This trebuchet has a curved axle, a feature that it shares with the pole-framed traction trebuchet illustrated in Ibn Urunbughā al-Zaradkāsh's *Kitāb anīq fī al-manājanīq* shown in Figure 8.

11. A trestle-framed traction trebuchet as it is about to discharge a stone-shot from its sling. The pulling crew—obscured by knights charging in the foreground—is hauling down the ropes attached to the butt-end of the beam. The traction power of the pulling-crew swings the throwing arm of the beam upward, sending the operator of the machine aloft. By holding on to the sling for a moment and then releasing it, the operator increases the efficiency of the machine by utilizing the force generated by the flexion of the beam. From the "Maciejowski Bible" produced in Paris around 1250. New York, The Pierpont Morgan Library, MS M.638, fol. 23v.

Map (p. xxiv)

1. Medieval Spain

LIST OF CONTRIBUTORS

Nicholas Agrait
  Fordham University

James W. Brodman
  University of Central Arkansas

James A. Brundage
  University of Kansas

Robert I. Burns, S.J.
  University of California Los Angeles

Paul E. Chevedden
  Virginia Military Institute

Steven Isaac
  Louisiana State University

Donald J. Kagay
  Albany State University

Lawrence J. McCrank
  ITT Technical Institute

Nina Melechen
  Fordham University

Paulette L. Pepin
  University of New Haven

William D. Phillips Jr.
  University of Minnesota

Teofilo F. Ruiz
  Brooklyn College

Jean A. Truax
  University of Houston

Theresa M. Vann
  Hill Monastic Manuscript Library, St. John's University

ACKNOWLEDGMENTS

On September 8–11, 1994, the students and colleagues of Joseph F. O'Callaghan presented a colloquium during the annual meeting of the Texas Medieval Association to commemorate his forty years of service at Fordham University. Most of the essays included in this volume were initially presented at the colloquium. Joseph O'Callaghan's friends and colleagues presented a pre-publication copy of the collected essays to him on January 4, 1997, during a reception at the Spanish Institute in New York City.

The editors would like to thank the individuals and organizations that helped with the colloquium and the subsequent volume: Anne Mannion, Anne O'Callaghan, Catherine O'Callaghan, Louis Pascoe S.J., Robert Himmelberg, Teo Ruiz, Robert I. Burns S.J., the Texas Medieval Association, the Hill Monastic Manuscript Library, the American Academy of Research Historians of Medieval Spain, Fordham University, and the Spanish Institute. We also thank Julian Deahl of E.J. Brill for his help and patience.

ABBREVIATIONS

A pobreza ...	*A pobreza e a assistencia aos pobres na peninsula Ibérica durante a Idade Media. Actas das Ias jornadas luso-espanholas de historia medieval*, 2 vols. (Lisbon, 1973)
ACA	Archivo de Corona de Aragón, Barcelona
ACB	Archivo de la Catedral de Burgos
ACT	Archivo de la Catedral de Toledo
AEM	*Anuario de Estudios Medievales*
AHN	Archivo Historico Naciónal, Madrid
ASC	*Anglo-Saxon Chronicle*
BAE	*Biblioteca de Autores Españoles*
BCT	Biblioteca del Cabildo de Toledo
BH	*Bulletin Hispanique*
BRAH	*Boletín de la Real Academia de la Historia*
CAVC	*Colección de las Cortes de los antiguos reinos de Aragón y de Valencia y el principado de Cataluña*, eds. Fidel Fita y Colomé and Bienvenido Oliver y Esteller, 27 vols. (Madrid, 1806–1922)
CDACA	*Colección de documentos inéditos del Archivo General de la Corona de Aragón*, ed. Prospero de Bofarull y Moscaró, 42 vols. (Barcelona, 1850–1856)
CFIV	Antonio Benavides, ed., *Memorias de Fernando IV de Castilla, Crónica del rey don Fernando IV*, 2 vols. (Madrid, 1860)
CHE	*Cuadernos de Historia de España*
CHR	*Catholic Historical Review*
Cortes	*Cortes de los antiguos reinos de León y de Castilla*, ed. Real Academia de la Historia, 7 vols. (Madrid, 1861–1903)
CSCO	*Corpus Scriptorum Christianorum Orientalium*
Ar	*Scriptores Arabici*
Iber.	*Scriptores Iberici*
Scr. Syri	*Scriptores Syri*
EHR	*English Historical Review*
*EI*²	*Encyclopedia of Islam, New Edition*, eds. H.A.R. Gibb, J.H. Kramers, E. Lévi-Provençal, J. Schacht, et al., 9 vols. to date (Leiden, 1960–)

Ep	*Epistola*
ES	*España Sagrada*, ed. Henríque Flórez (Madrid, 1765)
GS	*Gesta Stephani*
HN	William of Malmesbury, *Historia novella* (London, 1955)
JL	Philip Jaffé, *Regesta pontificum romanorum* (AD 882–1198), 2nd ed., by S. Löwenfeld, 2 vols. (Leipzig, 1885–1888; reprint, 1956)
LF	Jaume I, *Llibre dels Feyts del Rei En Jaume*, ed. Joroi Bruguera, 2 vols. (Barcelona, 1991)
LFM	*Liber feuorum maior*, ed. Francisco Miguel Rosell, 2 vols. (Barcelona, 1945–1947)
MFIV	Benavides, *Colección diplomatíca*
MGH SS	*Monumenta Germaniae Historica. Scriptores*
OV	Oderic Vitalis, *The Ecclesiastical History*, ed. Marjorie Chibnall, 6 vols. (Oxford, 1969–1980)
PL	*Patrilogiae Latina Cursus Completus*, ed. J.P. Migne
RR	*Regesta Regum Anglo-Normanorum*
RS	*Rolls Series*

BIBLIOGRAPHY OF JOSEPH F. O'CALLAGHAN,
1958–1996

1958

"*Difiniciones* of the Order of Calatrava enacted by Abbot William II of Morimond, April 2, 1468." *Traditio* 14 (1958): 231–268.

1960

"The Affiliation of the Order of Calatrava with the Order of Cîteaux." *Analecta Sacri Ordinis Cisterciensis* 15 (1960): 3–59, 255–292.

1961

"The Earliest *Difiniciones* of the Order of Calatrava, 1304–1383." *Traditio* 17 (1961): 255–284.
"Don Pedro Girón, Master of the Order of Calatrava, 1445–1466." *Hispania* 21 (1961): 342–390.

1962

"Martin Pérez de Siones, Maestre de Salvatierre." *Hispania* 22 (1962): 163–170.
"The Foundation of the Order of Alcántara, 1176–1218." *CHR* 47 (1962): 471–486.

1963

"Sobre los orígenes de Calatrava la Nueva." *Hispania* 23 (1963): 494–504.

1966

Hermandades entre las Ordenes Militares de Calatrava y Santiago durante los reinados de Alfonso VIII y Fernando III de Castilla. Ciudad Real: Instituto de Estudios Manchegos, 1966.

1969

"The Beginnings of the Cortes of León-Castille." *AHR* 74 (1969): 1503–1537.
"Hermandades between the Military Orders of Calatrava and Santiago during the Castilian Reconquest, 1158–1252." *Speculum* 44 (1969): 609–618.

1971

Editor, *Studies in Medieval Cistercian History presented to Professor Jeremiah F. O'Sullivan.* Spencer, MA: Cistercian Publications, 1971.
"The Order of Calatrava and the Archbishops of Toledo, 1158–1245." in *Studies in Medieval Cistercian History presented to Professor Jeremiah F. O'Sullivan* (Spencer, MA: Cistercian Publications, 1971), 63–87.
"The Cortes and Royal Taxation during the Reign of Alfonso X of Castile." *Traditio* 27 (1971): 379–398.

1972

"Las definiciones medievales de la Orden de Montesa, 1325–1468." *Miscelánea de Textos Medievales* 1 (1972): 213–251.

1974

Translator. *The Autobiography of St. Ignatius de Loyola,* ed. John C. Olin. New York: Harper & Row, 1974. Reprint, New York: Fordham University Press, 1992.

1975

The Spanish Military Order of Calatrava and its Affiliates. London: Variorum Press, 1975.
A History of Medieval Spain. Ithaca, NY: Cornell University Press, 1975.

1980

"The Masters of Calatrava and the Castilian Civil War, 1350–1389." in *Die geistlichen Ritterorden Europas,* eds. Josef Fleckenstein and Manfred Hellmann (Sigmaringen: Jan Thorbecke, 1980), 353–374.

1981

"The Ecclesiastical Estate in the Cortes of León-Castile, 1252–1350." *CHR* 67 (1981): 185–231.

1983

"Don Fernan Pérez, un Maestre desconocido de la Orden de Calatrava, 1234–1235." *Hispania* 43 (1983): 433–439.
"Una Nota sobre las llamadas Cortes de Benavente." *Archivos Leoneses* 37 (1983): 97–100.

1985

"Paths to Ruin: The Economic and Financial Policies of Alfonso the Learned." *The Worlds of Alfonso the Learned and James the Conqueror*, ed. Robert I. Burns, S.J. (Princeton: Princeton University Press, 1985), 41–67.
Spanish translation: "Senderos de ruina: La política económica y financiera de Alfonso el Sabio," *Los mundos de Alfonso el Sabio y Jaime el Conquistador*, ed. Robert I. Burns (Madrid, 1990).
"Sobre la promulgación del Espéculo y del Fuero Real." *Estudios en homenaje a Don Claudio Sánchez Albornoz en sus 90 años*. 3 vols. (Buenos Aires: Instituto de Historia de España, Universidad de Buenos Aires, 1985), 1:167–179.
"Alfonso X and the Castilian Church." *Thought* 60 (1985): 417–425.
"The Integration of Christian Spain into Europe: The Role of Alfonso VI of León-Castile." *Santiago, Saint Denis and Saint Peter*, ed. Bernard F. Reilly (New York: Fordham University Press, 1985), 101–120.

1986

"The Order of Calatrava: Years of Crisis and Survival, 1158–1212." *The Meeting of Two Worlds: Cultural Exchange between East and West during the Period of the Crusades*, ed. Vladimir P. Goss (Kalamazoo: Western Michigan University, 1986), 419–430.

1987

"The O'Callaghans of Kilcranathan." *Journal of the Cork Historical and Archeological Society* 92 (1987): 106–112.

"The Cantigas de Santa María as an Historical Source: Two Examples (nos. 321 and 386)." *Studies on the Cantigas de Santa María: Art, Music and Poetry*, eds. John Esten Keller and Israel Katz (Madison: The Hispanic Seminary of Medieval Studies, University of Wisconsin, 1987), 387–402.

"Las Cortes de Fernando IV: Cuadernos inéditos de Valladolid 1300 y Burgos 1308," *Historia, Instituciones, Documentos* 13 (1987): 315–328.

1988

The Cortes of Castile and León, 1188–1350. Philadelphia: University of Pennsylvania, Press, 1988.

"Las Cortes de Castilla y León (1230–1350)." *Las Cortes de Castilla y León en la Edad Media. Actas de la Primera Etapa del Congreso científico sobre la Historia de las Cortes de Castilla y León, Burgos, 30 de Septiembre a 3 de Octubre de 1986*, 2 vols. (Valladolid: Las Cortes de Castilla y León, 1988), 1:155–181.

1989

Las Cortes de Castilla y León, 1188–1350. Trans. Carlos Herrero Quiros. Valladolid: Cortes de Castilla y León and Ambito, 1989.

"Las Cortes de Valladolid-Tordesillas de 1401: Un Relato de los Procuradores de Burgos." *En la España Medieval* 12 (1989): 243–247.

1990

"Image and Reality: The King Creates his Kingdom." *Emperor of Culture: Alfonso X the Learned of Castile and his Thirteenth-Century Renaissance*, ed. Robert I. Burns, S.J. (Philadelphia: University of Pennsylvania Press, 1990), 14–32.

"The Mudéjars of Castile and Portugal in the Twelfth and Thirteenth Centuries." *Muslims under Latin Rule, 1100–1300*, ed. James M. Powell (Princeton: Princeton University Press, 1990), 11–56.

"The O'Callaghans during the Rebellion of 1641." *Journal of the Cork Historical and Archeological Society* 95 (1990): 30–40.

1992

"'To Know God and all Good Things,'" *Conflict and Community: New Studies in Thomistic Thought*, ed. Michael B. Lukens (New York: Peter Lang, 1992), 3–11.

"The Ideology of Government in the Realm of Alfonso X of Castile." *Exemplaria Hispanica* 1 (1991–1992): 1–17.
"Catálogo de los Cuadernos de las Cortes de Castilla y León, 1252–1348." *Anuario de Historia del Derecho Español* 62 (1992): 501–531.

1993

The Learned King: The Reign of Alfonso X of Castile. Philadelphia: University of Pennsylvania Press, 1993.
"Algunas peticiones de los Frailes conventuales de la Orden de Calatrava." *En la España Medieval* 16 (1993): 55–58.
"Castile, Portugal, and the Canary Islands: Claims and Counterclaims, 1344–1479." *Viator* 24 (1993): 287–309.
"Origin and Development of Archival Record-Keeping in the Crown of Castile-León." *Primary Sources and Original Works* 2 (1993): 3–18.

1994

"Los estudios medievales en los Estados Unidos y el Canadá." *Medievalismo. Boletín de la Sociedad Española de Estudios Medievales* 4 (1994): 201–204.

1996

"Pedro López de Ayala and the State of the Fourteenth-Century Church." *Medieval Iberia: Essays on the History and Literature of Medieval Spain*, eds. Donald J. Kagay and Joseph T. Snow (New York: Peter Lang, 1996), 229–241.
"Kings and Lords in Conflict in Late Thirteenth-Century Castile and Aragón." *Iberia and the Mediterranean World of the Middle Ages. Essays in Honor of Robert I. Burns, S.J.*, eds. P.E. Chevedden, D.J. Kagay and P.G. Padilla (Leiden: E.J. Brill, 1996), 117–135.
El Rey Sabio: El reinado de Alfonso X de Castilla (1252–1284). Trans. Manuel González Jiménez. Sevilla: Universidad de Sevilla, 1996.
"La vida de las Ordenes Militares de España según sus estatutos primitivos." *Alarcos 1195. Actas del Congreso Internacional Commemorativo del VIII Centenario de la Batalla de Alarcos*, eds. Ricardo Izquierdo Benito and Francisco Ruiz Gómez (Cuenca: Estudios de la Universidad de Castilla-La Mancha, 1996), 7–29.
"Las definiciones de la Orden de Calatrava, 1383–1418." *En la España Medieval* 19 (1996): 99–124.

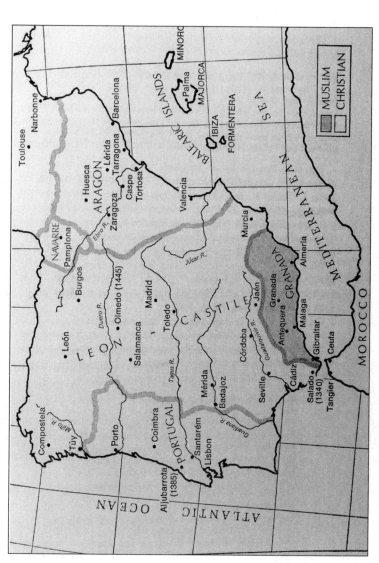

Medieval Spain

INTRODUCTION

We compiled this volume of essays to commemorate Joseph F. O'Callaghan's forty years at Fordham University. During those forty years he raised a family with his wife Anne; taught medieval history to two generations of undergraduate and graduate students; rose from the rank of instructor to full professor; and wrote *A History of Medieval Spain*, a classic book in the field of Iberian studies. Any one of these accomplishments would constitute a rich life. But the wider historical profession best knows Joseph O'Callaghan as a pioneer of medieval Spanish historical studies in the United States. It is hard for graduate students today to appreciate that even ten years ago the extensive program of the International Medieval Congress at Western Michigan University in Kalamazoo might contain only one panel on Spanish history. O'Callaghan himself tells the story of how he attended a meeting of the American Historical Association and met only one other scholar there who shared his interests—Robert I. Burns, S.J., now professor emeritus of the University of California Los Angeles. The current popularity of the study of medieval Spanish history has been fueled by O'Callaghan, Burns, Charles Julian Bishko (the third pioneer of Iberian studies in this country) and the students of these men.

O'Callaghan's interest in Spain began when he was a doctoral student with Jeremiah O'Sullivan, the noted Cistercian scholar. O'Callaghan became interested in the Spanish military religious orders, specifically, the Order of Calatrava. He was awarded his first Fulbright to conduct this research. This study eventually emerged in his dissertation entitled "The Affiliation of the Order of Calatrava with the Order of Cîteaux."

In the subsequent years O'Callaghan published articles culled from his dissertation research on the military religious orders, which have since been collected into a Variorum volume. During this early part of his career he found time to pursue his interest in the history of parliament. *The Cortes of Castile-León* exemplifies O'Callaghan's interests in the origins and development of medieval institutions. Despite the intense focus that English-speaking historians have placed on Britain's parliamentary development, O'Callaghan firmly believes and taught that the development of parliamentary institutions was a European-wide phenomenon. The Spanish kingdoms were unique because urban representatives attended the *Cortes* in 1188 as a recognized estate of the realm, predating town representation elsewhere in Western Europe.

O'Callaghan's first major work was *A History of Medieval Spain*, which appeared in 1975 and was literally years in the making. It is a bravura performance that also typifies O'Callaghan's scholarship: the ability to identify existing gaps in historical investigation, combined with a deceptively simple expository style and a discrete refusal to speculate beyond the bounds of the textual evidence. *A History of Medieval Spain* filled the need for a book explaining all aspects of medieval Spain to English-speaking readers. O'Callaghan identified the key Christian and Muslim people and events in Iberian government, religion, economy, society, and culture between 711 and 1492. He translated significant and illustrative poems, chronicles, and documents for inclusion in the text. His extensive bibliography, organized by period and topic, was an additional aid for further research. The resulting book is encyclopedic in nature and uncompromising in scholarly quality, yet it can be given to an undergraduate or recommended to a non-academic reader.

Retirement has, if anything, increased O'Callaghan's productivity, as illustrated by his first monograph to appear after his retirement, *The Learned King: Alfonso X*. O'Callaghan has long been interested by the tumultuous reign of this complex man who may be one of the most influential monarchs in history. Alfonso X presents a paradox to the modern world: the learned institutional reformer who patronized the bookarts yet alienated his realms in the pursuit of the imperial crown. O'Callaghan's book is the only monograph in English that examines all the elements that made up this complex individual, and yet O'Callaghan himself would say that Alfonso requires more extensive study. Even now his work on the *Cantigas de Santa Maria*, Alfonso X's illuminated collection of songs of the miracles of the Virgin, is in press.

This collection of articles, however, does not focus on Alfonso X or even solely on medieval Spain, because Joseph O'Callaghan has pursued other scholarly interests in the course of forty years. For example, he translated the *Spiritual Exercises* of Ignatius of Loyala, the Spanish founder of the Society of Jesus. He also made a foray into Irish history with an article on the O'Callaghan clan. The research on this article, appropriately enough, also led to Spain, since he found that the current head of the clan resides in Madrid. Therefore, this collection of essays, written by O'Callaghan's friends, students, and colleagues, finds its subject matter spreading out from the Iberian peninsula into England and even China. Spain is, after all, a very heterogeneous society, with wide-ranging influences, and O'Callaghan's life's work helped place it at the center rather than the periphery of European history. The title of this book reflects O'Callaghan's basic approach to the discipline of history. Alongside his other scholarly strengths, such as his ability to identify essential scholarly research, his clear prose, and his exhaustive knowledge of primary and secondary source material, is his recognition that he is dealing with people, whether they are living or dead.

The contributions to this volume have been divided into two categories that reflect Joseph O'Callaghan's research and teaching interests. These categories are the Influence of Law on Society and the Relationship between Government and War. The first selection, James A. Brundage's "Force and Fear: A Marriage Case from Eleventh-Century Aragón," examines Pope Urban II's decision involving the marriage of a niece of Sancho I Ramírez of Aragon (1063–1094). This decision, which Gratian and later canonists collected into their decretals, ruled that a valid Christian marriage required the free consent of both parties. Urban's ruling, which was essentially pastoral rather than canonical in nature, was intended to advise Sancho rather than set a precedent. But it later acquired the force of law, illustrating that the reign of Ramiro the Monk, which initially destabilized Aragonese dynastic policies, had a longer-reaching effect.

Nina Melechen's "Calling Names: The Identification of Jews in Christian Documents from Medieval Toledo," asks the question of why Toledan notaries, unlike others in the peninsula, often redundantly identified Jews as Jews in their documents? She finds that Toledan documents identified Jews by the title "Don" and by the label "Jew." These two labels, in addition to Biblical names that were unique to Toledan Jews, meant that documents from Toledo contained three ways to identify Jews. Part of the reason for this practice was the early development of vernacular notarial practices in Toledo, which drew on other traditions including Arabic customs. But Melechen also argues that notaries in Toledo used this system of identification to reinforce Jewish separateness from Christian society.

James Brodman, in "Shelter and Segregation: Lepers in Medieval Catalonia," examines the specialized hospitals in Catalonia, Toulouse, and Majorca that catered to lepers. The leprosaria were organized as a religious community that lived a common life and owned property. Brodman focuses on the organization and finances of the Hospitals in Barcelona, Lerida, and elsewhere in Catalonia, and finds that these institutions were organized as asylums, or residences, not as places for the cure of the sick. He finds that such hospitals catered to wealthy lepers, except in Barcelona, where poor residents were given preference in the leprosaria.

Leprosy and plague were the great scourges of medieval life. William D. Phillips examines the fourteenth-century plague epidemics in Iberia, which have not been as well studied as those in the rest of Europe. There have been extensive local studies examining the mortality rates of specific groups, but Phillips is the first to provide an overview of the situation in Iberia resulting from the plague. Phillips finds that the Iberian outbreaks of the plague follow identifiable patterns similar to the rest of Europe: the plague struck the coast, large urban centers, the urban poor, and members of specific professions like the clergy, notaries, and the medical profession. The results of the plague, however, differed in Iberia. Catalan villages remained inhabited, whereas post-plague villages in Old Castile were deserted. The Castilians may have begun migrating before the plague, but in Portugal the plague initiated desertion. Kings and *Cortes* tried to regulate prices and the movement of population. The change in social relationships following the plague was most marked. Yet Phillips would not argue that the plague drastically changed Iberian politics, society, or economy, and that if any such changes occurred they were primarily psychological and cultural.

Teofilo F. Ruiz looks at Castilian wills in terms of "The Business of Salvation." Similar to the case of the lepers of Barcelona, Ruiz finds that testators prior to 1350 were reluctant to waste money on the undeserving poor. Instead, they preferred to give bequests to *envergoñados*, poor neighbors who were ashamed to beg. This attitude was in sharp contrast to charitable attitudes in sixteenth-century Spain, which, in reaction to Luther's attacks upon almsgiving, urged generous charitable donations. Ruiz finds that there were no medieval precedents for Spain's assumed tolerance towards the poor in the early modern period. Instead, he finds a ceremonialization of poverty that suggests a different concept of salvation from that of simple charity given with love.

The next group of papers examines the relationship between government and war. Theresa M. Vann takes a "New Look at the Foundation of the Order of Calatrava." O'Callaghan's doctoral thesis found that Spanish Order of Calatrava was part of European-wide phenomena inspired by Bernard of Clairvaux and the crusading Order of the Temple, and not a unique Spanish creation inspired by the Muslim *ribat*. Since he wrote his thesis, new historical arguments have emerged for the influence of the *ribat* based upon anthropology, and new interpretations of narrative sources argue that they should be treated as literary constructs. Vann re-examines the already-known evidence and introduces new evidence that suggest that O'Callaghan's traditional interpretation remains the most likely one.

Two of the contributors indirectly demonstrate the holes that still exist in English-language Spanish historiography. Lawrence J. McCrank rediscovers "The Lost Kingdom of Siurana," a Catalan *taifa* kingdom previously known through folklore and legend. McCrank cuts through the legend to find that the Catalan highlands retained pockets of resistance to both African and Christian invaders, in the process recapitulating all the evidence available for this forgotten realm.

Nicholas Agrait, in "The Reconquest during the Reign of Alfonso XI," reminds us of the importance of the Spanish theatre of the Hundred Years War. The career of Alfonso XI, prematurely cut short by the bubonic plague, marked the end of Castilian expansion until the reign of Ferdinand and Isabella.

Robert I. Burns, "The Many Crusades of Valencia's Conquest," also takes on historical paradigms: the artificial difference between crusade and reconquest. Burns argues that the campaigns of James the Conqueror in Valencia constitute a crusade, consonant with the character of the crusades to the Latin East, and part of the papal crusading program. Burns argues that the financial success of James' Valencian campaigns in no way denigrates the spiritual motives for them. Ignoring universal crusade history and substituting instead the reconquest mitigates the spirit of the Spanish campaigns.

Paul E. Chevedden introduces a new discovery, "The Hybrid Trebuchet: The Halfway Step to the Counterweight Trebuchet." The trebuchet, a type of pre-gunpowder artillery, originated in China between the fifth and fourth centuries BCE. It reached the Mediterranean by the time of the Islamic conquests during the sixth century CE. Chevedden has discovered evidence for a developmental stage between the human-powered traction trebuchet and the gravity-powered trebuchet. This link, which he has named the hybrid trebuchet, was both human and gravity powered. More powerful than previous versions, it was probably developed in the Islamic realms and may have been a significant factor in the Muslim conquest of Spain.

Donald J. Kagay analyzes a popular account of the *Corts* of Barcelona of 1228 in "The Emergence of 'Parliament' in the Thirteenth-Century Crown of Aragon." James I of Aragon, who called the assembly prior to his invasion of Majorca, described it in his "Book of Deeds," the *Liber dels Feyts*. But the "View from the Gallery" that Kagay has discovered provides a slightly different point of view from the monarch's. The most notable difference is that while James recalls his oratory as spellbinding, the Catalan townsmen remembered that they could not understand a word. Kagay also found that the townspeople focused on administrative details that were beneath the king's notice. He concludes that the popular account provides more evidence for the interplay between memory and written record.

Paulette L. Pepin reconstructs the struggle over the *libertas ecclesiastica* between the Castilian crown and the church during the thirteenth century, which culminated with the Council of Peñafiel in 1302. While the church claimed exemption from royal taxation, they could not refuse to help finance Fernando III's campaigns against the Muslims. The church found that the rewards for the conquest of Seville in 1252 did not compensate for their sacrifices, and their liberties steadily eroded through the rest of the thirteenth century. Finally, during the minority of Fernando IV, the church was barred from the *Cortes*. Lacking a political forum, the Castilian church rebelled against Fernando IV in 1301. The Council of Peñafiel ended the rebellion and restored the church's rights. But Pepin finds this was not a permanent solution, because the Castilian church was too faction riven for the bishops to maintain a position of strength.

Steven Isaac and Jean Truax examine the tangled relations and succession of Henry I of England. Issacs probes the essential weakness of King Stephen, who undermined his reign while at the height of his success. Isaac argues that Stephen's release of the Empress Matilda in 1139, an act designed to demonstrate the monarch's strength, instead sowed the seed for his own discomfiture when Matilda refused to retire and gained unexpected support. Jean Truax also looks at the political vicissitudes in Henry I's circle in "Politics Makes Uneasy Bedfellows: Henry I of England and Theobald of Blois." Truax focuses on Theobald, nephew of Henry I and brother to Stephen. The two Angevins gained more prominence when Henry's only legitimate son died in the wreck of the White Ship. Theobald, who expected to inherit Normandy if his brother became King of England, did not realize all his territorial aspirations. Like Henry, he failed to create a dynasty, although Truax believes that he did well to maintain his independence.

The papers in this volume follow clearly-defined themes: how society's concerns leave their mark in the law, and how warfare shapes government and politics. Each contributor challenges a traditional historical construct. Each argument is based upon archival and textual evidence. The overall result is a view of both northern and southern medieval European societies, which were marked as much by their commonalities as by their differences. It is our hope that the papers in this collection will serve to expand the knowledge of the vast hinterland known as the Middle Ages, while paying tribute to a colleague and teacher whose unprecedented career, coupled with decades of careful and insightful research, stands as a clear guide to a variegated, and often confusing, landscape.

Theresa M. Vann

Donald J. Kagay

THE INFLUENCE OF LAW ON SOCIETY

FORCE AND FEAR: A MARRIAGE CASE FROM ELEVENTH-CENTURY ARAGON

James A. Brundage

The thesis of this paper centers on the bundle of legal and pastoral problems that arose from marriages that one partner entered unwillingly—in other words, from what we might call "shotgun marriages." More specifically, I propose to examine one particular case decided by Pope Urban II (1088–1099) on 1 July 1089.[1] This case arose in the royal family of the Kingdom of Aragon and was brought to the pope by King Sancho I Ramírez (1063–1094). Sancho's query to the pope has apparently not survived, but the pope's reply struck canonists in the late eleventh and early twelfth centuries as sufficiently interesting that several of them included it among the papal decisions they reported in their collections of canon law.[2] Sometime around 1140 a Bolognese law teacher named Gratian incorporated the text of Pope Urban's letter into his *Decretum*, which soon became (and long remained) the basic textbook in medieval schools of canon law.[3] The decision in this Aragonese case thus entered the mainstream of canonical doctrine on the difficult legal issues that cluster around the problem of marriages contracted through force or fear.[4]

Canonists considered that only part of Pope Urban's letter to King Sancho held much legal interest and they therefore incorporated only that segment of it in their collections. In that portion of his letter the pope wrote:

---

[1] JL 5399; also see Appendix A. I am greatly indebted to Robert Somerville, who first directed my attention to the legal problems that this text raises.

[2] The letter first appeared in the *Collectio Britannica*. Ivo of Chartres reproduced it in his *Decretum* 8.24 and *Panormia* 6.109, as well as the *Collectio trium partium* 3.15(16).22.

[3] See James A. Brundage, *Medieval Canon Law* (London, 1996) on Gratian and the schools of law.

[4] The studies collected in Angeliki E. Laiou, *Consent and Coercion to Sex and Marriage in Ancient and Medieval Societies* (Washington, 1993), present a useful historical introduction to the issues and their treatment in various regions and periods, as well as numerous references to the abundant literature on this topic. I have also addressed some of these issues in a paper on "Coerced Consent and the 'Constant Man' Standard in Medieval Canon Law," presented at the Davis Center colloquium on *Reason, Coercion, and the Law*, in November, 1993.

> Concerning the marriage of your niece, whom you declare that you
> have promised under oath will be given (because of urgent necessity)
> to a certain knight, We decree, as fairness demands, that if (as reported)
> she totally rejects that man, and willfully persists [in her rejection], so
> that she altogether refuses to marry him, you may in no way force her,
> unwilling and objecting, to be joined to that man in marriage. Those
> who are of one body should also be of one mind, lest perchance a
> young woman joined to someone against her will may risk the guilt
> of desertion (against the command of the Lord and the Apostle) or the
> crime of fornication. It appears indeed [that] the evil of the sin spills
> over onto him who married the unwilling woman. Much the same
> may be held concerning a man.[5]

Let me briefly sketch the facts of the situation that gave rise to this
decision before turning to the legal problems that it raises. Sancho
Ramírez I of Aragón married Felicia, daughter of Hilduin de Roucy.[6]
The niece whose marriage was an issue in this case was almost certainly not one of Felicia's relatives. It is extremely unlikely that the
Roucy family would have permitted Sancho to intervene in marriage
arrangements among their own kin.

We must look for the niece, therefore, among the family of King
Sancho I Ramírez himself.[7] One of the king's brothers, García, was
bishop of Jaca and died in 1086 leaving no known children. Sancho's
sister, Sancha, married an elderly man, Count Ermengau of Urgel,
about 1058. They had no children and he died in military action
in 1064. Sancha then returned to Aragón, where she had admirers,
but she did not remarry and died without children. A second sister,
Teresa, married Guillem Beltran, Count of Toulouse. Guillem died
childless in 1112. A nun who entered the monastery of Santa Cruz
as a child may possibly have been a third sister of Sancho I, although
the identification is doubtful and, in any event, she is not known to
have had any children. So far no niece. But King Sancho had one
further sibling, his illegitimate half-brother, Count Sancho, lord of
Aibar, Benabarre, Fantova, Javier, and Ribagorza. Count Sancho, the
eldest of King Ramíro's children, is said to have left five sons and,
more important for our purposes, two daughters. One daughter,

---

[5] Urban II in JL 5399 = Gratian, *Decretum* C. 31 q. 2 c. 3. See Appendix A for
Latin text.
[6] *The Chronicle of San Juan de la Peña: A Fourteenth-Century Official History of the Crown
of Aragon*, trans. Lynn H. Nelson (Philadelphia, 1991), p. 19.
[7] See genealogy, p. 15.

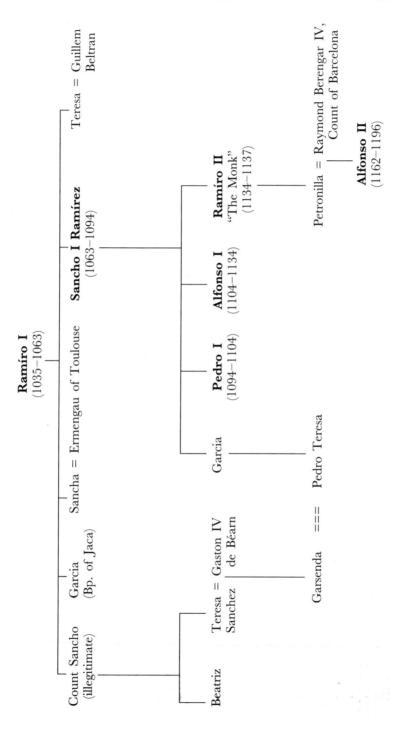

Rulers of Aragon

Count Sancho (illegitimate)

Garcia (Bp. of Jaca)

Sancha = Ermengau of Toulouse

Ramíro I (1035–1063)

Teresa = Guillem Beltran

Beatriz

Teresa = Gaston IV de Béarn
Sanchez

Garcia

Pedro Teresa

Garsenda === Pedro

Pedro I (1094–1104)

Alfonso I (1104–1134)

Sancho I Ramírez (1063–1094)

Ramíro II "The Monk" (1134–1137)

Petronilla = Raymond Berengar IV, Count of Barcelona

Alfonso II (1162–1196)

Beatriz, apparently did not marry, but the other, Teresa, married Gaston IV, Viscount of Béarn.[8]

Teresa Sanchez, daughter of Count Sancho, thus seems likely to have been the niece whose marriage Pope Urban ruled upon. Circumstantial considerations reinforce this identification. Since Sancho Ramírez consistently attempted to strengthen his ties with the southern French nobility, it would have been entirely in keeping with his general policy to use his niece's marriage for that purpose.[9]

As for Teresa herself, her ties to her family of origin seem to have remained strong. Sancho I died in 1096, as we have seen, while King Alfonso and Teresa's husband, Gaston, both died in 1134. The Aragonese acclaimed the remaining brother of their late monarch, Ramíro the Monk, as their king. The next in the line of succession to the Aragonese throne was Teresa Sanchez's nephew, Pedro Teresa, son of Teresa's brother, Garcia, and thus grandson of Count Sancho. Pedro Teresa apparently married his cousin, Garsenda, who was the daughter of Teresa Sanchez. Teresa Sanchez seems to have played some role in a conflict with King Ramíro the Monk in 1135 and drew upon forces loyal to her late husband, Gaston, to safeguard Cinco Villas, a region of recent Béarnaise settlement. Although the king prevailed in the conflict, Teresa Sanchez does not appear to have suffered any adverse consequences for her part in it.[10]

These not particularly edifying circumstances make it abundantly clear that the marriage of King Sancho I's niece, Teresa Sanchez, played an important role in the political schemes that swirled around the Aragonese royal family. Given the family entanglements I have described, any difficulties that arose in the arrangements for her marriage might reasonably have justified an appeal for a definitive verdict on the matter.

Let me return now to the text of Pope Urban's decretal. The pope ruled on the point at issue that the free consent of both parties

---

[8] *Chronicle of San Juan de la Peña*, p. 17; Joseph F. O'Callaghan, *A History of Medieval Spain* (Ithaca, NY, 1975), pp. 219, 222.

[9] O'Callaghan, p. 197; Thomas N. Bisson, *The Medieval Crown of Aragon: A Short History* (Oxford, 1986), p. 13.

[10] Teresa Sanchez's son, Centulo, and her daughter, Guiscarda, were the founders of two branches of the family of the viscounts of Béarn. Her other daughter, Garsenda, who married Pedro Talesa, was the ancestress of the lords of Borja and the Italian branch of that family was known, of course, as the Borgias. I am grateful to my colleague, Lynn Nelson, for guidance through this dynastic maze.

(in this case, of King Sancho's niece) was absolutely essential for a valid Christian marriage. Although this may seem self-evident to us, it was in fact anything but obvious in the late eleventh century. Parents and other kinsfolk, particularly among the ruling elite, routinely arranged the marriages of their children. The prospective bride and groom might not be consulted about the matter until late in the process, and their wishes were in any event secondary to the demands of dynastic policy. Pope Urban held in this decretal, however, that valid marriage cannot take place unless the parties themselves consent to the union. Their consent, moreover, must be free. If procured under duress, the marriage was invalid. In the pope's words, "*[N]equaquam eam inuitam et renitentem eiusdem uiri cogas sociari coniugio.*"[11] The rule of this case, as Georges Duby (among others) has pointed out, flatly contradicted the interests of eleventh century potentates—such as King Sancho I of Aragón—in negotiating dynastic marriage alliances.[12]

The pope concluded his letter with two speculative observations (which lawyers would classify as *dicta*) in which he addressed matters that were not strictly at issue in this case. In the first *dictum* Pope Urban asserted that a person unwillingly bound in marriage might be liable either to desert the unwanted spouse or to seek unlawful sexual gratification with another, presumably more attractive, partner. This statement merely expressed the pope's opinion as to the probable outcome of marriages entered under duress. It had no binding authority in law. Other judges might perhaps find the *dictum* persuasive, and no doubt some did, but it established no rule of law.

The final sentences of the decretal comprise Pope Urban's second *dictum* in this case. In them the pope addressed the problem of assigning moral guilt when a forced marriage resulted in desertion or adultery. The precise meaning of these two sentences has puzzled both medieval and modern readers. The pope's statements are ambiguous (perhaps they were deliberately so) and seem open to any of three interpretations. Urban may have meant that:

---

[11] Urban II in JL 5399 = Gratian, *Decretum* C. 31 q. 2 c. 3.

[12] Georges Duby, *Medieval Marriage: Two Models from Twelfth-Century France*, trans. Elborg Forster (Baltimore, 1978), pp. 5–12, 15–22; idem, *The Knight, The Lady and the Priest: The Making of Modern Marriage in Medieval France*, trans. Barbara Bray (New York, 1983), pp. 170–172.

1) A person who forces a woman to marry someone against her will thereby becomes morally liable for any matrimonial offenses that may follow;

or

2) If an unwilling bride subsequently deserts her husband or commits adultery, the guilt for her action will fall upon her husband;

or

3) If a woman who married against her will should later leave her husband or take an extramarital lover, both her husband and the person who forced her to marry will share in the guilt for her deed.

Scholars continue to disagree about the proper reading of *De neptis*. John Noonan and Michael Sheehan understood Pope Urban's words to mean that the guilt for subsequent desertion or adultery would fall upon the person who forced a woman to accept an unwelcome husband.[13] Others, however, have maintained that the pope assigned moral guilt in these circumstances to the husband.[14]

The phrase *pari tenore* in the concluding sentence of Urban's letter, taken together with the circumstances of the case, however, seems to favor the third interpretation. The pope appears to be warning King Sancho not to pressure his niece into a marriage she does not want, since he and his niece's husband will both share in the guilt should his niece subsequently abandon her husband or take up with some more desirable man. This seems a reasonably simple and direct interpretation of the pope's intent. Alternative readings of *pari tenore* assume that the pope took the occasion of Sancho's query to issue a speculative ruling on a hypothetical situation in which the roles of bride and groom were reversed and a man was being forced to marry against his will. This seems unlikely.

Johannes Teutonicus, the author of the authoritative *Glossa ordinaria* on Gratian's *Decretum*, also understood *De neptis* to mean that both the unwanted husband and the person who applied duress would share in the guilt arising from subsequent desertion or adultery. Addressing the meaning of the verb *redundare* in this text, Johannes advised law students:

---

[13] John T. Noonan, Jr., "Power to Choose," *Viator* 4 (1973): 421; Michael M. Sheehan, "Choice of Marriage Partner in the Middle Ages: Development and Mode of Application of a Theory of Marriage," *Studies in Medieval and Renaissance History*, n.s. 1 (1978): 11–12.

[14] This, for example was the view of Benencasus who in his *Casus Decreti* placed the onus on the husband: "*Nam eorum munus debet esse consensus, quorum unum corpus efficitur, et qui eam inuitam copulauerit, tenetur ex fornicatione, si qua postea sequeretur, uel ex dissicio uel adulterio, quod inde postea fuerit subsecutum.*"

Note the rule. He who furnishes the occasion for harm appears to have caused the harm, as in the Decretal *De cetero*, on homicide, the canon *Si tu* in [Gratian's] Case 27 question 2, and the canon *Est iniusta* in Case 23, question 4.[15]

The references here plainly support this understanding of Johannes' gloss on the closing passage on Urban's letter.

Equally interesting, I think, is what Pope Urban did not say in this decretal. He avoided addressing directly the juristic issues of consent or validity. A century later, during or after the time of Pope Alexander III (1159–1181), those issues would surely have been the central focus of any papal ruling on this situation. Urban II, however, simply did not confront the question of whether such a marriage was valid, an issue that would greatly concern twelfth-century decretists.[16] Nor did he try to define any sort of scale of duress or to identify any specific benchmark, beyond which duress was morally and legally unacceptable, as later popes would do.[17] Still less did he attempt to define the circumstances under which a person coerced into marriage might be justified in attempting to escape from the undesired union.

Instead, Pope Urban approached the situation as a pastoral, rather than a legal problem. He centered his attention on the moral consequences of forcing a woman to agree, at least verbally, to marriage with a partner whom she does not wish to marry. He told King Sancho, in effect, "Don't do it, because it would be wrong. Even worse, it would be rash; for if you force your niece to marry you will leave both yourself and her husband open to the horrible moral consequences that will follow if she later runs away or takes up with someone she likes better." This is an admonition, not a command. It contrasts strikingly from the approach to these problems that would emerge during the next two or three generations.

Perhaps because of this, twelfth-century commentators on Gratian's *Decretum* (the decretists) paid scant attention to this canon. The *Summa*

---

[15] *Glos. ord.* to C. 31 q. 2 c. 3 v. *redundare: Nota regulam: qui occasionem damni dat, damnum decisse uidetur, ut extra De homic.*, De cetero [X 5.12.11], C. 27 q. 2 Si tu [c. 24] and C. 23 q. 4 Est iniusta [c. 33].

[16] E.g., the *Summa* "Elegantius in iure diuino" seu Coloniensis 13.55, eds. Gérard Fransen and Stephan Kuttner, *Monumenta iuris canonici, Corpus glossatorum*, vol. 1 in 4 pts. (Vatican City, 1969–1990), 4:33: "[C]oactus consensus, qui nec uere consensus est, matrimonium non opereratur."

[17] Notably Pope Alexander III (1159–1181) in X 4.1.15 *Veniens ad nos*.

attributed to Gratian's earliest known disciple, Paucapalea, for example, simply stated that this canon means that women should not be
forced to marry men they do not wish to marry and, having said
that, passed on to the next topic.[18] Master Rolandus, another early
teacher of Gratian's text who was active in the late 1150's, likewise
ignored the final portion of the canon, as did the unknown author
of the *Summa Parisiensis*, who wrote just a few years later.[19] Rufinus,
too, ignored the issues raised in the final sentences of *De neptis*.[20]

The disinterest of the decretists in the closing section of Urban's
decretal almost certainly mirrored the academic context in which
they wrote. It is all too easy to forget that the decretist texts that
we now read as deliberate analytical commentaries originated as
classroom lectures in medieval law faculties. The teachers whose
Summas we ponder, while seated in an easy chair in our studies,
voiced their comments in the stale air of early morning lecture halls,
where they were trying to teach law students what they would need
to know in order to practice as advocates or to make decisions as
judges in courtrooms scattered through the length and breadth of
Western Christendom. Looked at from the viewpoint of a judge or
practitioner in the courts, the concluding sentences of *De neptis*, while
they no doubt had some theoretical interest as pastoral advice, simply failed to cut the mustard as law. A law teacher could very well
look at this passage and think something along the lines of, "The
pope's advice in this case, although no doubt sound enough, is not
the sort of thing that's going to be much use in a domestic relations
lawsuit." Having thought that, he might well decide to move smartly
along to the next canon in his text. It is very likely, I think, that some
such train of thought accounts for the scant notice that *De neptis*,
and particularly its closing sentences, received from the twelfth-century
decretists.

---

[18] *Die Summa des Paucapalea über das Decretum Gratiani* to C. 31 q. 2 c. 3, ed. J.F.
von Schulte (Giessen, 1890), p. 124. Rudolf Weigand, "Paucapalea und die frühe
Kanonistik," *Archiv für katholisches Kirchenrecht* 150 (1981): 139–141, however, argues
persuasively that the text edited by Schulte was not by Paucapalea. The *Summa* of
Paucapalea does not exist in a single manuscript. Paucapalea's views must be searched
for in the early glosses on the *Decretum*.

[19] *De summa Magistri Rolandi* to C. 31 q. 2 c. 3, ed. Friedrich Thaner (Innsbruck,
1874), p. 157; *The Summa Parisiensis on the Decretum of Gratian*, ed. Terence P. McLaughlin
(Toronto, 1952), p. 239.

[20] Rufinus, *Summa decretorum*, ed. Heinrich Singer (1902; Aalen, 1963), p. 473.

APPENDIX A

Urban II in JL 5399 = Gratian, Decretum C. 31 q. 2 c. 3

De neptis tuae coniugio, quam te cuidam militi daturum necessitatis instante articulo sub fidei pollicitatione firmasti, hoc equitate dictante decernimus, ut, si illa uirum illum, ut dicitur, omnino renuit, et in eadem uoluntatis auctoritate persistit, ut uiro illi prorsus se deneget nupturam, nequaquam eam inuitam et renitentem eiusdem uiri cogas sociari coniugio. Quorum enim unum corpus est, unus debet esse et animus, ne forte, cum uirgo fuerit alicui inuita copulata, contra Domini Apostolique preceptum aut reatum discidii, aut crimen fornicationis incurrat. Cuius uidelicet peccati malum in eum redundare constat, qui eam coniunxit inuitam. Quod pari tenore de uiro est sentiendum.

[Concerning the marriage of your niece, whom you declare that you have promised under oath will be given (because of urgent necessity) to a certain knight. We decree, as fairness demands, that if (as reported) she totally rejects that man, and willfully persists [in her rejection], so that she altogether refuses to marry him, you may in no way force her, unwilling and objecting, to be joined to that man in marriage. Those who are of one body should also be of one mind, lest perchance a young woman joined to someone against her will may risk the guilt of desertion (against the command of the Lord and the Apostle) or the crime of fornication. It appears indeed [that] the evil of the sin spills over onto him who married the unwilling woman. Much the same may be held concerning a man.]

Trans. James A. Brundage

CALLING NAMES: THE IDENTIFICATION OF JEWS IN CHRISTIAN DOCUMENTS FROM MEDIEVAL TOLEDO

Nina Melechen

Identifying Jews—specifically, Jewish men—in Christian documents from Toledo and its diocese between the twelfth and fourteenth century is strikingly easy. But it is not so clear why such precise identification, which was not universal in the medieval Iberian Peninsula, developed in Toledo. The redundancy of identification used there saves the historian from confusion about who, in the available records, was a Jew, but it raises other very important questions. Why, in fact, did the Christians of Toledo call attention to Jews by over-identifying them, when the Jewish behavior described in their records was not in itself odd, and was mirrored by Christian behavior? And why did the scribes of Toledo develop such redundancy of identification when other Iberian Christians did not? The patterns of identification used in Toledo evidently resulted from the early use of the vernacular there, which permitted scribes to create new forms to distinguish members of minority groups. They worked to reinforce the symbolic boundaries between Jews and Christians and to reestablish the distinctions between the groups that were undermined by the very interactions the documents recorded.

From the thirteenth century onward, whenever individual Jewish men were mentioned as participants in Toledan vernacular contracts, bills of sale, records of lawsuits, or similar documents, they were over-identified as Jews. These same documents also named Jews as witnesses, neighbors, or authorities, in which cases they were frequently, but not inevitably, as heavily over-identified. At the first reference, a Jew's name was preceded by the term "don," a separator which at that time had no honorific connotations but simply indicated that he was not Christian.[1] The Jew's given name and surname also identified him as a Jew, since Toledan Jews shared a pool

---

[1] See Manuel Ferrer-Chivite, "El factor judeo-converso en el proceso de consolidación del título 'Don'," *Sefarad* 45 (1985): 133–134, 140–141. By the fourteenth century, "doña" was increasingly used to distinguish women from men, and thus

of mostly Biblical names that were not used by Christians.[2] Finally, in case this indirect information was not enough, a Jew was explicitly described as a "judío." A typical first reference to a Jew was "don Abraham Ibn Halegua, Jew."[3] Similarly, Toledan vernacular documents identified Jewish women with the labels "doña" and "judía" to avoid any ambiguity.

This triple identification by separator, Jewish name, and religious descriptor stood in stark contrast to the naming of Christian men in the same documents. The first reference to a Christian included his given name and surname, a reference to a parent and often to a spouse, and a place of residence; that was all. Christians were not identified as members of a religious group, nor, after the twelfth century, were they usually identified by ethnicity or place of origin outside Toledo. And the Christian men of Toledo, as the normative inhabitants there, had no separators attached to their names. A Christian, therefore, might first appear as "Juan Alfonso son of Alfonso Esteban of Alcabón."[4]

---

ceased to be useful in distinguishing Jewish from Christian women. Around the same time "don" was also used to distinguish nobles from the non-noble.

[2] Twelfth-century Jews were more likely to use non-Biblical names than were their later descendants. Apparently, the shift among Castilian Jews to a restricted pool of names took place during the thirteenth century, antedating the first national legislation requiring such restriction, which was not passed until 1313. Given names were not useful for identifying Jewish women, since they rarely used Biblical names and used many names that were shared by Muslim and Christian women. Many Jewish surnames also suggested that the bearers were not Christian. Most, though by no means all, Toledan Jewish families during the twelfth and thirteenth centuries bore Arabic surnames. With some ambiguity, therefore, due to the presence in Toledo of Mozarabic families with Arabic surnames, they suggested that the families were not Christian, though, of course, they did not firmly identify them as Jewish. See José Godoy Alcántara, *Ensayo histórico etimológico filológico sobre los apellidos castellanos* (Madrid, 1871; reprint ed., Barcelona, 1975), pp. 40–44.

[3] AHN, Clero, carpeta 2985, no. 13: "don abrahem aben halegua judio morador enel dicho lugar". See Luisa Cuesta Gutiérrez, ed., *Formulario notarial castellano del siglo XV* (Madrid, 1947), for an example of a Castilian notarial formulary from the second quarter of the fifteenth century, probably from Toledo, which gives no examples of how to name Jews in documents. This omission is all the more striking because the formulary does give numerous examples of how to refer to Christians. Possibly the formula for naming Jews was so well known that its divergence from the formula for naming Christians needed no comment, or possibly the compiler of the formulary considered it a matter of local practice. Although the formulary's origin is not stated, the prevalence of references to Toledo make it likely that it was produced in that city.

[4] AHN Clero, carp. 2985, no. 13: "johan alfonso fijo de alfonso esteuan de alcauon." See Cuesta Gutiérrez, p. 179, for the formula from the fifteenth-century formulary: "fulano, fijo de fulano, vesino de tal lugar."

The distinction became even more pronounced with second and subsequent allusions to an individual in the same document. These references were abridged to "the said" followed by a short version of the identification. Christians at this point lost the citation of family members and residence; they were generally simply called by name and surname, for instance "the said Juan Alfonso." Brief references to Jews, on the other hand, continued to emphasize their membership in a minority group, as they were referred to both by recognizable (Jewish) given name—not by surname—and by separator, as in "the said don Abraham."[5]

The thoroughness of the Toledan triple identification was in fact unusual. In the Crown of Aragon, in contrast, Jews were not limited to the relatively small pool of names they shared in Castile, and they tended to change their Hebrew names for Romance or Arabic names of similar sound or meaning in their dealings with Christians or Muslims, recorded in Latin or Arabic documents. Moreover, they were not always explicitly identified as Jews and they were not always given the separator "don." Robert I. Burns has noted that this ambiguity has caused some historians—and must have caused many contemporaries—considerable confusion in distinguishing between Aragonese Christians and Jews by names alone.[6] And in the kingdom

---

[5] Even in places where the formal triple identification was not used consistently, such as the kingdom of Navarre and parts of Castile, "don" was often included in second references to Jews. In these cases, over-identification was not felt to be necessary in the first reference, but subsequent references insisted on the individual's separation from the norm. See Rogelio Pérez Bustamante, ed., *El registro notarial de Dueñas* (Palencia, 1985), p. 83 (item 1). The disappearance of Jewish surnames in short references may have been intended as another sign of distinction, since Christians kept their surnames in short references.

[6] See Robert I. Burns, *Muslims, Christians, and Jews in the Crusader Kingdom of Valencia: Societies in Symbiosis* (Cambridge, 1984), p. 138, and idem, *Diplomatarium of the Crusader Kingdom of Valencia: The Registered Charters of Its Conqueror, Jaume I, 1257–1276*, 2 vols. to date (Princeton, 1985–), 1:101–102, 2:292–304, for the names used by Jews; idem, *Jews in the Notarial Culture: Latinate Wills in Mediterranean Spain, 1250–1350* (Princeton, 1996), pp. 4–8; and see idem, *Muslims, Christians, and Jews*, pp. 134–135, for the case of a Christian moneylender long thought by historians to have been a Jew. Typical Aragonese full and short references to Jews can also be found in Maria-Teresa Ferrer i Mallol, "La redacció de l'instrument notarial a Catalunya. Cèdules, manuals, llibres i cartes," *Estudios históricos y documentos de los Archivos de Protocolos* 4 (1974): 113–116. Document 2 of Appendix I (the minute and the registration of a document dated February 28, 1359; AHPB, Francesc de Ladernosa, *Quintum manuala*, fol. 35v and AHPB, Francesc de Ladernosa, *Capibrevium comune*, fol. 16r–v, respectively) shows that both the notary's minute of the document to be written and his full registration of the document (which was then copied onto parchment as a formal charter; p. 81) refer to "Issachus Astrugi Mercadelli, iudeus Barchinone,

of Navarre, as another example, Jews were generally distinguishable in documents by given name, or by separator, or by explicit identification, but rarely by all three at once.[7]

The redundancy found in business and legal records from Toledo was also different from the naming patterns found in other kinds of Castilian records, such as Latin and vernacular chronicles and charters from the royal chancery. Such records, which by definition dealt with exceptional events and behavior rather than daily business dealings, treated all the individuals they mentioned as unique. Both royal charters and Castilian chronicles sometimes did over-identify Jews but just as often omitted part of the triple identification.[8] And those occasional chroniclers who did rely on triple identification used a

---

filius . . . Isaachi Mercadelli, quondam iudei de Barchinone," and that in subsequent references the Jew was called "prefato Issacho Mercadelli," "eidem Issacho," and "dicto Issacho." See David Romano, "Otros casamenteros judíos (Barcelona-Gerona 1357)," *Estudios históricos y documentos de los Archivos de Protocolos* 5 (1977): 300–301, for the Barcelonese document of 27 November 1357, which first calls two Jews "vos Vitalis Caravida, judeus Gerunde, et Salamon Caravida, judeus Barchinone" and then refers to them simply as "vobis" throughout.

[7] In the kingdom of Navarre most Jews did take recognizably Jewish given names, and they were identified as "judío" in most vernacular documents. But they rarely were assigned the separator "don," and were not redundantly identified as Jews in short references. See the "Apéndice documental" to Béatrice Leroy, "Los judíos de Navarra al final de la Edad Media," trans. Juan Ignacio de Laiglesia, in Mercedes García-Arenal and Béatrice Leroy, *Moros y judíos en Navarra en la Baja Edad Media* (Madrid, 1981), pp. 199–249, for a variety of types of documents including references to Jews, from a number of Navarrese towns. Even in other parts of Castile the emphasis on identifying Jews was not as strong as in Toledo. An early fifteenth-century notarial register from Dueñas (province of Palencia), for example, actually names Jews according to the usual formula for naming Christians at the first reference (i.e., as "fulano fijo de fulano," as it is phrased in Cuesta Gutiérrez, p. 179), with no separator or explicit identification as Jews; apparently the Jewish given name was considered sufficiently obvious there. But on second and subsequent references, the separator "don" was introduced, so that redundant identification was maintained throughout most of the document. For instance, a Jew was introduced as "Ça Odara fijo de Sento Odara," but his father is referred to thereafter as "el dicho don Sento;" see Pérez Bustamante, p. 83. ("Ça" may have been a mistake for "Çag.") For references to Jews without any redundancy see *ibid.*, pp. 85, 95–96 (items 4, 17).

[8] Some of the chronicles are: Jofré de Loaysa, *Crónica de los Reyes de Castilla Fernando III, Alfonso X, Sancho IV y Fernando IV (1248–1305)*, trans. and ed. by Antonio García Martínez, 2nd ed. (Murcia, 1982); Luis Charlo Brea, ed. and trans., *Crónica latina de los reyes de Castilla* (Cadiz, 1984); Rodrigo Jiménez de Rada, *Historia de los hechos de España*, trans. and intro. by Juan Fernández Valverde (Madrid, 1989); and the *Crónica de don Alfonso décimo*, *Crónica de don Sancho el bravo*, *Crónica de don Alfonso el onceno*, and *Crónica de don Pedro primero* in *Crónicas de los reyes de Castilla desde don Alfonso el sabio, hasta los católicos don Fernando y doña Isabel*, vol. 1, ed. Cayetano Rosell, *BAE*, vol. 66 (Madrid, 1875).

variant of it for all the persons whose deeds they recounted, not for Jews alone. At first reference in these chronicles, most individuals' given names were preceded by some form of identifier, whether a title of royalty, nobility, or secular or religious office (for instance: "*infante*," "*conde*," "*frayle*," "*alcalde*"), or, for both Jews and Christians, the vaguer "don." Most also were identified by descriptors following their names, referring to religion or ethnicity, to citizenship, or to occupation, for example "*judío*," "*mozarab*," "*gallego*," "*vecino de* . . .," "*morador de* . . .," "*monedero*," "*criado de*. . . ." In these records, therefore, Jews, though clearly members of a distinct group, appeared to be acting as individuals, not as persons who must be identified according to their minority status.

Redundant identification was also absent from the Arabic-language documents that Christians in Toledo sometimes prepared during this period. These derived in part from Islamic models followed in the city before the Christian conquest, and were produced well into the thirteenth century by Mozarabic scribes there. As in Arabic documents from the Crown of Aragon, almost all the individuals mentioned in this group of records used Arabic or Arabicized names. Moreover, though in these documents Jews were always clearly called Jews, such a description was both ethnic and religious, since it mirrored the identification of Christians according to their ethnic origins. Christians were identified either culturally, as Mozarabs, or geographically, as those with backgrounds in Castile, Aragon, Galicia, Barcelona, or elsewhere.

Finally, but very significantly, Muslims who appeared in Christian vernacular documents from Toledo did not receive the triple intitulation applied to Jews there. They were identifiable as Muslims through their given names and surnames and were explicitly called Muslims when first cited, but they were not assigned the title "don" and on subsequent references they, like Christians, were called by their names and surnames alone.

But Toledan scribes over-identified Jews as Jews. An examination of more than eleven hundred vernacular business and legal documents from the province of Toledo yields some 350 references to Jews.[9] Among these documents, which detail the economic life of Toledo

---

[9] Based upon my survey of the eleven hundred Toledan documents in AHN, Seccíon Clero (excluding those written in Arabic), and the holdings of the ACT, I estimate that the overall percentage of all surviving Toledan documents from the

and shed light on its land market, are fewer than a dozen exceptions to over-identification. The effect on the reader is to make Jewish
identity and distinct status evident at all times.[10] In the world described
by Toledan vernacular records, a place of ordinary economic and
legal competition and cooperation between Christians and Jews,
Jews acted much like Christians. But one could not read a Toledan

---

twelfth through fourteenth centuries that contain references to Jews is between eight
and ten percent, since the Arabic documents, which do not include the royal grants
and ecclesiastical correspondence sometimes found in Latin and Castilian, were
more likely to refer to Jews. Jews were not mentioned in documents that dealt with
the foundation of Christian religious institutions, donations, and ecclesiastical correspondence, and subtracting these documents from the total leaves about five hundred documents. Thus Jews are shown as participating in twenty or twenty-five
percent of Toledo's business activities (they appear as neighbors or witnesses in
about as many more), indicating that they were disproportionately active in the
Toledan economy but hardly dominated it.

Attempts to specify either the total or the Jewish population of Toledo have been
contradictory. Leopoldo Torres Balbás, "Extensión y demografía de los ciudades
hispanomusulmanas," *Studia Islamica* 3 (1955): 55–56, has estimated that around the
time of the Christian conquest Toledo's population was about 37,000, but there is
no reliable information on how that population developed in the following centuries. Norman Roth, "New Light on the Jews of Mozarabic Toledo," *AJS Review*
11 (1986): 196, contrasts this with the figure of over 12,000 Jews in the city in the
early thirteenth century, which he takes from a fifteenth-century reference to a statement by a thirteenth-century resident. This estimate, however, like all medieval estimates of population, should not be taken seriously; certainly it is misleading to
imply, as Roth does by the juxtaposition of the figures, that the Jews of Toledo at
any time accounted for one-third of the town's population. Nevertheless, Yitzhak
Baer, *A History of the Jews in Christian Spain*, 2nd ed., trans. Lotte Levensohn and
Hillel Halkin (Philadelphia, 1961), pp. 190, 418–419, notes 1, 2, suggests that at
the end of the thirteenth century there were only about 350 Jewish families in
Toledo, which seems too low a figure. I estimate that Jews made up from fifteen
to twenty percent of Toledo's population. This suggestion is very approximate, based
on the proportion of the total surface area of Toledo taken up by Jewish neighborhoods. The method has its own problems, not least of which is that Toledo is very
hilly, and not all areas of the city are equally habitable; see Julio Porres Martín-
Cleto, "Los barrios judíos de Toledo," in *Simposio "Toledo judaico" (Toledo 20–22 Abril
1972)* (Toledo, 1973[?]), 1:46. However, it does suggest that during the twelfth century the Jewish population of Toledo expanded from about ten percent of the total
(under the Muslims the *Madīna al-Yahūd* took up about that proportion of the city's
area, while in the thirteenth century the *juderías* took up roughly between one-sixth
and one-fifth), an impression confirmed by what we know of Jewish migration to
Toledo.

[10] In this way, Toledan documents had the same effect as did medieval iconography, in which Jewish men appeared in distinctive dress and with distinctive facial
characteristics. For examples of thirteenth-century pictures of Jewish men see the
illuminations of Cantigas #2, 3, 4, 6, 12, 25, 27, 34, 85, 107, 108, and 109 in *El
"Códice rico" de las Cantigas de Alfonso X el Sabio: MS T.I.1 de la Biblioteca de El Escorial*
(Madrid, 1979).

vernacular document in which a Jewish man appeared without being made aware that he was a Jew and that his religion implied characteristics and status that made him very different indeed from Christians. Why, then, did Toledan Christians find it necessary to insist so strongly and so unusually on Jewish difference?

Part of the impetus for the development of the triple identification was the necessity in Toledo of combining a variety of models into a single vernacular pattern. Toledan vernacular formulas began to develop relatively early in the thirteenth century, and drew on other traditions. One set of influences came from the Latin practices followed by the Castilian chancery and in the city itself into the middle third of the thirteenth century.[11] Another was the Arabic formulas that had been used in Toledo until the Christian conquest of 1085 and which continued to be followed by some sections of the Christian population there through the thirteenth century.[12] Each contributed some elements to the Toledan vernacular formulation.

Castilian Latin practice did not use the triple identifier for Jews. Although most Jews mentioned in Castilian Latin documents used Biblical names, others were referred to by Arabic or Latin names. Where the name or the context was ambiguous, the Jew was explicitly called a Jew, but where his religion was clear this identification was sometimes omitted. And the Latin "dominus," the source of the vernacular "don," was used in Castilian Latin documents as an honorific, not a separator; hence it was not always applied to Jews and was more often applied to Christians. So Jews appearing

---

[11] For Latin documents issued by the Castilian chancery (and by the Leonese chancery before the final union of the two kingdoms), see Julio González, *Regesta de Fernando II* (Madrid, 1943), pp. 239–341 (documents issued 1158–1187); idem, *El reino de Castilla en la epoca de Alfonso VIII*, 3 vols. (Madrid, 1960), vols. 2–3 (documents issued 1145–1216); idem, *Alfonso IX*, 2 vols. (Madrid, 1944), vol. 2 (documents issued 1188–1230); idem, *Reinado y diplomas de Fernando III*, 3 vols. (Cordoba, 1980–1986), vols. 2–3 (documents issued 1217–1253). For other Castilian Latin documents see Fritz Baer, *Die Juden im Christlichen Spanien: Urkunden und Regesten*, 2 vols. (Berlin, 1929–1936).

The Castilian vernacular was first heavily used in documents issued by Fernando III during the 1230s and was the language generally used by the end of the 1240s.

[12] See Angel González Palencia, *Los mozárabes de Toledo en los siglos XII y XIII*, 4 vols. (Madrid, 1926–1930); and Francisco J. Hernández, comp. and ed., *Los cartularios de Toledo* (Madrid, 1985). In González Palencia's collection of 1,140 documents, 54 date from the period from 1101 to 1150, 368 from 1151 to 1200, and 448 from 1201 to 1250. The number then decreased to 316 from 1251 to 1300, and almost disappeared in the fourteenth century.

in Toledan Latin documents could be identified, but were not over-identified, as Jews.

There was also no triple identification of Jews in Islamic documentary practice. These forms had influenced the Arabic-language records that the Mozarabs of Toledo preferred even after the Christian conquest.[13] Mozarabs, Christians whose ancestors had lived under Muslim rule and had adopted Arabic language and culture, generally had Arabic names. Many Christians and Jews who settled in Toledo after 1085 also adopted Arabic names for the purpose of dealing with Mozarabs.[14] Names alone, therefore, could not serve to distinguish between Jews and Christians in these records, and so explicit religious identifiers were used. The Mozarabs themselves had been a religious minority under Islam and were identified as Mozarabs in Islamic documents; this practice continued under Christian rule into the late eleventh and the twelfth century.[15] At times during this period they extended ethnic identification to other Christian groups in their records. During the thirteenth century, as cultural distinctions between Toledan Christians of various backgrounds began to blur, ethnic descriptors of Christians began to be dropped from Mozarabic documents, but identification of Jews and Muslims continued.

Most of the examples of Christian ethnic identifications in these documents come from the first half of the thirteenth century, though there are a few from the last half of the century. The Mozarabs' continued use of Arabic at that late date was a deliberate attempt to maintain their distinct identity within Toledo. But in fact, they did gradually adapt to the Toledan Christian norm, as is seen by their own adoption of Castilian names. During the twelfth century,

---

[13] González Palencia, 4:360–361, states that the notarial formulas found in Toledan Mozarabic documents were transferred almost word for word from the formulas for similar transactions found in Islamic formularies. The main difference between the two traditions was that Islamic documents explained that business was being carried out "according to the law of the Muslims," while Mozarabic documents referred to "the law of the Christians." He finds no traces of Visigothic notarial practice in the documents in his collection.

[14] See González Palencia, 4:117–40, for Mozarabs in general; see examples in ibid. and Hernández for Toledan Jews and Christians of other backgrounds using Arabic names; see the many references in S[helomo] D[ov] Goitein, *A Mediterranean Society: The Jewish Communities of the Arab World as Portrayed in the Documents of the Cairo Geniza*, 5 vols. (Berkeley, 1967–1988), for other examples and for letters written in Arabic by Toledan Jews.

[15] See González Palencia, 4:122–123, for documents from the last half of the twelfth century that illustrate this practice, which apparently died out after that time.

it became increasingly common for Mozarab individuals with Arabic names and surnames to use vernacular variants of those names as cognomens, and the practice became pronounced after that time. Moreover, by the end of the twelfth century it was normal for these Arabic-language documents to contain clauses stating that the contents had been explained (to the Mozarabic participants) in the vernacular, and had been understood. This was a clear sign that the use of Arabic had become a type of formal identification but was no longer a cultural trait.[16]

So the explicit identification of Jews as Jews had precedents in both the Latin and the Arabic traditions which influenced Toledan vernacular practice. The earliest vernacular documents from Toledo also routinely recorded individuals' ethnicity. The most salient element of group identity was religion. Thus non-Christians were simply defined as Jews or Muslims. But differences among Christians were acknowledged as well, and vernacular documents recorded the activities of Mozarabs, Castilians, migrants from Galicia, Navarre, Aragon, and the frontier, and even former residents of specific cities like Gerona and Barcelona. For a while these distinctions seem to have been applied to descendants of the various settlers as well. But during the course of the thirteenth century the Christian residents of Toledo began to be integrated into a single Toledan identity, and identification of Christian ethnicity dropped out of vernacular documents at the same time that it was dropped from Mozarabic documents. In some cases, the ethnic identification became a family surname, but it was more often dropped altogether, with a patronymic providing a surname when one was adopted.

Jews and Muslims were left as the only groups requiring special identification.[17] In these circumstances, the use in vernacular documents of the explicit identifiers "judío" and "moro" to describe members

---

[16] See González Palencia, 4:123–125, 129. Mozarabic documents also had no equivalent to the vernacular "don." An Arabic honorific, "mair" (sometimes "maior"), was used in the earliest Mozarabic documents as the equivalent of the Latin "dominus," but this term died out around the end of the twelfth century. For the final fifty years of its use, it appeared interchangeably with "dominus" and "domina" in Arabic transliteration. At first honorifics, the use of these Latin terms was generalized so greatly that during the thirteenth century they were applied to every individual in the documents almost without exception, becoming the equivalent of the modern "señor" and "señora."

[17] Muslims appeared relatively rarely in Toledan documents, and almost always as the objects, not the subjects, of the activities recorded. The local population of Muslims grew smaller and poorer as most of them left Toledo after the Christian

of religious minorities was obvious, and was carried over from both the Latin and the Arabic documentary traditions. And for the Muslims, militarily defeated and economically insignificant, this identification sufficed. But, despite the obvious tendency of Toledan scribes to streamline traditional practice where it had become unnecessary, as with dropping the ethnic identification of Christian groups, they began adding the prefix "don" to Jewish names, complicating the issue of notarial identification of Jews.[18]

The use of the title "don" and the insistence on recognizably Jewish names were Castilian vernacular developments. As has been seen, "don" evolved from "dominus," a Castilian Latin honorific or sign of noteworthiness. In its transition to the vulgar tongue, it kept the second of these meanings, and came to be a signal of difference. Local vernacular documents applied it to nobles, who had a different legal status than non-nobles; they increasingly used "doña" for women, to differentiate them from the masculine norm; and they applied it to Jews, who were different from Christians. Only in the fifteenth century did its long association with the nobility give it honorific connotations once again, at which time Jews were prohibited from using it.[19]

From a much earlier date, the Castilian parliament, the *Cortes*, also had attempted to keep Jewish names distinct from Christian names. The townsmen at the *Cortes* held at Palencia in 1313 were the first to petition successfully for such legislation, when the guardians

---

conquest, and the remaining community was not enlarged by new immigration, as were the area's Christians and Jews. See Joseph F. O'Callaghan, "The Mudejars of Castile and Portugal in the Twelfth and Thirteenth Centuries," in *Muslims under Latin Rule, 1100–1300*, ed. James M. Powell (Princeton, 1990), pp. 14, 18–20, 26–40.

[18] For example, Cuesta Gutiérrez records an interesting early-fifteenth-century Castilian notarial formulary that gives numerous examples of how to describe Christians, from the basic "fulano fijo de fulano, vesino de tal lugar" (p. 179), through an example of how to refer to a priest who wants to leave property to his children (he is first called "fulano clerigo, vesino de ..." and his priestly character is mentioned in each subsequent reference, as "el dicho fulano clerigo" (p. 66). Yet the formulary contains no examples of how to refer to Jews; evidently, this was such common knowledge that it did not need to be explained.

[19] The prohibition formed article 12 of the Ordenamiento de las leyes de Ayllón, which Queen Catalina, acting as regent for her son Juan II, issued on 2 January 1412. It stated "Que ningun judio nin judia usara de palabra nin por escrito ti-tulo de don, inponiendose al que lo contrario hiziera el castigo de cien azotes." See Ferrer-Chivite, pp. 135–36 and note 11. Ferrer-Chivite notes that Jews routinely ignored the prohibition, and certainly the Jews of Toledo continued to feature in Toledan documents as "don," though there are signs that it was taking on honorific connotations there too, expressing status within the Jewish community.

of Alfonso XI reported that "they petitioned us that from now on [neither] the Jews nor the Moors should call themselves Christian names and if they do use such names [the townsmen] should judge them as heretics."[20] In Toledo, however, Jews had avoided Christian names, or perhaps Christian scribes had refused to record Christian names for them, long before this enactment. The scribes not only preempted the national legislation on Jewish names; in the fifteenth century, after Jews were forbidden to call themselves "don," Toledan documents continued to apply the term to them. Obviously, the need to maintain the Toledan tradition of multiple identification of Jews superseded obedience to national law.

In fact, the naming patterns in Toledan documental practice developed in response to the need to create new forms in a new language, reflecting contemporary ideas of group identity. The transition to the vernacular gave scribes in Toledo the chance to devise formulas that generally reflected the social and legal realities of their society. And the model to which Toledan scribes wished to hold Jews was one of fundamental difference from and conceptual separation from Christians. Once the new formulas had been established, however, they themselves became a tradition that had increasingly little contact with reality but merely reinforced the conceptual paradigm. The fact that most documents in which Jews appeared recorded economic and legal interactions that showed Jews and Christians in similar roles contradicted this model but evidently strengthened the need to insist on it.

Christians since Augustine had believed that Jews could be permitted to live beside them, as a distinct group whose humiliation would point out the supersession of their beliefs. Such a system obviously required an emphasis on Jewish difference, often expressed as a demand that Jews wear distinguishing badges or clothing. In Castile, the emphasis on Jewish humiliation, difference, and separation was fully endorsed by the *Siete Partidas*, the comprehensive legal code compiled in the mid-thirteenth century for Alfonso X and finally formally promulgated as national law in 1348 by Alfonso XI.[21] But

[20] *Cortes*, 1:244–245, clause 42: "Otrossi nos pidieron que da qui adelante los judios nin los moros non se llamen nonbres de cristianos e ssilo llamaren que ffagan justiçia dellos commo de hereges. . . . Tenemos por bien e otorgamos gelo."
[21] See Dwayne Eugene Carpenter, *Alfonso X and the Jews: An Edition of and Commentary on Siete Partidas 7.24 "De los judíos"* (Berkeley, 1986), esp. pp. 57–58 for the description

Castilian authorities were notorious for not enforcing such regulations, and so clothing could not mark the boundary between Christians and Jews in Toledo, or point to Jewish humiliation.[22] The triple identification, however, could function as a sign of Jewish difference whenever Jews' activities were recorded.[23]

Jewish commerce with Christians also revealed a reality which did not correspond to the Christian image of Jewish difference and inferiority. Jews regularly engaged in commercial and financial relations with Christians. The fact that Christians and Jews were seen in Toledan documents acting in similar ways and filling similar roles blurred the inherent boundaries which, both Christians and Jews taught, ought to exist between the groups. Jewish leaders had very real concerns about conversion to Christianity. As the events of the end of the fourteenth and the fifteenth century make clear, Christian prosyletizing became more effective in politically and economically vulnerable Jewish communities. Even a large and vibrant Jewish community had to be aware of the dangers of conversion to Christianity. At the best of times, Jewish social contacts with Christians were problematic in an allegorical tradition that discussed idolatry and apostasy in social, especially sexual, terms.[24] As Robert I. Burns and

---

of Jews living among Christians on royal sufferance, and on the necessary degradation of the Jewish condition.

[22] Indeed, Jewish legislation in 1432 suggests that Jewish dress was more likely to present visions of opulence. See Yolanda Moreno Koch, ed. and trans., *De iure hispano-hebraico. Las Taqqanot de Valladolid de 1432: un estatuto comunal renovador* (Salamanca, 1987), for Jewish nervousness about reactions to rich clothing. The reluctance of the Christian authorities to enforce the more extreme elements of distinctive dress on religious minorities was in some ways a continuation of Iberian Islamic practice. The Muslim rulers of the peninsula were noted for not enforcing extremely humiliating requirements on their Christian and Jewish subjects. See Bat Ye'or [Yahudiya Masriya], *The Dhimmi. Jews and Christians under Islam*, revised and enlarged English edition, translated by David Maisel, Paul Fenton, and David Littman (Rutherford, NJ, 1985), p. 78.

[23] There may have been another theological element to the need for distinction as well. Jeremy Cohen points out that by the thirteenth century Christians criticized the Jews they knew for being different from Biblical Jews; whether by creating and adhering to the Talmud or by being the descendants of the legalistic Pharisees who had corrupted the pure Biblical text, Jews disturbed Christians by defining themselves differently than Christians thought they ought. See Jeremy Cohen, *The Friars and the Jews: The Evolution of Medieval Anti-Judaism* (Ithaca, 1982). Perhaps the triple identification was one way that Christians could reassert their authority to define and describe Jews the way they wished, and to freeze them in time by freezing the formulaic references to them.

[24] See Moshe Halbertal and Avishai Margalit, *Idolatry*, trans. by Naomi Goldblum (Cambridge, MA, 1992), pp. 11–14.

Joseph Shatzmiller have pointed out for other regions, Jewish economic activity served to integrate Jews into the surrounding society;
it did not divide them from their Christian neighbors.[25] In this sense,
Jews were more like Christians than they were like the other religious minority in Toledo, the Muslims. Muslims were most likely to
appear in Toledan documents as clients, tenants, servants, or slaves
of Christians, and could not, from these contexts, possibly be thought
of as the equals of Christians.[26] Jews, on the other hand, could appear
on an equal footing with Christians.

So Jews, unlike the Muslims whose inferiority and distinctive social
position could be understood from the texts of the documents, had
to be put in their place with the use of the triple identifier. The title
"don" emphasized Jewish separation and inferiority despite their
apparently normative behavior. The identifiably Jewish names also
served to reinforce boundaries: persons with such names were not
part of the Christian community. And the explicit identification of
Jews as Jews suggests the desire to show why these individuals stood
out—because they were part of a group that was inherently separate from Christians.[27]

It is clear, then, that the choices made in Toledo in writing about
Jews served a number of purposes. At the most basic, practical level,
the identification as a Jew gave anyone concerned a clear piece of
useful information about an individual; for instance, that he lived
in one of the Jewish neighborhoods of Toledo, or that he did not
do business on Saturdays. By also insisting that a Jew was a non-
Christian, the formula taught that Jews were different, with different

---

[25] Burns, *Muslims, Christians, and Jews*, pp. 133–134; Joseph Shatzmiller, *Shylock
Reconsidered: Jews, Moneylending, and Medieval Society* (Berkeley, 1990), pp. 67–70, 123–126.

[26] O'Callaghan, "Mudejars," pp. 25–30.

[27] Like the ideal of separation between the religious communities, this denigra-
tion of the spiritual standing of the other was not a uniquely Christian attitude. In
the first half of the fourteenth century, regulations of the Toledan Jewish community
continued to refer to Christians (as distinct from both Jews and Muslims) as idol
worshipers; see Judah ben Asher, *Zikhron Yehuda, ve-hu sefer she'elot u-teshuvot* (Berlin,
1846), #45: "U-ve-nidui ha-qahal ha-qadosh qahal Tulaitulah, yishmeru tsuro ve-
go'alo, ve-'al kol mi she-yode'a be-havero she-b'a 'al yishm'a'elit 'o 'al 'ovedet 'elilim
she-yodi'uhu la-dayyanim" [And under the ban of the holy community the community of Toledo, may its rock and its redeemer keep it, and on everyone who
knows about his companion that he went to an Ishmaelite woman or to a woman
who worships idols {i.e., to a Muslim or to a Christian woman}, that they should
make him known to the judges]. For a more general treatment of medieval Jewish
attitudes to Christianity, see Jacob Katz, *Exclusiveness and Tolerance: Studies in Jewish-
Gentile Relations in Medieval and Modern Times* (Oxford, 1961), pp. 39–40.

beliefs, habits, and intrinsic worth. The whole value of the triple identification lay in its over-emphasis on an individual's separation and difference from the Toledan norm. It ensured that anyone who might encounter Toledan vernacular documents would envision the Jews who appeared in them as strange and think of their activities as unusual. And here it revealed its true meaning: by denying the Toledan reality of economic integration, the use of deliberately divisive language upheld the theoretical forms of organization of Toledan and Castilian society.

SHELTER AND SEGREGATION:
LEPERS IN MEDIEVAL CATALONIA

James W. Brodman

Medieval hospitals, whether located in Catalonia or elsewhere in Europe, functioned principally as shelters rather than as providers of medical services. The need of their clientele was viewed as arising more out of "poverty" than from any particular malady, with the consequence that many shelters intermingled individuals who suffered from disease with those who were afflicted with old age or economic distress. While it might be argued that blindness, age or disease was itself the primary cause of the poverty that beset the inmates of hospitals, nevertheless, the tendency of the medieval documents to label these folk as being poor or "the poor of Christ" frequently obscures the specific nature of their distress. Indeed, it seems that many medieval hospitals made no fundamental distinctions among inmates and limited their services to the basics of bed and bread, served with a measure of religious consolation. Thus, throughout the medieval period, there are notices of the foundation and operation of shelters that served pilgrims, the indigent, and the sick. Yet, the mid-twelfth century marks something of a watershed, for it is in this era that a new category of asylum begins to appear, one dedicated to particular groups of the needy, like lepers, the victims of ergotism, and orphans. Of these, the earliest, and by far the most numerous, were leprosaria.

The first leper colonies developed in Europe when instances of leprosy increased after 1100. These rural gatherings initially were organized not too differently from the early communities of Augustinian canons, and frequently were headed by the oldest surviving leper. Gradually a process of institutionalization and definition set in, as the lepers acquired a legal status and formal title to the property they occupied, and organized themselves through statutes into some sort of regime. This process was advanced by Canon 23 of the Third Lateran Council (1179), which gave such communities official status within the Church: "When these men are gathered in a number sufficient to lead a common life, we enact that they can have a

church and a cemetery, and the benefit of a priest among them."
The foundation of a chapel, or the conferral of donations in property or cash, eventually brought such communities to notice, often
under the invocation of a saint, as a leper hospice or hospital.[1]

If leprosaria began to appear ca. 1100, the numbers of new foundations peaked between 1150 and 1250, and then fell off rapidly.[2]
Few genuinely new foundations date from either the fourteenth or
fifteenth centuries. It is impossible to estimate the numbers of these
hospices, because most were small, with perhaps a half-dozen inmates,
and have left few if any documentary traces. Furthermore, because
this work never was taken up in any consistent way by the religious
orders, leprosaria were generally local institutions. The Order of
St. Lazarus, whose work included the care of lepers, never grew to
any size, and the many leper hospitals that bore the name of this
saint rarely had any connection to the order.[3] There were, however,

---

[1] Françoise Beriac, *Histoire des lépreux au moyen âge, une société d'exclus* (Paris, 1988),
pp. 155–161. Most frequently the invocation was that of St. Lazarus, whom medieval
people tended to identify as both the brother of Mary and Martha and the pau-
per at the gate of Dives: Patricia Cullum, *Hospitals and Charitable Provision in Medieval
Yorkshire 936–1547* (1989), p. 32.

[2] Medieval Toulouse, for example, had seven leprosaria, the earliest in existence
in 1167, with the last having its first mention in 1246. See John H. Mundy, "Charity
and Social Work in Toulouse, 1100–1250," *Traditio* 22 (1966): 227–230.

[3] The Franciscans, the Order of the Holy Spirit and the Hospitallers cared for
lepers, but more by way of accident than intention. Jill R. Webster, *Els menorets:
The Franciscans in the Realms of Aragon From St. Francis to the Black Death* (Toronto, 1993),
p. 186; Beriac, pp. 233–234. The Order of St. Lazarus was founded in Jerusalem
during the 1120's as a confraternity that cared for the sick and lepers. In Palestine,
particularly under King Baldwin IV of Jerusalem, the Order acquired military
responsibilities, and its grand master up until 1253 was required to be a leper. The
Order of St. Lazarus was introduced into France after the Second Crusade by Louis
VII, who is said to have given it a hospital in Paris to care for lepers, although
others assert that even this remained under the jurisdiction of the bishop of Paris.
André Mutel, "Recherchés sur l'ordre de Saint-Lazare de Jérusalem en Normandie,"
Annales de Normandie 33 (1983): 121–142, indicates that their primary function was
property management (initially for the benefit of the brethren in the Near East),
not the care of lepers, and that the Leprosarium of Saint-Lazare in Montpellier
was a laic foundation with no connection to the Order. In the Crown of Aragon,
towns like Valencia, Gerona and Lerida had Hospitals of San Llàtzer, but their
connection to the Order is uncertain. Studies of similar hospitals in the region of
Asturias show no affiliation to the Order of St. Lazarus. In August 1265, Pope
Clement IV issued a bull directing that all lepers be placed under the Order's protection and care, but this proved to be completely impractical and came to naught.
See J. Tolivar Faes, *Hospitales de leprosos en Asturias durante las edades media y moderna*
(Oviedo, 1966), p. 261; Robert I. Burns, S.J., *The Crusader Kingdom of Valencia:*

large numbers of these local institutions. Louis VIII of France, for example, in the early thirteenth century bequeathed money to some two thousand leper shelters in his kingdom, but there must have been more than these in France since major regions at that date were still outside of royal control.[4] A quarter of all hospitals in the English county of Yorkshire were leprosaria, and included rural foundations of aristocratic patronage as well as shelters in approximately half of the towns.[5]

In Spain, leper hospitals also proliferated in the twelfth century, and their appearance might well coincide with the development of the Santiago pilgrimage route, whose traffic likely introduced numbers of lepers into the peninsula. According to one estimate, there were twenty thousand lepers in medieval Spain and approximately two hundred leper shelters. If true, this means that many, or most, lepers were left to fend for themselves in the countryside on the margins of society. While no one has yet been able to gauge the inmate population of Iberian leprosaria, J.H. Mundy's estimate of ten inmates per house in nearby Toulouse, if true for Spain as well, would yield a hospital capacity far below the estimated leper population.[6] Tradition holds that one of the earliest leper hospitals in Iberia was established at Palencia in 1067 by the Cid, who is said to have met and cared for a leper-pilgrim to Santiago, later revealed to be San Lázaro.[7] In the province of Asturias, through which a branch of the Santiago road ran, over twenty leprosaria were established between the mid-twelfth and later thirteenth centuries.[8] At Burgos, in Castile, there were two shelters, both under the invocation of San Lázaro, one just outside the walls on the Santiago road, and the other in a more rural

---

Reconstruction on a Thirteenth-Century Frontier, 2 vols. (Cambridge, MA, 1967), 1:242; W.G. Rödel, "San Lazzaro, di Gerusalemme," *Dizionario degli istituti di perfezione* (Rome, 1974–), 8:579; Pierre Edme Gautier de Sibert, *Histoire de l'Ordre Militaire et Hospitalier de Saint-Lazare de Jérusalem* (1772; Paris, 1983), pp. 48–63; Charles Moeller, "Lazarus, Saint, Order of," *The Catholic Encyclopedia* (New York, 1910), 9:96–97; Marcel Baudot, "La Gestation d'une léprosarie du XIVe siècle: La maladrerie Saint-Lazare de Montpellier," *Actes du 110e Congrès national des sociétés savants* (Paris, 1987), 1:411; Malcolm Barber, "The Order of Saint Lazarus and the Crusades," *CHR* 80 (1994): 454.

[4] Beriac, pp. 163–166.
[5] Cullum, pp. 20–26.
[6] Mundy, p. 253.
[7] Carmen López Alonso, *La pobreza en España medieval* (Madrid, 1986), pp. 439–440.
[8] Toliver Faes, pp. 251–254.

locale.[9] León had its own asylum in 1171, as did Seville and Córdoba not long after their conquest in the mid-thirteenth century.[10]

In Catalonia, the best known leprosarium was located in Barcelona, and variously called the *Casa del Malalts* or *Masells* or *Mesells*, the Hospital of *Sant Llàtzer*, or the *Domus Infirmorum*. No act of foundation for it has survived but, despite traditions that date its origins in the mid-ninth century, it began to function, like so many others, in the second half of the twelfth century. Some credit its foundation to Bishop Guillem de Torroja (1144–1171), but the earliest direct reference to the leper hospital is not dated until 1200. The hospice itself was located across the modern Ramblas from the twelfth-century city, in the Plaza Pedró, an agricultural district of small gardens that did not become fully urbanized until the fourteenth century. At first, the chapel was dedicated to Santa María dels Malalts, but in the fourteenth century to Sant Llàtzer al Pedró. As an indication of an episcopal or capitular foundation, the hospice continued to be supervised by the bishop and the chapter, who held powers of appointing rectors, conducting visitations, and legislating customs. The rector initially was both the house's administrator and a chaplain who served at the altar of Santa Margarita, which was endowed in 1218 by a powerful court official, Ramon de Plegamans, and later in 1295 by his grandson Marimon de Plegamans. Sant Llàtzer endured as an independent institution until 1401, when it was joined, first to the hospital of Santa Eulàlia, and then to Barcelona's new general hospital of Santa Creu. Subsequently, due to a rise in the incidence of leprosy in Catalonia during the fifteenth century, there was an attempt by the city council to establish a new, and larger, leper hospital outside the Porto Nou. This effort, however, floundered, not only because of the projected cost, six thousand florins, but also because of a fear that such a facility would only encourage the immigration of lepers into city. Ultimately, the council decided to make do with the cur-

---

[9] L. Martínez García, "La asistencia material en los hospitales de Burgos a fines de la Edad Media," *Colloque de Nice: Manger et boire au moyen âge, 1982,* 2 vols. (Nice, 1984), 1:353.

[10] José Sánchez Herrero, "Cofradías, hospitales y beneficencia en algunes dióce-sis del valle del Duero, siglos XIV y XV," *Hispania* 34 (1974): 5–51; Juan Ignacio Carmona García, *El sistema de hospitalidad publica en la Sevilla del antiguo Regimen* (Seville, 1979), p. 26; Antonio García del Moral, *El Hospital Mayor de San Sebastian de Córdoba: Cinco siglos de asistencia médico-sanitaria institucional (1363–1816)* (Córdoba, 1984), pp. 39–40.

rent facilities by denying admission to lepers who originated from outside of Barcelona itself.

Bishop Ponç de Gualba carried out a pastoral inspection of Sant Llàtzer on 24 February 1307. The record of that visitation lists the hospital's personnel at that time: Bernat d'Orts, the rector; Jaume de Rocafort, a cleric and a leper who disliked the rector; Berenguer de Canal, the chaplain, and three male attendants. In 1379, the staff had grown to include an administrator, several chaplains, six full-time staff, and several part-time alms collectors and neighborhood retainers.

Statutes concerning Sant Llàtzer's operation are extant from a reform by Bishop Ponç de Gualba in 1326, instituted to correct problems in the hospital's administration. Evidently, the rector, reacting to charges that the leper-inmates were improperly cared for, had responded by proposing a reduction in the number of admissions. The bishop's response was to overhaul the hospital's administration. First of all, the duties of the rector were reduced to serving as chaplain, with his administrative functions now turned over to a procurator, who was to be a layman appointed by the bishop. The reform was intended to correct fiscal irregularities, because presumably the lay administrator would be better trained in finance than his clerical predecessor. In addition, by limiting the rector's duties to the chapel, it also improved the inmates' access to daily mass and the sacraments.[11]

Financial accounts for Sant Llàtzer survive for the eleven-month period from May, 1379 to April, 1380, and these give us a snapshot of its economic well-being, the sources of its support, and some indication of its internal operation. The overall figures suggest that the hospital was prospering, with a budgetary surplus of over 1,200 *solidos* from revenues of almost 4,600 *solidos*, yet this conclusion is somewhat problematic given the source of most of this income. Approximately one-half came from short-term giving: the sale of bread alms (30%), alms collected in town (11%), legacies (6%), and chapel offerings (3%). Only a quarter came from permanent endowment:

---

[11] Aurora Pérez Santamaría, "El hospital de Sant Lázaro o Casa dels Malalats o Maselles," in *La pobreza y la asistencia a los pobres en la Cataluña medieval*, ed. Manuel Riu (Barcelona, 1980–1982), 1:77–89, 105–106, 114–115; C. Batlle Gallart and C. Casas, "La caritat privada i les institucions benèfiques de Barcelona (segle XIII)," ibid., 1:144; Carmen Batlle Gallart, *L'assistència als pobres a la Barcelona medieval (s. XIII)* (Barcelona, 1987), pp. 67–69.

investments, rentals, and bursaries established for anniversaries. The remainder derived from the sale of wine and other agricultural products (20%) and money contributed by leper-inmates (5%). Thus, three-fourths of Sant Llàtzer's revenues was subject to the vagaries of Barcelona's economy and could be expected to fluctuate with the times. Lacking comparative figures, it is impossible to determine whether 1379 was a typical year, or an unusually good one.[12]

As befitting its function more as an asylum than as a hospital in the modern sense, the largest expenditure at Sant Llàtzer was for food (38%), followed by wine (31%). While almost the entire expense of the latter was recovered through the sale of surplus vintage to others, all of the former went to feed both staff and inmates. While imprecise to be sure, this evidence suggests something of the configuration of the house and the treatment of its residents. Because more was budgeted per capita to feed the staff, we can assume that they ate better than the lepers.[13] In 1379, furthermore, we know that the staff included an administrator, two or three chaplains, five staff members and a slave. That being so, the food budget would seem to have allowed for the support of fourteen or fifteen lepers, a modest population indeed given a staff of approximately ten. This, however, did not evidently translate into a high level of care for the leper-residents, because of the ten staff members listed only one female attendant was directly charged with the care of inmates.[14]

Outside of Barcelona, one of the earliest leprosaria was founded at Lérida, where a hospital of Sant Llàtzer is cited in Berenguer de Boixadors' will of 1185. The hospice was located on inexpensive land on the left bank of the Segre, near the Hospital of Nicolau, that contained an old mosque and a half dozen buildings. In the next century, a confraternity that enrolled men, women and clergy was established to provide support, to which King Jaume II is said

---

[12] Pérez Santamaría, 1:92–93.

[13] Ibid., 1:99–100. For example, the statutes permitted 2 *diners* to be spent per day on each staff member for food, while inmates were allotted only 12 *diners* per week. On feast days, a single *diner* could be spent on each leper, and staff member, but the administrator and chaplains were to receive food worth 3 *diners* each.

[14] Ibid., pp. 99–100, 104–106. Besides the administrator and chaplains, the staff included a porter, three individuals who collected bread as alms for the hospital (whose subsequent sale represented 30% of the hospital's income), a slave, a laundress and the attendant.

to have belonged. Another hospice on the road to Gardeny seems
to have been established early in the thirteenth century.[15] At Gerona,
the Hospital of Sant Jaume de Pedreto, or Le Pedret, was located
outside the walls.[16] The Hospital of Santa Maria Magdalena was
probably a mid-thirteenth-century foundation at Urgell, with 1284
being its first citation. Like others, its location was outside of the
walls. It was a popular charity, with over a third of the wills extant
for 1287–1291 remembering it with small legacies. Leprosy, however, must have soon declined here since, in the early part of the
next century, the property was made into a residence for hermits.[17]
At Vich, the arrangements for lepers were less distinct. They were
cared for at a hospice operated by the church of Sant Bartomeu
that seems to date from the mid-thirteenth century; this, however,
was soon annexed into the Hospital of En Cloquer, which also shel-
tered travellers and vagrants. Similarly, Ramon de Malla in 1275
built a chapel and hospital for the poor, but this also came to serve
lepers and plague victims in an annex building staffed by *donats*.[18]
At Cevera, Santa Magdelena is first mentioned in a will of 1235.
The hospital and church must have existed under some sort of municipal jurisdiction because in 1246 town officers ousted the hospital's
administrators in a dispute over its expansion.[19]

A decline of leprosy in Catalonia during the fourteenth century
is suggested in the conferral of leprosaria at both Tàrrega (1322)
and Cervera to the Franciscans for use as residences. At Tàrrega
four years later, the Franciscans were given permission to sell the
leper house and use its proceeds toward construction of a new convent on the condition that they would care for all present and future
lepers born in the town, but without the need for a separate leprosarium their numbers must have been few. At Cervera there is no
indication that the friars cared for lepers at all, but Duran argues

---

[15] Josep F. Tarragó i Valentines, *Hospitales en Lérida durante los siglos XII al XVI* (Lerida, 1975), pp. 31, 36, 69.

[16] Christian Guilleré, *Girona medieval. L'etapa d'apogeu, 1285–1360* (Gerona, 1991), p. 89; idem, "Assistance et charité á Gérone au début du XIVème siècle," *La pobreza*, 1:196.

[17] Carmen Batlle Gallart, *La Seu d'Urgell medieval: La ciutat i els seus habitants* (Barcelona, 1985), pp. 139–141.

[18] Eduard Junyent, *La ciutat de Vic i la seva història* (Barcelona, 1976), pp. 87–88.

[19] Josep Danon, *Visió històrica de L'Hospital General de Santa Creu de Barcelona* (Barcelona, 1978), p. 16; Agustí Duran i Sanpere, *Llibre de Cervera*, (Barcelona, 1977), pp. 213–214.

that in any case the Franciscans returned Santa Magdalena to the town in 1328, along with some sort of endowment.[20]

In Christian Majorca, the oldest known citation of leprosy is in the *Constitutions of the Monastery of Santa Margarita* (circa 1330) that address the problem of leper-monks. In the fifteenth century, Majorca had an officer called the *morbería* who was charged with keeping those carrying infectious diseases, which included the plague, tuberculosis and leprosy, from entering the island. Under him were various officials who dealt specifically with leprosy. First of all there was the *vesador i instigador dels massells*, who was charged with identifying cases of leprosy. But the disease here, as elsewhere, was evidently in decline because in 1468 this position was consolidated with that of the second official, the examiner of lepers. Then there was the Hospital dels Massells, that was functioning in 1440 with a physician to oversee the care of lepers. This was located outside the walls, near the gate of Santa Catalina, where lepers could beg alms at a safe distance from town residents. Frequently in the fifteenth century, the *instigador dels massells* also served as governor of the leper hospice.[21]

Were all lepers treated alike? Certainly all partook of a certain marginalization. They were segregated from society and, whether or not they actually underwent the ritual of civil death, lepers were regarded as terminal patients, and thus not as apt candidates for any sort of medical treatment. Yet various studies, for example, in the Asturias region of Castile as well as in Catalonia, suggest that rich and poor lepers received different levels of care. Unlike cases of the sick, where the rich were tended at home and the poor in public shelters, affluent lepers tended to reside in endowed hospitals where they were provided with decent accommodations, a bed and even some recreation, while the poor were more likely to end up as members of rural communities supported by begging. Hospital admission, in addition to being influenced by factors of family and wealth, also could be conditioned by geography, in that residents of a locality would be given priority over outsiders for the limited number of

---

[20] J.R. Webster, "La reina doña Constanza y los hospitales de Barcelona y Valencia," *Archivo Ibero-Americano* (1991): 278; idem, *Els menorets*, pp. 55, 186. Duran, *Llibre de Cervera*, pp. 214–215, adds that the hospital was reconstructed with 200 *sous* left by merchant, Joan Llop, in his will of 1377, and the church with money willed by another merchant, Betran dels Archs, in 1389.

[21] Antonio Contreras Mas, *La asistencia publica a los leprosos en Mallorca; Siglos XIV al XIX* (Malloca, 1990), pp. 21–22, 42, 57–59.

places.[22] At Barcelona, after 1326, a committee composed of the bishop's almoners and two upstanding citizens of Barcelona decided whom to admit to Sant Llàtzer. First priority was to be given to lepers from the city itself, followed by those from the diocese, then other Catalan lepers, and finally transients. Given our earlier estimate of fourteen or so places at Sant Llàtzer, one can assume that there was little room for the latter.[23]

Perhaps the most important concern in deciding matters of admission was the cost of care, since anyone admitted might well remain in residence for several years. In France, and perhaps elsewhere, the presumption was that the property of the perspective inmate would now belong to the leprosarium.[24] By the end of the thirteenth century, notarial manuals contained contracts that recorded various agreements between lepers and shelters concerning the disposal of the former's property.[25] But many lepers were too poor to underwrite the cost of their care. In some instances, they were required to provide at least their own clothing and bedding; in other instances, alms from the community supported poor lepers. At Barcelona, lepers, or their families, were obligated to pay nothing in theory, but in fact those with means were expected to defray, in whole or in part, the cost of their care, if for no other reason than to preserve Sant Llàtzer's resources for the truly poor. But, on the other hand, indigents seem to have constituted most, if not all, of Sant Llàtzer's inmates, since the records of 1379, for example, show that lepers contributed just over five percent of the house's total income. Beriac's study of French asylums, indeed, reveals no consistent pattern of admission. There was a bias against the poor and against strangers, but these were not absolute. The ability to pay, on the other hand, was

---

[22] López Alonso, pp. 435–436.

[23] Pérez Santamaría, pp. 88–89. This prioritization is contained in statutes promulgated in 1326.

[24] James W. Brodman, "What is a Soul Worth? *Pro anima* Bequests in the Municipal Legislation of Reconquest Spain," *Medievalia et Humanistica*, n.s. 20 (1993): 20–21, shows that, for the most part, families would automatically inherit all of a decedent's real property and up to 80% of his personal property, with the remainder disposable at the testator's wish. See Beriac, p. 226, for France, where the Customs of Beauvais in effect give the leprosarium the family's right to a leper's property, leaving the deposition of only a fifth of those goods to the leper.

[25] Beriac, p. 226. For example, a leper at Castelsarrasias gave 6 *sous* in 1300 for his admission, while in 1280 a father promised his daughter's future inheritance to the commander of the leprosarium at Capdenac.

also no guarantee of admission. The leper community itself and its leader had a great deal of discretion in deciding these matters.[26]

Canon law imposed no particular form of governance upon leper communities, and the chaplains appointed by bishops did not always serve as rectors or administrators, as was the case at Barcelona. At Toulouse, for example, the leper houses seem to have had no single head, but instead to have been governed by a council or chapter composed of hospitallers and/or the lepers themselves. In the thirteenth century, some bishops promulgated statutes for leprosaria that placed lepers and/or their healthy aides under some sort of observance.[27] Those at Meaux in 1300, for example, had to promise to live without property, observing chastity, obedience and silence. At St.-Lazare of Montpellier, inmates were forbidden to fornicate, quarrel, sell the house's property to outsiders, or steal, and were enjoined to pray together in Church in silence at the appointed hours. But the archdeacon of Paris argued that lepers should not be treated like religious because many were married and had purchased their place in the asylum. For similar reasons, Bishop Ponç de Gaulbes of Barcelona in 1326 eliminated the requirement that inmates at Sant Llàtzer take vows of chastity and obedience, although he did express the wish that the lepers would live chastely and avoid sin. In the interests of maintaining order, however, even municipal authorities attempted to impose a semi-religious regimen upon lepers, but the promulgation of statutes against theft, assault and battery also demonstrates that the ideal was rarely attained.[28]

Leprosy was a terminal disease from which no recovery was expected, and consequently leprosaria were, like most medieval hospitals, places of residence rather than centers of treatment. Lepers would be fed and clothed; at Barcelona's hospital of Sant Llàtzer they were also given a small amount of spending money, one *dinar* on each of the fifteen major feasts celebrated in the house. While

---

[26] Beriac, pp. 228–231; Pérez Santamaría, pp. 88, 92–93, 111.

[27] Mundy, p. 249. The leper hospital at Chartres, the Grand Beaulieu, imposed its statutes, based loosely upon the Rule of St. Augustine, on both healthy and leprous, although these were separated by condition as well as by gender. Since this hospital was successful and of note, its usages were imitated by other leprosaria, such as that of Saint Gilles, established in 1135 in the Norman town of Pont-Audemer. See Simone C. Mesmin, "Waleran, count of Meulan and the Leper Hospital of S. Gilles de Pont-Audemer," *Annales de Normandie* 32 (1982): 8–11.

[28] Beriac, pp. 235–244, 249; Pérez Santamaría, p. 89.

those who became too ill to join in the communal meal were given special food, the hospital's *Libre dels Comptes* reveal only minor provisions made for medical care. Regulations did permit a portion of the 12 *dinars* that were set aside each week for an inmate's food to be used for lancets and bandages, but there is only a single reference to a physician visiting an inmate. Furthermore, the accounts indicate that virtually nothing was spent on any products that might be of a therapeutic nature.[29]

Leprosaria in Catalonia seemed to have developed somewhat later than those of France, or even northern Spain. In the thirteenth century, however, as the region, through its port of Barcelona and its expansionary thrusts into Valencia, the Balearics and Italy, became more closely tied to the outside world, leprosy and the need to shelter lepers from society became more evident. The institutions founded to this purpose, for the most part, mirrored those of other European regions: they were small, of local origin and governance, generally located on the edge of town, and served as places of residence, rather than centers of care. Given the limits on inmate population, the lepers so served were privileged among their compeers. While the latter led lives of mendicancy and itinerancy, the former had the reasonable security of bed and board. In Barcelona, if our slender evidence is at all typical, those selected for this care were chosen principally on the basis of their residency, and were supported by public alms rather than by their own resources. They were the *pauperes verecundi* (or *vergonzantes, vergonyants*), the worthy poor, as opposed to outsiders and vagrants who were likewise shunned by homeless shelters and soup kitchens and parochial almoners. Charity in fourteenth-century Barcelona, it seems, began at home.

---

[29] Pérez Santamaría, pp. 112–113. The physician's charge was three *solidi* per visit, suggesting *inter alia* an economic motive for avoiding medical care.

PESTE NEGRA: THE FOURTEENTH-CENTURY PLAGUE EPIDEMICS IN IBERIA[1]

William D. Phillips, Jr.

In the mid-fourteenth century, plague epidemics assaulted wide portions of Eurasia and Africa. The scholarly literature on the plague in many parts of Europe is well developed, but less so for Spain and Portugal, where there has never been a book-length study of the topic.[2] Fortunately, it is possible to track the incidence of plague in various regions by using contemporary chronicles, parliamentary and municipal records, and the wealth of detailed local histories and case studies produced in the last few decades. Those same records provide information about the consequences of the plague in the aftermath of the initial outbreak, when epidemics recurred every ten or twenty years. They also allow a series of comparisons with experiences elsewhere in Europe and the Middle East.

For Europe as a whole, the general outlines of the story are clear. Beginning in the eleventh century, population grew in the wake of the medieval agricultural revolution. Better diets and less work for women allowed more and healthier babies to be born, and an eventual increase in the labor supply and the demand for food. Plowing more land increased the food supply, and the population rose still higher. By the end of the thirteenth century, however, Europe's population approached the maximum that could be sustained by existing agricultural technology. Famines and epidemics began to reduce the population and consequently lessened the demand for

---

[1] An earlier version of this paper was delivered as the annual Bertie Wilkinson Memorial Lecture at the University of Toronto, February 3, 1994.

[2] I am currently at work on a study of the topic. Several general surveys have been published in article form. See, for example, Jaime Sobrequés Callicó, "La peste negra en la Península Ibérica," *EM* 7 (1970–1971): 67–102; Julio Valdeón Baruque, "La Peste Negra: La muerte negra en la península. El impacto de la peste." *Historia* 16 (1980): 60–71. For a general treatment of Spanish demography, see Vicente Pérez Moreda and David S. Reher, eds., *Demografía histórica en España* (Madrid, 1988); Charles Verlinden, "La grande peste de 1348 en Espagne: Contribution à la étude de ses conséquences économiques et sociales," *Revue Belge de Philologie et Histoire* 17 (1938): 103–146.

food. Farms on marginal lands, whose soils were by then wearing out, were abandoned in a process that left entire villages deserted in northern Europe in the early fourteenth century.

Then, at mid-century, bubonic plague struck. In the course of less than four years, the plague killed between one-quarter and one-third of the entire European population. The initial wave of the Black Death was the greatest demographic disaster Europeans have ever experienced.[3] Over the same period, the Muslim world of North Africa and the Middle East suffered roughly comparable losses. Following the acute decline of population, and in part because of it, Europe underwent economic changes and social alterations that in many cases led to mob violence and rebellion.

Plague is most commonly a disease of rodents. It is caused by a bacillus (*Yersinia pestis*) which is often transmitted by a particular species of flea, one of whose favorite hosts is the black rat (*Rattus rattus*). When plague breaks out in the rat population, the flea ingests infected blood, and the bacilli multiply in its stomach. Eventually, it becomes blocked by the growth of the bacilli and can no longer feed properly, disgorging rather than engorging the blood of its host. When the flea moves to another host and attempts to feed, it injects tainted blood into a new victim.

Of the several varieties of plague, the bubonic form is most common. The characteristic buboes or swellings form along the lymphatic system, accompanied by fever, pain, swelling, and hemorrhages beneath the skin. The buboes ultimately break, if the patient can survive four or five days in great pain. At that point, the victim either dies or recovers. Bubonic plague kills about 30 to 40% of those infected. Once an epidemic of the bubonic form is in progress, another form can develop, called pneumonic plague. Spread directly from person to person by droplet infection as a patient coughs into the air, pneumonic plague is nearly 100% fatal. Some researchers have identified a third form as well, septicaemic plague, in which the bacillus multiplies so rapidly in the victim's bloodstream that death occurs very quickly and almost without symptoms.

We know a great deal about the plague, because it has persisted in many parts of the world since the Middle Ages. In the late nineteenth and early twentieth century, public health officials monitored

---

[3] By comparison, in neither World War I nor World War II did the death toll reach 10% of the European population.

epidemic outbreaks in India and China, when modern hospitals were available and when modern statistics were kept. During those epidemics, researchers finally determined the mechanism by which the plague spread, but they still could not cure it, in the absence of modern antibiotics. Plague still exists, but it is easily cured with antibiotics if it is diagnosed in time. In the western and southwestern United States, a few people contract bubonic plague every year, usually from contact with wild rodents, but it is rarely fatal. In fourteenth-century Europe, lacking modern hospitals and antibiotics, and having no clear idea of how the disease was spread, the demographic consequences would have been devastating regardless of the underlying state of the economy. But the plague struck a Europe already weakened by overpopulation, harvest failures, famine, and epidemics. In that precarious situation, the Black Death sent shock waves through the whole structure of civilization and caused damage that took a century to repair.[4]

The first, and what turned out to be the worst, outbreak of plague in the Iberian peninsula began in March of 1348. According to various contemporary reports, it seems to have appeared first on the island of Mallorca and then in Rosellón and Cerdaña, the Pyrenean frontier counties, sometime around April. Barcelona was affected by early May, as was Tarragona and elsewhere in Catalonia. Almería, still a Muslim port in the mid-fourteenth century, joined the ranks of stricken towns in the last days of May. By June, plague broke out in the great pilgrimage center of Santiago de Compostela in the far

---

[4] For a selection of general works on the plague in Europe, see Jean Noël Biraben, *Les hommes et la peste en France et dans les pays européens et méditerranéens* (Paris, 1975–1976); William M. Bowsky, ed., *The Black Death: A Turning Point in History?* (Huntington, NY, 1978); A. R. Bridbury, "The Black Death," *Economic History Review*, 2nd ser., 24 (1973): 577–592; Ann G. Carmichael, *Plague and the poor in Renaissance Florence* (Cambridge, 1986); Elisabeth Carpentier, "Autour de la Peste Noire, famines et épidémies dans l'histoire du 14ᵉ siècle," *Annales E.S.C.* 6 (1962): 1062–1090; Samuel Kline Cohn, *The Cult of Remembrance and the Black Death: Six Renaissance Cities in Central Italy* (Baltimore, 1992); Geoffrey Marks, *The Medieval Plague; the Black Death of the Middle Ages* (Garden City, NY, 1971); William Hardy McNeill, *Plagues and Peoples* (Garden City, NY, 1976); Mario da Costa Roque, *As pestes medievais europeias e o "regimento" proueytoso contra ha pestinença* (Paris, 1979); Josiah Cox Russell, "The Effect of Pestilence and Plague, 1315–1385," *Comparative Studies in Society & History* 8 (1966): 463–473; Daniel Williman, ed., *The Black Death: The Impact of the Fourteenth-Century Plague* (Binghamton, NY, 1982); Sylvia Thrupp, "Plague Effects in Medieval Europe," *Comparative Studies in Society and History* 8 (July, 1966): 474–483; Graham Twigg, *The Black Death: A Biological Reappraisal* (New York, 1985); Philip Ziegler, *The Black Death* (New York, 1969).

northwest. Most, if not all, of the outbreaks in 1348 assumedly were introduced from outside the peninsula, rather than spreading from one initial point of infection. Once established in port towns, however, the plague spread inland. From Barcelona and Valencia it advanced along separate routes to the inland city of Zaragoza, arriving in September. By October the city registered some 300 deaths each month. By 1349, the peninsula as a whole was infected, and the Black Death in its various forms reportedly claimed its largest number of victims in that year.[5] All told, the first plague epidemic in Iberia lasted until March of 1350.

Studies of the Black Death must often rely on indirect evidence for many of their conclusions. All over Europe, scholars have used the mortality records of bishops and archbishops, cathedral canons, monks and members of military orders, notaries and city councilors, as proxies for their fellow citizens. Corporate groups and prominent individuals claim places in the written records that usually ignore ordinary mortals. The famous plague accounts of Florence and Fiesole are exceptions to the normal pattern, because they had Giovanni Boccaccio to chronicle their misfortunes. Most of the thousands of towns in Europe had no Boccaccio to describe the suffering of their citizens. Civil and ecclesiastical officials who kept records were often among the first to die, because their offices put them at great risk. The record-keeping of Spain and Portugal suffered from the same deficiencies common throughout plague-stricken Europe, even though several precious medical treatises from Islamic and Christian Spain exist to enlighten us, along with a few other contemporary descriptions.

A feature of plague studies in Spain is their local nature, which is characteristic of similar studies throughout Europe. The variations in Iberia's topography and the deeply entrenched localism of the peninsula have meant that local histories and limited regional surveys dominate the published works dealing with the plague. That is

---

[5] Antonio Ubieto Arteta, "Cronología del desarrollo de la Pesta Negra en la peninsula ibérica," *Cuadernos de Historia: Anexos de la Revista Hispania* (Madrid, 1975), vol. 5, *Estudios sobre el Reino de Valencia*, pp. 47–66. I should add a warning at this point that this chronology is based on the work of Antonio Ubieto, whose methodology has been legitimately questioned. He relied for much of his chronology on the deaths of bishops and archbishops, events which are hardly precise markers of the progress of a disease. Nonetheless, his is the most complete account to date, and it does possess an internal logic. The bishops' deaths do plot a geographical progression; only further research will tell if its only basis was coincidence.

not all bad; a synthesis of focused local studies with an eye for specific detail can help us to construct a peninsula-wide mosaic.[6]

Many local studies of Iberian mortality from the Black Death already exist, but there is no consensus about whether or not distinct regional patterns developed.[7] To date, the local studies that

---

[6] Robert-Henri Bautier, "Un nouvel ensemble documentaire pour l'histoire des pestes du XIVe siècle: l'exemple de la ville de Vich en Catalogne," *Académie des inscriptions et Belles-Lettres, comptes rendu* (1988): 432–56; Sérgio Luís P. Carvalho, "A peste de 1348 em Sintra," *1383–1385 e a crise geral dos seculos XIV/XV: Actas* (Lisboa, 1985): 129–135; Maria Helena da Cruz Coelho, "Um testamento redigido em Coimbra no tempo da Peste Negra," *Homens, espaços e poderes (séculos XI–XVI)* vol. 1, *Notas do Viver Social* (Lisboa, 1990), pp. 60–77; M. Grau Monserrat, "La peste negra en Morella," *Boletín de la Sociedad Castellonense de Cultura* 46 (1970): 148–60; José M. Doñate Sebastia, "Datos negativos referidos a la Plana de Castellón, en relación con la peste negra de 1348," *VIII Congreso de Historia de la Corona de Aragón* (Valencia, 1967), 2:27–43; Richard W. Emery, "The Black Death of 1348 in Perpignan," *Speculum* 62 (1967): 611–23; María Estela González de Fauve, "Testimonios de la crisis del siglo XIV en Aguilar de Campoo," *Estudios en Homenaje a Don Claudio Sánchez Albornoz en sus 90 Años* (Buenos Aires, 1986) 4:25–33; Christian Guilleré, "La Peste Noire a Gérone (1348)," *Annals de l'Institut d'Estudis Gironins* 27 (1984): 87–161; Jordi Gunzberg Moll, "Las crisis de mortalidad en la Barcelona del siglo XIV," *Boletín de la Asociación de Demografía Histórica* 7 (1989): 9–35; Richard Francis Gyug, ed., *The Diocese of Barcelona during the Black Death: The Register Notule Communium 15 (1348–1349)* (Toronto, 1994); idem, "The Effects and Extent of the Black Death of 1348: New Evidence for Clerical Mortality in Barcelona;" *Mediæval Studies* 45 (1983): 385–398; Jocelyn Nigel Hillgarth and Giulio Silano, eds., *The Register "Notule Communium" 14 of the Diocese of Barcelona (1345–1348): A Calendar of Selected Documents* (Toronto, 1983); Amada López de Meneses, "La peste negra en Cerdeña," *Homenaje a Jaime Vicens Vives* 1 (Barcelona, 1967), pp. 533–542; idem, "La peste negra en Las Islas Baleares," *VI Congreso de Historia de la Corona de Aragón* (Madrid, 1959), pp. 331–344; idem, "Una consecuencia de la peste negra en Cataluña: el 'pogrom' de 1348," *Sefarad* 19 (1959): 92–131; Anthony Luttrell, "Los hospitalarios en Aragón y la peste negra," *EM* 3 (1966): 499–514; Agustín Rubio Vela, "La ciudad de Valencia en 1348: la peste negra," *Primer Congreso de Historia del País Valenciano* 3 (1980): 519–526; Alvaro Santamaría Aránzdez, "Mallorca en el siglo XIV," *EM* 7 (1970–1971): 165–238; idem, "Peste negra en Mallorca." *VIII Congreso de Historia de la Corona de Aragón*, 2 vols. (Valencia, 1967), 2:103–130; Melanie Shirk, "The Black Death in Aragon, 1348–1351," *Journal of Medieval History* 7 (1981): 357–367; idem, "Violence and the Plague in Aragon, 1348–1351," *Journal of the Rocky Mountain Medieval and Renaissance Association* 5 (1984): 31–39; Robert Sidney Smith, "Fourteenth-Century Population Records of Catalonia," *Speculum* 19 (1944): 494–501; Juan Torres Fontes, "Tres epidemias de peste en Murcia en el siglo XIV," *Anales de la Universidad de Murcia. Medicina* 1 (1977): 123–161; idem, *De Historia Médica Murciana. II. Las Epidemias* (Murcia, 1981); José Trenchs Odena, "La diócesis de Zaragoza y la peste de 1348," *Instituto Jerónimo de Zurita. Cuadernos de Historia* 25–26 (1973): 119–140; idem, "Documentos pontificios sobre la peste negra en la diócesis de Gerona," *Cuadernos de trabajos de la escuela española de historia y arqueología en Roma* 14 (1980): 183–230; Albert Villaró, "La Pesta Negra, el 1348, a la Seu d'Urgell," *Urgellia* 8 (1986–1987): 281–28; M.V. Amasuno Sarraga, *La peste en la Corona de Castilla durante la segunda mitad del siglo XIV* (Salamanca, 1996).

[7] Antonio Arjona Castro, "Las epidemias de peste bubónica en Andalucía en el

exist have either focused on special categories of people for whom statistics can be developed, such as public officials and members of military and religious orders, or they are extrapolations from such studies. Other proxies for mortality rates have been derived from the few notarial archives that exist, which almost uniformly show an elevated number of wills following the initial appearance of the plague. Presumably, the wills reflected both the reality of plague mortality and the public fear of it. Given the wide regional variations in record keeping, there may never be a comprehensive accounting of plague mortality for the peninsula as a whole.

Beyond the trajectory and overall mortality of the disease, observations about the Iberian case follow patterns well-known in other areas of Europe. Coastal regions were, on average, hit harder than the interior. Larger towns and cities suffered more severe losses than smaller towns. Mountainous areas often escaped the infection altogether, while population centers on the plains seem to have been disproportionately afflicted, in part because they were connected by trade routes to one another and to the ports of entry.

While the epidemic raged, the overall death rates were elevated, but all of the deaths cannot be attributed to plague, and the death rates varied considerably from place to place. There were occupational hazards. Members of the clergy, medical personnel, and notaries perished in great numbers, placed in harm's way by the nature of their offices. Representatives of all three groups frequented the bedsides of clients stricken by the plague, attending to their spiritual

siglo XIV," *Boletín de la Real Academia de Cordóba* 56 (1985): 49–58; Maurice M. Berthe, "Famines et épidémies dans le monde paysan de Navarre aux XIVe et XVe siècles," *Académie des Inscriptions et Belles Lettres. Comptes rendus des seánces* 2 (Paris, 1983), pp. 299–314; Jean Pierre Cuvillier, "La population catalane au XIVe siècle. Comportaments sociaux et niveaux de vie d'aprés les actes privés," *Mélanges de la Casa de Velázquez* 5 (1969): 159–187; J. Gautier-Dalché, "La peste noire dans les états de la Couronne d'Aragon," *Bulletin Hispanique* 64 (1962): 65–80; Josep Iglesias Fort, "El fogaje de 1365–1370. Contribución al conocimiento de la población de Cataluña en la segunda mitad del siglo XIV," *Memorias de la Real Academia de Ciencias y Artes de Barcelona* 34, 3ª ep. (1962): 249–356; Amada López de Meneses, "Documentos acerca de la peste negra en la Corona de Aragón," *Estudios de Edad Media de la Corona de Aragón* 6 (1956): 291–447; Emilio Mitre Fernández, "Algunas cuestiones demográficas en la Castilla de fines del siglo XIV," *EM* 7 (1970–1971): 615–622; Gunnar Tilander, *Fueros aragoneses desconocidos promulgados a consecuencia de la gran peste de 1348*, in *Leges Hispanicae Medii Aevi* 9 (Stockholm, 1959); Julio Valdeón Baruque, "Aspectos de la crisis castellana en el primera mitad del siglo XIV," *Hispania* 29 (1969): 5–24; idem, "Reflexiones sobre la crisis bajomedieval en Castilla," *En la España Medieval* 4 (Madrid, 1984), pp. 1047–1066.

concerns, attempting to cure their bodily ills, and recording their wills.[8] In the course of their activities, they could hardly escape becoming infected themselves. Within towns, the poorer neighborhoods typically experienced the plague first and suffered more than their wealthier neighbors. Nevertheless, no class escaped the disease, and it was in Spain that the plague claimed its highest ranking victims in all of Europe. Queen Leonor, wife of King Pedro (the Ceremonious) of Aragon and daughter of Alfonso IV of Portugal, died at the end of October 1348.[9] King Alfonso XI of Castile died from the plague in March 1350, while his army was besieging Gibraltar.[10]

The general economic and social consequences of the plague in Europe as a whole are familiar to students of medieval history. Through an inheritance effect, survivors of the plague tended to have more money *per capita* and were willing to spend that money on higher quality, more expensive goods. Rural and urban workers, their numbers thinned by the epidemic, sought and obtained higher wages and more favorable contracts. When they could not secure higher wages and better conditions locally, they moved to places where they could. Often that meant moving into the cities, in a process that left many villages totally abandoned. Although historians once attributed the desertion of villages in northern Europe mainly to the plague, they now see it as part of a broader demographic fluctuations and alterations in patterns of land use. There is little question, however, that the plague accelerated the phenomenon.

Influential urban leaders and landed nobles felt the effects of the changed economic context. They had to pay higher wages to their workers and offer other blandishments to keep them from going elsewhere. The market for land collapsed, which led to lower rental incomes for landowners. Before long urban leaders and nobles urged

---

[8] Jon Arrizabalaga, "Facing the Black Death: Perceptions and Reactions of University Medical Practitioners," in *Practical Medicine from Salerno to The Black Death*, ed. Luis García-Ballester, et al. (Cambridge, 1994), pp. 237–288; Hanspeter Kern, "La peste negra y su influjo en la provisión de los beneficios eclesiásticos," *VIII Congreso de Historia de la Corona de Aragón* (Valencia, 1967), 2:71–83; Michael R. McVaugh, *Medicine Before the Plague: Practitioners and their Patients in the Crown of Aragon, 1285–1345* (Cambridge, 1993); José Trenchs Odena, "La archidiócesis de Tarragona y la peste negra: los cargos de la catedral," *VIII Congreso de Historia de la Corona de Aragón* (Valencia, 1967), 2:45–64.

[9] José Martínez Ortiz, "Una víctima de la peste, la reina doña Leonor," *VIII Congreso de Historia de la Corona de Aragón* (Valencia, 1969), 2:9–25.

[10] *Crónica de don Alfonso el Onceno*, attributed to Juan Núñez de Villazan (fl. 14th century), ed. Francisco Cerda y Rico (Madrid, 1787), pp. 624–626.

representative assemblies and monarchs to cap wages and place restrictions on workers' freedom of movement. When those measures were put into effect, they provoked serious rebellions in England, France, and Italy.

The Christian kingdoms of Iberia felt equally profound consequences from the plague and the economic and social disruptions that followed. Their experiences varied region to region, however, and often followed different patterns from their neighbors across the Pyrenees. According to recent research, Catalonia "did not experience the complete abandonment of villages in the aftermath of the Black Death."[11] Individual farmsteads were abandoned, especially in areas of marginal productivity, but villages remained inhabited. In the mountains abandoned farms tended to remain vacant, but in the more favored valleys they were quickly reoccupied after the epidemic passed. Surviving peasants left marginal holdings and moved to more productive ones. Other peasant families simply absorbed deserted farms into their holdings. As a consequence, few if any villages disappeared.

The situation was different in Old Castile, where many of the villages in existence in the thirteenth century were ghost towns by the fifteenth. The question, however, is to what extent the Black Death caused the desertions. The answer, on the basis of most studies, is that the Black Death provoked an acute phase within a chronic problem. The abandonment of villages in Old Castile was part of a process that began in the thirteenth century, as in northern Europe, but with significant differences and local variations.[12]

In the the heartland of Old Castile, the region between the Duero and the Tajo rivers, Christian settlement had become reestablished in the tenth and eleventh centuries. During the twelfth and thirteenth centuries, as the front line of the reconquest moved south and left the region more secure, population increased and marginal lands were cultivated. Lords, lay, clerical, and royal, devised ways of extracting greater profits from agricultural production in general and peasant

---

[11] Paul Freedman, *The Origins of Peasant Servitude in Medieval Catalonia* (Cambridge, 1991), p. 168.

[12] Nicolás Cabrillana, "La crisis del siglo XIV en Castilla: La Peste Negra en el Obispado de Palencia," *Hispania* 28 (1968): 245–258; idem, "Los despoblados en Castilla la Vieja," *Hispania* 31 (1971): 450–550, (1972): 5–60; Patricia de Forteza, "Yermos y despoblados: Problemas de terminología," *Estudios en Homenaje a Don Claudio Sánchez Albornoz en sus 90 Años* (Buenos Aires, 1985), 3:73–85.

farmers in particular. Faced with heavier dues owed to their lords, farmers had a variety of incentives for abandoning their lands, either to seek work in the cities or to find more favorable conditions to continue farming. After Andalusia came under Christian control in the mid-thirteenth century, villagers from northern Spain could easily find work in the cities or better conditions for farming in the Andalusian countryside. In either case, they could escape the harsh obligations owed to their lords in Old Castile. The Black Death did not initiate the southward migration, but it certainly accelerated it.

A similar process took place in Portugal, but historians think that the Black Death initiated the process. Surviving peasants fled the countryside, using the scarcity of labor to improve their lives. A Portuguese version of the inheritance effect provided resources for dependent peasants to move up the social scale and to escape from labor dues to landlords. In the exodus from farm to town and city in Portugal, fields and villages were abandoned. Portuguese historians have argued that the situation was so altered that the country could no longer even supply its own food and turned to overseas trade to bring in grain. The lords, for their part, complained loudly about the scarcity of labor in the countryside and rued their inability to force peasants to pay labor dues. Nobles found themselves impoverished if they relied solely on their traditional income from farm rents. Consequently, they flocked to the royal court and lobbied for overseas adventures.[13]

Throughout the Iberian peninsula monarchs listened to the complaints of elite groups in society, and what they heard was similar everywhere.[14] At the base of the complaints were noticeable alterations in the ways society and the economy functioned, alterations that in the immediate term gave better opportunities to the laboring classes and reduced the control exercised by the elite. Lower class people moved from place to place seeking and often securing better conditions and higher wages. With rising wages came higher prices. In response, throughout the peninsula the elite sought ordinances and regulations that would restore conditions prevailing before

---

[13] Virginia Rau, *Sesmarias medievais portuguesas* (Lisboa, 1982); idem, "Para o estudo da peste negra em Portugal," *Actas do Congresso Histórico de Portugal Medievo. Guia oficial en Bracara Augusta* 14–15 (Braga, 1963), pp. 210–239.

[14] Angel Vaca, "Una manifestación de la crisis castellana del siglo XIV: La caída de las rentas de los señores feudales," *Studia Historica. Historia Medieval Salamanca* 1 (1983): 157–166.

the plague. These can be grouped into three categories. One was to place restrictions on freedom of movement, often phrased as measures to end vagabondage but really designed to keep workers in the fields or in their towns of origin. The other two categories were more straightforward: to cap both prices and wages at pre-plague levels.

In Aragon, the *Cortes* of Zaragoza of 1350 attempted to thwart the market pressures on both wages and prices as a result of plague mortality. Detailed regulations for artisans specified their wages and their conditions of work, and threatened those who violated the regulations with fines. Similarly, the prices for goods made by artisans were fixed by the government.

In Castile, King Pedro I, responding to the demands of the *Cortes* of 1351, issued restrictions on personal movement, wages, and prices. Conditions of work were also established for artisans and farm workers of various kinds, including plowmen, harvesters, vineyard workers, and day laborers. Among the provisions was a prohibition on the formation of workers' confraternities, presumably feared as a source of unrest. Pedro I faced an acute crisis, but most of his provisions invented nothing new. A century earlier Alfonso X had ordered many of the same measures, without the plague as a goad, and his successors endorsed similar decrees through to the end of the fifteenth century. In other words, the plague stimulated royal governments to intervene in the economy, but they had found other occasions to do so long before the plague. Perhaps historians would find it profitable to analyze these post-plague regulations as part of a long-term effort at increasing royal control, as well as a response to the Black Death.

In Portugal, the picture was much the same, and the Portuguese *Cortes* was particularly upset about perceived gains made by the church. The *Cortes* of 1352 noted that so many people were dying and leaving bequests to the church that before long, it feared, all Portugal would belong to the church.[15] The complaints of the Portuguese elite were similar to those elsewhere in the peninsula. Rural workers were abandoning their fields and moving to the cities, and those who remained were refusing to perform their labor services. Workers were also demanding and getting higher wages, while so-called vagabonds had become another sort of plague. As a consequence, the Portuguese *Cortes* of 1349 tried to restrict freedom of

---

[15] Humberto Carlos Baquero Moreno, "A Peste Negra e os Legados a Igreja," *Revista de Ciencias Historicas* 6 (Porto, 1991): 133–143.

movement.[16] Throughout the peninsula, monarchs listened sympathetically to complaints about the consequences of the plague, in part because royal income from taxes had fallen along with the population.[17] Yet their efforts to reverse changes in the economic and social structure of their kingdoms were not always successful, largely because the changes *were* structural, and not just conjunctural. As research on the late medieval centuries becomes more sophisticated, historians are realizing that the Black Death was only one factor in a broad-based evolution of Iberian economy and society.

Throughout the peninsula, the post-plague period witnessed a series of fundamental shifts in the relations between town and countryside and between proprietors and workers both urban and rural. Just as certainly, many of those changes had been in progress before the plague and continued long after its acute phase. Plague survivors could afford to abandon marginal lands and concentrate on the most productive ones, and to shift to the production of crops that would produce the highest returns in urban markets. They could also shift from farming to herding. As Julio Valdeón Baruque has written,

> It has been said, perhaps with a certain dose of ingenuity, that Castilian sheep raising was the child of the plague. Doubtless the reduction of the supply of labor, and definitely the reduction of cultivated fields, favored the expansion of spaces devoted to pasturage. But beyond that elemental statement we cannot go any further.[18]

Castilian stock-raising, especially sheep herding, rose in the two centuries following the plague. It is not clear, however, whether the demographic decline freed more marginal land for pasture or whether sufficient pasture had always been available, and stock-raising, especially for the production of fine Merino wool, simply offered better market returns in the aftermath of the Black Death. Portugal also witnessed a shift from cultivation to herding in many places, but there, too, the relation between land use and the plague is not clear.

Throughout Europe, popular revolts were a consequence of the Black Death. The Peasants' Revolt in England, the *Jacquerie* in France,

---

[16] Victor Deodato da Silva, *A legislação económica e social consecutiva á Peste Negra de 1348 e sua significação no contexto da depressão do fim da Idade Média* (São Paulo, 1976).

[17] See for example, Winfried Küchler, "La influencia de la peste negra sobre la Hacienda Real," *VIII Congreso de Historia de la Corona de Aragón* (Valencia, 1967), 2:65–70.

[18] Julio Valdeón Baruque, "Reflexiones sobre la crisis bajomedieval en Castilla," *En la España Medieval* 4 (1984) p. 1054.

and the *Ciompi* in Italy have all been characterized as reactions to government attempts to thwart the gains made by peasants and urban workers following the Black Death. In Iberia some anti-Jewish popular violence erupted in Barcelona and other eastern cities in the late 1340's, but the large-scale revolts only arose in the 1390's, two generations after the great epidemics.[19] Those later revolts are problematical for various reasons. Scholars still have not reached a consensus on whether they were primarily anti-Jewish in origin or whether they were motivated more by socio-economic aims. In either case, or in a combination of both (which seems more likely), they were responses to conditions in late medieval Spain that were longstanding by the late fourteenth century and that continued to spark unrest throughout the fifteenth.

One fruitful way to examine the consequences of the plague in Iberia is to compare and contrast what happened in the Christian and Islamic portions of the peninsula; in other words, to ask how Christians and Muslims responded to the plague. Medical treatises exist for both Islamic Spain and Christian Spain that allow a direct comparison for certain aspects of the epidemic.

The general assumption among scholars is that the Islamic world of the Middle East and North Africa suffered roughly similar demographic effects to those experienced in Christian Europe. Yet the attitudes of the populace and their leaders to the disaster were not the same. Michael Dols and others argue that Muslims and Christians differed substantially in their responses to the plague. Moreover, and perhaps a related development, the long-term consequences of the plague differed for the two economies.[20]

Fourteenth-century western Christians believed the plague was God's punishment for a sinful society, that the disease was contagious, and that measures to avoid contagion such as quarantine and flight would be effective. At the same period, Muslims believed that the plague was God's will but that God's will was unknowable and unavoidable. They further believed that disease could be seen as a purification for the soul, not a punishment, and that the plague was not contagious. For all these reasons, it followed logically that they

---

[19] Amada López de Meneses, "Una consecuencia de la peste negra en Cataluña: el 'pogrom' de 1348," *Sefarad* 19 (1959): 92–131; Shirk, 31–39.

[20] Michael Dols, *The Black Death in the Middle East* (Princeton, 1977); Lawrence I. Conrad, "TĀ'ŪN and WABĀ': Conceptions of Plague and Pestilence in Early Islam," *Journal of the Economic and Social History of the Orient* 25 (1982): 268–307.

did not believe flight or any human response would be effective against it. Gatherings for Friday prayers in the mosques continued, and commerce and pilgrimages continued without interruption. Such attitudes and the patterns of behavior to which they led may have produced a higher death toll in Muslim lands, though figures are lacking to test that hypothesis. A fatalistic view toward the plague may have insulated the Muslim population from some of the doubt and despair that assailed Christian Europe, or it may have led to a paralyzing terror. In the current state of research, the consequences are not clear.

Three important treatises on the Black Death in the fourteenth century were written by Spanish Muslims. The earliest, from February 1349, was the work of ibn Khatima, a physician and philosopher living in Almería, the port through which plague first entered Islamic Spain.[21] The author of the second treatise was ibn al-Khatib, a scholar in Granada and a friend of ibn Khatima.[22] He wrote in the aftermath of the plague, sometime between 1353 and 1363. The third writer, a Granadan student of ibn al-Khatib, was ibn Ali ash-Shaquri.[23] In general terms, all three scholars shared similar ideas about the causes of the plague, blaming it on miasmal disturbances in the air, due to imbalances of moisture and to corrupting gases from rotting bodies, manure, or stagnant waters. Interestingly enough, al-Khatib offered an explanation for the spread of the disease that violated the orthodoxy of Islamic medicine. He believed in contagion, postulating that the disease could be contracted through contact with an infected person or with that person's clothing and other belongings. Michael Dols described his view as "a clear example of innovation,

---

[21] M. Antuña, "Abenjátima de Almería y su tratado de la peste," *Religión y Cultura* 1 (1928): 68–90; Miguel Casiri, *Bibliotheca arabico-hispanica escurialensis* (Matriti, 1760–1770); Taha Dinanah, "Die Schrift von Abï Djafar Ahmed b. 'Alí b. Mohammed b. 'Alí b. Hátima aus Almerian über die Pest," *Archiv für Geschichte der Medizin* 19 (1927): 37–81; Emilio Molina López, "La obra histórica de Ibn Játima de Almería y algunos datos más en su Tratado de Peste," *Al-Qantara* 10 (Madrid, 1989): 151–173.

[22] Ibn al Jatïb, *Libro del cuidado de la salud durante las estaciones del año o "libro de higiene,"* ed. and trans. María de la Concepción Vázquez de Benito (Salamanca, 1984); Marcus Joseph Müller, "Ibnulkhatïbs Bericht über die Pest," *Sitzungsberichte der Königlich Bayerische Akademie der Wissenschaften* 2 (Munich, 1863), pp. 1–34; William B. Ober, "The Plague at Granada, 1348–49: Ibn al-Khatib and ideas of contagion," in *Bottoms up!: A Pathologist's Essays on Medicine and the Humanities* (Carbondale, 1987).

[23] Rachel Arie, "Un opuscule grenadin sur la Peste Noire de 1348: La 'Nasiha' de Muhammad al Saquiri," *Boletin de la Asociacion Española de Orientalistas* 3 (1967): 189–199.

at a time of crisis, within a traditional and authoritative body of thought."[24] Al-Khatib's views on contagion may have contributed to his persecution for heresy and his eventual exile. In any case, his treatise and the work of his two contemporaries offer comparative data that expands our understanding of the experience of plague in Islamic Spain.

So far I have been describing what happened as a consequence of the Black Death. Before concluding, I should mention two developments that did *not* take place, or, more precisely, two developments that may have been delayed by the Black Death: the reconquest and overseas expansion. In 1348, the Muslims successfully defended Granada. In 1350 Alfonso XI died while besieging Gibraltar with a large army. According to a chronicler of Seville, he died of a tumor on the neck, a classic plague symptom, and the campaign was abandoned soon after. From then until the 1470's Castilian monarchs declined to mount full-scale efforts to complete the reconquest. Was their reluctance a consequence of the Black Death? Only very indirectly, in my view.

A number of factors determined the rhythm of the reconquest, and most of them had little if anything to do with the plague. Castilian monarchs throughout the late fourteenth and the fifteenth century were preoccupied with civil wars and wars against the Crown of Aragon and Portugal. Once the Trastámaras sat on the thrones of both Castile and Aragon in the early fifteenth century, their struggle had many elements of civil war, or even a family feud. During the same period, the Granadan kings were not provocative adversaries and seldom attacked Castile. Granada was falling apart internally and no longer received much support from Morocco. At the same time, it was nominally Castile's vassal state and had agreed to provide an annual subsidy to Castile in African gold. Taken together, those conditions sufficiently explain why Castilian rulers were less than eager to commit the effort and expense necessary to finish the reconquest in the late fourteenth and early fifteenth centuries, even without the advent of plague.

I think it is possible to make a case, on the other hand, that the Black Death delayed the beginning of one of the most important undertakings of late medieval Castile and Portugal: the expansion into the Atlantic that ultimately led Columbus to the Caribbean and

---

[24] Dols, p. 94.

Vasco da Gama to India. By contrast, I admit, the Crown of Aragon continued its Mediterranean expansion during this same period, seemingly unaffected by the plague in this regard at least. But Atlantic exploration was another matter.

On the eve of the Black Death, Atlantic exploration seems to have been poised to increase in intensity. The Canary Islands, known to classical antiquity as the Fortunate Isles, began to interest Italians and Iberians in the early fourteenth century, and they appeared on Angelino Dulcert's portolan chart of 1339. In 1341, the king of Portugal sent a well-supplied expedition to conquer the Canary islanders, but it seems to have come to nothing. Another major but curious effort to conquer and colonize the Canaries began in the 1340's, when pope Clement VI in Avignon gave lordship over an ill-defined collection of Atlantic and Mediterranean islands to Don Luis de la Cerda, also called Don Luis de España, a great-grandson of Alfonso X of Castile and Louis IX of France. The kings of Portugal and Castile were not disposed to see the islands granted to Don Luis and each claimed prior rights in the names of their kingdoms. Undeterred, Don Luis set about raising an expedition in France and secured the aid of the king of Aragon. Although he died before launching his campaign, he bequeathed his claim to his eldest son in 1348—an ominous year. By then Europe was in the grips of the Black Death, which suspended plans for any large-scale attempts at conquest.

In the second half of the fourteenth century, a series of smaller expeditions, mostly from the Crown of Aragon and often with missionary aims, probed the Canaries and nearby areas. Nonetheless, no major effort to conquer the islands emerged for a half century after the outbreak of the plague. Only in 1402 did the Bethencourt and La Salle expedition begin the definitive conquest of the Canaries.[25] I would argue that the disruptions in Iberian society and economy after the Black Death played a major role in retarding exploration of the Atlantic.

---

[25] For the history of European exploration and conquest of the Canaries, see Felipe Fernández Armesto, *Before Columbus: Exploration and Colonization from the Mediterranean to the Atlantic, 1229–1492* (Philadelphia, 1987); Florentino Pérez Embid, *Los descubrimientos en el Atlántico y la rivalidad castellano-portuguesa hasta el Tratado de Tordesillas* (Seville, 1948); Antonio Rumeu de Armas, *España en el África atlántica* 2 vols. (Madrid, 1956); John Mercer, *The Canary Islanders: Their Prehistory, Conquest, and Survival* (London, 1980); Miguel Angel Ladero Quesada, *Los primeros europeos en Canarias (Siglos XVI y XV)* (Las Palmas de Gran Canaria, 1979).

A similar, though weaker, case can be made for Portuguese exploration of the African coast. Portugal had a long-standing interest in tapping into the Moroccan grain trade and the Saharan caravan trade. Control of possessions in Morocco could accomplish those aims and also allow support for Portuguese fishing fleets in Moroccan waters. The disruptions caused by the Black Death played a role in delaying Portuguese ambitions in Africa, though not the dominant role. Equally important were the long wars against Castile that absorbed so much Portuguese energy. Those wars did not end until 1411, and the Portuguese conquest of Ceuta occurred four years later.

Early in the twentieth century, historians assigned the Black Death a pivotal role in European development, ending one era and beginning another, marking the transition from medieval to modern times. In the final decade of the twentieth century, most historians would not make such sweeping claims.

Charles Verlinden was ahead of his time in 1938, when he concluded his survey article on the plague in Spain by observing that "the Black Death caused many upheavals but did not really change the fundamental character of any political, social, or economic institution."[26] Five decades later, after countless investigations of aspects of life in many Spanish and Portuguese localities, Verlinden's conclusion can still stand with little modification. But he left out, and so have I, attention to the psychological and cultural ramifications of the plague. Artistic and literary reactions to the Black Death were widespread, persistent, and influential in the century and a half after 1350. Abiding psychological and emotional reactions, as Iberians absorbed the horrible realities of the death toll and lived with the fear and insecurity that the plague engendered, shaped individual and collective actions in all fields.

In Iberia, as elsewhere in Europe and the Islamic world, the plague must be seen in a broad context that includes the relations between lords and peasants, the growth of urban institutions, the expansion of monarchical power against aristocratic opposition, and the relations between Christians and non-Christians. The Black Death became one more player in an unfolding drama that was already well-advanced by 1348.

---

[26] Verlinden, "Grande Peste," 145.

THE BUSINESS OF SALVATION: CASTILIAN WILLS IN THE LATE MIDDLE AGES[1]

Teofilo F. Ruiz

In early September of 1347 Martín Ortiz de Agonçiello, a merchant and citizen of Logroño (a town in the Rioja, in the northwestern region of Old Castile), lay sick in bed awaiting death. He was probably still quite young for his children had not yet come of age and his mother, Elvira Jiménez, was alive and active. Wishing to put his affairs in order, Martín sent for the royal scribe of Logroño, Ruy García, and for witnesses and relatives. In their presence, "being of good memory and good understanding and *cobdiciando* (coveting, greedy for) the glory of Paradise," Martín dictated his will. Obviously, this was mainly an impromptu testament dictated from his bedside. In it he moves from one concern to another in no apparent order, trying to make certain that nothing has been left out. Yet he had given some thought to the matter. Martín had selected beforehand the thirty poor *envergoñados* who were to be fed and clothed the day of his burial. In fact, he had already given the chaplain Pedro González and his wife María Pérez a list of their names. But, above all, what is evident in these final dispositions is Martín's desire to settle his property on those of his own blood. Half of his earthly goods was to go his wife but with the condition that she not remarry and that for the next fifteen years she care for the children. If she married before the established period, María would have to relinquish

---

[1] The inspiration to write this paper came from two presentations to the Davis Center Seminar by Professor Peter Brown and, above all, Dr. Judith Herrin. A short version of this article was presented to the Denys Hay Seminar in Medieval and Renaissance History of the Antiquary Program at the University of Edinburgh and a full version to the Davis Center at Princeton University. I greatly benefitted from the many useful suggestions made in both seminars. In particular I owe many thanks to Robert Bartlett, Giles Constable, Olivia Constable, Natalie Z. Davis, John H. Elliott, Angus MacKay and Lawrence Stone. In addition I also owe many thanks to Elizabeth A. R. Brown, Paul Freedman, Scarlett Freund, Ruth Behar, David Frye, Peter A. Linehan, Hilario Casado, Adeline Rucquoi, Raymond S. Willis, and specially to Charles M. Radding and Xavier Gil Pujol for their most valuable comments. In truth this has been a collective enterprise, though for the opinions and mistakes, I am solely to blame.

both the property and the children to Martín's relatives. Moreover, once the children reached their majority, most of the property was to be settled on them. Funds were also provided for bequests to churches and monasteries, to give bread, wine and meat (or fish if required by the liturgical calendar) to thirty poor *envergoñados*, citizens of Logroño, on the day of his burial. Moreover, Martín donated one hundred *varas* (about 85 yards) of *sayal* (sackcloth) to dress the poor "for the love of God (and) for my soul," but undoubtedly also in memory of his name, as a reaffirmation of his social standing.[2]

There was nothing unique in this will. It had, as did other testaments in this period (including those from clerics), a secular spirit which more than balanced Martín's pious and charitable concerns. Greedy for Paradise—the word is in itself significant—the salvation of his soul was purchased in a businesslike manner: donations to churches and monasteries here and there in return for masses, pilgrimages to famous shrines, and a ceremonial funeral feast. All in all this was a shrewd yet, monetarily, very small investment in eternity. But in his last hours, with one eye aimed at the afterlife and the other at this world, Martín's driving wish was the preservation and rational distribution of his fortune among his kin. He also assigned money to the brotherhoods to which he belonged, to the neighborhood of the Market district where he probably transacted business, and to the poor *envergoñados*. By means of these gestures, Martín was making a final statement about the distance which separated him from the poor, and marking his place in the social hierarchy of the town.

Neither the tone of the will nor Martín's concerns for kin and social status was unusual; rather, its uniqueness lay in that Martín's testament was just one of a small number of wills drawn up before 1350 in which we find specific provisions for feeding and clothing the poor. But even in this particular case, Martín did not just select any of the poor but a small and carefully chosen number of neighbors who had fallen into penury yet were ashamed of begging, the *envergoñados*.[3] This limited concern for the plight of the poor evident in Castilian wills before 1350 was paralleled, to a certain extent, by legal, literary and popular attitudes in this period. As such they con-

---

[2] *Colección diplomática de las colegiatas de Albelda y Logroño, I, 924–1399*, ed. E. Saínz Ripa (Logroño, 1981), pp. 269–273. For *envergoñados*, see below.
[3] Linda Martz, *Poverty and Welfare in Habsburg Spain. The Example of Toledo* (Cambridge, 1983), p. 5.

trast sharply with the passionate defense of the poor and of Christian charity which Domingo de Soto, Cristobal Pérez de Herrera, and others advanced in sixteenth-century Spain. In their works these writers sought to answer the attacks which Catholics, such as Juan Luis Vives, and Protestants, such as Martin Luther, had directed against begging and the concept of alms-giving itself. Quoting from St. Paul's I Corinthians, Cristobal Pérez de Herrera stressed that to love one's neighbor, meaning here specifically the poor, was, to a large degree, the foundation of individual salvation. Similarly, earlier in the sixteenth century Domingo de Soto in his *Deliberación en la causa de los pobres* argued that alms-giving was indeed the duty of all Christians and that to deny charity to one's neighbor was a mortal sin.[4]

Implicitly, and, at times, explicitly, their views reflected the notion of a transformation in the way in which de Soto and Pérez de Herrera's contemporaries dealt with the poor as compared with a more sympathetic treatment in an earlier time. This change was evident, in other parts of early modern Europe and in Spain itself, in the repressive legislation against beggars and their freedom of movement, as well as by attacks on indiscriminate alms-giving. In recent scholarship the debate on poverty and charity undertaken in sixteenth-century Spain has been viewed as an anomaly when compared to developments elsewhere in Europe. Either because of Spain's economic backwardness and/or its military and aristocratic ideology, historians such as Gutton, Lis and Soly, have argued that harsh condemnations of the idle and of beggars, which could be found in the rest of pre-capitalist Europe, were either absent from the Iberian peninsula or softened by the survival of indiscriminate charity. Linda Martz has already dealt most aptly with these contentions, and there is no need here to rehearse her arguments.[5] The question remains, however, whether Spain's assumed tolerance towards the poor and benign views of charity in the early modern period were grounded on medieval precedents. Michael Cavillac, for example, in his thorough and valuable introduction to Cristobal Pérez de Herrera's *Amparo de pobres*, places special emphasis on the evangelical dignity of the poor in

---

[4] Cristobal Pérez de Herrera, *Amparo de pobres*, intro. Michael Cavillac (Madrid, 1975), pp. 86–88; Domingo de Soto, *Deliberación en la causa de los pobres* (Madrid, 1965), pp. 62–70. For a discussion on the debate on the poor in early modern Spain see Cavillac's introduction, l–clxxix; Martz, pp. 7–91.

[5] Jean Pierre Gutton, *La société et les pauvres en Europe (XVIe–XVIIIe siècles)* (Paris, 1974), pp. 97–115; Martz, pp. 1–91.

medieval Castile and on the survival of traditional Christian concepts of charity into the early modern period. As was the case in France and England, where already in the Middle Ages the sanctity of poverty began to be rejected, in Castile we also find such measures after the disasters of the mid-fourteenth century, specifically the Plague. But in Castile, argues Cavillac, "the apostolic dignity of the poor had far deeper roots since it was supported by aristocratic disdain for manual work."[6] In this, however, early modern apologists and recent scholars have been mistaken. The most perfunctory glance at the extant documentation for the period before 1350 shows that medieval Castile was not a place where the poor were invested with "apostolic dignity" or any kind of dignity for that matter. In many ways, both medieval Castile and early modern Spain were "different" from England and France, but not, however, in their treatment of the poor.

In the following pages I will examine those few instances in which the sources show examples of private charity, here understood as the feeding and clothing of the poor. Furthermore, I wish to show how, whenever such legacies or donations can be found, they do not adhere to the ideal of Christian charity, meaning here, giving with love in the spirit of St. Paul, without reservation. Obviously, as Christians, medieval Castilians could not cast aside the mental baggage of centuries of Church teachings and the lessons taught almost daily by the Gospels, the Epistles and Church Fathers. As pettynoblemen, merchants, and landholders, they were also part of a world in the midst of important economic, social, and cultural changes. It is my contention here that although Castilians, and men and women elsewhere in the medieval West, had an understanding of what charity was according to evangelical prescriptions, few practiced it as a constant in their lives. It can be argued, of course, that heroic examples of true Christian charity have been few and far between in any age, regardless of how insistently the love of the poor is presented as a guiding model for all to follow. Nevertheless, at the moment of death, when charity must have been most poignantly urgent, those executing their wills left nothing to the poor, or did so in a limited, almost formalized manner. I wish, therefore, to examine how and why private and even ecclesiastic feeding and clothing

---

[6] Cavillac, lxxiv–lxxix; Gutton, pp. 93–97.

of the poor often turned into highly ceremonial and public displays wholly alien to the original message of the Gospel. In doing so, we can see how this ritualized giving reaffirmed the existing social distance between rich and poor, reminding those receiving charity of their place in a well-defined hierarchy of eating and dressing.

This inquiry into the nature of northern medieval Castilian charity reveals a much broader transformation taking place in this period. This involved new ways of thinking about salvation and the after life, as well as new attitudes towards property, city and kingdom. Here I will examine briefly the condition of the poor in northern Castile before the Black Death and legal and literary attitudes towards poverty and charity. This will be followed by an analysis of those wills which did indeed provide for the feeding and clothing of the poor, and I hope to do so within the context of the wider transformation of values revealed by extant testaments. Finally, I would like to suggest why this was so. There is something else which requires brief mention. We must keep in mind throughout this discussion other types of private charity which cannot be documented by historians. I refer here to the impromptu giving of alms and food to beggars in the street, on the steps outside the church, or at the door of the house, when they come asking for charity "for the love of God." Before 1350 there is little or no evidence for this type of charity though we must assume that it existed. Later, in early modern Spain, this direct charity could reach impressive and well-documented levels. In fifteenth-century Valladolid, members of the urban patriciate kept careful accounts of their daily alms-giving to the poor—which is in itself revealing of new attitudes towards charity. The Count-Duke of Olivares, as a child, was expected to devote ten percent of his monthly expenditure to charity, and Ruth Behar has shown how until a few years ago private charity was "institutionalized" in Leonese villages. Such activities, however, whether documented or not, only represent the other side of more ritualized forms of charity.[7]

---

[7] See Adeline Rucquoi, *Valladolid en la edad media*, 2 vols. (Valladolid, 1987). Also John H. Elliott, *The Count-Duke of Olivares. The Statesman in an Age of Decline* (New Haven and London, 1986), p. 16; Ruth Behar, *Santa Maria del Monte. The Presence of the Past in a Spanish Village* (Princeton, 1986), pp. 183–184.

I. *Poverty and the Poor in Northern Castile Before 1350*

In the late Middle Ages, the kingdom of Castile had to face serious economic, social, and political problems. Endemic political and noble violence, troubled royal minorities, civil wars, and demographic dislocations beset the realm from the mid-thirteenth to the late fifteenth century.[8] These conditions influenced the number and status of the poor and forced Castilians first to take notice of the needy in their midst and eventually to make half-hearted attempts to help as well as to control the poor.

In thirteenth- and fourteenth-century Castile it is next to impossible to define most of the time what the sources meant by the "poor," or indeed to calculate their number. Historians have already dealt with specific aspects of poverty, such as attitudes towards the poor and social assistance in medieval Castile, but to my knowledge no one has yet examined private charitable efforts as a whole nor has anyone studied charity in this period.[9] What is clear, however, is that the sources for the first half of the fourteenth century seem to indicate that the number of the poor was on the rise, their plight evident for anyone to see, and this was poverty made more visible by being concentrated in urban centers.

With the growing number of the poor and their greater visibility also came a transformation in social attitudes towards poverty. As was the case elsewhere in the West, hostile views of poverty and of

---

[8] On the late medieval Castilian crisis see Julio Valdeón Baruque, "Aspectos de la crisis castellana en la primera mitad del siglo XIV," *Hispania* 29 (1969): 5–24; Teofilo F. Ruiz, "Expansion et changement: La conquête de Seville et la société castillane (1248–1350)," *Annales Economies Societés Civilisations* 3 (1979): 548–565; and idem, *Crisis and Continuity. Land and Town in Late Medieval Castile* (Philadelphia, 1994), esp. bibliography pp. 329–341.

[9] The bibliography on the history of poverty and charity in western Europe is quite extensive, and a few references will suffice. See Michel Mollat, *Les pauvres au Moyen Age* (Paris, 1978); *Études sur l'histoire de la pauvreté (moyen âge–XVIᵉ siècle)*, ed. Michel Mollat, 2 vols. (Paris, 1974) and extensive bibliographies included in both works. For the Iberian peninsula, especially northern Castile, see the articles collected in *A pobreza e a assistencia aos pobres na peninsula Ibérica durante a Idade Media. Actas das Ias jornadas luso-espanholas de historia medieval*, 2 vols. (Lisboa, 1973) (hereafter cited as *A pobreza*). Also Carmen López Alónso, *Los rostros, la realidad de la pobreza en la sociedad castellana medieval (siglos XIII–XV)* (Madrid, 1983); and idem, *La pobreza en la España medieval. Estudio histórico social* (Madrid, 1986); Antonio Rumeu de Armas, *Historia de la previsión social en España. Cofradías, gremios, hermandades, montepíos* (Madrid, 1944); Luis Martínez García, *La asistencia a los pobres en Burgos en la baja edad media. El hospital de Santa María la Real, 1341–1500* (Burgos, 1981). For the early modern period see Martz, *Poverty and Welfare*, and her extensive bibliography.

the poor appear in the legal and literary sources of the period.[10] Even the Christian command of alms-giving was redefined, establishing gradations and categories which ran counter to the teachings of the Gospel. Alfonso X's (1252–1284) great legal code, the *Siete partidas*, recommended the following guidelines for those unable to give to all the needy: 1) help Christians before non-Christians; 2) poor men captive in Moorish lands should be helped first; 3) those in prison because of debt should be next; 4) choose the appropriate time to give alms; 5) do not give excessively or to just one person—divide your alms among many; 6) be charitable to poor relatives before helping strangers; 7) give to the aged before the young; 8) help the handicapped or sick before the healthy; and 9) give to noblemen or to those who were rich and have fallen on hard times before giving to those who have always been poor. Some of these recommendations sought a more rational utilization of alms-giving (help the aged, the poor and the sick first), but others reflected the martial and aristocratic character of Castilian society, as well as the rigid hierarchical distinctions in existence then.[11]

Moreover, Castilian legal codes before 1350 sought to protect the family's right of inheritance, above all the rights of children and grandchildren, against excessive donations to the Church, often limiting donations to just one fifth of the estate. Yet, in the typical ambivalence of the period, the *Partidas* allowed the testator to name the poor as his heirs, but establishing once again a clear order as to how the estate was to be divided: first to those sick in hospitals and unable to beg; second to the handicapped and orphan children; third to the very old. Although still emphasizing the spiritual nature of charity, that is, alms without love are no aid to salvation, the *Partidas* also commanded "that alms should not be given to those who were healthy and refused to work the land." Even if the *Partidas* did not have the force of law until 1348, they represent the normative legal vision of that age. As such Castilian law before 1350 reflected the traditional concerns with the poor but also growing intolerance with the idle and with beggars. The harshness of such legal commands

---

[10] For antagonisms against the poor in other parts of Europe see M. Mollat, "Pauvres et assistés au moyen âge," in *A pobreza*, 1:26–7; Frantisek Graus, "Au bas Moyen Âge: pauvres des villes et pauvres de campagnes," *Annales Economies Societés Civilisations* 16 (1961): 1056–1057.

[11] *Partida* I, 23.7–10 in *Los códigos españoles concordados y anotados*, ed., M. Rivadeneyra, 12 vols. (Madrid, 1847–1851), 2:310–312.

is also evident in the legislation of the *Cortes*. Beginning as early as 1268, and continuing throughout the next century and a half, the edicts of the *Cortes* of Castile and León encouraged royal and municipal officials to arrest idle able-bodied peasants and to force them to work.[12]

At the same time as these coercive measures were being introduced to force the idle to work and to define the deserving poor as just the aged, the sick, the very young, and widows, the act of begging came under attack. In the fourteenth century even religious orders had to obtain royal licenses to beg, and in 1338, when Alfonso XI granted such a permit to the monks of Silos, he did so because "many men go around the land (begging) with lies and tricks, and the simple men of the land receive much harm." Moreover, late medieval Castile witnessed the emergence of a new category of the poor, the *envergoñado*, that is, the known poor who until recently had enough means to live. Not surprisingly, most of the relief allocations in the 1338 accounts of Santo Domingo de Silos, one of the most important Benedictine houses in northern Castile, were destined for the poor *envergoñados*.[13]

In thirteenth- and early fourteenth-century Castile, poverty began to be justified "because of man's necessity to give alms as a way to cleanse his sins," but more often, as in the *Poema de Alfonso XI*, in the writings of López de Ayala, and in the *Libro de miseria de omne*, poverty was the outcome of royal and noble violence and excessive fiscal demands.[14] In Juan Ruiz's *Libro de buen amor*, where to be rich was certainly more desirable than to be poor, and to eat well far better than an ascetic life, one also finds that giving to the poor is simply not enough. The giver must, in the true spirit of charity,

---

[12] For rights of inheritance *Fuero juzgo* IV, 5.i; also IV, 2 in *Códigos*, 1:132–137; *Fuero real* III, 6.x in *Códigos*, 1:382. See also *Partida* VI, 3.20 in *Códigos*, 4:42. For attacks against the idle, see *Partida* II, 20.4 in *Códigos*, 2:463; *Cortes*, 1:78; 2:76, 92, 112 et passim. On the martial and noble character of Castilian society see Teofilo F. Ruiz, "Une royaute sans sacre: La monarchie castillane du bas Moyen Âge," *Annales Economies Sociétés Civilisations* 3 (1984): 429–453. For repressive measures in early modern Spain see Martz, pp. 14–21, 27; William A. Christian, Jr., *Local Religion in Sixteenth-Century Spain* (Princeton, 1981), p. 24.

[13] Marius Ferotin, *Recueil de chartes de l'abbaye de Silos* (Paris, 1897), pp. 380, 389, 390–391, 403. In his testament, Martín Ibáñez, prior of the cathedral chapter of Burgos, left 200 *maravedís* to clothe "*pobres envergoñados*." ACB, vol. 48, f. 319 (30 July 1333).

[14] See Luis Martín, "La pobreza y los pobres en los textos literarios del siglo XIV," in *A pobreza*, 2:601, 611–612, 614.

share also in the pain of the needy. It must be done with love. It must be both a spiritual and a material gift. And yet Juan Ruiz cannot help but emphasize with a touch of irony the reciprocity of all giving. As the poor scholar begs for money, he promises to his credulous listeners that "for every ration that you give, God will return a hundred," and in the bargain will even cure your cough.[15]

True charity must be, following the example of St. Martin of Tours, at least sharing fully what one has. In the *Libro de Apolonio* a poor and destitute fisherman finds King Apolonio on the shore reduced to abject poverty. After hearing his plight the fisherman presents Apolonio with half of his only garment and half of his meager dinner. In Gonzalo de Berceo's *Milagros de Nuestra Señora* a beggar for the love of God and the Virgin shared half of the alms he received with other beggars. At his death the Mother of God herself came to take him to heaven where he was fed "as the angels are" with *candeal* (white wheat) bread.[16] Between the ideals of society and the reality of daily life there is often a great gap, and for all the worthy descriptions of charity present in literary sources, I have yet to find a similar real example in the documents of thirteenth- and fourteenth-century northern Castile.

II. *Feeding and Clothing the Poor*

a) *The Evidence of the Wills*

We have no notarial records in northern Castile for the period before 1350. There are, nonetheless, hundreds of charitable donations and testaments extant for this period in Castilian archives or published in documentary collections. They provide a rich source for our inquiry.[17] The wills and living gifts examined below can be divided

---

[15] Juan Ruiz, *Libro de buen amor*, 2nd ed. (Valencia, 1960), p. 269 (1590a–d), pp. 282–283 (1650a–1660d).

[16] *Libro de Apolonio* (Madrid, 1982), pp. 59–61; Gonzalo de Berceo, *Milagros de Nuestra Señora* (Madrid, 1982), milagro v, 38–39.

[17] The extant wills and donations come *in toto* from ecclesiastical holdings. They were there because they included legacies of property or income which had been donated to a particular church or monastery, or which eventually became part of the ecclesiastical domain. As with most medieval documentation, however, these sources probably represent only a fraction of far larger documentation. For the use of wills as a source for medieval history see W.K. Jordan, *Philanthropy in England*

into two distinctive chronological sets. The first includes documents
running from the early ninth century, when the county of Castile first
emerged into political life, to the mid-thirteenth century. For the second chronological set, beginning in the 1250s, the mid-fourteenth
century and the Plague serve as a clear terminus. Although my focus
is here on settlements to feed and clothe the poor, this is of course
a modern and narrow understanding of charity which does not always
correspond to how medieval men and women perceived alms-giving.
This must be stressed, since Castilians in the Middle Ages may have
thought that they fulfilled their duties to Christ and the poor by
giving to churches and monasteries.[18]

On 6 May 1107, the count Gómez González and his wife Urraca,
pro remedio animarum nostrarum, donated land, a vineyard, and the parochial church of San Miguel to Michaeli Didaz, abbot of the monastery
of San Miguel de Busto. The opening paragraph of the donation,
obviously a formulaic device since it is often repeated verbatim elsewhere in Castile, expressed, in corrupted Latin, the general equating
of pious and charitable gifts: *Evangelius preceptis ammonitus, in quibus
dicitur; date elimosinam et omnia munda erunt vobis; ceterisque in quibus subin-
fertur; abscondite elimosinam in sinu pauperis et ipsa orabit pro uobis ad
Dominum, qui sicut aqua extinguit ignem ita elimosina extinguit peccatum; ob
peccatorum meorum diminitionem et infernalis ignis feci hanc scedulam.*[19]

The theme of *elimosina* extinguishing sins as water does fire is a
common one before 1250, but for all the references to the poor, the
donation is to the monastery and not directly to the secular poor.
It can be argued of course that these types of indiscriminate giving
did eventually make their way to the stomach of the needy through
monastic charity. After all monastic property was in theory the patrimony of the poor. But this specific donation, as well as many others
in northern Castile, shows clearly that their purpose was not to feed
or clothe beggars but to assure salvation and to fend off those men-
acing infernal fires.[20]

1480–1660. A Study of the Changing Pattern of English Social Aspirations (New York, 1959),
p. 22; Joel T. Rosenthal, *The Purchase of Paradise. Gift Giving and the Aristocracy, 1307–
1485* (London, 1972), pp. 29, 81 and following.

    [18] Rosenthal, 9.

    [19] José M. Garrido Garrido, ed., *Documentación de la catedral de Burgos (804–1183)*
in *Fuentes medievales castellano-leonesas*, 13 (Burgos, 1983), pp. 155–156; Luciano Serrano,
ed. *Fuentes para la historia de Castilla*, 3 vols. (Valladolid, 1906–1910), 3:336.

    [20] Rosenthal, pp. 11–15. Most of the early donations and wills in northern Castile

In the accompanying table, we can see a detailed breakdown of donations and wills in northern Castile from the ninth to the mid-fourteenth century and for what purpose pious and charitable gifts were made. A perfunctory examination of this table and a closer reading of the sources reveal specific patterns. Living gifts and wills in the chronological set running up to 1250 show an overwhelming uniformity. They were mostly straightforward settlements of property and, to a lesser extent, income on one single ecclesiastical institution *pro remedio anima (sic) mee, pro remissione peccatorum nostrorum*, or as often for the souls or the remission of sins of parents and other close relatives.

A good number of the testaments and donations also requested burial in the church or monastery to which the donation was being made. Far less often in this earlier period the donors requested such specific services as anniversaries, lighting of candles, chantries or similar pious bequests. Rarely did they settle part of their gifts on the needy. Almost without exception, the testaments before 1250 chose a single monastery or church as the recipient of private largesse, rather than spreading donations among diverse ecclesiastical institutions. One must also assume that before the early thirteenth century, settlements on relatives, friends, other religious institutions, and perhaps even the poor did take place before death, or concurrent with pious donations to one specific church, but very seldom do we find documentary evidence to guide us on these matters.[21]

Moreover, though I have made a distinction between donations and testaments, using the wording of the documents as the guiding criteria, the immense majority of these living gifts—excepting royal and comital ones—took place late in life or after the death of close relatives. Most of the donations in the early period were, in fact if not textually, wills, and they expressed the wishes of the donors for the settlement of their spiritual affairs and the hope of forgiveness for their sins. There was no need to specify how the gifts were to be used, and the reciprocal aspects of the act of giving, although only implied, are clear. What was important, then, was the giving, and the intermediaries between the secular and the divine—priests and monks—chose the most efficacious ways (prayers, feeding the poor,

---

contains such expressions as "*pro remedio anima mee (sic), ut evadam portas inferni,* and in a few occasions *pro extinguenda incendia gehenne ignis.*" Serrano, 3:108–110, 189–190.

[21] See Serrano, 1:31, 67–70, for two rare examples of donations to relatives before 1250 found in the documentation of San Salvador de El Moral.

inscription in the liturgical calendar, votive candles, and so on) to bring the donor's gift to God.

Of course churches, monasteries, and hospitals did care for the poor, but in the late Middle Ages, as shall be seen below, they did so in the same limited and ritual manner of their secular counterparts. In any case, in their charitable programs, here understood as feeding and clothing the poor, the Church could only make a small dent in the growing problem of poverty, and greater involvement by society was needed.

By the mid-thirteenth century a series of important transformations took place in the way in which Castilians made charitable and pious donations. The first important change was in language, from Latin to Castilian, as lay scribes replaced ecclesiastical ones. With this change, the formulaic, ritual expressions of earlier donations and wills disappeared. This is most evident in royal grants that, although at the beginning of this change, contained Castilian expressions which were literal translations of *pro remedio anima (sic) mee*, do so less and less after 1250. By the 1260s and 1270s, with few exceptions, the formulaic expressions had disappeared. Instead, donations by the crown became simply instruments of royal policy and largesse.

At the same time, either because the economic prosperity of the twelfth and early thirteenth century turned sour, or because of changing attitudes towards the church—what has been described as a breakdown of confidence in ecclesiastical institutions—as well as a new mentality emerging in this period, the number of donations to the Church dropped dramatically.[22] Northern Castilians, especially the bourgeoisie and the petty-nobility, still gave, but the Church could no longer expect the type of unrestricted giving of yesteryear which had been the foundations of its early economic prosperity.

Not coincidentally, in the late Middle Ages the Castilian Church faced severe economic difficulties. This was due in great part to the savage royal exactions and noble expropriations of ecclesiastical property but also to the sharp decrease in secular gifts.[23] Moreover, unlike

---

[22] For the new language of royal donations see F. Javier Pereda Llarena, *Documentación de la catedral de Burgos (1254–1293)* in *Fuentes medievales castellano-leonesas*, 16 (Burgos, 1984), 53–55; Ferotin, pp. 200–201, 241–242, and following. For the "breakdown of confidence in the Church" I follow the comments by Giles Constable during the presentation of this paper at the Davis Center.

[23] See Peter A. Linehan, *The Spanish Church and the Papacy in the Thirteenth Century* (Cambridge, 1971), pp. 112–116, 123–134, and ch. 8; José M. Nieto Soria, *Las*

previous donations and wills, those after 1250 demanded specific services in return. Money, which now often replaced property as the item donated, or rental income, often in kind, was given to churches and monasteries under very strict guidelines.[24] Ecclesiastical institutions still remained intermediaries between donor and recipient, between the secular and the divine, but priests and monks were asked now to perform specific services in return for gifts.

Furthermore, the terms of the giving were often so restricted that they allowed for little diversion of funds, and more and more as we move into the fourteenth century, the executors were relatives of the donor, secular overseers set to make sure that pious bequests and chaplaincies were reserved for relatives and that the terms of the will were fulfilled. Just as often, property was passed on to relatives, albeit with the obligation to direct part of the income for pious and charitable ends, but clearly the indiscriminate willing of property to the Church had now come to an end.[25] Finally, unlike the period before the mid-thirteenth century, ecclesiastical institutions not only faced increased competition for donations and gifts from family and friends of the donors but also from a growing number of quasi-religious institutions and activities: brotherhoods, sponsored pilgrimages, crusades, and others. Most testaments after 1250 showed an almost universal tendency to scatter donations as widely as possible. This was done probably to insure every possible mode of salvation, or to reduce the risk of damnation. Included in this new dispersal of gifts one finds also provisions for the feeding and clothing of the poor. Moreover, by the late Middle Ages one witnesses the first steps towards a partial transferring of the individual's responsibility for the destitute to secular bodies. Thus, the Crown and municipal corporations took steps to provide legal services for the poor, to set up hospitals and create a royal almonry.[26] To a certain extent, however, this also

relaciones monarquía-episcopado castellano como sistema de poder (1252–1312), 2 vols. (Madrid, 1983), 1:298–399.

[24] See AHN Clero, carpeta 227, no. 1 (18 June 1337) and below for a good example of this dispersion of gifts.

[25] For some examples see Colección diplomática de las colegiatas de Albelda y Logroño, pp. 49–52, 208–209, 269–273; in Pereda Llarena, 363–370 (1316), Don Julián legated 1,000 maravedís for the release of captives in the hands of the Moors, but he requested that those rescued with his money be shown to his executors. If the monks of the Trinity refused this condition, they were to receive nothing. For the reserving of chaplaincies for relatives, see ACB vol. 48, f. 319 (30 July 1333) where Martín Ibáñez reserved them for men of his lineage. Also see below.

[26] For institutionalized support for the poor in the Iberian peninsula, mostly after

marked a growing realization of the social benefits of controlling
the poor through confinement in hospitals and through welfare, a
transition from charity to control which paralleled the ceremonialization of private charity and pointed to similar developments in the
early modern period.

b) *Private Legacies to Feed and Clothe the Poor*

A statistical sampling of donations and wills conveys a general idea
of trends in pious and charitable giving and shows the minor role
which feeding and clothing the poor played in such bequests. We
must take, however, a closer look at the few wills which did indeed
include provisions for the poor. In them we can often see delineated
the terms of such aid, as well as attitudes towards the poor. Most
of the wills included in the table and those examined below were
generated by urban oligarchs or petty-nobles of northern Castile, but
in most respects these testaments did not differ a great deal from
those of kings and high nobility.[27]

On 15 April 1289, Doña Elvira Alfonso donated most of her property in Varenciella de Río Pisuerga to the monastery of Santa María
la Real de Aguilar de Campóo. She offered this gift "for her soul
and the soul of her children and husband." The abbot of Santa
María promised in return a perpetual chaplaincy for her soul in the
altar of St. John. Moreover, on the day of Our Lady (15 August)
fifty-four of the poor were to be fed every year. To this end Doña
Elvira allocated one *fanega* and a half of wheat, two *cántaras* of wine
and a piece of mutton for every two poor men or women (16 pieces
to the animal).[28] Doña Elvira's will allows us to reconstruct more
or less the typical fare of the poor at these ritual feedings, and thus

---

1350 see relevant articles in *A pobreza*. Outside Iberia see Mollat, pp. 169–176. For
a later period see Natalie Z. Davis, "Poor Relief, Humanism, and Heresy. The
Case of Lyon," *Studies in Medieval and Renaissance History*, 5 (1968): 240: "The other
major difference between the medieval period and the sixteenth century in redis-
tributing income to the poor is in administration."

[27] See Julio Valdeón, "Problemática para un estudio de los pobres y de la pobreza
en Castilla a fines de la Edad Media," in *A pobreza*, 2:911, for the wills of kings
which included provisions for the feeding of the poor after 1350. In their respec-
tive wills, Juan I and Enrique III ordered that 600 of the poor be clothed the day
of their burial and fed for the next nine days. On the other hand, neither of Alfonso
X's two wills included any provisions for the poor. See *MHE* 2:110–134.

[28] AHN Clero, carpeta 1662, no. 2 (15 April 1289).

to contrast it with the diet of other social groups. This testament also permits a rough estimate of the actual cost of such giving, and thus provides a way of assessing what percentage of the total cost of pious, charitable, and personal donations the feeding and clothing of the poor represented.

In her testament Doña Elvira requested wheat bread, which was not common fare for the destitute. Rye bread and a mix of grains (wheat, barley) was the bread of the poor: Doña Elvira's feast was one of those rare occasions in which the poor ate the bread of the rich. We do not know exactly how much grain made up the *fanega* at the standard measure of Aguilar de Campóo, but on average it comes out to between one half and three quarters of a kilogram of bread per person. This is a good amount for a seating but short of the kilogram of bread (mostly wheat) assigned to monks daily (between 12 and 14 *fanegas* a year) in 1338. Two *cántaras* of wine at 16 or 16.5 liters per *cántara* gives us around 0.61 liters per person. Although an account of travelers from 1352 shows a daily consumption close to two liters per person, the poor sitting at Doña Elvira's anniversary table certainly had enough. As to the meat, according to Braudel, in the late sixteenth century a ram provided an average of 11.96 kilograms of meat per unit.[29] Adhering to this calculation we can assume around 375 grams of meat per person, or a bit more than a third of a kilogram. Since the meat was probably accompanied by some greens or served in a stew, those poor people benefitting from Doña Elvira's largesse should have left the table, at least once a year, with full stomachs. These are, of course, very rough estimates and do not take into account waste or pilfering by ecclesiastical cooks or executors. And yet the price of such meal was indeed quite small. Even including expenses for preparation, vegetables and other incidentals the total budget for the meal should not have exceeded 30 *maravedís*.[30]

---

[29] Fernand Braudel, *The Mediterranean and the Mediterranean World in the Age of Philip II*, trans. Siân Reynolds, abr. Richard Ollard (New York, 1992), p. 180.

[30] What and how much the poor was fed at these charitable feasts or in hospitals remained constant throughout the next centuries. Similar portions were served in fifteenth-century Burgos and in sixteenth century Lyon. See Carlos Estepa, et al., *Burgos en la Edad Media* (Valladolid, 1984), p. 453; Davis, p. 244; Luis Martínez García, "La asistencia material en los hospitales de Burgos a fines de la Edad Media," in *Manger et boire au Moyen Âge. Actes du colloque de Nice*, 2 vols. (Nice, 1984), 1:335–347.

If we accept this tentative estimate of the cost of charity, then the gulf between the diet of the well-to-do and the poor was indeed extreme. The comparison can be drawn simply in monetary terms. Thirty *maravedís* was a paltry sum in 1289 and contrasts vividly with the 2,000 *maravedís* granted to each magnate and his retinue for daily expenses when at the court of Ferdinand IV in the early fourteenth century, or the daily allowance for food of 150 *maravedís* each to which Alfonso X and his wife promised to adhere as a measure of austerity in 1258. At this level the differences between the rich and the poor, already evident in terms of clothing and housing, becomes more poignant in terms of income assigned for food.

Equally revealing are the two extant wills of Ferrant Pérez, scribe of Frías, a small town north of Burgos. The first will dates from 1334, and it was drawn jointly with his wife Catalina Ruiz. By then, Ferrant was already a prosperous municipal official with properties in and around Frías. We also know that some of his income derived from money lending, for two months before the drawing up of his first will he had lent 900 *maravedís* to Ferrant Sánchez de Velasco, a powerful local noblemen. In their first testament Ferrant and Catalina made important donations to the Augustinian monks of the Hospital of Frías. In return they requested to be buried at the Hospital, a chaplain to "sing masses" for their souls forevermore, and anniversaries to be kept on the feast of Our Lady for Ferrant and on that of St. Catherine for Catalina. Moreover, they settled 20 *maravedís* annually on the Hospital for the upkeep of a lamp, and 300 *maravedís* for the repairs of the church. Finally, they made provisions for the clothing of fifteen poor men and women with cloth, half *sayal* (sackcloth), half *estopazo* (burlap).[31]

By 1344, when the second will was drawn, Catalina was already dead, and Ferrant's fortune had increased dramatically. The long list of debtors mentioned in the testament, his own debts and the many references to transactions with Jewish money lenders can only lead to the conclusion that he was an important usurer and perhaps an intermediary between Jewish bankers and Christian borrowers. By 1344, care for the poor had also become an important concern. The new will opened with a bequest of up to 1,000 *maravedís* to build a hospital of stone with ten beds to house and feed the poor.

---

[31] AHN Clero, carpeta 226, no. 17 (20 August 1334); carpeta 227, no. 2 (20 October 1334).

Separate settlements were made to support spiritual services at the hospital chapel, wax for candles, oil for lamps, purchase of a chalice. To the monastery of San Vicente he gave 300 *maravedís*, and an equal amount to pay for 500 masses because "he was a sinner and for those debts he owed and did not remember." There were other pious donations, including money to send men to Compostela, to Santa María of Roncesvalles, to Santa María of Rocamadour, and to Jerusalem. In addition there was also a modest contribution of five *maravedís* to the Crusade. In another entry he ordered his executors to dress 300 of the poor of the neighborhood of Frías (in garments of half wool, half burlap), and that on the day in which they received their vestments they also be fed. The amount to be spent on clothing and feeding the poor is not spelled out, but a later entry in the will assigned 70 *maravedís* to dress ten poor people. If these figures hold for the other three hundred, then 2,100 *maravedís* were required to clothe them, plus additional income for food.[32]

I have only found one other will in northern Castile before 1350 in which wool is requested as a fabric to clothe the poor—for other such donations explicitly asked for burlap or sackcloth—and, coincidentally, the testament also dates from the decade of 1340, a period of great need in northern Castile. In 1349 Don Gonzalo Pérez, canon of the cathedral of Burgos, bequeathed funds for the foundation of a ten-bed hospital for the poor. In addition he left instructions for 200 of the poor to be clothed, 100 with wool and the other 100 with linen cloth. This is also the only will, as far as I know, in which the poor are described as hungry. Gonzalo supplied his hospital with "good blankets, firewood to keep the poor warm and enough food for the *pobres flacos* (literally the thin poor)" but meaning the hungry poor. He did this "for the honor of God, (so) that He would wish to forgive my sins." Elsewhere in the will, besides a multitude of masses, anniversaries, oil for church lamps, money for the Crusade, and so forth, Gonzalo provided funds to feed 100 poor men. On the other hand, as with most wills in this period, settlements on relatives and friends took the lion's share of the estate. Moreover, Gonzalo insisted that the chaplaincies he had endowed were to be reserved for his kin as long as there were living relatives, and in their default by citizens of Aguilar de Campóo, his hometown.[33]

---

[32] AHN Clero, carpeta 227, no. 7 (13 April 1344).
[33] ACB, vol. 49, f. 438 (23 July 1349).

III. *The Ceremonialization of Charity*

Examples from wills do not bring us any closer to a better understanding of what medieval men and women intended to do in their
testaments or why. Nor does the use of such a expression as the ceremonialization of charity convey the complexities and pitfalls inherent
in dealing with this topic. For one, this implies perhaps an orderly transition from an ideal form of Christian charity and care, represented
by the normative lives and examples of Christian saints, to the oper-
ative instrumentality of a later age, as manifested by a few surviving
wills. The transition was, of course, neither simple nor orderly. After
all, regardless of how small a portion of the estate was bequeathed
to the poor or for what reasons, the examples we have seen above
are manifestations of Christian charity.

Part of the problem lies in the use of such words as charity, here
meaning love, and ritual or ceremonialization. Both terms can be understood and misunderstood at a diversity of levels, nor can we ignore
the different cultural contexts to which we apply these terms. When
defining *caritas* as Christian love, we refer to a peculiar kind of love,
involving a triangular relation between the giver, the poor and Christ.
What happened to that triangular relationship is essentially one of
the topics of this article.

In Castile, long before 1350, the poor began to lose their charis-
matic value and often were turned into a mere symbol. In this remak-
ing of the triangle into a dual relationship between the donor, whether
a private individual, a municipal corporation or the state, and the
needy, we already have the basis for modern attitudes towards social
assistance. And here it is worth noting the growing distinction between voluntary poverty, often assumed from positions of power and
wealth, and the lot of the involuntary poor, a condition more often
than not associated with weakness.

As to rituals or ceremonialization of giving, is one speaking of beliefs
or actions which resulted from things other than beliefs? Clearly,
there were and are today rituals which depend exclusively on the
faithful repetition of certain words or the faithful performance of
specific gestures. Examples of this are magical incantations, the mass
or the sacrament of baptism which are ineffectual if some words or
gestures are missing. Most of the examples I have given above, however, do not belong to this category of rituals, and if they do, they
do so only partially. Instead, the ceremonial feeding and clothing of

the poor was often meant to convey a message to other human beings through a vocabulary of gestures and actions. This difference is crucial, for in the case of formalized charity it allowed for insincerity. One gives, but not too much, and in such giving the donor reinforces the existence of social boundaries. Indeed, that in itself is part of the message, and this makes the range of possible actions wide and fluid, adaptable to differences of personality, circumstances and messages.[34]

As we have already seen, in the period before the mid-fourteenth century, to those near death or settling their affairs in anticipation of death, feeding and clothing the poor, though done more frequently than in the centuries before 1250, was often only a secondary concern or no concern at all. In fact, it may have appeared as only a function of that fragmentation of "good deeds" which we see in wills drawn after the 1230s. When such dispositions are found, and I must emphasize once more how scant the evidence is, with a few exceptions they were a ritualized form of giving, ritualized in the sense indicated in the paragraphs above.

This feeding and clothing of a pre-selected and symbolic small number of the poor on the day of the burial of the donor, on the anniversary of his or her death, or even over his or her tomb was in one sense a reciprocal arrangement: food for prayers, food and clothing for remembrance. The donors, however, often did not give because they loved or cared for the poor very much, but because the poor were, in a sense, symbolically Christ. This was of course not peculiar to Castile or to the late Middle Ages and echoes the command of the tenth-century English *Regularis concordia*, which admonished the monks to administer the maundy "with the greatest care to the poor, in whom Christ shall be adored." At yet another level, however, these practices harked back to ancient and pre-Christian traditions which survive to this day throughout the world in the form of the wake or the offering of food at funerals.[35]

---

[34] I owe much of this section to the comments of Charles M. Radding.

[35] For the selection of a symbolic number of the poor to be fed at special occasions or the endowing of a number of beds in hospitals see Mollat, p. 66; *Burgos en la Edad Media*, 452–453; *Regularis Concordia. Anglicae Nationis Monachorum Sanctimonialiumque*, trans. Thomas Symons (London, 1953), pp. xxxvii, 61–62. For giving bread to the poor over the tomb of the donor, see *Colección diplomática de las colegiatas de Albelda y Logroño*, p. 50; Carmen Batlle, "La ayuda a los pobres en la parroquia de San Justo de Barcelona," in *A pobreza*, 1:64. For feasting around tombs in early Christianity,

Furthermore, the gathering of canons, priests, and a number of the poor for a ceremonial feast on the day of the donor's burial spoke of the deceased's standing in the community. It showed to others, beyond the grip of death, the extent of his or her wealth and piety. But the food the poor ate was different from the food eaten by the rich. The quality of the wine, often the quality of the bread, and the types of meat consumed by the poor at these ritual feasts were indeed inferior to those served to the ecclesiastical administrators of private charity, inferior to what the donor himself had eaten before departing this world, and far inferior to what kings and magnates ate in late medieval Castile.

And so for that matter were their clothes. Dressed in burlap and sackcloth: 10, 12, 300 of the poor, symbolic representatives of Christ, came in ceremonial pilgrimage to partake of the funeral meal and to offer witness, to give confirmation by their clothes and by what they ate of the rigid social hierarchy, the social boundaries which existed in Castile and elsewhere in the West at the dusk of the Middle Ages. The information on the eating and clothing of the northern Castilian bourgeoisie, the high nobility, and the royal court points to a pattern of conspicuous consumption, a pattern reflected in sumptuary legislation, travel and monastic accounts, and literary works from the mid-thirteenth century on.

The ordinances of the *Cortes* dealing with these matters sought, often unsuccessfully, to restrain the eating, feasting, and clothing excesses of the high nobility and the ostentatious displays of the rising urban oligarchies. Yet, sumptuary edicts did not represent draconian measures; rather they were mild attempts at providing a ceiling to what appears to have been exaggerated and wasteful expenses.[36]

---

see Judith Herrin, "Women and the Faith in Icons in Early Christianity," *Culture, Ideology and Politics*, eds. R. Samuel and G. Steadman Jones (London, 1983), pp. 57–58; also Christian, p. 57. On the idea of "social asymmetry" I follow the comments of Peter Brown on Michael W. Dols's paper to the Davis center on 18 October 1985, "where the donor is to God as the poor is to the donor." On primitive forms of funeral feasts, see James G. Frazer, *The Golden Bough: A Study in Magic and Religion*, abridged ed. (New York, 1927), pp. 147–161; Richard Huntington, *Celebration of Death: The Anthropology of Mortuary Rites* (Cambridge, 1979), pp. 105–107.

[36] These distinctions went beyond the earthly boundaries. In heaven, the angels ate *pan candeal*, the purest white wheat bread. (See above.) Among the many agreements found in Castilian archives in which donations of property were made in return for maintenance for life, the quality of the bread, meat, and wine was often clearly spelled out. In Oña we find references to the *pan de señores* (bread of the lords) (AHN Clero, carpeta 312, no. 18 [8 August 1345]). In 1293, when Doña

These non-noble knights and merchants, who as we know dressed in gold, silk, and scarlet clothes,[37] insisted, in those few wills which included legacies to clothe the poor, on burlap and sackcloth, a confirmation to all of the widening gulf between those above and those below. Thus, while a few donations to the poor here and there added to each person's heavenly account of good deeds, they also reinforced and sharpened, whether consciously or unconsciously, social distinctions in northern Castile, as they did elsewhere.

Of course, the poor did not depend exclusively on this so-called charity. Otherwise, they would have faced impossible conditions. The feeding and clothing of the poor was largely the work of the Church but, increasingly after 1300, it became the work of municipal corporations. And yet, in the twilight centuries between charity and welfare, between the scattered-shot approach to giving and the early attempts to rationalize assistance to the poor which marked the coming of the early modern period, monastic efforts showed the same tendencies toward becoming ritualized which we have observed above. Here a few examples will suffice.

In monastic institutions, in this particular case Benedictine monasteries in northern Castile, the amounts dedicated to charity in 1338 were quite small when compared to other expenses. Moreover, the cost of administering monastic welfare was quite high, eating further into the monies or grain reserved for the needy. At the monastery of San Salvador de Oña of the 635 *fanegas* allotted to the office of the almonry only 429 were left for the poor after expenses. Of the total expenses of 5,290 *maravedís* assigned for alms annually, only 2,745 *maravedís* were left for charity while the other 2,545 *maravedís* went either to fatten the purses of those in charge or to general expenses. Of this money, the 200 *maravedís* reserved for the clothing of the almoner seems at first glance an obvious abuse, and a confirmation of the popular dictum that charity begins at home. Altogether, at Oña the total amount spent in charity represented 5.45% of the total budget of the monastery, and of that only 2.8% really went to the poor. Obviously, the monastery exercised its Christian duties in

María de Sagentes made arrangements for her support with the abbot and monastery of Santa María la Real, she insisted on around two liters of wine daily "of that which the abbot drinks," and meat on Sundays, Tuesdays and Thursdays (AHN Clero, carpeta 1662, no 12 [9 August 1293]).

[37] Teofilo F. Ruiz, "The Transformation of the Castilian Municipalities: The Case of Burgos, 1248–1350," *Past & Present*, 77 (1977): 17–20.

other ways: hospital care, teaching, burial of the poor, though some
of these expenses were already included in the figures mentioned
above.[38]

We must compare these expenses with what these same monks
ate in 1338. As García González has shown, the allocations for food
and wine for the monks was one of the most important items in
monastic budgets. Departing from a strict adherence to St. Benedict's
rule, meat was served around 160 days a year; in places such as
San Pedro de Cardeña, near Burgos, the monks ate fish every day
in addition to meat. Eggs were part of the menu three days a week
at Santo Domingo de Silos, and vegetables, fruits, bread (one kilogram daily), and large quantities of wine (more than two liters per
day) completed the rather splendid collation of monks. Altogether
between 250 and 295 *maravedís* a year were necessary for each monk,
almost 100 *maravedís* more than was required to feed one poor person for a year according to the terms of Doña Elvira's will.[39]

The amounts which monasteries reserved for the needs of the
poor allowed only for a specific and small number of them to be fed.
I have calculated the number of those fed at Oña to be between 52
and 55 daily, but no provisions were made to accommodate emer-
gencies, bad crops, or periods of extreme need. Likewise the cathedral chapter of Segovia, which had forty canons, fed forty poor men
and women daily, one for each canon regardless of actual necessity,
in a ceremonial act of charity.[40]

Hospitals, both ecclesiastical and secular, offered assistance as
well, but here again many of these institutions did not yet have a
clear concept of their functions. The case of Burgos is instructive in
this respect. With a large number of hospitals in the late medieval
period, some Burgalese hospitals took in the poor only when there
were not enough pilgrims to fill their beds. On the other hand, other
institutions founded towards the mid-fourteenth century, such as the
hospital endowed by Ferrant Pérez de Frías, were reserved exclusively
for the needy. In Burgos proper, the Hospital del Rey, the largest

---

[38] Juan José García González, *Vida económica de los monasterios benedictinos en el siglo
XIV* (Valladolid, 1972), pp. 115–116, and his edition of the accounts of northern
Castilian Benedictine monasteries (1338), 131ff.

[39] Ibid., pp. 91–99.

[40] I owe thanks to Miguel Santamaría Lancho for the information on Segovia.
See his *La gestión económica del cabildo de Segovia*, forthcoming. García González,
pp. 131ff.

in Castile, had as many as 87 beds and two infirmaries in the late fifteenth century, but this was exceptional. Most of the hospitals in Burgos and elsewhere in Castile in the late Middle Ages limited their number of beds to ten, twelve or thirteen, symbolic numbers in remembrance of Christ and the apostles.[41]

In the thirteenth century, with changes in the nature of poverty and a marked increase in the numbers of the urban poor, municipal authorities began to take a more active role in social assistance. Often, however, this did not come about as a result of a well planned program but was the outcome of pressing need or even from direct requests by the poor. In 1312 the poor blind of Burgos petitioned the city council to build a hospital for them in the neighborhood of San Gil. We know that the hospital was built for in 1338 Alfonso XI ordered the municipal authorities to forbid those who were not blind from living in the hospital. Already by 1366 the hospital housed not only the blind but also the lame and deformed of the city, but by then the unfortunate inmates were often robbed and subjected to other acts of violence.[42]

IV. *Conclusion*

Contrary to recent views on the idealized nature of Castilian private charity and of the apostolic dignity of the poor in the period before 1350, the evidence above shows that private donations for the feeding and clothing of the poor were meager and often ceremonialized forms of giving. Ecclesiastical and public efforts to deal with the poor also suffered from the same defects. Clearly if, as Gregory of Nazianzus insisted, to feed and clothe the poor was to feed and clothe Christ, then in terms of the charitable dispositions at the end of one's life, poor Jesus would have had a difficult time.

From the earliest examples of wills and donations to those in the mid-thirteenth century we observe a fairly uniform pattern. In this early period pious donations and testaments followed a pre-set formula; gifts to ecclesiastical institutions were on the whole unrestricted. In them the expectations of prayers or masses for the souls of the

---

[41] *Burgos*, 189–192, 446–461.
[42] ACB, vol. 44, ff. 178, 179, 180 (15 November 1312, 20 April 1338, 2 December 1366).

donors and their families were only implied. Seldom in this extensive documentation do we find direct settlement on the poor. After the mid-thirteenth century, donations decreased in number, reflecting perhaps worsening economic conditions and new secular concerns. At the same time, testaments became very specific.

The former unrestricted giving is replaced by very clear and explicit demands for masses, anniversaries and other pious and charitable ends. In return the donor settled a fixed amount of income or property on the Church. In those cases in which property was donated, however, a relative or executor kept some financial control. Moreover, most donors sought to spread their bequests among as many institutions as possible. Unlike the wills of an earlier period, the donor's family, friends, and business obligations, that is, his or her secular concerns, began to command the greatest attention.

We are left still with the question as to what prompted these changes. Why did they come about? The answers to these matters must remain tentative. In truth, I do not think that there is a single satisfactory explanation, but rather a combination of plausible suggestions. One of the most attractive answers to our query is found in Jacques Le Goff's formidable book, *The Birth of Purgatory*. Indeed, it could be easily argued that the birth of the notion of Purgatory, which Le Goff places in the later half of the twelfth century, spread to northern Castile by the following century. By the early thirteenth century, the bourgeois and petty-nobility of Castile began to demand pious services, such as masses, anniversaries, and candles in churches, in return for their donations. Ideally, these were the types of offering best suited to reduce time in Purgatory. Support for this link between the discovery and acceptance of an intermediate place between Heaven and Hell comes from iconography and from the geographical breakdown of donations and wills. One of the earliest pictorial representations of Purgatory (ca. 1300) comes from Salamanca, and there are strong indications that wills drawn in towns along the Road to Compostela (and thus more open to French influences) were the first to show a scattering of donations and the first to abandon the formula *pro remedio anima (sic) mee.*[43]

---

[43] Jacques Le Goff, *The Birth of Purgatory*, trans. Arthur Goldhammer (Chicago, 1984), pp. 167–168, 289–333, 368. A 1230 will from Logroño, one of the first stops in Castile of the Road to Compostela, is one of our earliest examples of dispersal of donations. *Documentación de las colegiatas de Albelda y Logroño*, pp. 49–52.

As attractive as this formulation is, and it has the sort of chronological symmetry and elegance which makes it very appealing, one must still show some caution. Before 1350, none of the wills I have examined ever used the term Purgatory, though the absence of the word does not necessarily imply that most people in this period did not know about it already. Moreover, as Le Goff himself has pointed out, in earlier centuries unrestricted donations for one's soul and for the souls of others already held an expectation of redemption and forgiveness beyond death.[44]

Another possibility is that the change from Latin to Castilian as the language of royal administration and private affairs, which also coincided chronologically with the changing patterns of the wills and donations, transferred the drawing of such instruments from ecclesiastical to lay hands. Donors and testators enjoyed now greater control over how their property was to be divided and on what they might expect in return for their gifts. A change from one language to another, one as swift and widespread as that which took place in Castile in the mid-thirteenth century, had to be underlined by a variegated set of other changes and transformations. Underneath linguistic change, there were religious, psychological, economic, and politica shifts of deep and lasting impact.

Not the least of these changes was the growing literacy of the petty-nobility and the bourgeoisie, an end to an illiteracy which had once, as Marc Bloch pointed out, masked selfish actions under a veneer of "simple piety." We must also consider the increased complexity and ceremonialization of daily life in the late Middle Ages. Eating became a ritualized and highly ceremonial affair in Castile as it did elsewhere in the West. Is there a connection between the ritual eating of the powerful and the ritual feeding of the poor? Such ties can be illustrated for a later period, but they can only be assumed for an earlier age. Moreover, shortly after 1350 the concept of *caritas* itself was expanded to include love for country. For here at the end of this inquiry and only in passing we must acknowledge the rise of the state as an important catalyst for change, and nowhere was this transition from Christian love to social duty as clearly stated as in the statement: *Quod non capit Christus, rapit fiscus.* The poor were slowly ceasing to be of Christ and more and more the responsibility of the state.[45]

---

[44] Le Goff, p. 134.
[45] Marc Bloch, *Feudal Society*, trans. L.A. Manyon, 2 vols. (Chicago, 1964), 1:80–81.

We can only see these transformations "through a glass darkly" and often, because the sources do not allow for more, assume that they took place. But the evidence of the donations and wills is incontrovertible; it tells us that significant changes were in the making. The ways in which Castilians, and medieval men and women elsewhere, saw themselves, discovered new economic roles, and new forms of expressing their feelings for God and community are far too complex to discuss in detail here. In Castile, the rise of urban mercantile elites and the final acceptance of primogeniture (significantly the kings of Castile and León did not stop the practice of dividing the kingdoms until 1252) had a great deal to do with changing attitudes towards property and the relations between the spiritual and the secular. After 1250 wills became the primary vehicle for the settlement of property among relatives and friends and for disposition of financial obligations, replacing what must have been arrangements *inter vivos* of an earlier age. To put it simply, people held on to their property a great deal longer, often until death.

All these hypotheses do not help us to understand fully changing attitudes towards the poor and towards the feeding and clothing of the needy. Mollat and others have emphasized the urban character of medieval poverty, and the role which the rise of an urban civilization in medieval western Europe, with its concomitant mercantile mentality, had on new attitudes towards the poor. And yet, the urban elites of Avila or Sepúlveda, to cite just two examples, derived their economic and political power almost exclusively from farming and ranching and did not share in the new economic changes. Still, their views of the poor and their relations with Church and crown did

---

For the ritualization and ceremonial aspects of eating see Mark Girouard, *Life in the English Country House. A Social and Architectural History* (Harmondsworth, Eng., 1980), pp. 22–26, 30–32, 47–52; Norbert Elias, *The Civilizing Process*, 2 vols. (New York, 1982), 1:60–88. For the new concept of charity see Ernst Kantorowicz, *"Pro patria mori* in Medieval Political Thought," in *Selected Studies* (Locust Valley, NY, 1965), 316: "Here the parallelism of 'love of God and love of his brothers' is of some importance because it was the Christian virtue of *caritas* which finally was to work as a lever to justify ethically, or even to sanctify, war and death for the fatherland." See also p. 321 and his "Mysteries of State. An Absolutist Concept and Its Late Medieval Origins," in *Selected Studies*, 393–395. It is worth noting, even if only in a note, that Christian attitudes towards charity in late medieval Castile differed quite markedly from Muslim examples and do not seem to have been influenced by them. In 1492 Hernando de Talavera commenting on the Moors stated that "We must adopt their works of charity and they our Faith." Quoted in K. Garrad, *The Cause of the Second Rebellion of the Alpujarras* and cited in John H. Elliott, *Imperial Spain 1469–1716* (Harmonsworth, Eng. 1970), p. 51.

not differ much from those of merchants in Burgos or Logroño.[46]

We must also remember that all the repressive legislation against the idle in thirteenth- and fourteenth-century Castile was directed against the rural poor. In northern Castile there was yet none of the striking urban poverty found in other parts of the West or later in early modern Spain. There was, however, widespread rural poverty and underemployment, and they only grew worse with time. Otherwise how can one explain the need for an extensive network of village hospitals to house the poor already in place by the mid-fifteenth century.[47] Thus, urbanization and a new mercantile mentality were not the only reasons for changes in attitudes towards the poor in Castile.

We are left, I fear, with tentative answers but not one single convincing explanation, except to be certain that private and ecclesiastical charity had become, with some exceptions, a repetition of gestures and actions, aimed at communicating a message to the poor. This process of routinization, to borrow Max Weber's term, is far too complex to be raised here. It is perhaps grounded in the human condition. In northern Castile before the Black Death, bread, meat and wine were given to a few of the poor in a symbolic and ceremonial manner. Sometimes this was done in full expectation of prayers for one's soul or remembrance but also as a confirmation and display of the donor's social status. Compare the heroic qualities of apostolic examples, that of the first Franciscans, or the words of early modern writers such as Domingo de Soto, the spirit in which they gave and shared, with the limited and formal way in which northern Castilians assigned a few coins to feed and clothe the poor, with food and fabrics which painfully reminded the needy of their station in life, which told the world, once a year, ceremonially, of the donor's munificence. It was bread and vestments given without love. It was not charity.

---

[46] For urban elites in Avila and Sepúlveda, see Angel Barrios García, *Estructuras agrarias y de poder en Castilla. El ejemplo de Avila (1085–1320)*, 1 (Salamanca, 1983); Jean Gautier-Dalché, "Sepúlveda a la fin du Moyen Age; evolution d'une ville castillane de la meseta," *Le Moyen Age* 69 (1963): 805–828.

[47] See Hilario Casado Alonso's superb book, *Señores, mercaderes y campesinos. La comarca de Burgos a fines de la edad media* (Valladolid, 1987).

Table
Pious and Charitable Dispositions in Wills and Donations. Northern Castile

Years	807 –899	900 –999	1000 –1099	1101 –1199	1200 –1250	Total	%	1250 –1350	%
Donations	9	137	210	137	39	532	85.8	170	71.1
Wills	1	29	39	12	7	88	14.1	69	28.8
Total	10	166	249	149	46	620		239	
For soul[a]	10	147	228	131	21	537	86.6	52	21.8
Burial	4	41	63	9	3	120	19.3	47	19.7
Anniversaries	0	0	0	10	10	20	3.2	59	24.7
Chantries/chaplaincy	0	0	1	3	1	5	0.8	37	15.5
Candles/oil for lamps	0	2	3	3	0	8	1.3	15	6.3
Pittance for the clergy	0	7	2	0	1	10	1.6	15	6.3
Feed/clothe the poor	0	2	1	4	1	8	1.3	18	7.5
Alms to hospitals	0	0	2	0	0	2	0.3	3	1.2
To more than one institution	0	0	0	4	12	16	2.6	72	30.1
Masses/prayers for the soul	0	6	0	2	2	10	1.6	32	13.4
Sponsorship of pilgrims	0	0	0	0	0	0	0.0	3	1.2
Aid for the crusade	0	0	0	0	1	1	0.2	5	2.1
Found hospital/monastery	0	2	0	0	1	3	0.5	6	2.5
Maintenance of self or kin	0	2	5	4	3	14	2.3	11	4.6
Others	0	0	1	3	0	4	0.6	10	4.2
Donations by king or counts	0	43	58	54	10	165	26.6	8	3.4

[a] In the period 1250–1350 a good number of donations used the formula "for my soul," which corresponds to the "pro remedio anima mee" of the period 807–1250. Most of the donations and wills containing such words, however, also included other types of bequests as well as specific demands for masses, burials, anniversaries, etc. In fact, this entry could very easily be considered as equal to masses or prayers for the soul of the donor. In another sense, however, all the donations in this period, whether explicitly stated or not, were made "for one's soul."

THE RELATIONSHIP BETWEEN
GOVERNMENT AND WAR

A NEW LOOK AT THE FOUNDATION OF THE
ORDER OF CALATRAVA

Theresa M. Vann

Joseph F. O'Callaghan's doctoral thesis, "The Affiliation of the Order of Calatrava with the Order of Cîteaux," identified a significant gap in Cistercian and Crusader studies.[1] The Spanish militar religious orders were not obscure, and previous histories of the crusades had mentioned them, usually as an afterthought to the better-known Orders of the Hospital and the Temple. But when O'Callaghan began his work no modern monograph of comparable critical scope focused on the native Iberian religious orders.[2] The only other available secondary works were antiquarian or pietistic accounts in Spanish that catered to Calatrava as a noble order of chivalry. Unlike the Hospitallers and Templars, there was no published corpus of archival material for O'Callaghan to draw upon, and that lacuna still exists.[3]

---

[1] Joseph F. O'Callaghan, "The Affiliation of the Order of Calatrava with the Order of Cîteaux," Ph.D. thesis, Fordham University, 1956.

[2] Some early works on the Order of Calatrava are: Francisco de Rades y Andrada, *Crónica de las tres Ordenes y Caballerías de Santiago, Calatrava y Alcántara* (Toledo, 1572; facsimilie ed., Barcelona, 1980); Francisco Caro de Torres, *Historia de las ordenes militares de Santiago, Calatrava y Alcántara* (Madrid, 1629); Giuseppe de Zuñiga, *Epitome historica dell'illustrissima religione et inclita cavalleria de Calatrava* (Lecce, 1669); J. Fernández Llamazares, *Historia compendiata de las cuatro ordenes militares de Santiago, Calatrava, Alcántara y Montesa* (Madrid, 1862); and Honorio Alonso Rodríguez, *Algo sobre la fundación de la Orden de Calatrava* (Barcelona, 1917). Some later monographs are: Francis Gutton, *L'Ordre de Calatrava* (Paris, 1955); Derek Lomax, *Las ordenes militares en la peninsula iberica durante la edad media* (Salamanca, 1976), discusses the sources for the study of the Spanish military orders; see pp. 71–109 for a comprehensive bibliography; and Emma Solano, *La Orden de Calatrava en el siglo xv: los senorios castellanos de la orden al fin de la edad media* (Seville, 1978), pp. 23–50, contains an annotated listing of the unedited sources and a listing of the published ones. Subsequent articles on the Order of Calatrava includes Clara Estow, "The Economic Development of the Order of Calatrava, 1158–1366," *Speculum* 57 (1982): 267–291. Similar monographs about the Order of Santiago also exist. The most useful of the older sources remains José López Agurleta, *Vida del venerable fundador de la orden de Santiago, y de las primeras casas de redempción de cautivos* (Madrid, 1731); and Bernabé de Chaves, *Apuntamiento legal sobre el dominio solar de la Orden de Santiago en todos sus pueblos* (Madrid, 1740; facsimilie ed., Barcelona, 1975).

[3] O'Callaghan used Francisco de Uhagón y Guardamino, "Indice de los documentos de la Orden Militar de Calatrava," *BRAH* 35 (1899): 5–167, which indexed

O'Callaghan selected the Order of Calatrava for his thesis because solid primary source material established a clear link with the Cisterican Order, enabling him to use archival material and narrative sources to produce a dissertation that made an important contribution to the history of the Order of Calatrava. It was published twice and is still cited today as an important source for the origins and foundation of the Order.[4]

O'Callaghan focused on five major points in his thesis:

(1) to attempt a clarification of the obscurities surrounding the foundation of Calatrava in 1158 and its subsequent incorporation into the Order of Cîteaux;

(2) to describe the internal regimen of the Order of Calatrava so as to demonstrate its dependence upon the Rule of St. Benedict and the customs of Cîteaux;

(3) to point up the role of the Cistercian general chapter as the supreme legislative assembly and final judicial tribunal for the Order of Calatrava;

(4) to describe the filiation of Calatrava with the abbey of Morimond and

(5) to trace the gradual transformation of the Order of Calatrava into an honorary society of noblemen and the consequent disintegration of its relations with Cîteaux during the sixteenth and seventeenth centuries.[5]

As O'Callaghan recognized, this focus would have equal significance for both Cistercian and Spanish studies since it linked the establishment of the Order of Calatrava with the writings of Bernard of Clairvaux. His work challenged the assertion made by José Antonio

---

most of the unpublished documents of Calatrava in the Archivo Histórico Nacional (Madrid). Ignatio Josef de Ortega y Cotes, *Bulario de la Orden Militar de Calatrava* (also entitled *Bullarium ordinis militiae de Calatrava*) (Madrid, 1761; facsimile edition, Barcelona, 1981) contains the papal bulls issued to the Order. In comparison to the Order of Calatrava, more documents pertaining to the early years of the Order of Santiago have been published: a partial list would include Antonio Francisco Aguado de Cordoba, *Bullarium Equestris Ordinis S. Iacobi de Spatha per annorum seriem nonnullis* (Madrid, 1719); Derek W. Lomax, *La Orden de Santiago (1170–1275)* (Madrid, 1965); José Luis Martín, *Orígenes de la orden militar de Santiago* (Barcelona, 1974); Milagros Rivera Garretas, *La encomienda, el priorato y la villa de Uclés en la Edad Media* (Madrid, 1985); and Enrique Gallego Blanco, *The Rule of the Spanish Military Order of Saint James* (Leiden, 1971).

[4] Joseph O'Callaghan, "The Affiliation of the Order of Calatrava with the Order of Cîteaux," *Analecta Sacri Ordinis Cisterciensis* 15 (1959): 161–193; 16 (1960): 3–59, 255–292; subsequent citations from the reprint in *The Spanish Military Order of Calatrava and its Affiliates* (London, 1975).

[5] Idem, "Affiliation," p. 161.

Conde that the military religious orders were inspired by the Islamic *ribat*.[6] According to Conde, the *ribat* was a fortress established along the Islamic frontiers, garrisoned by warrior ascetics. Like the Christian military religious orders, service in the *ribat* was considered meritorious and was supported by pious donations, but unlike the Christian convents the inhabitants could serve for limited periods, as opposed to taking lifetime vows. In refutation of this thesis, O'Callaghan established that the foundation of the Order of Calatrava was inspired by mainstream Cistercian thought, modeled upon the Order of the Temple, and connected to a specific event in Castilian history. O'Callaghan relied upon three primary sources that link the origins of Calatrava with the influence of Cistercian monasticism: Bernard of Clairvaux, *De laude novae militiae ad milites Templi*, the primitive texts outlining the *vivendi forma* of Calatrava, and Rodrigo Jiménez de Rada's *De rebus hispaniae*.[7]

Bernard addressed the treatise *De laude novae militiae* (ca. 1128–1136) to Hugh de Payens, founder of the Order of the Temple.[8] In it Bernard praised the new knights, the *militia*, who fought to defend Christ and the Church against their enemies. The bad knights, or *malitia*, preyed on their fellow Christians. This treatise provided a theme for later monastic writers, who used Bernard's play on words to contrast the *militia* and the *malitia*.[9] The *vivendi forma* that the Abbot of Cîteaux gave the Knights of Calatrava sometime around 1164 reflected this Latinate distinction between good and bad knights, for in it the Abbot praised the members of the order who converted from Knights of the World to Knights of God for the purpose of fighting the enemies of the faith.[10] Finally, Rodrigo Jiménez de Rada,

---

[6] O'Callaghan, "Affiliation," pp. 176–178; José Antonio Conde, *História de la dominación de los árabes en España*, 3 vols. (Madrid, 1820–1821), 1:619, n. 1.

[7] Contemporary scholars working on the origins of other military Orders, such as Jean LeClercq, "Un document sur les débuts des Templiers," *Revue d'Histoire Ecclesiastique* 52 (1957): 81–91, employed a similiar methodology using Bernard, the narrative account, and the rule as his sources.

[8] *PL* 182, cols. 921–940. J. LeClercq and H.M. Rochais, eds., "Liber ad Milites Templi: de laude novae militiae," *S. Bernardi opera* (Rome, 1963), 3:312–39, is the critical edition. See also the English translation by Conrad Greenia published in Bernard of Clairvaux, *Treatises III*, Cistercian Fathers Series 19 (Kalamazoo, MI, 1977). R.J. Zwi Werblowsky's "Introduction," pp. 115–123, identifies this treatise as Bernard's apologia for a new form of religious life.

[9] See Aryeh Grabois, "Militia and Malitia: The Bernardine Vision of Chivalry," in *The Second Crusade and the Cistercians*, ed. Michael Gervers (New York, 1992), pp. 49–56.

[10] O'Callaghan, "Affiliation," p. 188; *Bullarium*, pp. 3–4, no. 4: "*Laudabile propositum*

thirteenth-century archbishop of Toledo, wrote the only account of the origins of Calatrava, or, indeed, of the founding of any Iberian military religious order, in *De rebus hispanie*.[11] Rodrigo's description of how a Cistercian monastery, with the help of the archbishop and people of Toledo, undertook the defense of Calatrava when the Templars withdrew under the threat of a Muslim army provides a clear link between the Order of Calatrava and the Cistercians.

O'Callaghan placed the Cistercian documentation into the framework of Rodrigo's narrative, thus emphasizing the European influences of Bernard of Clairvaux and the Order of the Temple on the foundation of the Order of Calatrava. This contribution is the most-cited aspect of the thesis. Certain preconceptions, however, continue to influence Spanish historiography. Elena Lourie has revived the theory of the influence of the Muslim *ribat* on the Christian military orders, even though O'Callaghan and, more recently, A. J. Forey, have not found any textual evidence for such influence.[12] Lourie responded to this and to other observations that Islam lacked the concept of permanent religious vows by using the anthropological argument that borrowed elements can be completely changed by the receiving culture, so that Christian culture assimilated the idea of the *ribat* into a Christian context.[13] She suggests that the idea for the *Cofradía* of Belchite, an obscure military confraternity whose insti-

---

vestrum, quo a militia mundi ad dei militiam conversi, inimicos fidei expugnare statuistis, plurimum approbamus."

[11] Rodrigo Jiménez de Rada, *Historia de rebus hispanie sive historia gothica*, in *Corpus Christianorum, Continuatio Medievalis*, ed. Juan Fernández Valverde, vol. 72 (Turnholt, 1987).

[12] Elena Lourie, "A Society Organized for War: Medieval Spain," *Past and Present* 35 (1966): 67–68. Alan Forey, *The Military Orders from the Twelfth to the Early Fourteenth Centuries* (Toronto, 1992), pp. 8–10, argues that there is no proof that the first generation of crusaders in the Latin East knew of the *ribat*, nor that such *ribats* existed in the crusader states in the twelfth century, and that the original function of the Knights of the Temple differed from that of the *ribat*. J. Chabbi, "Ribat", *EI²*, 494, calls the identification of the *ribat* as a "Muslim military monastery" a misinterpretation of the word. For a fuller description of the *ribat*, see Robert I. Burns, S.J., *Islam under the Crusaders: Colonial Survival in the Thirteenth-Century Kingdom of Valencia* (Princeton, 1973), 197; Mikel de Epalza, "Islamic Social Structures in Muslim and Christian Valencia," in *Iberia & the Mediterranean World of the Middle Ages*, eds. P. Chevedden, D. Kagay & P. Padilla, 2 vols. (Leiden, 1996), 2:188–189; Pierre Guichard, *Les Musulmans de Valence et la Reconquête (XIᵉ–XIIIᵉ siècles)*, 2 vols. (Damascus, 1991), 1:205–210.

[13] Elena Lourie, "The Confraternity of Belchite, the Ribat, and the Temple," *Viator* 13 (1982): 170.

tutions survive in a charter confirmed by Alfonso VII in 1136, was culturally assimilated from the *ribat* since its members could serve for limited periods of time. Unfortunately, Belchite is the most prominent of the *cofradías*, and no other evidence of their organization survives in order to test Lourie's thesis.

Medieval Spanish historiography has also engaged in a form of cultural borrowing that has influenced the interpretation of the origins of the Order of Calatrava. Under the influence of Frederick Jackson Turner's frontier thesis, the fight against the Muslims, or the Reconquest, became a democratic struggle to defend the lands of free frontiersmen. The work of Claudio Sánchez-Albornoz and his students has fueled an interpretation in which the native Iberian military religious orders sprang from local soil, uncontaminated by any touch of Cistercian, Templar, or Hospitaller influence.[14] Therefore even though subsequent historians have recognized that O'Callaghan has established the Cistercian influence on the foundation of the Order of Calatrava, they have de-emphasized this influence by following Rodrigo's account literally. Sole reliance upon Rodrigo's version makes the foundation of Calatrava a unique Spanish event inspired by unique Spanish circumstances. In the debate over the *ribat* as an inspiration for Christian military religious orders, the presence of the Templars is an important factor in the argument for Cistercian influence. But to those following the argument for Spanish exceptionalism, the withdrawal of the Templars assumes greater importance for the development of native institutions. For example, Angus MacKay reported that Raimundo of Fitero and his knights not only stepped into the breach left by the Templars but also defended the town heroically, an extrapolation that Rodrigo does not support in his account.[15] Derek Lomax incorporated Rodrigo's account in his book, *The Reconquest of Spain*, and interpreted the events as demonstrative of the Templars' insistence that their real mission was to protect the Latin East, with only a token appearance in Spain.[16]

---

[14] Claudio Sánchez-Albornoz, *Spain, A Historical Enigma*, trans. Colette Joly Dees and David Sven Reher, 2 vols. (Buenos Aires, 1957), 2:621–706, chapt. 12, does not directly address the origins of the Order of Calatrava but he postulates the uniqueness of Spanish feudalism, especially in the sense that the repopulation of the Duero created a caste of free men in feudal Europe.

[15] Angus MacKay, *Spain in the Middle Ages: From Frontier to Empire, 1000–1500* (London, 1977), p. 32.

[16] Derek W. Lomax, *The Reconquest of Spain* (New York, 1978), p. 108.

Even Lourie accuses the Templars of "falling down on the job" in their failure to retain Calatrava.[17]

The focus on Rodrigo's account reemphasized the notion of Spanish exceptionalism. New historical research, instead of correcting this trend, treats Rodrigo, or indeed any chronicle, as a literary source. Interpreting Rodrigo's history as a literary source emphasizes the medieval author's aims and ambitions rather than his account of historical events. The foremost practitioner of this view is Peter Linehan, who in *History and Historians of Medieval Spain* postulates that Rodrigo's history was part of a literate ploy that manipulated written records in order to assert Toledo's claims to primacy.[18] Linehan's interpretation of Rodrigo follows a gradual reassessment that has been taking place since the beginning of this century. Prior to Linehan, work on Rodrigo changed from a movement for canonization to a detailed study of Rodrigo's activity as a medieval seignorial lord.[19] Linehan's work emphasizes that Rodrigo understood the uses of history and the advantage of establishing a written record in pursuing his goals.

In the light of Linehan's reevaluation of Rodrigo Jiménez de Rada as a historian, Rodrigo's account of the foundation of the Order of Calatrava should be reexamined. It is significant because it is the only narrative account of the founding of the Order of Calatrava, and it contains unique information about the military Orders in Spain.

Rodrigo Jiménez de Rada devotes book 7, chapter 14, of *De rebus hispaniae* to the story of the foundation of Calatrava. Since this is also one of the three chapters that comprise the life of Sancho III of Castile (1157–1158), the author obviously considers the story of Calatrava as one of the main events of the reign. According to Rodrigo, in the year 1157 King Sancho of Castile concluded a treaty with his younger brother, King Fernando of León (1157–1188).

---

[17] Lourie, "Society," 67.

[18] Peter Linehan, *History and the Historians of Medieval Spain* (Oxford, 1993), does not directly address the issue of Rodrigo's trustworthiness on the matter of the origins of the Order of Calatrava.

[19] For a pietistic interpretation, see Manuel Ballesteros Gaibrois, *Don Rodrigo Jiménez de Rada* (Madrid, 1943); Javier Gorosterratzu, *Don Rodrigo Jiménez de Rada* (Pamplona, 1925), which is laudatory yet nevertheless relies upon archival sources. Hilda Grassotti, "Don Rodrigo Ximénez de Rada, gran señor feudal y hombre de negocios en la Castille" *CHE* 55–56 (1972): 1–302, was perhaps the first attempt to reddress the balance by interpreting Rodrigo as a feudal lord.

Sancho then went immediately to the city of Toledo, where there were rumors of a Muslim advance on the fortress of Calatrava. The Templars, who held the fortress, feared that they could not withstand the Muslim army, so they asked Sancho to relieve them of the responsibility of Calatrava. After the Templars left, nobody else would take the fortress. At the same time Raimundo, the abbot of Fitero, and a monk named Diego Velásquez came to Toledo. Diego Velásquez was a former nobleman who had been raised with the king, and he persuaded his abbot to volunteer when Sancho sought defenders for Calatrava. Raimundo refused at first, but finally asked Sancho for Calatrava at Diego's insistence. Even though others thought it was foolish, Sancho agreed. Abbot Raimundo and Diego Velásquez then went to Juan, archbishop of Toledo, who immediately gave material aid and made a public pronouncement that all those who aided Calatrava merited remission of their sins. This pronouncement brought volunteers and donations of horses, weapons, and money. Sancho gave the village and castle of Calatrava to Raimundo and the monastery of Santa María de Fitero in perpetuity. Raimundo took possession of Calatrava with Diego Velásquez. The Muslim army did not appear, but the defenders of the castle nevertheless adopted monastic habits and began military operations against the Muslims. Raimundo garrisoned the castle with the members of the monastery of Fitero, troops, armaments, and surplus goods from Fitero. Raimundo died soon afterward, and was buried in Ciruelos; Diego Velásquez lived a while longer. The chapter ends with the death of King Sancho in August of that year, after a reign of one year and twelve days, and his burial in Toledo.

There are several reasons for treating this account with caution. First, Rodrigo's version of the sequence of events is not supported by the diplomatic evidence. Rodrigo assumed that Sancho returned to Toledo after the Treaty of Sahagún with Fernando II in 1157, and that he then solicited aid for Calatrava. Cristina Monterde thinks it more likely that after Sancho met with his brother he first went to Burgos, then to Soría.[20] Moreover, the Treaty of Sahagún was ratified in May 1158.[21] Sancho was in Almazán in January 1158 when he issued the charter giving Calatrava to Abbot Raimundo of Fitero.

---

[20] Cristina Monterde Albiac, *Colección diplomática del monasterio de Fitero (1140–1210)* (Zaragoza, 1978), p. 299.

[21] Julio González, *El reino de Castilla en la época de Alfonso VIII*, 3 vols. (Madrid, 1960) 2:79–82, no. 44. Monterde Albiac, p. 299, erroneously dates the treaty to 1157.

The meeting between the king and the abbot, therefore, took place in 1157, before the treaty of Sahagún in May 1158.[22] Since Sancho died in August 1158, he could not have reached an agreement with his brother and then go to Toledo to deal with the Muslim army. Nor did the abbot of Fitero attend him in Toledo, but in either Soría or Almazán. Either Rodrigo knew the events (but not their sequence) or he manipulated the timing and the locale to place the meeting between Sancho and Raimundo in the city of Toledo.

Second, the threatened attack upon Calatrava is not mentioned in any Muslim chronicle. Admittedly, the military and political situation in Castile had disintegrated considerably since 1156, and the situation in the city of Toledo would have encouraged panic in 1157. Sancho's father, Alfonso VII, had fallen ill in June of 1156. The illness was so severe that the chroniclers recorded it and the chancery referred to it in the dating of his documents.[23] At the same time, the political power of the Almoravids was disintegrating in Muslim Spain. A new Berber tribe, the Almohads of North Africa, had attempted the conquest of Córdoba. El Sayid Abū Saʿīd, son of the Almohad emir of Morocco, crossed into the Nasrid kingdom and captured Granada in 1156.[24] Saʿīd then sent an army to besiege Almería.[25] He also overran the Christian positions at Santa Eufemia, Pedroche, and Montoro.[26] There is speculation, based upon the disappearance of key officials from charters, that a major Christian defeat took place around this time.[27] Alfonso VII, in company with his ally Ibn Mardanīsh of Valencia, tried to relieve Almería in 1157, but he was unsuccessful. He died in Toledo upon his return from Almería in August, dividing his realms between his two sons, Sancho III of Castile and Fernando II of León.

---

[22] González, *Alfonso VIII*, 2:64–66, no. 35.

[23] Bernard F. Reilly, *The Contest of Christian and Muslim Spain 1031–1157* (Oxford, 1992), p. 212.

[24] Abu Marwan Ibn al-Kārdabus, *Historia del Andalus (España Musulmana)*, trans. Margarita La-Chica Garrido, Universidad de Alicante 6 (Alicante, 1984), pp. 310–311.

[25] Ibn al-Kārdabus, p. 311.

[26] Reilly, pp. 221–222.

[27] Reilly, pp. 221–222, postulates that a major defeat occurred in 1156 because that year Núño Pérez, the former royal alférez, disappeared from the documents. Ambrosio Huici Miranda, "Un nuevo manuscrito de 'al-Bayān al-Mugrib'," *Al-Andalus* 24 (1959): 63–84, dates such a defeat to 1155, based upon the literary evidence. Both of these dates occurred immediately prior to the formation of the Order of Calatrava. Therefore, a major defeat occurring in either 1155 or 1156 could predispose Toledans to panic in 1157.

Sancho had been born around 1133, so he was approximately twenty-four years old in 1157. He had been named king in his father's lifetime, sometime around 1149, and knighted in 1152.[28] According to the terms of his father's will, he became king of Castile, while his younger brother, Fernando, became king of León. The two young kings first sought treaties with each other to prevent a possible war. Meanwhile, the Almohads had already recaptured Baeza and Ubeda, and the Castilians expected them to press upon the area south of Calatrava.[29] The Almohads were planning a military campaign in Granada that would come to naught, but their Christian contemporaries were not to know that.[30]

The death of Alfonso VII, a young, untried king, a possible major defeat, a changed political situation that turned León into a potential rival, and the loss of Almería were all situations that could demoralize a city, let alone an entire kingdom. Rodrigo, however, mentions none of these as possible causes for the crisis in Toledo. He may have been correct about the rumors in Toledo of a possible Almohad advance against the castle of Calatrava, but his narrative account perceived these rumors and the resulting panic as the causes of the formation of the Order of Calatrava. This is a dramatic story that emphasizes the Almohad threat to the city of Toledo, but it also implies that Sancho was a poor leader. If Rodrigo's account is true, both the Templars and the Castilian court exhibited a massive lack of confidence in Sancho's ability to support the defense of a frontier fortress. His kingship would be seen as a failure if his soldiers doubted his ability to lead them against an Almohad advance. Rodrigo does not provide any mitigating factors that could explain the lack of faith in the king. In view of his death in 1158 Sancho's health could have begun deteriorating in 1157, but Rodrigo does not say that. The Castilian nobles could have been concerned about war with León because of Alfonso VII's will, but Rodrigo says that one of the first acts of Sancho's reign was a peace treaty with his brother. The Templars may have withdrawn because of a financial crisis. They had lent Louis VII of France money to finance the Second Crusade. This expedition had ended in disaster for Louis and financial losses for the knights, who then refused to participate in an expedition to

---

[28] Reilly, pp. 229–230.
[29] González, *Alfonso VIII*, 1:569.
[30] Ibn al-Kārdabus, pp. 308–315.

Egypt in 1158.[31] But Rodrigo mentions none of this. It is extraordinary and unprecedented that the only people the King of Castile could find to garrison a fortress were two Cistercian monks. It is unusual that the king could offer no material aid, and that their only supplies came from the church of Toledo, the monastery of Fitero, and the pious donations of the inhabitants of Toledo. Yet the other chapters about Sancho III in Rodrigo's history do not portray the king as an unfit ruler.[32] Thus contemporary interpretations that stress the panic and the improvised defense of the fortress are not considering the entire picture.

Rodrigo's history is also the only chronicle source for some important information about the Castilian frontier. First, he states that at some point between 1147 and 1157 Alfonso VII entrusted the fortress of Calatrava to the Order of the Templars. It is unfortunate that no contemporary royal charter referring to this donation survives.[33] This was the first and only occasion that the Castilian kings granted frontier property to the Templars, although the Order was active along the Toledo frontier.[34] The Order of the Temple and the Knights of the Hospital both had extensive land holdings in eastern Spain, and the Templar presence in Aragon is especially well documented.[35] In the absence of direct heirs, Alfonso I of Aragon (1104–1134) had bequeathed his kingdom in 1134 to these two military orders and to the Holy Sepulcher, but the Aragonese quickly acted to put his brother, the monk Ramiro, on the throne instead.[36] Lacking

---

[31] Malcolm Barber, *The New Knighthood: A History of the Order of the Temple* (Cambridge, 1994), p. 25; Steven Runciman, *A History of the Crusades*, 3 vols. (London, 1952), 2:312–313.

[32] See Rodrigo, *De rebus*, book 7, chapter 12, where the author praises Sancho's abilities and laments that he died before he reached his full potential.

[33] The *fuero* of Calatrava (1148), survives in an incomplete seventeenth-century transcription (AHN Ordines Militares, Registro de Escrituras de la Orden de Calatrava, I, fol. 4). It mentions *fratres*, possibly the Templars, in the first article.

[34] See, for example, Antonio Maya Sánchez, ed., *Chronica Adefonsi Imperatoris*, in *Corpus Christianorum Continuatio Mediaevalis* 71 (Turnholt, 1990), part 1, chapts. 47, 48, p. 172, for Templars at the castle of Escalona in the vincinity of Toledo in 1134.

[35] See Forey, *The Military Orders*, pp. 65–67; idem, *The Templars in the Corona de Aragon* (London, 1973).

[36] See Elena Lourie, "The Will of Alfonso I 'El Batallador', King of Aragon and Navarre: A Reassessment," *Speculum* 50 (1975): 635–651; José María Lacarra, *Alfonso el Batallador* (Zaragoza, 1978); A.J. Forey, "The Will of Alfonso I of Aragon and Navarre," *Durham University Journal* 73, no. 1 (December, 1980): 59–65; Clay Stalls, *Possessing the Land: Aragon's Expansion into Islam's Ebro Frontier under Alfonso the Battler, 1104–1134* (Leiden, 1995), 273–274.

similar sources, Castilian historians have attempted to reconstruct the circumstances under which Alfonso VII gave Calatrava to the Templars. Julio González reasons that Calatrava provided refuge for Jews expelled from Andalucía by the Almohads; once this group of settlers moved on, the town became depopulated, and Alfonso VII had to find someone to garrison it quickly.[37] But Alfonso VII had been able to find nobles willing to hold other towns and castles, or to appoint someone if there were no volunteers. At no other time did Alfonso VII turn to the Templars for help. The Templars of Calatrava are unique in Castilian history, and there is no supplementary evidence outside of Rodrigo Jiménez de Rada.

Archbishop Juan's issuance of a plenary indulgence is the second unusual incident. The original charter does not survive, and Rodrigo is Goñi Gatzambide's sole source for the identification of the archbishop's aid as a plenary indulgence. Goñi Gatzambide categorizes this twelfth-century episcopal plenary indulgence as a rare innovation.[38] During the twelfth century, the pope issued crusading indulgences; bishops only began issuing them in large numbers in the thirteenth century. Archbishop Juan may have granted the indulgence as Rodrigo says, since precedents existed for episcopal encouragement of Iberian crusaders.[39] Rodrigo may also have had his own circumstances in mind when he conferred such powers upon his predecessor. Innocent III had urged Rodrigo and other Iberian bishops to direct a crusade that resulted in the battle of Las Navas de Tolosa in 1212.[40] Honorius III had made Rodrigo a papal legate to call and direct a crusade in 1218, and directed the other Iberian bishops to obey him on this occasion.[41] Either Rodrigo assumed that the twelfth-century archbishop of Toledo had the same powers as he did to issue a crusading indulgence, or Rodrigo needed to create

---

[37] González, *Alfonso VIII*, 2:225. O'Callaghan, "Affiliation," 180, n. 2, follows the same lines of evidence as González and notes that there is no contemporary supporting charter giving Calatrava to the Templars.

[38] José Goñi Gaztambide, *Historia de la bula de la cruzada en España* (Vitoria, 1958), p. 89.

[39] Diego Gelmírez, archbishop of Santiago de Compostela, offered remission of sins in 1125 to soldiers of Christ who would open the way to the Holy Sepulchre via Spain (*Historia Compostelana, ES* 20:427–430, book 2, chapt. 78). In 1155 Cardinal Hyacinth at the Council of Valladolid offered remission of sins to those who defended Christianity, the same privilige as if they had gone to the Holy Land (Goñi Gaztambide, pp. 87–88). I am indebted to Joseph O'Callaghan for these citations.

[40] See Goñi Gaztambide, pp. 110–132.

[41] Ibid., p. 141.

a historical precedent for his actions in directing a crusade. Whatever happened, Rodrigo's account emphasizes the leading role of the archbishop of Toledo in creating an improvised crusading order.

Rodrigo's history omits Sancho's prior relationship with Abbot Raimundo and the monastery of Fitero, which, with additional diplomatic evidence, establishes the king's support of Cistercian monasticism. During Alfonso VII's lifetime, Sancho had patronized several monasteries, but Fitero, one of the first Cistercian monasteries in Spain, gradually won royal favor.[42] Sancho had given the castle of Tudején to Raimundo and the monastery of Fitero before Alfonso VII's death in 1157.[43] This early gift of a castle did not specify the monastery's responsibilities to garrison and defend it, but simply donated the property to God, the monastery, and the abbot in perpetuity.[44] In comparison, Sancho's grant of the village and castle of Calatrava to Abbot Raimundo in January 1158 included the Cistercian congregation among the recipients.[45] This charter contained the additional stipulation that the abbot defend the property against the Muslims, a provision that also appears in later royal Castilian grants to the military religious orders. Sancho's inclusion of the Cistercian congregation in a grant that specified military responsibilities implies that the king knew of Cistercian writing and preaching on the "new knights," and that such preaching probably inspired his creation of the new military religious order. By the following month, Sancho III gave Raimundo of Fitero the village of Ciruelos, but directed this donation to the monks and brothers of Calatrava, omitting any reference to Fitero or the Cistercian Order.[46] After one month the royal

---

[42] González, *Alfonso VIII*, 1:484–485, 510–512.

[43] Monterde Albiac, *Colección diplomática*, pp. 432–434, no. 92 (15 April 1157). Monterde, pp. 289–290, believes that an earlier charter dated 1156 in which Sancho takes the monastery under his protection is a forgery.

[44] Ibid., pp. 432–434, no. 92. The language of the charter does not indicate that the monastery had specific military responsibilities before the garrisoning of Calatrava: ". . . si que sint ad eum pertinentibus quecumque sint, uel ubicumque eas inuenire hereditario uos et omnes succesores uestri in perpetuum, et omnia iura ei pertinentia ut diximus que ad regiam spectant maiestatem."

[45] *Bullarium*, p. 2, no. 1. (January 1158): "sanctae congregationi Cisterciensi, et vobis domino Raymundo, abbati ecclesie Sancte Mariae de Fitero, et omnibus fratribus vestris. . . ."

[46] *Bullarium*, pp. 2–3, no. 2; González, *Alfonso VIII*, 2:69–70, no. 38: ". . . vobis [monachis] et fratribus de Calatrava. . . ." This charter survives in a copy of a notarial translation made in 1408. See Juan Francisco Rivera Recio, *La iglesia de Toledo en el siglo XII* (Rome, 1976), 2:218, for the identification of Cirugares with Ciruelos.

chancery recognized the brothers of Calatrava as an identifiable, separate entity from the abbey of Fitero.[47] The papacy, however, did not so recognize the brothers of Calatrava, nor did the Cistercian general chapter grant them a *vivendi forma*, until September 1164.[48]

The historian is left with the question of why Rodrigo might overemphasize the role of the archbishop and the people of Toledo. Other than simple aggrandizement, Rodrigo's reasons were the claims that his diocese had over the Order and lands of Calatrava. The castle of Calatrava was strategically located on the road between Andalusia and Toledo. According to Muslim sources the *imam* Muhammad first fortified Calatrava in 855–856.[49] Positioned just south of the eastern end of the mountains of Toledo, the castle provided a base for Almoravid raids against the city of Toledo. Sometime around 1102–1103, the Almoravid emir Tasufin made a tour of inspection of the region and poetically compared it to an eagle, with Toledo as the head and Calatrava as the beak.[50] Alfonso VII captured the castle and village of Calatrava in January 1147, prior to his campaign to take Almería.[51] Rodrigo Jiménez de Rada reports that Alfonso VII besieged Calatrava with war machines because it posed a great danger to the kingdom of Toledo.[52] A charter that Alfonso VII issued when he captured Calatrava supports Rodrigo's assessment of the strategic importance of the fortress to the safety of Toledo.[53] With its capitulation Calatrava ceased to be a base for Muslim raids against Toledo, and became part of the defenses of Toledo's eastern flank.

---

[47] The first donations to the Order named the recipient as the "brothers of Calatrava" ("fratribus de Calatrava"). The first Master of Calatrava named as the recipient of a royal donation was Fernando Escaza on 5 May 1169. See González, *Alfonso VIII*, 2:201–202, no. 118.

[48] *Bullarium*, pp. 3–4, no. 4; O'Callaghan, "Affiliation," pp. 188–189.

[49] Abū ʿAbd Allāh Muhammad Ibn ʿAbd al-Munʿim al-Himyārī, *Kitāb ar-Rawd al-miʿtar*, trans. María Pilar Maestro González, Textos Medievales <10> (Valencia, 1963), pp. 328–329.

[50] Ambrosio Huici Miranda, ed. and trans., *"Al-Hulal al Mawsiyya": Crónica árabe de las dinastías Almoravide, Almohade y Benimerín* (Tetuan, 1951), p. 91.

[51] Reilly, p. 212, indicates the capture took place by January 1147. The *Anales Toledanos, ES* 23:390, provides a date of 1146 (era 1184). Chronologically, the chronicler places it after Alfonso VII's attack on Córdoba and before his capture of Baeza (October 1147).

[52] Rodrigo, book 7, chapter 4.

[53] Fidel Fita, "Bula inédita de Honorio II," *BRAH* 7 (1885): 344–346; also José Antonio García Luján, *Privilegios reales de la catedral de Toledo (1086–1462)*, 2 vols. (Toledo, 1982), no. 18 (13 February 1147): "Quanta mala quanteque persecutiones

After recapturing Calatrava, Alfonso VII gave the mosque and its properties to Raimundo, archbishop of Toledo.[54] The same charter gave Archbishop Raimundo the right to populate the town according to the *fuero* (customs) of Toledo.[55] Also in 1148, Alfonso VII gave Calatrava a brief *fuero* that recognized the settlers' property rights and the boundaries of Calatrava.[56] Alfonso's donation of the mosque of Calatrava to the diocese of Toledo established its proprietary interest in Calatrava, and formed the basis for any later claims that the diocese exercised over the town. What happened between 1147 and 1157 in Calatrava, however, is not clear. No evidence survives to indicate that Raimundo established any settlements or improvements in Calatrava. Uncharacteristically, the diocese ignored this property. It did not press claims until 1180, when an activist archbishop, Cerebruno, challenged both the Orders of Santiago and Calatrava over the issue of diocesan rights in areas held by the military orders. Under Cerebruno's leadership, Toledo claimed its former properties based upon the evidence in its cartulary of royal grants and donations. But the diocese could not produce written proof in its cartularies that it established permanent settlements in the lands that the military religious orders had acquired. On this basis, the Order of Santiago soundly trounced Cerebruno in the royal courts and forced him to settle.[57]

On the issue of diocesan rights, no one, except the Masters of the military orders, was prepared to dispute that the orders owed tithes to the diocese of Toledo on these properties. The Order of Calatrava seized the diocesan real estate and tithes in Calatrava after Cerebruno's death in 1180.[58] In relation to a similar controversy in

---

per calatrava, dum in potestate sarracenorum maneret, toletane civitati et populo christiano assidue evenissent, omnibus hominibus per hyspaniam constitutis satis est manifestum." The same charter establishes that Calatrava fell after Alfonso VII captured Córdoba.

[54] Rodrigo, book 7, chapter 4. Fita, "Bula," 344–346 (13 February 1147).

[55] Fita, "Bula," 344–346 (13 February 1147); also Angel González Palencia, "Noticias sobre don Raimundo, arzobispo de Toledo," *Spanische Forschungen der Gorresgesellschaft* 6 (1937): 119.

[56] Julio González, *Repoblación de Castilla la Nueva*, 2 vols. (Madrid, 1975), 1:224; AHN Madrid, Ordenes Militares, Registro de Calatrava, I, f. 4.

[57] Martín, *Orígenes*, pp. 47–49, 299–300, nos. 115–117. The exact properties in question were Oreja, Alharilla, Salvanés, and Belinchón.

[58] See Joseph F. O'Callaghan, "The Order of Calatrava and the Archbishops of Toledo 1147–1242," in *The Spanish Military Order of Calatrava and its Affiliates* (London, 1975), pp. 67–68. O'Callaghan attributes the date of Cerebruno's death to 1181;

Portugal, Pope Alexander III had ruled that the knights of Calatrava were exempt from tithes on cultivated land because of their
affiliation to the Order of Cîteaux; however, he hoped that a compromise would recognize the rights of the diocese.[59] Likewise, the
Castilian king, Alfonso VIII, insisted that the archdiocese retained
its rights and revenues within the lands originally conferred by
Alfonso VII's charter.[60] A compromise reached in 1183 caused the
Order of Calatrava to seek full incorporation into the Order of
Cîteaux in 1187. The move gave the Knights of Calatrava the full
immunities of members of the Order of Cîteaux. The litigation between the archdiocese of Toledo and the Order of Calatrava finally
landed in the papal court 1236–1240, during Rodrigo's tenure as
archbishop. Rodrigo complained that the knights of the Order did
not render him canonical obedience, did not pay him tithes, had
taken over diocesan churches, had disputed his property rights and
boundaries, and had imposed tolls upon diocesan clerics and tenants.
A compromise in 1245 upheld the archbishop's rights over his properties.[61] In light of Rodrigo's longstanding litigation, he may have
found it useful to emphasize the primary role that the archbishop
of Toledo played in the founding of the Order of Calatrava and
to de-emphasize the influence of the Order of Cîteaux.

There is another important omission in Rodrigo's account of the
origins of the Order of Calatrava. Rodrigo did not mention that the
militia of Toledo, which had existed since at least 1099, played any
role in the defense of the city.[62] In addition, important new evidence suggests that a military *cofradía*, possibly linked to the militia,
existed in Toledo around the time of the foundation of Calatrava.[63]
The will of Pedro Moreda, a knight of Toledo, contains the earliest
lay bequest to the brothers of Calatrava and the only mention of the
confraternity of the militia.[64] It was dated September 1164, the same

---

Francisco Hernández, *Los cartularios de Toledo* (Madrid, 1985), pp. 189–190, no. 200,
puts it in 1180.

[59] O'Callaghan, "Order of Calatrava," 67.

[60] Ibid., 70.

[61] Ibid., 77–79.

[62] See Biblioteca Cabildo de Toledo, 42–20, ff. 10r–11v (23 April 1099), for the
earliest evidence of the Toledo militia's existence when its members witnessed a
royal charter.

[63] The will had been overlooked because it was preserved in the Toledan cartularies and not in the archives of the Order of Calatrava.

[64] Toledo, Biblioteca Catedral, 42–20, *Liber Privilegiorum*, fols. 72v–73v.

month as the papal recognition of the Order.[65] In comparison the earliest known secular, non-royal donation of real property to the Order of Calatrava was dated 1167.[66]

Pedro Moreda was a wealthy Toledan knight. His will distributed half of his estate to ecclesiastical institutions in Toledo, which included the Cathedral church of Santa María, various parish churches, and individual clerics. He left three major bequests to ecclesiastical institutions: the refectory of the cathedral of Santa María received a store that Pedro Moreda had purchased from Pedro of San Paulo in January of 1162 for 90 *maravedís*;[67] the archbishop and the canons inherited 300 gold *morabetinos*; and the brothers of Calatrava inherited Moreda's saddle horse, bridle, and all his weapons. Moreda reserved his yellow mule, however, to the Knights Hospitaller, who had received a royal grant of property in Toledo in 1162.[68]

Moreda's personal bequests to individual clerics included a horse saddle for Domingo, the chaplain of Santa Maria. Guillermo, the prior of the cathedral, inherited his new mule saddle. Pedro Moreda also divided his flock of sheep among the parish churches of Santa Leocadia outside the walls (30 sheep) Santa María de Sisla (20 sheep) and San Pablo (10 sheep). He allocated twelve *morabetinos* to the confraternity of the militia, and twenty-four *morabetinos* for captives. Moreda's family and familiars also received their share of the estate. His brother, Juan Meléndez, inherited the houses next to the cathedral that Moreda had bought from Saturno.[69] Master Aimerico got his green mantle, his shirts, his good trousers and his good bed cover. Coronello, a former servant of Alfonso VII, received five

---

[65] Rades y Andrada, *Crónica*, fol. 26, cites this will because other property that Pedro Moreda disposed of eventually wound up in the hands of the Order of Calatrava. Moreda's will was not otherwise included with the records of the Order's landholdings and property acquisitions because he did not leave the Order real property.

[66] Uhagón, *Indice*, 97, Particulares, no. 6, registers this as the donation of a vineyard, in the village of Nambroca, made by Pedro Parigi. This is suspect, though, since the donation is addressed to the Order of Salvatierra, by which name the order was known between 1195–1212. The *Bullarium*, p. 6, however, publishes the gift of a monastery from Urraca Pérez to the Brothers of Calatrava, dated 1167.

[67] Toledo, Biblioteca Catedral, 42–20, f. 72r–v. Alfonso VII had given Pedro of San Pablo the store 8 November 1154.

[68] González, *Repoblación*, 1:280.

[69] This may be the same as Saturnino Gauteri, who witnessed the purchase of the houses Pedro Moreda bought from Pedro of San Paulo in 1162. These houses eventually passed to the Order of Calatrava; see Rades y Andrada, *Crónica*, fol. 26.

measures (*cahizes*) of wheat. Moreda's widow, Semsi, received half of the estate. In addition, she kept anything that remained of the other half after the distribution of the bequests. The estate was so large Moreda named three executors in addition to his widow: Domingo, the chaplain of the cathedral,[70] Guillermo, the prior,[71] and Martin Abu-ʿali, who had earlier witnessed litigation involving the monastery of San Servando.[72]

The division of the estate demonstrates Pedro Moreda's strong ties to both the church and to the local military establishments. The horse, saddle, bridle, and weapons that Moreda left to the Brothers of Calatrava were possibly very valuable. Moreda may have referred to the animal that he left the Brothers of Calatrava as a saddle horse (*cauallum meum sellatum*) in order to distinguish it from draft animals; other sources understand the phrase to mean a war horse. The *fuero* of Toledo (1118) forbade sending saddle horses or weapons to Muslim lands.[73] Moreda's horse could have been worth as much as the property and the money he left to other ecclesiastical institutions. Between the tenth and the thirteenth centuries, Iberian horses cost anywhere from 30 and 3000 *maravedís*, although the average price was around 300–500.[74] The yellow mule that he bequeathed to the Order of St. John of Jerusalem may have been worth as

---

[70] Domingo, chaplain of the cathedral, flourished in Toledo between 1154 and 1164, when he witnessed many charters. See Hernández, *Los cartularios*, pp. 93–94, 101–105, 116–117, 122–123, 126–127, 129–130, 136–138, nos. 95, 103, 105, 106, 119, 125, 130, 134, 143, and 144.

[71] Guillermo, signed "W," prior of Santa María. Any number of clerics in Toledo named Guillermo witnessed charters with the initial W. during this period. Hernández, *Los cartularios*, pp. 54–55, 63, 79–80, 93–94, 101–102, 103–104, 108–109, 116–119, 122–123, 126–127, 129–131, 136–138, 143–145, 147–148, 152, 160–162, 167–168, 175, 177–178, 185–190, nos. 52, 60, 79, 80, 95, 103, 105, 109, 119, 121, 125, 130, 134, 135, 143, 144, 150, 152, 155, 159, 165, 166, 174, 182, 185, 195, 197, 198, and 200, found that the prior of the cathedral for the years 1146–1181 witnessed charters as "W," indicating that probably more than one Guillermo held this office.

[72] Hernández, *Los cartularios*, pp. 99–100, no. 101 (1154).

[73] Alfonso García-Gallo, "Los fueros de Toledo," *AHDE* 45 (1975): 473–483, no. 10. The earlier *fuero* survives in a recompilation of Toledan *fueros* from circa 1166.

[74] María del Carmen Carlé, "El precio de la vida en Castilla del rey Sabio al emplazado," *CHE* 15 (1951): 152; by the 13th century, the price went as high as 3,000 *maravedís*. Also see María Isabel Pérez Tudela y Velasco, *Infanzones y caballeros: su proyección en la esfera nobiliaria castellano-leonesa (s. IX–XIII)* (Madrid, 1979), pp. 103–106, 110–112, 208–211, who provides a wider number of prices of horses and mules for the tenth through the thirteenth century.

much, if not more, than the horse.[75] Weapons, depending upon the type, could cost as much as a horse. Pedro Moreda does not specify the type of weapon, so whether the Order got his sword or his shield is unspecified, although later wills are more specific. Moreda also provided twenty-four *morabetinos* for captives, or, presumably, for the redemption of captives. James Brodman has cited twelfth-century Catalan wills that leave similar amounts for captives, which demonstrates that a concern for captives was considered a meritorious bequest, one not reserved for members of municipal militias.[76]

In addition to his bequests to the two military religious Orders, Moreda left the confraternity of the militia twelve *morabetinos*. Moreda's reference to the confraternity of the militia confirms earlier speculations that such an organization existed.[77] Otherwise, little is known of the Iberian confraternities of the militia outside of the fact of their existence. The confraternity (*cofradía*) of Belchite or Zaragoza appears in a charter of Alfonso I of Aragón in 1122.[78] The *cofradía* of Belchite is clearly a military religious institution, composed of brothers who defended Christendom against its Muslim enemies. Anyone rendering this meritorious service or any other assistance in the form of pilgrimages, donations of alms, bequests of horses and weapons, and bequests to houses of captives, received indulgences. In addition, the members of the confraternity could retain any lands they had captured from the Muslims. The charter had originally been witnessed by Bernard, archbishop of Toledo and papal legate, and the bishops of Tarragona, Compostela, Osma, Zaragoza, Huesca, Barbastro, Calahorra, Tarazona, Loscar, Lescar, Sigüenza and Segovia.[79] Archbishop Raimundo of Toledo also witnessed Alfonso VII's reconfirmation of the *cofradía* in 1136. The charter was not a Rule, since it does not define a common life nor give the brothers a common goal other than fighting Muslims. Instead, it is a series of financial and spiritual privileges. The *cofradía* of Belchite itself disappeared soon after

---

[75] Carlé, p. 152.

[76] James Brodman, *Ransoming Captives in Crusader Spain* (Philadelphia, 1986), p. 12.

[77] Peter Rassow, "La Cofradía de Belchite," *AHDE* 3 (1926): 219.

[78] See Rassow, "Cofradía," 224–226, and Goñi Gaztambide, pp. 76–77, for the surviving text embedded in Alfonso VII's confirmation of 1136.

[79] Antonio Ubieto Arteta, "La creación de la cofradía militar de Belchite," *Estudios de Edad Media de la Corona de Aragón* 5 (1952): 427–434, established the date of the original as February–May 1122, based upon the listing of Iberian bishops.

1136. No one is sure what became of it, although it has been suggested that it merged into the military religious orders.

The terms of Moreda's will, specifically, his bequests of alms, horses, weapons, and redemptionary monies to the confraternity, the Hospitallers, and for captives are very similar to the provisions of the *cofradía* of Belchite. He also ties the confraternity with the militia of Toledo. Between 1099 and 1107, the militia of Toledo witnessed royal charters as a corporate body for Alfonso VI.[80] Its leader, like that of the *cofradía* of Belchite, bore the title of "*princeps.*"[81] The use of this title did not indicate royal status or overlordship, but instead was derived from the classical Latin term for the Iberian peninsula's tribal warlords.[82] By the mid-twelfth century the word "*princeps*" disappeared from Toledan charters and the Arabic word "*alcaid*" designated the military governor of the city. For example, the *Cronica Adefonsi Imperatoris*, composed toward the end of Alfonso VII's reign, used both the word "*alcaid*" and the word "*princeps*" to describe Gutierre Armíldez, who died in 1131.[83] Part II, which focused on Alfonso VII's campaigns in Toledo, describes the royal appointment of several "*principes,*" who then led the militia of Toledo in campaigns against the Muslims in Seville.[84]

The confraternity in Toledo could have been created by Alfonso VI, Alfonso I (who occupied Toledo and claimed it as part of his

---

[80] See Toledo, Biblioteca Catedral, ms. 42–20, ff. 10r–11v, "Guter Suariz princeps Toletane militie cf. . . . de Toletana militia: Johannes Ranemiriz cf., Garcia Vermudiz cf., Gonzaluo Sesfaniz cf., Claudio Johannis cf., Justo Pedrez cf." (23 April 1099); Toledo, Archivo Catedral, A.6.B.2.3., "Gutier Suarios princeps Toletane militie cf. . . . de Toletana militia Johannes Ranemiriz cf., Garcia Vermudiz cf., Gonzaluo Stefaniz cf., Claudio Iohannes cf., Iusto Petriz cf." (22 June 1103); A. García-Gallo, "Los Fueros de Toledo," *AHDE* 45 (1975): 461, "Michael Cidiz, princeps Toletane militie, conf . . . D[e mil]itie Toletane, . . . Garcia Ximenones, conf. Iohannie Ramiriz, conf. Gonzalvo Stephaniz, conf. Rodrigo Ordoniz, conf. Sancio Arnariz, conf. Iohanne Didaz, conf. Petro Didaz, conf. Pelagio Gudesteiz, conf." (19 March 1101); Toledo, Archivo Catedral, I.12.A.1.1., "Fernandus Telliz princebs toletane milicia . . . de Toletana milicia: Johannes Ramiriz cf., Claudius Iohannis cf., Johannes Didaz cf., Justus Petriz cf." (8 March 1107); also Hernández, *Los cartularios*, pp. 15–19, nos. 10, 12, 14.

[81] Rassow, "Cofradía," 215.

[82] Leonard Curchin, *The Local Magistrates in Roman Spain* (Toronto, 1990), p. 4. According to Donald J. Kagay, *The Usatges of Barcelona* (Philadelphia, 1994), pp. 34–36, the *principes* eventually assumed territorial sovereignty in Catalonia, although it would appear that the development of an effective monarchy in Castile prevented a similar development in Toledo.

[83] See *Cronica Adefonsi Imperatoris*, Part 2, chapts. 15, 24, pp. 202, 206.

[84] For example, see ibid., part 2, chapts. 24, 25, p. 206.

kingdom) or Alfonso VII; there is no written evidence, although Alfonso I and Alfonso VII were both associated with the *cofradía* of Belchite. The Toledo militia may have been organized as a para-religious body, whose members enjoyed spiritual as well as financial rewards. But the ultimate problem with the study of military confraternities is the lack of written evidence. Knowing that such a confraternity existed in Toledo does not answer any questions, although it advances new ones. Could the confraternity of the militia have defended the castle of Calatrava, or was it solely a spiritual organization? Did the confraternity facilitate the popular outpouring of men, money, and material for the defense of the fortress? Could the confraternity of the militia of Toledo have become part of the Order of Calatrava? It would seem that the confraternity was a religious organization, not the whole militia, because the men of Toledo continued to perform separate military service after the formation of the Order of Calatrava.[85] The spiritual benefits may have survived in the lay sphere, since the knights (*milites*) of the city were able to wrest exemption from tithes from Alfonso VIII in 1182.[86] But this remains speculation until more evidence comes to light.

The most valuable evidence from the will of Pedro Moreda is that a military confraternity existed in Toledo contemporary with the founding of the Order of Calatrava. Pedro Moreda, a knight of Toledo, was familiar with crusading ideology and the military religious orders that it spawned. His will linked the confraternity of the militia with the Brothers of Calatrava and the Order of the Hospital. The will of Pedro Moreda proves that the Cistercian idea of the "new Order of knights" found acceptance among the laity in the city of Toledo, and may have inspired popular support for the foundation of a native military religious order.

In conclusion, determining the origins of Calatrava relies upon a firm interrogation of written text. There may have been cultural borrowing of the concept of the *ribat* from the Almoravids, but there is no written proof linking the development of parallel institutions. The written evidence for Cistercian influence of Iberian military religious

---

[85] See González, *Alfonso VIII*, 3:391–93, no. 793 (3 February 1207), in which Alfonso VIII orders that the men of the surrounding towns (excepting those belonging to the archbishop or the Military Orders) had to perform military service with the town council of Toledo.
[86] García-Gallo, 447.

orders remains the most likely inspiration. Rodrigo Jiménez de Rada's account telescoped and compressed events, yet it probably contains the kernel of truth. The discriminating reader can identify those parts of Rodrigo's history that were motivated by self-interest; other aspects, while uncorroborated, are not entirely fantastic. Rodrigo remains our major source for the Templars in Calatrava and for the archbishop's crusading indulgence, two important aspects of the story that are not supported by diplomatic evidence but whose accuracy can be inferred. Certainly the Castilians saw the new Order of Calatrava as a continuation of the Templars' crusading mission. The diplomatic evidence does support the suggestion that Sancho III intended to create a military religious Order founded upon Cistercian ideology. Finally, the will of Pedro Moreda provides corroboration for the religious and military spirit of the times by indicating that a military confraternity already existed in Toledo. Whether or not the confraternity played a direct role in the founding of the Order of Calatrava, the existence of such an institution argues that the people of Toledo were already predisposed to a native military religious Order. The only aspect of Rodrigo's account that cannot be corroborated is his description of the outpouring of men, money, and material for the defense of the fortress. The will of Pedro Moreda provides a glimpse into the form of popular piety that inspired the creation of the Order of Calatrava, but it is only a glimpse that remains meaningless without Rodrigo's account to give it a context.

Appendix A

BCT 42–20 fol. 72v–73v
Will of Pedro Moreda, September 1164

Testamentum petri morede. in quo canonicis sancte marie predictam domum pro anniuersario suo sicut iam superius dictum est dedit.

In dei nomine et eius gratia. Ego P. moreda timens mortem quam nemo euadere potest, infirmus corpore sed sanus mente facio testamentum meum pro remissione anime mee. In primis dono refectorio sancte marie illam tendam quam ego acquisiui et comparaui de petro sancti pauli. Insuper dono archiepiscopo et canonicis sancte marie maioris in auro xxx morabetinos. Dono cauallum meum sellatum et frenatum et cum omnibus armis meis fratribus de calatrauah. Dono mulum meum amarellum ad hospitale iherusalem. Et sellam meam cum omni apparatu suo dominico capellano sancte marie dimitto. Dono ecclesie sancte leocadie extra muros xxx oues. Sancte marie de sisla dono xx oues. Sancto paulo x oues. Confraternie militantium xii morabetinos. Johanni melendez germano meo dono illas casas meas quas comparaui de saturno iuxta ecclesiam sancte marie magdalene. Dono magistro aimerico meum mantum uiride et meas camisias et braccas bonas et unam almuzallam bonam. W priori sancte marie meam sellam nouam mularem dono. Petro abbati sancte marie magadalene absoluo i morabetino quem mihi debet. Dono coronello v k de trigo et meam saiam et matri sue ii morabetinos. Mando clericis sancte marie magdalene v k de tritico. Dentur pro captiuis xxiiii morabetinos. Dominico subrino capellani et iohanni de iherusalem iii morabetinos. Fortoni qui testamentum hoc scripsit i morabetino. R. sacriste iii morabetinos. Hec omna que supra scripta sunt distribuantur per manus uxoris Semce et domni W prioris et dominici capellani atque Martini aboalin. Facta carta testamenti mense septembris. Era mccii. Hoc totum testificantur testes qui presentes fuerunt et ab ore eius audierunt et nomina sua scripserunt uel scribere preceperunt. Hec omnia que mandaui superius sint de medietate mea quia alia medietas uxoris mee est et si aliquid remanserit de medietate mea in manus uxoris mee sit omnibus diebus uite sue. Post mortem uero ipsius detur pro anima mea et sua ubicumque ipsa mandauerit. Magister aimericus testis. Ego forto presbyter qui hanc cartam scripsi testis. Arnaldus clericus sancte marie magdalene testis. Don clement de san antolin testis et scripserit pro eo.

THE LOST KINGDOM OF SIURANA: HIGHLAND RESISTANCE BY MUSLIMS TO CHRISTIAN RECONQUEST AND ASSIMILATION IN THE TWELFTH CENTURY

Lawrence J. McCrank

Imagine a Muslim highland pastoral and woodland paradise in north-eastern Spain, that after four centuries of prosperity and semi-autonomy due to its mountainous isolation, suddenly came to a cruel and bitter demise with the Christian Reconquest after the mid-twelfth century. It was a world lost to written history, except through folksong and legend embellished as tragedy and romance, reinforced by ruins and an awareness that the area, the Priorat of Catalunya Nova, is cultur-ally distinctive still to this day.

One tale tells of a beautiful Muslim princess, 'Abd al-'Azia (tran-scribed variously, i.e., Abd-elazia), devoted to her lover and lord "*el rey moro*," or "*rezuelo*," named Almira Almoniniz.[1] This is perhaps a corruption of the sobriquet *amir al-mu 'minin*, or "Prince of believers," rather than a personal name. Indeed, one Catalan chronicler, Pere Tomich, relying on some sources no longer extant, names a certain "Dentença" as the Muslim master of the Mountains of Prades who ruled from the castle of Siurana. He attempts to link this to a lat-ter surname associated with the barony of Falset in the mountains of Prades, as if to suggest that the Muslim lord of Siurana was a Mudejar who, after the Reconquest, had retained some holdings there, but this is assuredly a corruption.[2] So the exact identity of

---

[1] The story is recorded by Jaime Finestres y de Monsalvo, *Historia del real monas-terio de Poblet* (Barcelona, 1746; repr. 1947–55), 2:43–45; and was elaborated by Victor Balaguer, *Las ruinas de Poblet* (Madrid, 1885), pp. 55–93; and was retold in abbreviated form by Joaquin Guitert y Fontsere, *El real monasterio de Poblet* (Barcelona, 1929), pp. 107–109.

[2] Pere Tomich, *Histories e conquestes dels Reys d'Arago e Comtes de Catalunya* (Barcelona, 1534), facsimile ed., Antonio Ubieto Arteta, *Textos Medievales*, 29 (Valencia, 1970), p. 76: "*e empres de conquistar les muntanyes de Prades que tenien moros: en les quals havia un Rey moro appellat Dentenca: lo qual ya per te[m]ps lo Reye de Aragon avien lancat de dites muntayes el die heretaren del castell Dentenca: e lo dit Dentenca recullis en lo castell de Siurana; e aqui lo dit Rey Aldefonsus lo pres a merce: e seulo lo ser Chrestia: e mes li nom Guillem Dentenca: e de aquell son exits los Dentenca e lur linatge: e lo Rey dona lo Mora e Falcet: e*

the Muslim prince remains a mystery. In the era of *mulūk al-tawāᶜif,*
or "party kings," the Muslim lord of these highlands was the military
commander of the Muslim *thagr,* that is, March of Siurana (in Spanish,
Ciurana). After the fall of the *taifa* kinglets of Lerida and Tortosa in
1148–1149 it existed briefly, depending on one's Muslim or Christian
perspective, either as a *taifa* or as one of many pockets of Mudejar
rebellion against the new Aragonese-Catalan regime.

According to legend, the Muslim princess was sent to this isolated
refuge for her own protection. Siurana castle was built in an enclosed
gorge on a precipice overlooking the headwaters of the Siurana River
(actually a mountain stream at this point) as it flowed toward a wider
valley that formed one of the two plateaus of the modern Priorat
region. Medieval chroniclers would later describe it repeatedly as
"extremely well fortified" when it became the Crown's favorite keep
for noble prisoners.[3] Early-modern Catalan chroniclers, like Friar
Francisco Diago in 1603 paraphrasing, almost word for word, his predecessor (1562), the Aragonese Jerónomo Zurita, continued to remark
how well fortified Siurana was, noting it was so ensconced in the
highest part of the mountains that it must have seemed inaccessible
to the Christians and impossible to take.[4] It lay at the center of what

---

total la Baronia qui es dita Dentenca en les dires muntanyes de Prades." Thus, claims Tomich,
this Guillem Dentença was the same as or the successor to the Moor King Dentenca
of Siurana. *"Dentenca"* seems to be a Catalan corruption of *"den t[in]enca"* from *tenen-*
cia, which really refers back to the original landholding rather than to a personal
name. Nor does it seem likely that the inheritor, Guillem, would have been a
Mudejar prince without clearer identification. Moreover, the root *Tenca* defies transliteration from Arabic or easy identification with any Muslim name, but it does reflect
similar post twelfth-century Latin-Romance corruptions that occurred in Cistercian
documents related to Poblet and her estates. In the case of Poblet's daughter house
midway between Tortosa and Valencia, Benifaza or Benifasa (from the Muslim
overlords of the district the Banu Hassa), the central domain or *tenencia* became
known simply as the *Tinença* of Benifasa, as noted by Robert I. Burns, *The Crusader*
Kingdom of Valencia: Reconstruction on a Thirteenth-Century Frontier (Cambridge, MA, 1967),
1:216.

[3] As described by an Aragonese monk in *The Chronicle of San Juan de la Peña. A*
Fourteenth-Century Official History of the Crown of Aragon, trans. Lynn H. Nelson (Philadelphia,
1991), pp. 51, 71, 85, King Peter (d. 1285) imprisoned in Siurana first the Count
of Urgel after the barons' revolt of 1280 and then "under the closest custody"
Prince Charles of Salerno. His son, King Alfonso III, later held twenty hostages of
the king of France at Siurana where "they were kept as King Charles would have
been, had he been there" according to *The Chronicle of Muntaner,* trans. Lady Goodenough, 2 vols. (London, 1920–1921), 2:407. The Catalan chronicler Pere Tomich,
p. 87, adds that King Peter used the castle of Miravet for the same purposes.

[4] *Mando primero combatir la mayor fuerça que llaman Siurana, ques es un Castillo muy*
enrificado en lo mas alto deaquellos montes, en uno dellos tan encumbrado que parece inaccessible

was already nature's fortress, defined then by geography rather than man's boundaries, with successive ridges that lead upward from the Ebro Valley at its back and massive connected cordilleras that rise from the Mediterranean coastal shelf on the right and on the left flank adjacent to the old Roman road into the hinterland from ancient Tarraco, i.e., medieval Tarragona. This was a vortex of mountain walls penetrated only through narrow, winding gorges protected by strategically placed fortifications, guarding upland valleys, small farming villages, surrounded by unfenced pastures and pine forests. Twelfth-century Catalans used a Romance derivation of the Latin word for scraper to describe the Siuranan mountains as "[sky]scrapers".[5] Indeed, Muslim geographers often confused this mountain chain as an extension of the Pyrenees; for them, Barcelona was ultra-Pyrenean and beyond Hispania. This elevated triangulation and furthermost Muslim occupation jutted northeast from the bases of Tortosa and Lerida toward the old Hispanic March. Between the two marches lay a frontier, sometimes referred to as a "no man's land," or figuratively, and in some cases literally, as a *locus desertus*, which was the Christian metaphor for borderlands made uninhabitable by the insecurity created between alternating conquest and reconquest over the centuries.[6] This particular frontier could be only a few kilometers at the northern narrows, or a wide expanse across the plains dominated by an ancient fortified city, Tarragona.[7]

---

para darle bateria. Y pusose tanta diligencia en tomar los passos y sierras a los Moros que no pudiendo por ningun modo ser socorrdios se huvieron de rendiry entregar el Castillo al Conde. Y entonces en breves dias se apodero el Conde de toda la sierra. Compare Tomic, p. 76; Francisco Diago, *Historia de los victoriosissimos antiguos Condes de Barcelona* (Barcelona, 1603; facsimile ed., *Biblioteca Hispanica Puvill*, 2 vols. [Valencia, 1974]), f. 244v, who relies on him, and in turn, therefore, on the commentary by Jerónimo Zurita, *Anales de la Corona de Aragón* (Zaragoza, 1562), edited by Angel Canellas López (Zaragoza, 1967–), 1:221–222.

[5] AHN, Clero, carp. 2001, no. 2 (26 August 1152) (Poblet mss., old legajo 1446, no. 117), which is a twelfth-century copy of a lost original donation by Ramon Berenguer IV of land around formerly Muslim Vinaixa to Christian settlers from Tarrega; Agustí Altisent, ed., *Diplomatari de Santi Maria de Poblet: I (960–1177)* (Barcelona, 1993), pp. 133–134, no. 149; and José María Font Rius, *Cartas de pobáción y franquicia de Cataluña, I, Textos.* 2 vols. (Madrid-Barcelona, 1969), 1:142–143, no. 90.

[6] Thomas F. Glick treats "The Frontier as an Image and as a Creator of Landscape" in his *Islamic and Christian Spain in the Early Middle Ages* (Princeton, NJ, 1979), pp. 58–65.

[7] This arena is described in Lawrence J. McCrank, *Frontier History in Medieval Catalonia* (London, 1996), which is based on idem, *Restoration and reconquest in Medieval Catalonia: The Church and Principality of Tarragona, 971–1177,* 2 vols. (Ph.D diss.,

The story recalls that the princess 'Abd al-'Azia was left by her lord with a small guard at Siurana castle when he and his warriors went to battle Christian invaders at some unspecified lower ground. Couriers notified her subsequently that the Moors had been routed and were in disarray, so people were fleeing to the mountains and such bastions as Siurana as their last refuge. Her lover, Almira, did not return. She learned that he had fallen in battle; distraught, she barricaded herself with her few defenders in the castle tower. As the Christian forces wound their way up narrow trails along the stream, she contemplated her fate. Siurana was sure to fall to Christian siege since the lowlands were occupied. The princess lamented her loss and the fate of her countrymen, but, rather than endure capture, when the knights approached the castle she mounted the parapets of Siurana and before their eyes hurled herself from the highest tower to the rocky crags and rushing waters below. Thus ended sadly this story and the *taifa* kingdom of Siurana. The year was 1153, since in that year Christian rulers gave lands in the area as fiefs.[8] This was also the end of an era, as folk memory was to commemorate for centuries to come. This romanticized story of love and war, a classic tragedy, was still being told in the nineteenth century when it was recorded by antiquarians like Victor Balaguer, Eduard Toda i Guell, and Antoni Palau i Dulcet.[9]

The legends of the mountain communities of the Priorat have certainly been embellished as an oral literature, but in formal histories of Catalonia as elsewhere oral tradition has been dismissed too often as if folklore is totally fiction, without adequate recognition of the semiotic importance and kernels of inner truth in tales around historic sites such as Siurana.[10] Moreover, the durability of such mythography is remarkable. For example, this storytelling may be traced to

---

University of Virginia, 1974), and idem, *The Development of a Monastic Domain on the Spanish Frontier by the Cistercians of Poblet, 1150–1276* (MA thesis, University of Kansas, 1970).

[8] AHN, Clero, carp. 2002, nos. 4r–v (Poblet mss.), *Diplomatari de Poblet*, pp. 141–142, nos. 159–160, both dating 30 November 1153 (*MCLIII, pridie kalendas decembris, anno quo capta est Siurana*). The official copy for the count's archives has been lost, but was inventoried in the marginalia of the *Engagenciones*, f. 499v: compare *LFM* 1:265, no. 248 (29 April 1153).

[9] Antoni Palau y Dulcet, *La Conca de Bárbera: Monografía histórica y descriptiva* (Barcelona, 1912), pp. 90–112, accepted the historical kernel of the legend because of other documentation in Poblet's archives.

[10] Luis Domenech y Montaner, *Historía y arquitectura del monasterio de Poblet* (Barcelona, 1927), pp. 7–8, for example, rejected all such legend as *tradiciones novelescas* and

the mid-fourteenth century, or earlier, when the monks of Poblet gave the tradition some credence by attempting to trace their land claims to this Muslim lord rather than the authentic and extant land grant from Count Ramon Berenguer IV of Barcelona, issued on 18 August 1151. Documents supporting the tradition were later manufactured when other authentic documents were copied during the 1340s from the Cistercian archives for the Crown's officers.[11] The charter in question reads as translated from the supposed Latin version of a non-extant Arabic original:

> In the name of the merciful and compassionate God, and may His salvation be upon Mohammed, his honored Prophet, on him and his people, and peace be to the honorable king Almira-Almoniniz. May God aid and help you with His assistance, you the hermit Poblet who lives in the district of Lardeta. May God aid you and help you, and may He hold you close to His great mercy. You were held captive within the house of the Moors in the time of war, and through your dignity and grace, which God has chosen to give you, you have been returned to your hermitage. For that reason the king Almira-Almoniniz gives to you the concession of all these mountains and lands which are in this district, for you and whomever you distinctly choose, without any revocation. And let no Moor dare go against my above-stated donation under penalty of losing his life. Moreover, I assure you that none of my people, not the Moors who may be near, will dare to harm your person or your possessions. And so I sign with an honorable subscription, and I swear to God that I will not go against what I have promised you. And I take God or my witness; there is no other Creator but Him. This letter was made on the 20th day of the month of February in the Era of I Muhammad, the year 613.[12]

This obviously controversial charter with its problematic date and diplomatic form is entwined with other local legends pertaining to the foundation of the famous Cistercian monastery of Santa Maria de Poblet, which in the high Middle Ages were purposefully confused

---

regarded the supporting documents from Poblet as *sin aspecto de fidelidad no caracter*. These *leyendas* are disdained as the result of popular piety and the imagination of commoners given to *intervenciones sobrenaturales*.

[11] Two manuscripts exist, one in the Fundos de Poblet at the AHN in Madrid, and another at the Museo-Biblioteca Balaguer in Villanova i Geltru north of Tarragona. The latter is considered to be the copy made by the Cistercian monk Fernando, the Mudejar son of the last King of Granada, Abu 'Abd Allah (in Spanish, Boabdil) Muhammad, who entered the community in 1493 after his father went into exile in Morocco.

[12] From the Spanish translation in "Documento arabigo del Monasterio de Poblet," *MHE* 6 (1853): 111–119 (esp. 112–113).

to push this abbey's foundation date earlier than its sister house and competitor, Santes Creus, and to bolster claims of independence and exemption from episcopal control and from royal taxation levied ostensibly to further crusades. Perhaps the charter was misdated after 1335, when many parchments were copied into bound cartularies, might be attributed to problems in the conversion from Arabic to Roman numerals or copyist error in the number of downstrokes used in the latter.[13] Not only would a simple correction of one century not take into account the difference between the Muslim lunar and Christian solar calendars, but this would place the transaction too late, in 1135 after Christian infringement on Muslim territory which might also create the possibility of nullification on grounds that the desperate donation transferred lands already retaken by the Christians and which were no longer Almoniniz's to give. A further correction into the early 1120s places it amidst Christian encroachment on Muslim territory around the counter-offensive launched by the Almoravids (al-Murabitum), when it would have been unlikely for any Muslim lord to aid and abet a Christian settler, hermit or not, and risk reprisal for treason. The Almoravids would have been in Tortosa while the remnant of the Hudid faction held out at Lerida and, by inference, in the march of Siurana as well, maintaining a precarious independence between the encroaching Africans from Marrakesh and Christians from the north.[14] Although the Almoravid governor from Valencia may have sought control of this frontier after raids in 1108 crossed it to penetrate the Christian March, the Counts of Barcelona who then claimed suzerainty over this region had done so theoretically for more than a century.[15] Catalan settlers had penetrated the out-

---

[13] Finestres, 2:44, transposed the dating to the Christian era as 1217 or 1218 and realized that the chronology did not fit, so he assumed the date should have been 514 in Arabic numerals which had been incorrectly transcribed into Roman numerals as 614, so that the date needed correction to ca. 1120.

[14] The classic study of E. Levi-Provençal, *Histoire de l'Espagne musulmane, 711–1031*, 3 vols. (Paris, 1950–1953), stops, as do many histories of Muslim Spain, after the fall of the caliphate in 1031, and its treatment of the northeastern march is weak. For the history of the Party Kingdoms and chaos in Islamic Spain or al-Andalus during this critical turning point in the reconquest, see Anwar G. Chejne, *Muslim Spain. Its History and Culture* (Minneapolis, 1974), pp. 50–96; Glick, pp. 35–102; and specifically for the Almoravids, J. Beraud-Villars, *Les Touareg au pays du Cid: Les invasions Almoravides en Espagne aux Xe et XIIe siècles* (Paris, 1946). The southern focus of most Islamic studies can be offset somewhat by Bosch Vila, *El oriente arabé en el desarallo de la cultura de la marca superior* (Madrid, 1954).

[15] Pierre Bonnassie, *La Catalogne du milieu du Xe a la fin du XIe siècle. Croissance et*

lying areas of this frontier long before the Leridan-Tortosan client states were weakened by the fall in 1118 of their Ebro capital at Zaragoza and the subsequent move of Catalan and Norman forces into Tarragona. The Almoravid advance from Valencia, resulting in subjugation by a foreign power rather than a real coalition of allies, added to the chaos and effectively closed the circle around these *taifa* states. Muslim historians later blamed the collapse of their northern frontier as much on Muslim internecine rivalry and the tyranny of the Almoravids as Christian might and foresighted strategy. Modern historians of the reconquest who liken the Christian advance to the Crusades also point to African intervention as the turning point in the character of Christian relations with the Muslims.

The purported concession refers to lands subsequently colonized by the Cistercians of Poblet in the Conca de Bárbera, referred to as the district of Lardeta, which lay north of the upper Plain of Tarragona and northeast of the central highlands of the Siurana March. The text claims that Lardeta had been settled and was still occupied by Muslims, but this area lay beyond the protection of the mountain fortresses and was already being encroached upon by Christian frontiersmen. Between 1118 and 1129 when a Christian coalition occupied Tarragona, Muslim control of Lardeta would have become increasingly tenuous. The Cistercians later also claimed that this donation had been confirmed ca. 1130 by the unspecified ruler of Lerida (the Hudid king displaced from Zaragoza, Ahmad III b. 'Abd al-Malik, Sayf al-Dawla [1110–1142]?), supposedly Almoniniz's overlord.[16] The ruse, of course, was to claim that the monastery had title to this donation before its foundation through inheritance when

---

mutations d'une société in *Publications de l'Université de Toulouse le Mirail*, ser. A, vols. 23, 29 (Toulouse, 1975–1976), 1:15, 161–169, 334–398, argues that a dramatic shift in foreign policy and the beginning of concerted Catalan encroachment into Muslim territory began under Count Ramon Berenguer I "El Vell," (1035–1076) who first imposed tribute payments or extortions of protection monies, i.e., *parias*, on Yusuf al-Mudaffar of Lerida. Barcelona's overt claims on Tarragona are likewise traced to this count in Lawrence J. McCrank, "La restauración eclesiastica y reconquista en la Cataluña del siglo XI: Ramon Berenguer I y la sede de Tarragona," *Analecta Sacra Tarraconensia*, 80 (1980): 5–39.

[16] Transliterated ms. transcribed by Juan Vallespinosa in Joaquin Guitert í Fontsere, ed., *Collectio de manuscrits inedits de monjos del Real Monestir de Santa Maria de Poblet* (Barcelona, 1947–1948), no. 5, cited also by Finestres, p. 120. A second spurious charter purports to be a confirmation, dated July 26, 1217, and it corrects the donor's name with a less Romance transliteration of Amir-el-momenin, thought to be Miramamolin or the honorific title of *amir al-mu'minīn*.

Poblet incorporated the former hermitage of the namesake of the abbey, the hermit Poblet, named in the document.[17] Not only did the forger force the act into a diplomatic format that did not mature until well after the alleged transaction, but its claim to authenticity was compromised further by not being able to place the donation precisely into the state of affairs in the old Muslim March of Zaragoza of which Siurana would have been an outpost. Such affairs were admittedly confusing, and have never been sorted out in detail because of lack of documentation from the Muslim side and fragmentary intelligence from the Christian perspective. Indeed, most Christian sources could not even deal accurately with Arabic nomenclature, but merely attempted rough phonetic renderings and haphazard transliterations that make identifications of places and persons difficult. No doubt the charter was always seen as fraudulent and such claims were never recognized by the Crown, but the concoction is nevertheless intriguing as a reflection of early oral tradition a century after the reconquest that posits the historical reality of a semi-autonomous governor of the march of Siurana in the decades immediately before the fall of Lerida and Tortosa. The outstanding question is whether the entwined legends of the hermit Poblet, his captor and then benefactor Almira Almoniniz, and the suicide of the princess 'Abd-al-'Azia, were later inventions or whether stories simply expanded and embellished the kernel of historic truth that survived in the oral tradition of this region? There is minimally a two-generation gap between the time of the episode and its supposed confirmation in non-extant documentation alleged to have existed in the early thirteenth century, and a longer hiatus of two centuries before its attestation in the extant forgeries of Poblet.

No doubt learned scribes, some of whom by the reign of James I were Arabic specialists, inspected such documents critically and dismissed them as having no juridical value. They may not have cared

---

[17] The etymology for Poblet's name is contested. Those seeking to discredit the connection between the Cistercian foundation and a previous hermitage, and the confusion between hermits named Poblet and Ramon (or were they the same, i.e., Ramon de Poblet?) argue that the place name was after the poplar trees that surrounded the site. This does not automatically rule reference to the same hermit when surnames of men without noble lineage were often attributed from place names, i.e., that hermit living in the poplar groves. See the modern history by Agustí Altisent, *Historia de Poblet* (Poblet, 1974), pp. 25–34, who accepts the descriptive toponymic and simply avoids the entanglement of the abbey's prefoundation history and alleged connection to a prior hermitage.

about their historical importance except to verify land claims and confirm rights, so no records inquire into the demise of the Siurana march as context for the earliest Christian occupation of Lardeta. The related stories, however, retained some credibility inside Poblet and were in the late eighteenth century recalled by the abbey's chronicler, Jaume Finestres i de Monsalvo as background for his history of the monastery.[18] The monks, after all, could be reminded of the former Muslim foundations of their domain in the ruins on their property and fortifications which had been converted to granges and outhouses. When, in the 1830s, the monastery was sacked and nearly destroyed and its community dispersed, continuity in oral tradition was interrupted, documentation was destroyed, the archives were saved only by a salvage effort, and subsequently everything historical has had to be reconstructed across a major interregnum. With the advent of scientific history and rigorous textual criticism to which this charter was further subjected, all twentieth-century scholars have denounced the document as spurious and have therefore given the text scant attention. Also tossed out of the realm of objective history into the domain of folklore, or worse, pure fantasy, were the legends of Poblet's community—including such stories as those about the miraculous lights signaling Count Ramon Berenguer IV's march through the Conca de Bárbera in 1148 and his subsequent victories against the infidel, attributed in part to the intercession of the hermit Poblet. So too were dismissed the tales of Siurana, and even the possibility of an historic personage lying behind the archetype "prince of [wrong] believers." No remnant of such tradition was seen as truthful in fact. Its mythological nature and inner spirit were likewise discounted. This skeptical and hyper-critical position should be reconsidered. Although no Arabic records remain to document Siurana's importance, a few extant and authentic monastic and town charters nevertheless allow a reconstruction more sympathetic with the old local oral tradition.

This complicated historiographic issue, namely the character and significance of the *taifa* of Siurana before its subjugation, must be revisited. Re-examination of fragmented and contested evidence seems required in light of the ethnology of this region with its lasting distinctiveness and preservation of stories in Catalan through an era of

---

[18] Finestres, 2:44–45.

Castilian cultural and political ascendancy. At the present time, contemporary notions about oral literature and folklore are less skeptical about collective oral memory and recognize metaphor, non-literal meaning, and the conservatism and hence continuity in such local historical narrative. After Fernan Braudel we can appreciate this landscape's ability to isolate and incubate oral tradition through generations and be sensitive of the region's geography and remoteness. Its visible and well-known monumental ruins have yet to be subjected to a thorough medieval archeological excavation even though they have been inventoried. The unusually rich horde of reliable documentation from the mid-twelfth century in the Cistercian cartularies of Poblet and Santes Creus provide hints of Muslim-Christian interaction during the decade before and following the reconquests of 1148–1154. Relief mapping and historical modeling, along with the extant documentation, permits a reconstruction of reconquest activities and resettlement patterns, drawing upon the better-known subjugation of Muslims to Christian control in the Aragó-Catalan reconquest that advanced past Tortosa toward Valencia.

Buried inside such myth-making as the romance of the Siuranan couple and their unfortunate demise are indirect evidences of: (1) the existence of a beni Hud outpost along the frontier between focal points in Barcelonan and Zaragoza, which may have begun simply as a captaincy but which became an increasingly independent and semi-autonomous highland enclave that paid nominal allegiance to Lerida-Tortosa and perhaps tribute also to Barcelona, that by default became a short-lived *taifa*, when these river-valley strongholds were reconquered; (2) Muslim highlander resistance to assimilation and conquest by either African invaders or Christian conquerors, resulting in an internal frontier behind the battle lines as the Christian trajectories after 1144 temporarily went around the mountainous vortex toward their objectives, the Ebro fortress of La Zuda at Tortosa and the mighty acropolis of Lerida which fell one after the other in 1148–1149, that required separate campaigns in 1151–1155 to bring under control; and (3) the very slow and gradual integration of this region after its annexation by the Crown of Aragon and incorporation into the New Catalonia after 1177. Resistance to assimilation there is exemplified by a century-long history of local rebuffs to both royal and episcopal authority including resistance to taxation, replete with social riots and skirmishes, persistent banditry along the coastal road between Tarragona and Tortosa, piracy upon the nearby sea, and the need for special forces of Knights Templars surrounding the periphery and in the center the establishment of a bailiff at Prades.[19]

Religious conversion, ownership reversion, reconstruction and land reclamation, and administrative reorganization were slow processes. The experiences of the new overlords in the sparsely populated outlying areas and the smaller cities of Lerida and Tortosa assuredly influenced subsequent policies in Valencia. What had been an intermittent uneasy truce interrupted by sporadic local warfare, had become regional and fought by international forces and large coalitions. The mix of peoples, including those like the Normans who had never known Muslims except as enemies, was far greater than it had been, and the former *convivencia* of proximity now became an even closer situation of adjacency, with a conquering minority living in pockets amidst a vanquished but not always subdued majority. Previously contact was in trade and the occasional raid, but now the penetration was lasting. The changes may be seen only from the documentation of the conquerors since no Muslim records survive and the Islamic chroniclers are very vague about any affairs so far north. Some of the change-over can be discerned in the Cistercian records, first of Santes Creus further east, and then of Poblet, which was founded on the piedmont of the Siuranan March; and subsequently those from Vallbona farther to the north, and still later but inside the March itself, scattered records from Bonrepós and the Carthusian house of Scala Dei.[20] Fuller documentation surely existed in the lost *Libri Antiquitatem* or cartularies of Tarragona and the destroyed archives of Lerida's cathedral; additional light may yet come from explorations of Tortosa's archives, but so far its records seem to pertain to the lowlands and river valley only—which supports the legendary link of Siurana to Lerida. If there were no dramatic suicide accompanying the capitulation of Siurana in 1153, a less literal

---

[19] Lawrence J. McCrank, "The Cistercians as of Poblet as Landlords: Protection, Litigation, and Violence on the Medieval Catalan Frontier," *Cîteaux: Commentari Cistercienses* 26 (1975): 255–283; reprinted in idem, *Frontier History*, study 4 (London, 1996).

[20] For the historical context for the formation of these archives and this documentation, see idem, "Documenting reconquest and Reform: The Growth of Archives in the Medieval Crown of Aragón," *The American Archivist* 56 (1993): 256–318 (reprinted in idem, *Frontier History*, study 1), and an alternate version, "A Medieval 'Information Age': Documentation and Archives in the Crown of Aragón," *Primary Sources and Original Works* 2 (1993): 19–102, co-published in *Discovery in the Archives of Spain and Portugal: Quincentenary Essays, 1492–1992* (Binghamton, NY, 1993): 19–102.

and negative, yet critical, but more sympathetic hearing of this tale would recognize the symbolism of the princesses' escape from violation and her own death as the symbolic death of a kingdom and the subjugation of a once thriving Muslim culture by Christian overlords. Among Mudejars the warrior death of Almira Almoniniz and suicide of ʿAbd al-ʿAzia were the epitome of resistance to the Christian reconquest and denial of the new regime. Does this suggest self-destruction by its own uncompromising will, or merely the futility of rebellion? Does the story's survival in Catalan lore denote a sub-culture of mountain folk or a lingering guilt of conquerors remembering the world they destroyed? Or is Siurana simply a curiosity? Finally, consider how one relates such local legend and regional folk-lore with the overall culture that developed, or with the higher thinking of Aragonese-Catalan theologians, poets and jurists alike in their lore, namely representation of a reconquest more righteous and legitimate, Christian and holy, homogeneous and uniform, deliberate and strategic, and definitive and thorough than it actually was. Historians too, may wonder about the gain and loss in the taking of Siurana. More than territory was at stake here; lives were lost, families routed, and a culture was destroyed. The local tradition of tragedy contradicts the myth of a glorious reconquest.

Siurana castle, unlike the citadels of Lerida and Tortosa, was a refuge of last resort rather than a center of commerce, culture, or political power. Christians with their sense of localization, measurement, and definition of space, may have thought it more than it was. Instead, the entire Muslim march, its highland core with two dozen or more villages, and scattered towers near communities and along perimeter defenses, must be taken as an entity to make sense of the prolonged reconquest and problematic annexation and assimilation of this area. Siurana itself may be seen more as a symbolic locus of authority than any grand castle in an era of peripatetic courts, itinerant retinues, distributed power, and local governance by custom and tradition as much as anything. Extended family units or clans with members living in proximity to each other created socio-economic areas rather than bounded lands, and their network created a cultural region that did not always operate as a coherent political entity. Behind the symbol of Siurana lay the more pervasive reality of a Muslim highland pastoral and woodland culture based in scattered dwellings and small villages. The March took its shape more from the rugged landscape that confined and defined it, than political territoriality. Thus the description of Lardeta as a "district" as if there were some sort of juridical definition or boundary other than nature's formations reflects a Christian rather than a Muslim attitude. The Conca de Bárbera, which today is a definite district, was then considered, as the metaphor "shell" implies, a concave shallow surrounded by a higher perimeter on all sides, in which a promontory as a lookout had been guarded by defenses since the ninth century when the Hispanic March was established by the Carolingians. So too, with reverse topology, can Siurana's march be viewed as an elevated saucer with one of its strongholds in a depression, actually a river gorge, that is better known than other fortified places simply because it was one of the last holdouts and its ruins survive. Other defenses are still extant, but they blend into the rugged natural landscape; they may be known only by local nomenclature and through tradition.

The whole region is relatively compact; it is a triangular massif jutting out from the more secure Muslim hold on the lower Ebro Valley. The main region identifiable with the highland march is no more than a thousand square kilometers, circumscribed by remarkable geographic but no other boundaries. The Ebro River itself, with its delta region and lower valley dominated by Tortosa to the south, flowed through an upper valley with its commercial center at Gandesa. The river's flow through narrows guarded by Flix marks the transition to Leridan territory with its center at the confluence of the Segre and Ebro, Rivers; further along, Fraga existed as a client state downriver from Zaragozan territory proper. The Ebro River line from Tortosa to Lerida forms the base of this triangular projection northeast toward the old Hispanic March or border counties of Old Catalonia, namely Ausona and Barcelona. The Mediterranean and a narrow coastal shelf below majestic escarpments marks the lower right angle of this vortex, and the upper angle goes inland with an ever wider piedmont dominated today by Reus below the mountain perimeter that reaches a point south of the separated Coll de Lilla, cut off from the rest of the formation by the gorge of the Francolí River. The upper left angle is a series of cordilleras that rise from a much-traversed semi-arid steppe land stretching southeast from Lerida toward the upper plain of Tarragona.

Muslim Spain after the end of the Umayyad caliphate in 1031 seldom presented a unified front against the Christian states, which were usually equally disunited and prone to internecine rivalry. Lerida

and Tortosa, combined at times or independently, had been subject
to but were also often at war with Zaragoza, especially after the
bifurcation of power in the 1080s between the brothers al-Mundhir
and al-Muʿtamin once wielded tribally by a more cohesive banu
Hūd. They were as likely to war on each other, sometimes in alliance
with Christians, as allying with each other against a Christian lord.
The reunification forced by the Almoravids only temporarily altered
this behavior, but it was a political change scary enough to unite the
Christians in reaction to the African threat. The turning point in the
reconquest, however, was that with the decline of Almoravid power
in the northeast, the Zaragozan, Leridan, and Tortosan Muslims
seem to have resumed their former posture as autonomous states,
fractionalized as if political and economic business would be conducted as usual. The Christians, on the other hand, formed coalitions and formal alliances cemented by intermarriage and backed
by a Gregorian reform-minded and increasingly militant Church.
The papacy, too long dismayed over Christian waffling in Spain and
foreign intervention with the Crusades, became more aggressive after
1112 and the 1118 conquests of both Zaragoza and Tarragona.

The Tarragona campaigns from 1050 onward eroded the neutral
borderland between Muslims and Christians to a mere five kilometers in some places. The Conca de Bárbera was one of the earliest
arenas for interaction because both Christians and Muslims had
descended from the highlands to lower ground with an eye on the
sparsely populated and potentially lucrative upper and lower plains
of Tarragona. Muslim Lerida is often depicted as extending southeast from the Segre to the Mediterranean coast, including the Campo
de Tarragona. The political and natural geographies of this district
do not support such a mapping; nor is such assumed political or
military control from Lerida well documented. More likely Muslim
power from Lerida dissipated into the largely unpopulated semi-arid
steppe land broken by deep ravines and barren hills that impeded
east-west travel except on the old Roman road. Christians charted
their newly conquered lands in terms of Lerida roads which went
upland from this "highway" to the north of the Muslim March.[21]

---

[21] AHN, Clero, carp. 1998, no. 5 (Poblet mss.), is a copy made by the Huescan
scribe Gil de Sangarren in 1269 (no. 6 is a still later copy by notary Arnau Sabater
in 1330), but the original is non-extant and the copy is undated by year. *Diplomatari
de Poblet*, no. 166, p. 146, places it in 1155, February 20. In it the scribes of Ramon

The Leridan corridor enters close confines at the confluence of the Anguera drainage of the Conca de Bárbera with the Francolí. The latter is a radical outcropping rising 581 meters from the plains and clearly separates the Conca de Bárbera from the lower plain of Tarragona and shoves the upper plain northeast toward the Gaya River. This stream demarcated Christian territory along this frontier as much as the Francolí served as a Muslim boundary. Both streams with winter run-off cut deep trenches in some places, but their shallow creek-like character and meandering in other places meant that neither acted as a determent to north-south travel. The Muslims in the ninth through the eleventh centuries had founded another two dozen villages on the plains in addition to occupying Tarragona and its coastal defenses to Tamarit castle and the point named by the Christians as Punta del Moro. Extant toponymies such as "La Pobla de Malumet" and a dozen sites beginning with the Arabic "al-" allow a mapping of the Muslim resettlement of the highlands and the lower plain. In addition to these aforementioned sites, Morera y Llaurado inventoried Muslim settlements, based on place names, ruins and ceramics.[22] The Ebro River valley and neighboring upland plains had been protected by Tortosa, and the coastal Campo de Tarragona could be defended from the march's mountain communities and from the fortress of Tarragona, but the upper plain was too vulnerable to Christian positions in the hills below Montmell to the north, and the Conca de Bárbera may always have been a militarized zone.

A topographic relief map of New Catalonia suggests clearly the extent of the Muslim occupation, distinct from periodic invasions across these formidable natural barriers and a very temporary deployment at Barcelona itself. The Christians had a highland march often

---

Berenguer IV refer to the road leading [south] *versus Siurana usque in podio de la Bataila, que affrontat in dicto camino,* ... referring to a ridge along the invasion route where the Muslims had obviously mounted a defense against the invaders. The numerous *coll de la batalla* in this mountainous area attest to several such battles around the perimeter of the Siuranan March.

[22] Emilio Morera y Llaurado, *Tarragona cristiana: Historia del arzobispado de Tarragona,* 2 vols. (Tarragona, 1899), 304–306. Some of the names are: Alforja, Aleixar, Almoster, Alcover, al-Muzara (Musara), Albiol, Arboli, [A]Vimbodi, Albinanya, Marsa, Asroig, and Tivisa. He counted twenty-seven highland villages: among them figure Alcanar, Alcover, Alfara, Asco, Almudefar, Algas, Arenys, Avin-Cabacer, Benifallet, Benisanet, Mas de Barberans, Mas den Verge; and those in evidence from the medieval *repartiments* such as Batea, Bot, Caseras, Corbera, Cherta, Fatarella, Figuera, Flix, Gandesa, Rasquera, Pinell and Villalba.

identified with the fortress of Olérdola facing that of Siurana; it was equally formidable and its mountains actually touch the sea, leaving no medieval coastal road to Barcelona. The thoroughfare then, as today, cut through highland passes to the Penedés, down the Anoía River Valley to the Llobregat, and then cut back toward the sea to the small plain occupied by Barcelona. This was indeed the Muslim invasion route whenever the city was attacked by land; conversely, it was the avenue for Christian troops to move on Tarragona and its defensive castles were backups for the frontier campaigns just as those in the Muslim march served offensives across the plains of Tarragona. The Christians had created what Josep Iglesias called "a rosary of fortresses" to defend this perimeter.[23] The core of the Muslim march, however, was so well protected on all three sides by mountains that the same kind of defense system was not necessary. Its natural walls rise sometimes at 90 degree angles and ascend 600–700 meters within a mere five kilometers from the sea, 400 kilometers from the Ebro, and a soaring 1054 kilometers (Musara) twelve kilometers from the Campo de Tarragona. This ring of mountains, the Sierra de Monstant, Sierra de Prades, Sierra de la Musara, Sierra de Balaguer, Montalt, and de la Greu, encircle a plateau marked by two valleys drained by the Siurana and small tributaries like the Prades and Febro, that flow west into the Ebro. Thus, although there was northern entry point for the Muslims into Barcelona, the Siurana River provided a back door from the Ebro Valley. But once on the tableland, following the Siurana River to the upper valley and Siurana castle would required negotiation of several gorges. The gorges could be circumvented by a treacherous pass known as the *Escalera al Cielo,*" or the "rocky staircase to the skies." This explains why, when the city-states of Lerida and Tortosa fell to the Christian allies, the Siurana March did not. Its conquest required a separate campaign, and demonstrates why the comital charters pertaining to the resettlement of Espluga de Francolí and other sites along the perimeter of the march, speak repeatedly about the need for defenses and the duty of knights who hold local castles as fiefs to protect settlers from potential harm coming from the mountains.[24]

---

[23] Josep Iglesias y Fort, *La reconquista a les valls de l'Anoia i el Gaia, Episodis de la historia* (Barcelona, 1963), p. 13.

[24] AHN, Clero, carp. 2005, no. 7 (29 February or 5 March 1160) (Poblet mss.), referring to Ramón de Cervera's knights at the castle of Espluga de Francolí:

The Aragonese *hueste* against Zaragoza was timed with the Catalan move across the plains of Tarragona. The occupation of the city was a prelude to the fall of Tortosa and Lerida, which ultimately meant the demise of Siurana. The expanse of the Tarragonan frontier had been diminishing for a century since the first foray against Tarragona and an unsuccessful attempt in 1050 to convert its territory into a viscounty of Barcelona. This premature ambition was reinforced by the Gregorian reformers who wanted to restore the Romano-Visigothic metropolitan see of Tarragona. By the twelfth century, moreover, it became strategically important as the ideal base of operations against the Ebro Valley fortresses. After that it and the neighboring harbor of Salou would be the staging points for the expeditions against the Balearics as well as a link with Tortosa in the crusade against Valencia. The reconquest of Tarragona without the subjugation of the Siurana march could be accomplished; but its holding under such circumstances was a different matter. All such attempts to permanently occupy Tarragona, rather than simply raid its territory, had failed. But the intermittent warfare of the late eleventh centuries, both against the Muslims and in league with them against such Christian enemies as the freelance El Cid, may have had deleterious effects on the Tarragona countryside and the city's population.

The history of Muslim Tarragona is largely conjectural, so it throws only inference rather than a direct light on the Siurana question.[25] The extent of Muslim occupation is debatable, although most Catalan historians have assumed that it was a flourishing Muslim city from its conquest in 718 to the reconquest and resettlement between 1118–1128. However, military conquest dates tell little about interim history about anything other than the rise and fall of fortifications or rather their damage and repair coterminous with the exchange of political allegiance. Certain alleged victories may be likened more to

---

Diplomatari de Poblet, pp. 176–177, no. 212; see nos. 135, 141, 166–167 for similar language, with references to defenses but also permission to campaign in the highlands.

[25] Morera y Llaurado, pp. 245–319, admirably places Tarragona in the larger arena of peninsular history, but he relies on evidence from Valencia and Zaragoza, and then areas adjacent to Tarragona, mostly Tortosa, rather than from Tarragona itself. Implicit in his treatment is the assumption that Tarragona was a Muslim city like Lerida and Tortosa, and perhaps it was for a century before ca. 1050, but thereafter he identified no evidence whatsoever for Tarragona's Muslim occupation even though he worked in the municipal and archiepiscopal archives before their destruction during the Spanish Civil War.

the unchallenged claims on desolate sites. Was this the case of Tarragona? Muslim sources are largely silent about the city. No Tarragonan Muslims are known, not even rulers or commanders from dealings with Lerida, Tortosa and Zaragoza, or Barcelona, in contrast to the physicians, jurists, poets, theologians, teachers, merchants and diplomats known from Tortosa. No Mozarabic community is documented for these intervening centuries. And when Muslim armies did mass in defense of Zaragoza against Christian forces or turn against themselves in internecine war within the Hudid realms, there is no indication of Muslim assistance from Tarragona or, for that matter, from the march of Siurana, or to them for the defense of the city. It is as if this frontier was alone, apart from the two worlds on either side which clashed more and more and which sent constant traffic through it. Might not a trace of its vitality in the region's history be expected? Or was Tarragona by the twelfth century a frontier ghost town and barren monument?

The claim that Tarragona was a functioning Muslim city is based on pre-mid-eleventh century evidence, inference, and thereafter largely an *argumentum ex silencio* that instead relies on fragmentary archeological evidence. This consists of some pottery remains, fine ceramics, restoration work on the ancient walls of Tarraco, repair of the Roman aqueduct which brought fresh water to the city's cisterns from the springs that fed the Gaya headwaters near Pont de Annentara; and inscriptional evidence confirming that from the time of 'Abd al-Rahman III (d. 963) the Roman temple of Jupiter had been converted into a mosque long before the same chiseled stones were turned inward to be used again two centuries later to build a Christian cathedral on the acropolis.[26] Other such reused blocks may eventually add more to the picture, but the considerable archeological work on the city was to recover ancient ruins and antique artifacts from the early

---

[26] Ibid.; compare Josep María Recasens i Comes, *La Ciutat de Tarragona*, 2 vols. (Barcelona, 1975), 2:30–46, who also asks "Tarragona, erma I despoblada quatre-cents?" (p. 34) following much earlier doubts by Luis Pons d'Icart, *Libro de las grandozas y cosas memorables de la metropolitana, insigne y famosa ciudad de Tarragona* (Lerida, 1572; facsimile ed., Lerida, 1883) and echoed by Sanç Capdevila, "Sobre la invasio arab i la reconquesta de Tarragona," *Boletin Arqueológica de Tarragona*, 64–65 ( ): 29–63 (esp. p. 44) about Tarragona's continuous occupation. Although Recasens tries to follow Morera's reconstruction and is compelled to argue for Arabic settlement in Tarragona until the reconquest, the ceramic fragments to which he refers, found on the acropolis of St. Fructuosus, cannot be dated beyond the mid-eleventh century.

Christian era, with little attention to the later Muslim period. Indeed, restoration of a Christian Tarragona could have obliterated its Muslim antecedents, but no Muslim monuments remain. Such a total discontinuity might be explained by major destruction and prolonged siege, but no major campaign of cumulative battle known in history even marks the date of the transfer of Tarragona to Christian hands as in the case of Zaragoza, Lerida, and Tortosa. The concession of Tarragona by Count Ramon Berenguer IV on 23 January 1118 to Bishop Olaguer of Barcelona unequivocally claims that Tarragona was then deserted and had been destroyed for years.[27] Even after the city's repopulation by the Normans, the Muslim geographer al-Idrisi referred to Tarragona as a town of Jews with no mention of Mudejars. His reference was either to the later Jewish *barrio* or a commercial district outside the walls near the port, rather than referring to the citadel itself.[28] His reference and the entry of al-Bakrī (d. 1094) in his geographic dictionary, the *Mu'jam mā ista 'jam*, influenced the later anthology of al-Himyarī who mentions Muslim "*Tarakuna*," even though his historical references are vague.[29] He refers to Tarragona's impressive Roman ruins and credits the Muslim's with rebuilding the city, but he assumed that it was deserted before the Christian occupation. He was more curious about its wind mills than its history, but he does assert that an informer told him about a certain Ibn Zāydan (Zaidin) from Siurana who had once been influential in the region of Tarragona. This Muslim, however, is characterized as a merchant with business interests in Tarragona rather than its rule, and the reference is historical rather than contemporary with his fourteenth-century travelogue. Thus al-Himyari also attests the

---

[27] *LFM*, no. 245 (23 enero 1118), 1:258. *dono et per hanc scripturam donacionis trado ecclesie sedis Tarraconensis, . . . ipsam civitatem Terracone, que diu per multos armus sub destruccione et eremo absque cultore et incolatu mansi.*

[28] Compare Abū 'Ubayd Allah al-Bakrī, *Mu'jam mā ista 'jam*, ed. F. Wustenfeld (Gottingen and Paris, 1876), 2 vols., reproduced in 4 vols. (Cairo, 1945); Abū 'Abd Allah al-Idrīsī, *Description de l'Afrique et de l'Espagne*, trans. Reinhart Dozy and M.J. De Goeje (1864–1866; Leiden, 1968). Josep Millas Vallicrosa, "Epigrafia hebraico-española," *Sefarad* 5 (1945): 288, thought that perhaps al-Idrīsī was simply mistaken about Tarragona's Jews, since the contemporary itinerary of Benjamin de Tudela (1173) does not mention a Jewish community there. He speculates, therefore, but without any evidence whatsoever, that the reference was to Muslim inhabitants.

[29] Muhammad Ibn 'Abd al-Mun 'im al-Himyari, *Kitab al-Rawd al-mi'tar*, trans. María del Pilar Maestro González, *Textos medievales*, 10 (Valencia, 1963), 256–258, cited also by Recasens, 43; compare al-Himyari's work ed. by Évariste Levi-Provençal, *La peninsule iberique au Moyen Âge* (Cairo, 1934; reprinted ed., Leiden, 1938).

historical importance of Siurana before the reconquest, but he does not necessarily thereby provide evidence for a thriving Muslim city of Tarragona anytime after the mid-eleventh century. Instead it is likely that Tarragona was abandoned as the comital sources claim, or else it had been reduced to a mere military fortification with a garrison drawn from scattered villages, as might have been the case as well for the outpost at Tamarit. The occupation of Tarragona may be likened more to a prolonged series of raids, rather than any momentous campaign, battle, or siege. For decades the critical issue for Muslim and Christian alike was not the taking of Tarragona, but occupying her long enough to secure something more than a foray and tenuous grip, when the enemy lay in such close proximity and could counterattack whenever the political winds shifted. While both sides might amass the manpower on a temporary basis for a campaign, neither could repopulate the city. By the twelfth century Tarragona was very likely a city with a grand past, an empty presence, and a precarious future.

There is more evidence of a thriving village life along the perimeter of the march of Siurana than for the sustenance of urban life at Tarragona. The silver mines at Albiol and other sites were still productive. Mills operated on the upper Francolí when the water flow permitted. The pine-forested slopes of the mountains southwest of Tarragona were lumbered for shipbuilding at Salou. Sheep grazed on the Campo. Muslims farmed small garden plots, or *huertas*; they developed vineyards and olive orchards. Extant ceramics provide evidence for trade with both Lerida and Tortosa, and beyond, to Valencia and Denia. These artifacts, however, are evidence of cottage industries and agricultural village life rather than the economy of a great seaport and flourishing city.

Rather than the modern interpretation of a Muslim conquest and maintenance of a Romano-Visigothic city-state, one might look for a different model than that which seems to apply better to Zaragoza and Tortosa, and to a lesser extent, Lerida. In those cases ample textual, archeological, and monumental evidence exists of a fortified urban center which controlled a *territorium* and promoted suburban development, and whose influence spread out to surrounding villages to create a regional socio-economic, cultural and political entity. Instead, we may speculate that Muslim political power lay behind Tarragona, not in it, that agricultural village life prevailed on the Campo as in the highlands rather than any one dominating urban

center, and that the Muslim Tarragonians were far more tribal and
clan oriented than they were city dwellers or organized into a tight
regime. They may have had a rich oral tradition, deep religious
attachment, customs that produced an ordered life, familial relations
which led to an interlocking social structure, and local industries and
a healthy and diverse mixture of rural agricultural, pastoral, woodland, and trade economies. But in the absence of strong evidence to
the contrary, the older assumption that Tarragona remained a vital
urban center should be discarded. Substituted instead should be models drawn from Muslim experiences elsewhere in the peninsula. These
also call for a revision of the notions promulgated by Sánchez-
Albornoz of an indigenous feudalism which closely resembled the
French model for either Muslims or Christians. Rather than concentrate on their military importance alone, recent studies of castles
have stressed their value as social nuclei, bringing together at certain times people who were scattered across the countryside. In other
cases castles served as centers from which to mount offensive action
as much as self-defense. The *hissam-albacar* model of the castle as an
enclosed space for refuge rather than a residence or permanently
occupied fortification, seems appropriate for the small towers and
enclosed natural defenses used by Muslims throughout the march of
Siurana, at Siurana itself, and around Tarragona. Some of the stone
structures were enlarged to accommodate an extended family. The
Carolingian farmhouse (*mansus*) was thus transformed into the fortified quarters which constituted the principal Catalan farm structure
or *mas*.[30] Such an adaptable model might explain the defensive situation of Tarragona's citadel. The long-deserted city might have
been occupied by a temporary Muslim garrison which simply abandoned the city to the Christian invaders without any real defense.
Indeed, the Christian occupation of Tarragona is not documented
with so much as a skirmish, even though the Christian forces that
descended onto the Campo were so numerous that it took three
Christian interior castles to house them as the *hueste* was being formed.
The formation of the expedition is thus known, but not details about
any siege or major skirmish at Tarragona. The real battle was to
hold onto the site once taken, to occupy its immense area, and to

---

[30] The Catalan *masia* are surveyed by Joaquim de Camps i Arboix, *La Masia
Catalana: Historia- Arquitectura-Sociologia* (Barcelona, 1969), who sees their origins in
fortified country houses built in imitation of Roman villas.

guard against Muslim raids and guerilla warfare tactics from the surrounding countryside. This would account for the emphases on the recruitment of knights to form a mobile cavalry to range over the Campo. Such a revisionist interpretation explains so much more than the dominant assumption of a major military confrontation at Tarragona city.

Other scenarios suggest what may have been the situation at Tarragona. In the case of Majorca, as the earliest of its *repartiments* indicate, refuge castles intermittently occupied seem more prevalent than permanently-settled or continually-defended fortresses. As Julio González for the lands south of Toledo, Muslim lands had few boundaries because they were held by clans as communal clusters of plots, fields, pastures, and open spaces.[31] He associates this with Roman precedents, but Thomas Glick and others attribute such an unsurveyed and certainly therefore unfenced landscapes with Muslim familial association and the tradition of the extended family.[32] Robert I. Burns refers to "amorphous *alquerias*" in Valencia (i.e., farm-hamlets with lands held in common), that had only customary and vague notions of area, but no real boundaries.[33] Christians with their notions of defined property and individual ownership, and predilection for alods or freeholdings, could not understand Muslim land organization based on social structure, anymore than could nineteenth-century Europeans discern tribal territoriality and the sense of ancestral homelands among native Americans. Thus the above-mentioned forgery at Poblet may have misconstrued as a land grant what might have been a permit or edict of toleration by one People of the Book for another, namely a Christian hermit, to live in close proximity to them without harm. Moreover, the hermit may have been more peripatetic, like pre-Carolingian wandering monks, than stationary like the post-Benedictine reformers would have it, since in other instances the Muslims seemed also to have tolerated a hermit in the arid land of Cérvoles. These hermits may have been assimilated into the Cistercian Order by the early community. The monks would have then assumed that the land around their dwellings could be

[31] Findings based on Julio González, *Repartimiento de Sevilla*, 2 vols. (Madrid, 1951), and idem, *El reino de Castilla en la época de Alfonso VIII*, 3 vols. (Madrid, 1960).

[32] Thomas F. Glick, *Irrigation and Society in Medieval Valencia* (Cambridge, MA, 1970), pp. 31–51.

[33] Robert I. Burns, *Islam under the Crusaders. Colonial Survival in the Thirteenth-Century Kingdom of Valencia* (Princeton, 1973), pp. 55–63.

inherited by the community rather than revert back to communal unoccupied Muslim land. The monks did not occupy the land either, but claimed it, surveyed it, and thereby converted open space into a defined, organized monastic domain.[34] Such transfer would then have placed any Mudejars on the land in the position of squatters; with no clear land claim, they were subject to expulsion or conversion and assimilation. In the same spirit, the *repartiment* restructured the landscape, counted and measured, surveyed and defined territories into specific landholdings. The concession charters which predate the *repartiment* in the reconquest of Tarragona and the March of Siurana did the same thing. Without any visible boundaries left by the Muslim occupation, the Christians subdivided land and took great pains to specify certain natural landmarks in their charters. Many of these are still recognizable, so it is possible to delineate the Christian reorganization more than it is to map Muslim occupation, except where nature's boundaries were so formidable that they imposed limitations on both. Fortunately scribes sometimes refer to former owners and clan leaders, so we can obtain a few traces of former Muslim occupation, but mostly by inference and reliance on natural geography. In time, after less than one generation, even these vague inferences disappear.

As in Orihuela and other areas later reconquered, the rezoning of the land and the seigniorial allocation with subdivision of these land grants into farms, ranches, villages, and so on, resulted in the de-tribalization of remaining Muslim society. This contributed to the death of Muslim culture perhaps more pervasively than the military reconquest itself or any systematic expulsion of Muslim tenants. Rather than expel Mudejar farmers, shepherds, lumbermen and craftsmen, the stage was simply reset to assimilate them over the years. There may not have been so much forced emigration from the region, as from Tortosa to Valencia, but a continually pressured migration within the region, which nevertheless destroyed familial life and the local infrastructure that had sustained Muslim society. A society thus fragmented was easier to assimilate than one left intact. While there is no evidence that Muslims in large numbers fled to Tortosa in the wake of a sudden assault on their villages in the Campo de

---

[34] Lawrence J. McCrank, "The Frontier of the Spanish reconquest and the Land Acquisitions of Poblet, 1150–1276," *Analecta Cisterciensia* 29 (1973): 57–68; reprinted in idem, *Frontier History*, study 3.

Tarragona with the Christian occupation of the city, perhaps assimilation occurred in time in the lowland rural areas. However, the highlands proved to be a different matter. Even when force was applied in a series of campaigns to quell resistance there after the fall of Lerida and Tortosa, there is still no indication of southward migration to or through these centers or massive flight from these homelands to Valencia. Nor is there any admission of genocide, forced conversions, coerced resettlement, or the kind of tragic end that came of the legendary princess of Siurana

Understanding Muslim familial association as the key to land holding, coupled with the fragmentation of the region's natural geography, and a documented history of immigration and encroachment of Christians on Muslim territory throughout the eleventh century makes more plausible the notion of a constant infiltration by Christians of a sparsely populated Campo and a gradual shifting of the frontier, than any dramatic episodes of military encounter or a vision of claim hopping and boundary jumping as seen from a Christian perspective. This more fluid, interactive, and continuous transformation rather than sudden, discordant, revolutionary change and discontinuity, however, pertains to the gradual absorption of Tarragona into the Christian regime rather than any definitive reconquest, was altered significantly with the intervention of northern crusaders after 1096 and the African Almoravids after 1106–1108. The decade-long transition in Tarragona between 1118 and 1128, and transformation that took a generation longer until, as shall be seen, does not hold for the much more sudden and violent reconquest of the Siuranan march.

The formal claims on Tarragona by the Church and its reestablishment as a metropolitan see by the papacy in 1118 coincided with the grand alliance against a resurgent Islam designed and orchestrated by Count Ramon Berenguer III and his remarkable bishop of Barcelona, Oleguer Bonestruga.[35] Although the bishop became the archbishop of Tarragona while holding the see of Barcelona, he never took up residence in Tarragona. But he did install there a protector, or *vidaume*, the Norman Robert Burdet and his followers, who were recruited by the prelate's whirlwind preaching expedition

---

[35] This episode is explored fully in Lawrence J. McCrank, *Restoration and reconquest*; idem, "The Foundation of the Confraternity of Tarragona by Archbishop Oleguer Bonestruga," *Viator* 9 (1978): 157–177, and idem, "Norman Intervention in the Catalan reconquest: Robert Burdet and the Principality of Tarragona, 1129–1155," *Journal of Medieval History*, 7 (1981): 67–82.

into France that even attracted the attention of Oderic Vitalis.[36] No record exists for a siege or great battle in this reconquest. Instead, it seems that the troops simply rode into the city, dislodged its defenders, and then proceeded to take over the citadel and convert the old tower overlooking the sea into a residence for the new "prince of Tarragona." The bishop's biographer Renald of Barcelona asserts that while the Normans were bringing the Campo under control and serving the Count of Barcelona on expeditions farther away, the walls of Tarragona needed defending and constant armed guard. At one point, in the absence of her husband, Robert Burdet's wife donned armor and walked the walls to keep her men vigilant.[37] But the real military action seems to have been elsewhere.

The naval blockade by Pisan and Genoese ships reinforcing the fledgling navy of Barcelona, coordinated assaults on Lerida and Tortosa by Ramon Berenguer IV and his allies from Montpellier and the Knights Templars, and funding by the Church enabled the Normans to retain control of Tarragona.[38] Movement of the military frontier to the Ebro encouraged resettlement of the Campo, but no penetration of the Siuranan highlands. No archbishop resided in Tarragona until after the fall of Lerida and Tortosa, and the reorganization of a Christian Tarragona did not occur until the menace from the highlands was subdued with a series of military campaigns from 1151 through 1155. At this time the Cistercians were moved closer to the Muslim highlands to resettle above the principality of Tarragona, while the Templars from Bárbera were strategically moved to the new town of Montblanch. Commercial centers were developed at Reus and later Valls. Ultimately the Normans and French were also assimilated, and after the death of Robert Burdet his sons were undone by the archbishops, all from Barcelona, in league with the counts of Barcelona. Ramón Berenguer IV had married Petronilla, Queen of Aragon, to cement the grand alliance formed against Islam.

---

[36] Oderic portrayed Tarragona as depopulated and in ruins, which Recasens, p. 44, regards as sheer "fantasy," but the chronicler's source was most likely Oleguer himself while preaching in Normandy and soliciting recruits for the retaking of his see. *OV*, 6:252–277, 402.

[37] Renald of Barcelona, *Vitae sancti Ollegarii*, in *ES* 29:472–499.

[38] The overall strategy of the reconquest in New Catalonia is delineated in Lawrence J. McCrank, "Monastic Inland Empires and the Mediterranean Coastal Reconquest in New Catalonia, 1050–1276," *Spain and the Mediterranean*, ed. Benjamin F. Taggie, Richard W. Clement, James E. Caraway (Kirksville, MO, 1992), pp. 21–34.

Their son, Alfonso II of Aragon, could not tolerate a Norman principality in the midst of his growing realm any more than his father could
afford to leave the march of Siurana intact after the fall of Lerida
and Tortosa. After the assassination of Archbishop Hug de Cervelló
in 1171 a civil war broke out in Tarragona, the Norman lords were
expelled thereafter by the Catalans and exiled to the Balearics, creating an ecclesiastical principality under the archbishops.

What, in the meantime, happened to the march of Siurana? Do
the legends of ʿAbd-al-ʿAzia and Almira Almoniniz contain any historical elements that can be substantiated? Actually no; metaphori-
cally yes. The demise of the Muslim march can be reconstructed in
considerable detail and the story's context delineated, but the his-
toricity of the Muslim lovers cannot be substantiated.

The military alliance that was forged by the House of Barcelona
and the Church was far-reaching, pulling into the frontier southern
French and Norman knights, Italian naval contingents, and even
English crusaders, to add to the strength of the combined forces of
Barcelona, Urgel, and Aragon. Ultimately, an estimated 2,000 warriors descended upon Tortosa and Lerida in 1148–1149, and there
was no last minute Muslim reprieve. After the reign of Ali ibn Yusuf
(1107–1143) whose intervention had so thwarted Christian designs
on the entire Zaragozan realm, the African unification of the *taifa*
kingdoms proved short lived. Valencia had three governors between
1144 and 1145 and the leader to bring stability to this *taifa* kingdom, Abū ʿAbdallāh Mūhammad b. Saʿd, Ibn Mardanīsh (1147–1172)
was too busy consolidating power in the capital to render assistance
to the north. No clear leadership is identifiable at Tortosa in the
absence of direction from Valencia, and at Lerida no Muslim ruler
can be identified after Ahmad III b. ʿAbd al-Malik, Sayf al-Dawla
(1141). Three Almoravid rulers in succession lasted no more than
two years each. An interregnum occurred after 1146 when the Christians took swift advantage of the chaos in the Muslim world, and
the last Almoravid governor in Spain, Yahjā ibn Ghania, died in
1151. The second wave of African invaders, the Almohads, arrived
too late to undo the reconquest of the Ebro kingdoms. Muslim
Siurana, surrounded, was left on its own.

Catalan castellans were promised huge land concessions as early
as 1146 for their part in subjugating the March, but they were preoccupied in the Ebro Valley until after the capitulation of the Muslim
fortress cities. Thereafter, the problem of an internal frontier was

addressed swiftly by a series of mopping-up operations. The drive toward the Ebro cities had been a strategic multi-pronged attack requiring considerable coordination, involving a naval blockade and forays upriver, while land forces isolated and neutralized such outposts as Amposta, which protected the Ebro delta. Templars from Bárbera not only ensconced themselves at Montblanch, but occupied Granesa and from there attacked Flix and other Muslim fortresses guarding the Ebro connection between Lerida and Tortosa.[39] Once the two *taifas* were divided at this bottleneck, separate but coordinated campaigns began to specialize with each city and its territory. The assault on the Siuranan highland march was initiated by the Templars, who advanced simultaneously from the Ebro Valley along the Siurana River to the plateau, and from the opposite direction, from Espluga to Prades. Ramón Berenguer IV promised Berenguer Arnau portions of the Siurana estates, thinking they could be carved up like Tortosa to pay his debts and reward the besiegers. The crusade, now a half-decade in the making, had overtaxed the fragile realm that was not yet fully formed by draining manpower and money to the frontier. The unruly Christian lords from across the Pyrenees and looting crusaders had to be controlled and pacified themselves, and some Aragonese nobles who feared the pending union with Barcelona rose in revolt in 1151 and 1152, precisely when the pacification of the March was undertaken.

Consequently, the Muslims of the Siuranan regions continued to resist Christian overlordship when the count could least afford additional campaigns. While they may have thought of themselves as free Muslims defending their homeland and continuing the war against the crusaders, the perspective from count's position would have cast them as rebellious Mudejars assisting dissident elements in his realm. Ramón Berenguer IV therefore did not rely on either the coalition or the triumvirate that now governed Tortosa for support, but instead trusted a few Catalan nobles to subjugate the highlands while he turned his attention elsewhere to the marriage alliance with Aragon and the pacification of the Ebro Valley. The result may have been a brutal campaign without much negotiation, and the entrapment of the highland Muslims limited immigration and escape to

---

[39] See A.J. Forey, *The Templars in the Corona de Aragón* (London, 1973), pp. 5–86, for the role of the Templars and their subsequent rewards with the enfeoffments of major Muslim castles.

the south. The strategy was to keep Lerida and Tortosa separated, maintain control of the coastal shelf from Tarragona to Ampolla and guard the mouth of the Ebro Ampolla so no assistance could arrive by sea from the southern *taifas*, and to blockade the rebels in the highlands so they could not relieve Tortosa. He besieged the Muslim castle of Mirabet, which was taken in August, 1153. The military orders encircled the march from Montblanc to Xerta and joined their colleagues in the Ebro operations, from where they ventured into the highlands. Simultaneously, a two-pronged attack divided the Muslim defenders and prevented them from mounting a united front to protect their strongholds. Invading forces from the Ausona March under the command of Ponce de Cervera first reduced the piedmont villages of Avinaixa, Avimbodi, and L'Espluga, and then conquered Castellfullit and Prades. The Tarragonan Normans and Catalan castellans who held coastal castles as fiefs met at Castelvell, and from there advanced into the highland areas of Aleixar and La Musara. It was there, along a ridge above La Selva, became most fierce. The standoff failed, however, so that capture of Siurana castle on 29 April 1153 by Bertran de Castelet was the end of the campaign.[40] The chronicler of San Juan de la Peña much later counted the capture of Siurana among the great deeds of the count-king, as a natural consequence to the occupation of Tortosa:

> After he [Ramón Berenguer IV] returned from the capture [i.e., raid] of Almeria, he besieged the city of Tortosa with the aid of the Genoese. He gathered two thousand fighting men there, with whom he attacked the city vigorously and at last took it, in the Year of Our Lord 1148. He built a cathedral church there. In the following year, he besieged the city of Lérida. Ermengol of Castilla, Count of Urgell, participated along with the other barons and nobles. After a furious assault on the city, he took it on the same day of the year following that in which he took Tortosa; that is on the eight of the calends of November [25 October]. Afterward, in the Year of Our Lord 1154, he captured Fraga and the extremely strong castle of Miravet. The he captured the wonderfully well-fortified castle of Ciurana and many other fortresses and castles located

---

[40] The capitulation of Siurana is usually dated from the concession by Ramon Berenguer IV of its lands to Bertran de Castelet on 29 April 1153: AHN, Clero, carp. 2001, no. 20 (Poblet mss.); *Diplomatari de Poblet*, pp. 138–139, no. 155. In this charter the count-king gave the "universe" of populations in Siurana the same freedoms as bestowed on the inhabitants of Lerida after its capitulation to the Christians. These presumably formed the basis for the *usages* of Siurana that are mentioned in charters after 1166.

on the banks of the Ebro, and, at lenght, the places and lands that lie between Tortosa and Zaragoza. He exalted the Name of God through the three hundred churches that he built in His honor and glory.[41]

1154 may be remembered more accurately as a period of pacification by the Christian forces and consolidation of a Catalan regime in the lower March. By 1155 all of the Muslim highland fortresses had surrendered, and through 1158 with the disposition of Alforja their lands were redistributed by the count-king in a series of concessions and enfeoffments.[42] Thus one can trace the stranglehold on the Muslim March immediately before 1153 and its subjugation by the end of the decade when the count-king turned again to the rivalry of Aragon-Catalonia with Castile-León. The count stationed a castellan, Arbert de Castelvell, at Siurana and together they began the reconstruction of society in the hills according to Christian norms, which were apparently codified before 1166 into the *usages* of Siurana that dated to the conquest after 1153.[43] By 1164 a chaplain, Petrus, was assigned to the castle.[44] Christian settlers moved throughout the 1170s into the lower Campo and coastal shelf, but the highlands may have been more difficult to occupy. They were never completely pacified during the twelfth century. Almoravid power in Spain

----

[41] *Chronicle of San Juan de la Peña*, trans. Nelson, p. 51. As Nelson correctly points out (p. 119, n. 190), Fraga capitulated with Lerida on 24 October 1149, not 1154 as the chronicler maintained, and the author was also mistaken about the date of the fall of Siurana.

[42] Enumerated and mapped by Recasens, 2:71–74: Els Mangons (1149); La Boella and Riudoms (1150) and Cambrils (1151) by the Normans; then Centelles, and Albarca by the Cervera family (1151); Villafortuny (1152); Siurana itself (1153) followed by the quick takeover of Arcs, Colldejou, Borges, Reus, Alforja, Alcover, Vallmoll, Alio, El Codony, Sant Joan del Consell, Villalonga, and Pratdip all in one year (1154) after the fall of Siurana castle; Vilavert, Rocabruna, El Rourell, Espinaversa (Valls), and Barenys (1155); El Burgar, Cambrils, and Salou (1157); L'Albiol (1158) and Constanti (1159). Eight sites are specified as ecclesiastical properties by a papal bull of 25 March 1154; others are identified by their enfeoffments or foundation charters, i.e., *franquicias* or freedoms to attract colonists before the formalization of the *repartiment* system at Tortosa. Most of these have been edited by Font Rius, *Cartas de población* (see his map insert for the resettlement of the frontier of New Catalonia). For the final reconstruction and layout of the diocese of Tarragona and its border with Tortosa, including all settlements having parishes in the former Muslim March, see Lawrence J. McCrank, "La anatomía fiscal del periodo de post-restauración de la Iglesia de Tarragona: una revisión de las *Rationes decimarum hispaniae* (1279–1280)," *Hispania* 35 (1985): 245–298.

[43] AHN, Clero, carp. 2022, no. 11 (Poblet mss.), an original dating to January 1175; *Diplomatari de Poblet*, p. 382, no. 517; compare nos. 278 (1166) and 380 (1170) for other references to the usages of Siurana.

[44] AHN, Clero, carp. 2008, no. 16 (Poblet mss.); *Diplomatari de Poblet*, p. 209, no. 264.

collapsed soon thereafter, with Ibn Mardanīsh (d. 1172), who resurrected an independent state centered at Valencia, but who allied with the Christians rather than repelling them from the frontier of his newly won kingdom. The historian al-Marrākushī did not blame the Christians so much as the blatant despotism of the Almoravids and their corruption by power and luxury.[45] The loss of the upper frontier was lamented by peninsular Muslims therefore as a classic tragedy, identifying the fault as their own, deploring their own suicidal tendency toward internecine warfare, and like the Christians, blaming the Africans for the ruin of the old regime. Thus ended abruptly the would-be *taifa* of Siurana in as sudden and tragic a death as depicted in the legendary suicide of its princess, ʿAbd al-ʿAzia.

The charters of the time, subsequent *franquicias* of town *fueros* given to the new Christian colonists of some of the conquered villages, and retrospective comments embedded in latter Cistercian documents from the 1170s when the monks first began to exploit their domain, provide testimony to the reconquest of Siurana and forced subjugation of the entire March by 1158. The reconquest of the highlands had taken over a decade. The decade-long mopping-up operations in the highlands behind this new battle line along the Ebro has failed to attract much attention except for local historians. However, it is evident from the aftermath of the Leridan-Tortosan victories that there is more to the story than the conquest of the major cities that bordered this triangle of Muslim power that had survived for more than four centuries. Did the final reconquest obliterate Muslim highland culture? Probably not; this occurred during the next generation with the breakup of the land, resettlement and colonization by the Catalans, and passing of the justice system to comital appointees and local governance by castellans. Also influential was the consolidation of the monastic domain of Poblet, which not only converted several Muslim defenses into Cistercian granges but also open pasturage across the steppe lands into a zoned properties, and perhaps with some of the same depopulation measures taken by the White Monks in England and other places.

Mudejar history from this early period, and this area in particular, remains unknown. Resistance to assimilation apparently continued

---

[45] Al-Marrākushī, *al-Muʿjib talkhis akhbar al-Magrib*, excerpted by Reinhardt Dozy, *Recherches sur l'histoire et la littérature des Arabes d'Espagne pendant de Moyen Âge* (Leiden, 1848), 2:278; compare Muhammad Saʿd al-ʿIryan (Cairo, 1963), cited by Cheyne, p. 79.

throughout the century, which would imply that Mudejars survived as a minority among an increasing majority of Christian Catalan immigrants. The see of Tarragona and suffragan at Tortosa did not get their dioceses organized until after the 1170s, and the parishes in the old March seemed to have suffered unrest sometime between 1155 and 1160. Land transfers from former owners with Muslim names attest to a Mudejar substrata. Rarely are Christian charters so explicit as to identify the former Muslim tenure as explicitly as a donation to Poblet by Guillem Aimieric of the *hort*, or garden plot, of Petrola on the banks of Ebro River above Tortosa, which identifies the property clearly as such.[46] In another transfer between Christians in 1156 of orchards near the castle of Baells, the prior owners are identified as "Muza Ibnateli and his brother."[47] Two Muslim slaves appear as property exchanges in Poblet charters, and later the monastery had to contend with local resistance and social unrest among inhabitants of the old Muslim villages from Avimbodi to Espluga that remained inside its domain.[48] Given al-Idrīsī's description of Tarragona in 1154 just after the fall of Siurana, and his mention of the new city's Jews but nothing of an urban Mudejar community, it is likely that Muslim highlanders and lowlanders alike remained on their lands for the time being as peasant farmers, herdsmen, and woodsmen. Indeed, in 1174 a Mudejar named Ramón Sarrai (*Raimundus Sarracenus*) and his wife Nina were able to sell some land to Ramón de Vilar after paying off a debt of two *sous* in Agramunt coinage, which sometime after the reconquest had created a lien on their property.[49] In an unusual instance, when on 20 February 1167 Arnau de Jaca joined the confraternity of Poblet and bequeathed to

---

[46] AHN, Clero, carp. 2002, no. 16 (Poblet mss.) (12th-century copy of lost original) dated by Altisent, *Diplomatari de Poblet*, pp. 142–143, no. 161, as 6 March 1154 or 1155: *Fuit autem ortus iste de hereditate Abi Servat sarraceni.*

[47] AHN, Clero, carp. 2004, no. 4 (Poblet mss.), an original dating 23 August 1156; *Diplomatari de Poblet*, pp. 161–162, no. 191.

[48] AHN, Clero, carp. 2006, no. 13 (Poblet mss.), an original from Tortosa dating 29 November but without a specific year. *Diplomatari de Poblet*, pp. 280–281, no. 369, places it ca. 1170 based on subscriptors who appear in other dated documents at this time. Altisent prefers to see the donation from Alfonso II of the Muslim Meferiz Avinimel as a vassal rather than slave, but the text is clear about the gift of *servicium*. Jaime Santacana Tort, *El monasterio de Poblet (1151–1181)* (Barcelona, 1974), pp. 711–712, doc. 255, refers to the donation as one of *el servicio*. Both Cistercian editors were confronted with the problem of their monastery having had Muslim slaves in violation of the Order's statutes.

[49] AHN, Clero, carp. 2021, no. 20 (Poblet mss.), an original ms. dated 4 September 1174; *Diplomatari de Poblet*, p. 374, no. 50.

the abbey some pasture land around Ulldecona which was clearly delineated by Muslim-named landmarks (*usque ad Alzinam, et de Auzina usque ad Pinnam Rubeam que est in rego*), the transaction was witnessed by and subscribed in Arabic script by a certain Mohammed ibn al-Husain ibn Hasana.[50] Perhaps he was needed to verify the boundaries and assist in the conquerors' mapping of the territory. Thus piece by piece the rule of Barcelona and the diocese (but not the ecclesiastical seigneury of Tarragona) was extended between 1155 and 1171 into the piedmont country, but the highlands proper remained separate under a military governor. To this day the area, like the steppe lands east of Lerida, was labeled as a *comarc*, which designates it as a militarized zone remaining under a governorship and authority imposed from outside.[51] But such mere traces are all that remain of Siurana's Muslims one generation later.

Some inferences can be drawn from later experiences further south, but in Valencia the circumstances were considerably different with the new Christian colonists remaining for decades as a ruling minority among overwhelmingly superior numbers of Mudejars. They inherited there a culture that had another century to develop and accommodate itself to Christian overlordship and an enduring pluralism, which was in the first place more sophisticated, urban, and cosmopolitan than in the smaller frontier cities and rural villages to the north, and which was more connected socially and economically by irrigation systems and land supervision in an area of more coherent regional geography than the fragmented regionalism of the northeastern March. One experience in common, however, was a military reconquest and continued resistance to assimilation. How the prior experience in the Lerida-Tarragona-Tortosa arena affected the subsequent developments in the annexation of Valencia to the Crown of Aragon is mostly speculation. However, one of the most telling developments about the differences between Valencia's reconquest

---

[50] AHN, Clero, carp. 2011, no. 3 (Poblet mss.), an original dating 20 February 1167; *Diplomatari de Poblet*, pp. 235–236, no. 305. A thirteenth-century copy was included in the codified cartulary of Poblet (Biblioteca Provincial de Tarragona, ms. 241, f. 139r) edited by J. Pons i Marques, *Cartulari de Poblet: Edició del manuscrit de Tarragona* (Barcelona, 1938), p. 127, doc. 214, and by Santacana Tort, p. 505, doc. 61, but without retention of the original's Arabic subscription.

[51] AHN, Clero, carp. 2005, no. 5 (Poblet mss.), dating in 1160, verifies that the count constituted Siurana as a Christian "march" lying south of the frontier of the Rio Francoli; *Diplomatari de Poblet*, pp. 176–177, no. 212.

and consequent assimilation into the Crown and the experience a century earlier along and northeast of the Ebro Valley, is that as in the case of Zaragoza which was so thoroughly absorbed as to become the New Aragon distinct from the old mountain kingdom, the post-Tarragona conquests resulted in a New Catalonia, while Valencia retained its identity as a separate kingdom, region, and cultural entity. It seems mistaken to infer from Valencia a century later to the remote Muslim frontier above the Ebro that Muslim societies were all uniform and of high culture. The evidence from crusade tithing registers from a century later, 1279–1280 and 1285, indicate that these highlands remained rural, sparsely populated, and their villages, or at least their parishes, were less than a third the size of counterparts in the lowlands or on the plains.[52] The disappearance of the ultra-Ebro Muslim peoples from history therefore seems to reflect their rural, local, oral culture, without much of a written history in the first place, more than a deliberate purge of their memory from history by the new Christian regime. When the political and economic restructuring also altered social structures, continuity was broken and history was lost. Such historical lacunae are always troubling for historians, especially when looking for lost kingdoms and trying to unravel the mysteries of ghost towns; the problem is frustrating and perplexing. The problem of looking for what may have never been there may be compared with the New World explorers who tried to discover cities of gold but found rude settlements of adobe instead, or medieval reconquerors trying to capture something too amorphous to hold onto; Siurana, like Tarragona, could be taken physically, but not kept the way it was or as the conquerors thought it should be. These entities had to be recreated anew.

We should not be so anxious to disregard what little memory exists, therefore, whether in ruins or folksong, for in some cases it is all that we have. These relics provide insights to discern social and cultural traces of the lingering Muslim substrata. The reality of the Muslim existence survives in monuments, place names, physiological characteristics, and folk memory as in such stories about the heros of the reconquest era that form a national mythology, and remembrance as well of the lost kingdom of Siurana, a culture that is no more, and perhaps the brave death of one Muslim lord and

---

[52] McCrank, "Anatomía fiscal," 265–266.

the tragic suicide of his distraught princess. While such mythology may turn fanciful and be imbued with Romantic overlays and embellishments, behind the story line seems to lurk an enduring historical reality that is well enough documented from the records of the era to give it credibility in ethos if not in fact. Such legends seem relevant in a countryside that is still distinctive and geographically isolated despite the modern freeway that cuts through these mountains today. Their social diversity and pluralism, regionalism and parochialism, multi-culturalism and tri-lingualism with Castilian as an educated overlay, Catalan as common parlance, and a distinctive dialect, to this day defy national unity, withhold allegiance to external authority, and accommodate local cults and practices in its Catholicism. The oral memory of a different past can survive in such an ambient and closed society. Thus the ghosts of Siurana seem mysteriously real in the mountains of New Catalonia.

THE RECONQUEST DURING THE REIGN OF
ALFONSO XI (1312–1350)

Nicholás Agrait

Although acknowledged as a distinctive and important period in Spanish medieval history, the reign of Alfonso XI (1312–1350) has been neglected until very recently. For most European and American historians, Castilian history has traditionally taken second stage to such topics as the Hundred Years War, the development of the English and French national monarchies, and the conflict between the Holy Roman Emperor and the Papacy, to name a few. What is truly puzzling is that Spanish historians themselves have not adequately researched the circumstances and processes of Alfonso's distinguished monarchy. Interest in this subject has increased as of late, but the focus has more often been on legal and parliamentary developments or diplomatic and political trends which began in Alfonso's reign.[1] Even within reconquest historiography, Alfonso's military contributions have generally received only cursory treatment.[2] One possible reason could be that, in contrast to the great reconquest of the thirteenth century, his triumphs were not always accompanied by great territorial or monetary rewards. By these criteria of personal and territorial gain, Alfonso's accomplishments barely merit attention; yet Joseph O'Callaghan has speculated that had the king not died

---

[1] Among the most important works one should consult Joseph F. O'Callaghan, *The Cortes of Castile-León, 1188–1350* (Philadelphia, 1989) as well as the collection of essays edited by Adeline Rucquoi, *Génesis medieval del estado moderno-Castilla y Navarra (1250–1370)* (Valladolid, 1987) and Emilio Cabrera, ed., *Andalucía entre oriente y occidente (1236–1492)* (Córdoba, 1988). The historian who devoted a great deal of attention to this reign was Salvador de Moxó. His conclusions on the reign were edited and published as "Época de Alfonso XI," in *La expansión peninsular y mediterránea (c. 1212–c. 1350)* vol. 13 of *Historia de España*, ed. José María Jover Zamora (Madrid, 1990), 279–428; idem, "La sociedad política en la época de Alfonso XI," *Cuadernos de Historia* 6 (1975): 187–326; idem, *La alcábala: sobre sus orígenes, concepto y naturaleza* (Madrid, 1963).

[2] For general treatments of the reconquest, see Joseph F. O'Callaghan, *A History of Medieval Spain* (Ithaca, 1975); Angus McKay, *Spain in the Middle Ages: From Frontier to Empire, 1000–1500* (New York, 1989); Derek Lomax, *The Reconquest of Spain* (London, 1978).

suddenly while besieging Gibraltar in 1350, Alfonso might have captured it and gone on to complete the *reconquista* over one hundred
years before the ascendancy of the Catholic Kings.[3] In this case, the
image that arises of Alfonso is of a great conqueror unable to fully
realize his potential. It is my contention that the last decade of the
reign of Alfonso constitutes an important point in the reconquest
worthy of further consideration. First, Alfonso's campaigns may illustrate a transition in the practice of warfare in the Iberian Peninsula.
Second, his military triumphs at the battle of Salado (1340) and the
siege and capture of Algeciras (1342–1344) virtually eliminated any
threat of Marinid invasion into the Peninsula from Morocco, further
isolated the kingdom of Granada, and cemented Castile's dominant
position in the Straits.

Though it advanced during the 1340's and it remained an integral
part of Castilian identity, the war on Spanish Islam largely stalled
during Alfonso's reign. The general conditions were hardly encouraging when he assumed the throne as a child in 1312 after the sudden
death of his father, Fernando IV (1295–1312). Castile had emerged
from a period of expansion in the late thirteenth century marked by
the capture of many parts of Extremadura, Andalusia and the kingdom of Murcia. This great territorial expansion caused immediate
administrative problems for the Castilian Crown in maintaining the
political stability of the kingdom's old and new lands.[4] The kingdom
also faced foreign threats. While relations with Aragon were mostly
peaceful, Portugal and Navarre were not always on friendly terms
with the Castilians.[5] To the south, the Nasrid kingdom of Granada
could proved a formidable foe for all the states of Christian Iberia.
It also served as a staging point for the Marinids of Morocco, who
stood as an ever-present danger to peninsular diplomatic and military equilibrium.[6]

The political and military triumphs and failures of his immediate
successors made Alfonso's minority a period of great strife. With no

---

[3] O'Callaghan, *History*, p. 414.

[4] J. Gautier Dalaché, "L'histoire castillane dans la première moitié XIVᵉ," *AEM*
7 (1970–1971): 241–242.

[5] Julian Bishko, "The Spanish and Portuguese Reconquest, 1095–1492," in *A
History of the Crusades*, 6 vols., Kenneth Setton et al. (Madison, 1975), 3:436; Norman
Housley, *The Later Crusades From Lyons to Alcazar 1274–1580* (Oxford, 1992), pp. 277–278.

[6] L.P. Harvey, *Islamic Spain, 1250–1500* (Chicago, 1990), p. 156; Richard Fletcher,
Moorish Spain (Berkeley, 1992), pp. 163–165.

clear provision for the administration of the young king's lands, the regency became the focus of internecine war between the queen mother, Maria de Molina, the older princes, and the Castilian nobility.[7] After several episodes of civil war which led to rival royal courts, they finally reached an accommodation in 1315.[8] Despite the return of peace, the divided regency left a legacy of baronial banditry and urban violence which caused a downward economic spiral for kingdom and Crown alike.[9]

Even when domestic peace was only partially restored, the pressure to continue military forays against Muslim *Hispania* continued. In 1316, the *infante* Pedro mounted an expedition to the borders of the kingdom of Granada, where he first gained a great victory and then unsuccessfully besieged two Muslim castles.[10] In 1317 he again invaded Muslim territory, first relieving a Muslim siege of Gibraltar and then capping a series of raids into Granada's northern lands with the capture of the castle of Belmez. Drawn from this triumph by rivalry with his brother Juan over the regency, Pedro eventually accepted papal arbitration to end Castile's domestic woes, which named him and Juan as coregents. Then Pedro, bolstered by a recently-issued crusading bull, led a force into Muslim lands in early 1319. Not wanting to lose the benefits of a crusading opportunity, Juan joined his brother in the expedition that attacked the fortress town of Tiscar. Ineptly separating their forces, the two princes in June 1319 were surprised by a Muslim army. In the ensuing panic, much of the Castilian army was massacred and the two princes met their deaths either on the battlefield or in flight from it.[11] With this military disaster fresh in the minds of the Castilians, defense against any possible Granadan attack became the order of the day. Defense

[7] Moxó, "Epoca," p. 284; Mercedes Gaibrois de Ballesteros, *Doña María de Molina, tres veces reina* (Madrid, 1967).

[8] Cayetano Rosell, ed., *Crónica del rey Alfonso, el Onceno* [hereafter, *Crónica*] in *Crónicas de los Reyes de Castilla*, 3 vols., *BAE*, vol. 66 (Madrid, 1953), p. 177; *Cortes* [Burgos, 1317], 1:272–273, art. 39.

[9] *Cortes* [Carrión, 1317], 1:309, art. 14. Manuel García Fernández, "La Hermandad General de Andalucía durante la minoría de Alfonso XI de Castilla," *Historia, Instituciones, Documentos* 12 (1985): 354.

[10] *Crónica*, p. 180; Harvey, pp. 180–181. Contemporaneous Arab sources do not mention a Christian victory stressing instead the heroism of the Muslim troops.

[11] *Crónica*, pp. 181–184; for Alfonso's knighthood, see Peter Linehan, "The Mechanics of Monarchy: Knighting Castile's King, 1332," *History Today* 43 (March, 1993): 26–32.

of the frontier zones was left to the *Hermandad General de Andalucía*, a brotherhood of Castilian towns that bordered on Muslim territory.[12] By 1320, the *hermandad* had brokered a truce with Granada and a foreign crisis gave way to a domestic one.[13] With the two regents dead, civil war again loomed in Castile until a new regency council, composed of the queen mother and two male members of royal family, was appointed. This ruling arrangement persisted until 1325 when Alfonso, an adolescent of thirteen, began to rule for himself.[14]

Despite greatly diminished royal authority and revenues, Alfonso soon showed himself to be an adept political and military leader. The principal bane of his early reign were such over-mighty subjects as Juan Manuel, a member of the second regency council, and Juan Nuñez de Lara, an Andalusian noble who built a redoubtable power base which centered on Lerma.[15] Even when such epicenters of baronial dissent undiminished during his reign, Alfonso emerged as a monarch largely successful in balancing his own power against the traditional privileges of his nobles. He offset the influence of the great families by promoting members of lesser noble families and rewarding non-noble knights. Like many an Iberian sovereign before him, Alfonso used the prospect of war on a Muslim enemy to divert the opposition and banditry of his baronial rivals.[16]

While Granada did not launch any major offensives during Alfonso's minority, it took advantage of the 1319 defeat to capture the Castilian towns of Huesca, Ores, Galera, and Martos in 1325. The Granadan emir, Ismail I (1314–1325), may well have reclaimed more Christian territory if not assassinated in 1325, leaving a divided realm to his successor, Muhammad IV (1325–1333). As the Granadan danger temporarily abated, Alfonso took the initiative and launched several operations across the Muslim border. Between 1325 and 1327 he

---

[12] García Fernández, pp. 354–355. The *Hermandad General de Andalucía* was an agreement entered by the councils of the Andalusian towns in order to defend their local interests in the very uncertain times of Alfonso's minority. It was formed in 1312 and managed to last until 1325 when Alfonso abolished it because he felt it constituted a threat to this power.

[13] Manuel Nieto Cumplido, *Orígenes del regionalismo andaluz (1235–1325)* (Cordoba, 1979), pp. 65–66.

[14] Andrés Giménez Soler, *Don Juan Manuel. Biografía y estudio crítico* (Zaragoza, 1932), p. 484, doc. 453; *Cortes*, 1:372, art. 45 [Valladolid-1325].

[15] *Cortes*, p. 373; Giménez Soler, pp. 518, 539, 543–544, 551–558, docs. 401, 430 436, 450.

[16] Moxó, "Época," pp. 335–342.

captured Ronda, Pruna and Teba. This drive against Islam was stalled in late 1325, when the king's archenemy, Juan Manuel, allied himself with Granada and launched a damaging series of raids around Toledo. An alliance between Juan Manuel and Pedro IV, king of Aragon (1337–1338), seemed immanent.[17] In spite of the dire consequences such an alliance might produce, Alfonso refused to be deterred from his war on Granada. In the *Cortes* held at Madrid in 1329, he asked for and was granted more funding in order to continue his campaign to recover the lands held by the "Moors, the enemies of the faith."[18] This continued the conflict until 1331, when it was apparent that the whole affair lost momentum. Alfonso thus agreed to a truce with Muhammad IV which named Granada as a tributary state of Castile.

The hiatus in the Granada war reflected not a lessening in Alfonso's reconquest resolve, but rather growing instability in Castile's economy coupled with the need to isolate Juan Manuel.[19] The peninsular situation worsened for Alfonso when Muhammad IV, feeling threatened by Castile, asked the Marinid rulers of Morocco for military aid.[20] The Marinids quickly assembled and sent an army across the Straits and laid siege to Gibraltar. Alfonso was obviously concerned but unable to do much since he was busy dealing with the rebellions of his Castilian nobles headed by Juan Manuel. Instead, the Castilian border towns responded and organized to help Gibraltar. But Muhammad IV gathered his forces and staged a series of raids along the border. He attacked a castle at Castro, and later destroyed a fortress at Cabra, ravaging the adjacent areas.[21] These raids, while not producing stellar results, occupied the Christian forces in Andalusia and prevented the relief of the Christian garrison of Gibraltar. Without any hope of reinforcement, Gibraltar was forced to surrender to the Marinids. Alfonso gathered an army and tried to retake the city, but the lack of provisions and the constant military distractions posed by Juan Manuel and Granada hampered his efforts. Buying time, he made a treaty with the Muslims conceding the loss of Gibraltar in return for peace between Castile, Granada, and Morocco. Granada

---

[17] *Crónica*, pp. 206–210.
[18] Ibid., p. 223.
[19] Ibid., pp. 227–228.
[20] Harvey, p. 187; Anwar G. Chejne, *Muslim Spain: Its History and Culture* (Minneapolis, 1974), p. 100.
[21] *Crónica*, pp. 244–245.

agreed to remain a vassal kingdom of Castile.[22] In 1334, after Muhammad had been killed by a rebel group, the new emir, Yūsuf I (1333–1354), extended this agreement for another four years.[23] This renewed treaty with Granada freed Alfonso to deal with the other problems of his kingdom.

Through the mid-1330's, Alfonso also faced Christian enemies and domestic obstacles to the escalation of the Granadan war.[24] In 1335, he faced attacks from both Navarre and Portugal. To meet the invasion of his northern neighbor, Alfonso called a meeting of the *Cortes* at Valladolid in 1335. Although he secured the support of the nobility in this meeting, military funding was another matter. Despite the grudging help of the *Cortes*, the Castilian army proved itself superior to the Navarrese force with a chrushing defeat at Tudela. Not long after gaining peace with the Navarrese in late 1335, Alfonso was forced to deal with a Portuguese invasion occasioned by the treatment of his wife, Maria of Portugal. Preferring his mistress Leonor de Guzman, Alfonso had very little to do with his wife, whom he kept as a virtual prisoner.[25] To avenge his daughter, the Portuguese king Alfonso IV (1325–1357) attacked Extramadura near Badajoz in 1336 but was quickly repelled by Castilian troops. In 1337, Alfonso XI carried the border war to Portugal with a complex four-pronged invasion, which was only halted when Pope Benedict XII called for peace so the two Iberian monarchs could mount a united invasion against Granada.[26] Before the papal wishes could be realized, however, Alfonso had to deal with his rebellious barons. In 1334, he besieged Lerma, Juan Nuñez de Lara's power base, forcing him to capitulate two years later. Lara's rival, Juan Alfonso de Haro, posed a domestic problem of equal proportions to the king. By 1337, however, Alfonso had cornered Haro in the town of Agunciello. Rather than pardoning him, the king declared Haro a traitor and executed him.[27] This era of bloody pacification was capped in 1337, when Alfonso received Juan Manuel, his longtime rival, into his service.[28]

---

[22] Ibid., pp. 252–258.

[23] Harvey, pp. 192–193; Rachel Arié, *L'Espagne musulmane au temps des Nasrides* (Paris, 1990), pp. 101–121.

[24] Ibid., pp. 267–271.

[25] O'Callaghan, *History*, p. 410; Clara Estow, *Pedro the Cruel of Castile, 1350–1369* (Leiden, 1995), pp. 5–6; Antonio Ballesteros Beretta, "Doña Leonor de Guzman a la muerte de Alfonso XI," *BRAH* 100 (1932): 624–632; Moxó, "Sociedad política," pp. 259–264.

[26] *Crónica*, pp. 287–292.

[27] Giménez Soler, pp. 631–632, doc. 550.

[28] *Crónica*, pp. 306–310.

With his position and authority finally secured, Alfonso received the news in fall, 1330, that the Marinids had been transporting troops from Morocco into the Iberian Peninsula for some time. Alfonso signed a pact with Peter IV of Aragon in which the two monarchs pledged mutual assistance against the Muslims. While Alfonso was gathering his forces, Abd al-Malik, the leader of the Marinids, set off from Algeciras attacking Seville and its surroundings. Though causing great damage along the frontier, the Muslim army was quickly repulsed by Christian frontier garrisons. A setback for the Christians came in 1340 with the defeat of the Castilian fleet. Alfonso's admiral, Juan Jufre Tenorio, engaged the Marinids in order to halt their troop transfer. His fleet, badly outnumbered, was thoroughly routed, and the Muslims executed Jufre Tenorio shortly after his capture.

Shortly after this naval disaster, Alfonso turned to his former enemy, Alfonso IV of Portugal, to arrange an alliance which would help to make up for his naval losses.[29] Alfonso set out to meet the Moroccan and Granadan armies once he learned they had placed Tarifa under siege. He carried with him a crusading indulgence, which granted him a share of the ecclesiastical *tercias* and *decimas*, and a papal standard.[30] A Portuguese army led by Alfonso IV himself, and a number of European crusaders accompanied Alfonso's army. A fleet composed of Aragonese, Catalan and Portuguese ships attacked Tarifa from the sea in September 1340.[31] Prior to the battle, Alfonso, at the advice of Juan Manuel, sent a contingent of knights to reinforce the garrison at Tarifa. These reinforcements broke through the Muslim lines and entered the city. The main Christian army arrived on the scene in late October and sent a communique to the Muslim commanders, offering them the options of pitched battle or peaceful retreat from Tarifa. On 29 October the Muslims decided to fight and the two armies clashed at the the Salado River near Tarifa. The Christian forces were arranged into three groups: 1) the vanguard composed of the high nobility, members of the Military Orders, and the urban militias of Seville, led by Juan Manuel and Juan Núñez de Lara, master of the Order of Santiago; 2) the main body, with infantry led by Alfonso; and,

---

[29] *Crónica*, pp. 306–310; Housely, p. 279.
[30] Jose Goñi Gatzambide, *Historia de la bula de cruzada en España* (Vitoria, 1958), pp. 325–332.
[31] *Crónica*, pp. 318–325; Housely, p. 293.

3) the Portuguese army marching alongside Alfonso's group. The vanguard and Alfonso's contingent would engage the Marinids, while Portuguese were to fight the Granadan army.[32] Apparently, both sides spent some time staring each other down since neither wanted to be the first to cross the river. Finally they engaged in battle. The Muslims, fighting in a very confined space, were hit hard by the more heavily armored and armed Christian forces. When they started to flee back towards Tarifa, the Castilian garrison in the town launched an attack upon the rear of the Marinid army. The Muslims, forced to fight on two flanks, were soon slaughtered by the Christians. Ibn al-Hassan, the Marinid general, took flight and safely reached Morocco because Alfonso's forces were slowed by their excessive pillaging. In the melée after the Salado battle, Alfonso considered pressing his advantage by besieging nearby Algeciras but did not have sufficient provisions to do so. He fortified Tarifa and then returned to Seville loaded down with booty.[33]

How could the Christians, who by all accounts were outnumbered by the Muslims, achieve such a decisive and significant military victory in the battle of Salado? L. P. Harvey suggests that the Muslims lacked the proper leadership. The Berber army was more suited to fighting in open spaces where it could take advantage of its mobility. On the banks of the Salado river, they were no match for the heavily-armored Christian knights, who literally ran them down.[34] Salvador de Moxó felt that the Christian triumph was assured by their strategy of making the Muslims fight on two flanks. In this way, the contributions of the king of Portugal in defeating the Granadan army were instrumental.[35] No matter why it took place, the Christian victory at Salado proved a very significant event. Derek Lomax, Joseph O'Callaghan, and Salvador de Moxó agree that this battle effectively eliminated the Moroccan threat since it made military forays from North Africa all but impossible. Salado, then, was a true landmark in a reconquest journey that began centuries before.[36] Both Norman Housley and Julian Bishko, however, disagree, arguing that the Salado victory was not in itself the decisive blow to the Marinids. In their

---

[32] Moxó, "Época," pp. 402–403.

[33] *Crónica*, pp. 325–328; O'Callaghan, *History*, pp. 412–413; Arié, pp. 229–276; Ambrosio Huici y Miranda, *Las grandes batallas de la Reconquista* (Madrid, 1956), pp. 331–337.

[34] Harvey, p. 193.

[35] Moxó, *Expansión*, pp. 404–406.

[36] Lomax, p. 167; O'Callaghan, *History*, pp. 412–413; Moxó, *Expansión*, p. 400.

view, the later conquest of strategic points near the Straits was necessary to cement Castile's position vis-à-vis Morocco.[37] Regardless of
the magnitude of the 1340 battle, the fact remains that it marked
the last great offensive launched from North Africa into the Iberian
Peninsula. Granada was consequently left isolated since it could not
rely on Moroccan help.

Even though the Castilians won substantial booty at Salado, the
economic woes of the kingdom continued unabated. Alfonso, undaunted
in his war plans, convoked a *Cortes* at Arena in 1341, but only
requested a small amount of funding due to Castile's weakened
finances.[38] With this grant, he led a small force into Granadan territory and captured all the important villages above Algeciras. He
then returned to Castile and announced his plans for an Algeciras
campaign.[39] In order to raise the necessary funds, Alfonso, with the
approval of the *Cortes*, instituted a new royal sales tax, the *alcábala*.[40]
Yet even with this new source of funding, the ruinous state of Castile's
economy limited the range of Alfonso's military activities. Despite
these difficulties, the king began operations against Algeciras in August
of 1342. His armies were composed of all the traditional groups one
would expect from a late medieval besieging force: 1) heavy and
light cavalry; 2) infantry; 3) corps of "engineers" dedicated to the
building of siege engines; 4) *almogávares* (light skirmishers); 5) *adalides*
(expert warriors); and, 6) foreigners.[41] Since Algeciras was an important port city, a Christian fleet composed of Castilian, Genoese, and
Aragonese ships assisted Alfonso's ground forces. During this first
stage of the conflict in late summer 1342, the Muslim garrison of

---

[37] Housley, p. 280; Bishko, p. 438.

[38] *Crónica*, p. 331.

[39] There are not that many works on Algeciras but some of the most important
are: G. Daumet, "Jean de Rye au siege d'Algeciras," *Bulletin Hispanique* 12 (1910):
265–274; C. Martínez Valverde, "La campaña de Algeciras y la conquista de esta
plaza," *Revista de Historia Militar* 25 (1981): 7–40, E. Mitre Fernández, "De la toma
de Algeciras a la campaña de Antequera," *Hispania* 32 (1972): 71–122, L. Serrano,
"Alfonso XI y el Papa Clemente VI durante el cerco de Algeciras," *Cuadernos de los
Trabajos de la Escuela Española de Arqueología e Historia de Roma* 3 (1912): 1–35. The
most comprehensive works are: Antonio Torremocha Silva's *Algeciras entre la Cristiandad
y el Islam: estudio sobre el cerco y la conquista de Algeciras por el rey Alfonso XI de Castilla,
asi como de la ciudad y sus terminos hasta el final de la Edad Media* (Algeciras, 1994); and
*El ordenamiento de Algeciras (1345): datos sobre la conquista, repoblación y organización de
la ciudad en el siglo XIV* (Algeciras, 1983).

[40] Ibid., p. 335; Miguel Angel Ladero Quesada, *Fiscalidad y poder real en Castilla
(1252–1369)*, (Madrid, 1993), Moxó, *La alcábala*, p. 22.

[41] Moxó, "Época," pp. 410–411.

Algeciras harassed the besieging Christian armies, cutting off any reinforcements from the nearby city of Tarifa and holding positions beyond the city walls. They also held positions beyond the city walls from which the Christians could not initially dislodge them.[42] As the fall set in, torrential rains caused great damage to the Castilian siegeworks and artillery.[43] In addition, Alfonso soon found himself in financial difficulties which forced him to send diplomatic missions seeking loans to France, Portugal and the Papacy.[44] The fact remains that during the last months of 1342, despite all their siegecraft, the Castilian host was unable to encircle Algeciras by land or blockade it by sea. It encountered fierce Muslim resistance, which attempted to break through the besieging lines and launched heavy cannonade from the city walls. In fact, this siege constituted one of the first recorded instances of cannon use in the Iberian Peninsula.[45] Its effect, however, was minimal compared to that inflicted by the archers and crossbowmen.

As the operation dragged into the new year, the Castilian forces gradually gained the upper hand over the Algeciran garrison. They were able to move war engines such as trebuchets and siege towers close enough to the walls to inflict significant damage. The Muslims had increasing difficulty in breaking out of the city, suffering heavier losses with each attempt. The Christian naval blockade also prevented all but a few Muslim ships from entering or leaving the port of Algeciras. But the financial difficulties that had plagued the Christian forces in the previous months became ever more critical. By February, Alfonso had received no word from Philip VI of France or Pope

---

[42] *Crónica*, p. 344.

[43] For artillery in medieval Europe, see Paul E. Chevedden, "The Artillery of King James I the Conqueror," in *Iberian and the Mediterranean World of the Middle Ages: Essays in Honor of Robert I. Burns, S.J.*, ed. P. Chevedden, D. Kagay and P. Padilla (Leiden, 1996), pp. 47–94; Contamine, pp. 194–196; R. Rogers, *Latin Siege Warfare in the Twelfth Century* (Oxford, 1992), app. III, pp. 255–273.

[44] *Crónica*, pp. 347–348.

[45] Ibid., p. 344: *Et los Moros de la ciubdat lanzaban muchos truenos contra la hueste, en que lanzaban pellas de fierro muy grandes; et lanzabanlas tan lexos de la ciubdat, que pasaban allende de la hueste algunas dellas, et algunas ferian en la hueste: et otrosí lanzaban con los truenos saetas muy grandes y muy gruesas.* For cannon use in this era, see Contamine, pp. 133–134; Malcolm Vale, "New Techniques and Old Ideas: The Impact of Artillery on War and Chivalry at the End of the Hundred Year's War," in *War, Literature and Politics in the Late Midde Ages*, ed. C.T. Almond (Liverpool, 1976), pp. 57–72; Westin F. Cook, Jr., "Warfare and Firearms in Fifteenth Century Morocco, 1420–1492," *War and Society* 11 (1993): 125–144; Andrew C. Hess, *The Forgotten Frontier*, (Chicago, 1978).

Clement VI; Portugal, on the other hand, flatly turned down the Castilian request for assistance.[46] Alfonso XI threatened to debase the currency, which brought an outcry from across Castile, but also induced the Castilian townsmen gathered at the siege to grant a kingdom-wide *moneda forera* to continue operations.[47]

The next two months proved to be one of the most intense periods of the operation. In March, 1343, fully eight months after they had arrived, the Castilians succeeded in cutting off land access to Algeciras. They then attempted to solidify their position by placement of siege engines and extension of the siege works. The Muslims, realizing their critical situation, unleashed heavy artillery fire. This fusillade, combined with Muslim forays outside the walls, kept the Christians from completely reinforcing their position until late April. Though Algeciras was far from defeated, the Castilians had taken the first great step towards victory.[48]

Despite his clear dominance, Alfonso almost saw the siege operation disintegrate during the summer of 1343. The Genoese mercenary fleet threatened to leave if not promptly paid. Alfonso knew that their departure would be disastrous. The collapse of the naval blockade would have allowed the Marinids to restock Algeciras, enabling it to resist the Christians indefinitely. He quickly gathered the necessary sums, borrowing heavily from his own subjects and some local merchants.[49] During the rest of the summer, the Christian armies experienced serious shortages, made worse by a fire that swept through the camp. Again the siege was faced with a complete collapse. Yet Alfonso received some good news in August. His representative to Clement VI arrived and announced that the pope had granted his request for a loan. Alfonso XI had the money shipped directly to the Genoese fleet, keeping none for the support of his own armies. He also received word from a cleric in the service of the archbishop of Toledo that Philip VI of France had also agreed to lend money to Alfonso's war efforts. Yet even this fresh money could not be spent on resupplying his own men but was also consumed by the great debts Alfonso owed the Genoese. Since these loans were not enough to resolve the financial crisis facing the siege,

---

[46] Goñi Gatzambide, pp. 332–334.
[47] O'Callaghan, *Cortes*, p. 134; Ladero Quesada, pp. 54–57.
[48] *Crónica*, pp. 350–360.
[49] Ibid., p. 379.

Alfonso convened an *ayuntamiento* (assembly) of all the prelates, high nobles, knights and townsmen present in Algeciras. He requested more money and those present consented to a new tax to be imposed on the entire kingdom.[50] These grants certainly kept the operation from foundering but were actually little more than stopgap measures, By the fall, the shortages in the Christian camp, aggravated by the fire, grew so acute that starvation and price gouging became commonplace. The lack of supplies and currency made Alfonso's control over the Christian host increasingly difficult. The Genoese, in particular, threatened to leave or defect to the Muslims. In September 1343, one Genoese ship attempted to intercept and capture the Granadan emir's vessel while it was en route to a meeting with Alfonso. This lost Alfonso the service of one Genoese ship, which left to avoid his punishment, and a great opportunity to negotiate for the capture of Algeciras.[51] Dissent and despair within the Christian forces, which had been on the rise for months, led to a great increase in desertion. Yet in the midst of all the difficulties, there were encouraging signs that the resistance Algeciras itself was starting to weaken under the constant Christian pressure. It became increasingly clear to the Muslim garrison that without immediate relief their cause was lost.

The last months of 1343 and early 1344 witnessed the final attempts by the Granadans and the Marinids to save Algeciras. Both kingdoms gathered their armies and set off from Gibraltar. They were met by Christian forces near the Palmones river, which emptied into the Mediterranean east of Algeciras. But during November 1343, neither side committed to a pitched land battle, limiting their actions to skirmishing. On the sea, however, the two fleets jockeyed for position. After nearly a month, in December 1343, Alfonso led his forces into battle and promptly defeated the combined Muslim army. This victory determined the outcome of the siege.[52] In the following month, the Muslim relief force again attempted to break the naval blockade of the Algeciran port by slipping in a ship full of provisions. Apparently warned of this tactic, the Christian fleet was able to capture the intruder. Though the Muslims did get a supply ship into the port of Algeciras by February, the garrison was already near

---

[50] Ibid., pp. 367–368; O'Callaghan, *Cortes*, p. 38.
[51] Ibid., pp. 379–381.
[52] *CDACA*, 7:171–173, doc. 48; *Crónica*, pp. 381–385.

starvation.[53] By March 1344, the emirs of both Granada and Morocco sent envoys to Alfonso XI to negotiate terms. Alfonso XI, after discussing their offer carefully with his council, chose to accept the surrender of Algeciras. The peace treaty proclaimed an end of hostilities for ten years between the combatants. Yūsuf I, the emir of Granada, agreed to remain Alfonso's vassal.[54] On 26 March 1344, Palm Sunday, Algeciras was handed over to Alfonso. In a particularly astute political move, Alfonso allowed Juan Manuel to take possession of the city before making his own triumphal entrance. When the king did enter the city, one of his first moves was to turn the largest mosque into a church named Santa María de Palma. He stayed in the city until Easter before returning to Tarifa.[55]

The last six years of Alfonso XI's life were given over to the jurisdictional organization of Castile. The king expanded his control over Castilian cities with the appointment of royal *regidores* and tried to regulate the economy with the issuance of the *Ordenamiento de Alcalá* in 1348.[56] Yet even then, he was still looking for fresh conquests in the Muslim south. In the last year of his reign, he was making preparations for the conquest of Gibraltar. Despite his plans for further conquest, the siege of Algeciras remained his final military triumph. While he was besieging Gibraltar, the outbreak of bubonic plague that had been buffeting Europe reached southern Spain. Despite repeated warnings that he should desist in his efforts, Alfonso refused to lift the siege and became the only medieval monarch to die of the Black Death.[57]

In the realm of later medieval military history, the battle of Salado and the siege of Algeciras present a particularly intriguing set of circumstances. Few sieges of the reconquest were more multifaceted than that of Algeciras, which, like the later campaign against Granada

---

[53] *Crónica*, pp. 386–388.

[54] Giménez Soler, pp. 642–643, doc. 574; *Crónica*, pp. 388–389; O'Callaghan, *Medieval Spain*, p. 413.

[55] *Crónica*, pp. 388–389.

[56] María del Carmen de León-Sotelo Casado and Esther González Crespo, "Notas para el itinerario de Alfonso XI en el período de 1344 a 1350," *En la España Medieval* 5 (1986): 589; *Cortes*, 1:542 [Alcalá, 1348: no. 64]; Estow, pp. 16–17; O'Callaghan, *Cortes*, pp. 176–178.

[57] *Crónica*, pp. 390–391; Philip Ziegler, *The Black Death* (New York, 1969), p. 113; Rosemary Horrox, *The Black Death* (Manchester, 1994), doc. 77, p. 250; William D. Phillips, Jr. "*Peste Negra*: The Fourteenth-Century Plague Epidemics in Iberia," in this volume.

(1490–1492), combined integrated ground and naval operations. In some ways, such campaigns stand as a microcosm of the later medieval Castilian world marked by the increasing militarization of society, the manipulation of religious and military ideologies, and the emergence of a Crown complex enough to administer the increasingly international war on Spanish Islam.[58] In military terms, Alfonso's later campaigns are important for the development of counterweight and gunpowder artillery as well as the emergence of an "end game" strategy which would soon be applied to Granada. While Castile had fairly impressive naval resources, the scope of the Algeciras campaign and the disastrous Marinid victory over the Castilian fleet in 1340 emphasized the need for an international naval force.[59] Alfonso's ground forces stood as a cross section of Castilian and later medieval Mediterranean society and pointed the way to the polyglot forces of *siglo de oro* Spain which came to expand Iberian domiance from the Mediterranean to the Caribbean.[60]

The composition of Alfonso's ground forces was certainly more complex that that of his naval enterprises. It has been argued that, except for small contingents of Navarrese and other European crusaders, most of the Algeciras army was Castilian. One of the most significant sources of military manpower for Alfonso was the Castilian high nobility who brought their private troops or retainers to the battlefield. In the *Ordenamiento* of Burgos of 1338, Alfonso decreed that the high nobility had to equip and maintain troops in proportion to the amount of rent income they received. In addition, all of the royal vassals were required to equip and maintain mounted warriors or peons depending on how much support they received from the Crown.[61] The core of the royal army was constituted by troops outfitted by the crown and any knights who were in the service of

---

[58] For Granada war, see Harvey, pp. 307–323; O'Callaghan, *History*, pp. 666–669; Antonio de la Torre, *Los Reyes Católicos y Granada* (Madrid, 1952); María Angel Ladero Quesada, *Castilla y la conquista del reino de Granada* (Seville, 1971); idem, *Milicia y economía en la guerra de Granada* (Valladolid, 1964); Felipe Fernández-Armesto, *Ferdinand & Isabella* (New York, 1975), pp. 89–105. For later medieval Castile, see Luis Suárez Fernández, "The Kingdom of Castile in the Fifteenth Century," in *Spain in the Fifteenth Century, 1369–1516: Essays and Extracts by Historians of Spain*, ed. Roger Highfield, trans. Frances M. Lopez-Morillas (New York, 1972), pp. 80–113.

[59] Archibald R. Lewis and Timothy J. Runyan, *European Naval and Maritime History, 300–1500* (Bloomington, IN: 1985), pp. 144–161.

[60] John Lynch, *Spain Under the Hapsburgs*, 2 vols. (Oxford, 1965), 1:76–79.

[61] *Cortes*, 1:450; Moxó, "Época," p. 399.

the king. Other important components were the cavalry and infantry corps provided by the Military Orders. To these forces, one had to add the support of the town militias, in particular those of the prominent border cities such as Cordoba and Seville.[62] In addition to the infantrymen provided by the town militias, there was also a great number of non-noble knights. Alfonso had taken great interest in increasing the availability of these mounted warriors. He relied to some extent on the practice of granting certain privileges to those who would voluntarily agree to equip and maintain a horse. He utilized to a much greater extent, however, the *caballería de cuantía*, which required the outfit and maintenance of a horse by anyone who possessed more than a determined amount of patrimonial wealth.[63] From all the aforementioned sectors, Alfonso certainly could have raised a substantial fighting force. Yet considering that the siege of Algeciras was a military operation of such large proportions, could he have raised a force large enough to sustain the operation and triumph? Perhaps. But there are certainly some indications that he may have needed more manpower than that provided by traditional means. First, the town militias had certainly played a large role in the past. During this time, however, not all would have participated, at least not fully. The fact remained that while Alfonso had pacified the high nobility, the towns were still subject to attacks from noble bands. Moreover, those towns located along the Christian-Muslim frontier would have had to defend against possible intrusions from the Muslims. In short, even when participating, they would have to leave contingents at home for defense. There is also the difficulty of figuring out just how numerous these militias would have been.

There are some passages in the chronicles that refer to mercenary forces. Besides the Genoese ships employed by Alfonso, he also hired groups of Genoese fighting ground forces who served as siege engineers, footsoldiers, and most importantly, as archers.[64] The passages

---

[62] For further information on the town militias, one should refer to James Power, *A Society Organized for War: The Iberian Municipal Militias in the Central Middle Ages, 1000–1284* (Berkeley, 1988) and Elena Lourie, "A Society Organized for War: Medieval Spain," *Past & Present* 35 (1966): 54–76.

[63] Moxó, "Época," p. 399.

[64] *Crónica*, pp. 350–351: *Et por esto el Rey mandó a poner en el fonsario dos trabucos de los que avian fecho en Sevilla los Gioneses . . . Et el Rey mandó que fuesen y estar gentes de los Ginoses ballesteros, et otros omes que defendiesen à los que lo posiesen, si los de la ciubdat saliesen . . . Et estando los Christianos faciendo una cava en el fonsario dó posiesen estos trabucos, los de la ciubdat salieron, ca eran muy cerca de la su barrera, et eran muchas compañas,*

do not provide information as to the exact origin of the Genoese soldiers, so it has been impossible so far to determine if they came along with the Genoese ships or on their own to fight with the ground forces. Yet their presence opens the possibility that Alfonso's use of mercenary forces may have extended well beyond hiring naval squadrons. This, in turn, would throw into doubt the argument that Alfonso's armed forces at Algeciras were drawn strictly from Castilian resources. It is important to note that the practice of hiring mercenary armies would not have been unknown to the Castilians. In fact, they were quite prominent later on during the Castilian civil war in the 1360's between Pedro I and Enrique of Trastámara (1369–1379).[65] The beginnings of such foreign mercenary involvement in Spain, however, are far from clear and require a great deal more research to understand the militarily-fluid fifteenth century which saw shifting alliance across both territorial and religious boundaries.[66] With Castile's later penchant for many different types of troops in one military action, it seems likely that the Christian force at Algeciras was "combined" one, integrating both in-grown talent, foreign crusaders, as well as mercenaries.

To conclude, the period between 1344 and 1349, the era of Alfonso XI's great reconquest victories, has not been given the attention and credit it deserves. One possible reason for this is that his victories did not produce the large territorial expansion attained by his predecessors in the thirteenth century. Since the only Muslim possessions left in the peninsula were the heavily fortified cities in the Straits of Gibraltar and the kingdom of Granada, reconquest activity took the form of longer and more costly sieges and battles with less potential for plunder. Military operations grew increasingly expensive without the great rewards of the previous centuries. That said, it is my contention that in the context of the reconquest this time period is very significant. The threat of military invasion from Morocco into the

---

et comenzaron la pelea con los Ginoeses ... Et los Ginoeses ovieran à ser vencidos; pero estaban todos muy bien armados de todas sus armas, et eran muchos dellos ballesteros, et tenian muy buenas ballestas.

[65] Estow, pp. 207–231.

[66] Julio Valdeón Baruque, "La Incidencia de la Guerra de los Cien Años en la península íberica," in Pere el Cerimoniós i la seva època, ed. María Teresa Ferrer i Mallol; Manuel Sánchez Martínez, "La Relaciones de la Corona de Aragon con los paises musulmanes en la época de Pedro el Ceremonioso," Pere el Cerimoniós, pp. 79–97.

Iberian Peninsula was eliminated. With the battle of Salado, the Marinid army was routed and scattered. With the capture of Algeciras, Castile assumed improved access to the Straits, allowing them to protect more fully their strategic and commercial interests from any North African intervention. The importance of this rests not only in delivering a series of blows to the Marinids but also in the further isolation of the kingdom of Granada, the ultimate prize in the eyes of the Castilians. Viewed in this light, the reign of Alfonso XI marks the end of an era of great Castilian expansion stretching back to the thirteenth century. The only task left was the conquest of Granada, but this would have to await another set of inspiring and canny reconquest warriors, Ferdinand and Isabella.

THE MANY CRUSADES OF VALENCIA'S CONQUEST (1225–1280): AN HISTORIOGRAPHICAL LABYRINTH[1]

Robert I. Burns, S.J.

A major historiographical problem is the reluctance of many historians to abandon beguiling general concepts and terminology that mask a very different reality. In the face of steady erosion of such concepts, they cling to the old labels. When I first began my researches into the conquest of Islamic Valencia, nearly fifty years ago, hardly any Spanish scholars thought of it as a "crusade," but rather as part of the Reconquest, a relatively secular expansion of Iberian states along their southern borders. Not even the monumental history of crusade bulls in Spain by José Goñi Gaztambide in 1958 changed this attitude.[2]

The traditional paradigm was giving way in the wider world, however, to a Mediterranean-wide view of the crusades in a number of theaters of war, not excluding the naval and corsair elements. Eventually the Spanish crusades would have their monograph even in the multi-volume, multi-author history of the crusades organized by Kenneth Setton; and Spanish crusades play a prominent role in the international Society for the Study of the Crusades. My own books and articles have relentlessly used the phrase "Crusader Valencia" in their titles.

1. *Anti-Crusade Objections*

Intimidated by these developments, some students of the conquest of the Islamic coastal regions that the crusaders called the Kingdom of

---

[1] The present article is dedicated to Professor Joseph F. O'Callaghan on his assumption of emeritus status at Fordham University. It was delivered as an address at the 110th annual convention of the American Historical Association at Atlanta, Georgia, on 6 January 1996. A companion homage to Professor O'Callaghan is my "The *Guidaticum* Safe-Conduct in Medieval Arago-Catalonia: A Mini-Institution for Muslims, Christians, and Jews," *Medieval Encounters* 1 (1995): 51–113.

[2] José Goñi Gaztambide, *Historia de la bula de la cruzada en España* (Vitoria, 1958).

Valencia have cautiously begun using the term crusade but distancing themselves by placing quotation marks around it. Unable to deny that at least in the *Cortes* of 1236 King James the Conqueror went through all the motions of taking the cross, these historians diminish the role of crusading in the king's subsequent activities or empty the term of meaning, for example by denying the war was a real crusade because it lacked international participation, or because economic motives were to the fore, or because "religious" attitudes were not worn on the crusaders' sleeves. Thus in his recent study of King James's attitude toward Muslims, Vicente García Edo concludes that "I believe that the understanding of 'crusade' must be revised, which some authors attribute to the Valencian military crusade, because surely it only bore that designation on paper, that is to say as the result of papal bulls issued *al respecto* and nothing more."[3]

Similarly Pierre Guichard's current work on the Valencian conquest puts the term crusade within quotes; his position is still that of a previous study in which he concluded that "I would hesitate to employ, as several authors have done, the term 'crusade'" for this political or national war of expansion. He also believes that "the enterprise was formally decorated with the title 'crusade' only tardily [*tardivement*], when the conquest of Valencia was largely engaged" and a 1236 crusade *Cortes* was needed to supply funds.[4] The very influential historian of the Valencian conquest Antonio Ubieto Arteta always applies 'crusade' within quotes; admitting only the formalities at the Monzón *Cortes* and its papal bull, but as tangential and ineffective.[5] It is important to counter these paradigms, left over from a traditionalist nineteenth-century historiography, with factual data

---

[3] Vicente García Edo, "Actitud de Jaime I en relación con los musulmanes del reino de Valencia durante los años de la conquista (1232–1245): Notas para su estudio," in *Ibn al-Abbar, polític i escriptor àrab valencià (1199–1260): Actes del Congrés internacional "Ibn Al-Abbar i el seu temps," Onda, 20–22 febrer, 1989* (Valencia, 1990), p. 294.

[4] Pierre Guichard, "Participation des méridionaux à la Reconquista dans la royaume de Valence," in *Islam et chrétiens du Midi (XIIᵉ–XIVᵉs.)*, Cahiers de Fanjeaux no. 18 (Toulouse, 1983), 124. The same position is strongly affirmed in his *Les musulmans de Valence et la reconquête (XIᵉ–XIIIᵉ siècles)*, 2 vols. (Damascus, 1990–1991), 2:397, 403 and notes. See 2:431 on the al-Azraq crusade: "on ne discerne, de part et d'autre, que peu de motivations religieuses, et on ne perçoit aucune ambiance de 'guerre sainte'"; on the al-Azraq crusade see below, note 8.

[5] Antonio Ubieto Arteta, *Orígenes del reino de Valencia: cuestiones cronológicas sobre su conquista* (Valencia: Anubar, 1977), ch. 4 on "La 'cruzada' contra Valencia," and revised in 1979, ch. 4, especially sections on "la 'cruzada'."

on the crusade status of the Valencian conquest and to challenge redefinitions as to what constituted a genuine crusade. In that task, the present paper has a modest scope: to show in outline that this conquest involved not only a crusade but at least seven separate crusades. The chief objections of the traditionalists also need to be briefly addressed.

A main objection is the local or "national" character of Valencia's conquest. This is no objection at all. The popes deliberately programmed and preached this local focus as wholly consonant with the essential crusading character. Honorius III wrote to Castile, on 26 September 1226, a year after King James led his first crusade into Valencia: "Though the crusade [*negotium*] against the Saracens of Spain belongs to all the faithful, because it belongs to Christ and to the Christian faith, there is no doubt that it pertains in a special way to you and the other kings of Spain since they hold your land captive, even though as an injury to all Christendom." Consequently, he reminded them that Spain's *crucesignati* were always to get the identical indulgences decreed by the ecumenical Lateran Council in 1215 for the Holy Land and extended to Spain. The collateral objection that the Holy Land theater-of-war was more attractive means little; it did indeed have a unique appeal, priority, and danger, so that the papacy in King James's century was finally urging even Spanish rulers to send money and men to that particularly threatened and particularly sacrosanct theater. But the battlefield and the enterprise were common, as the popes repeatedly stated.[6]

The Valencian crusades were formally proclaimed as such by the papacy. They were closely monitored from Rome. Indeed they were even instigated ("*ad commonitionem nostram*") as well as applauded by Rome. They involved the latest Holy Land indulgences-of-crusade, the cross-taking, vows, and crusader protections. They had their papal legates and preaching programs, enjoyed funding arrangements as subsidy, and were called by the same names as their Holy Land

---

[6] I have studied each of the papal documents cited in this paper in its archival original in the Vatican Archives' registers, as well as in the well-known series of transcriptions and abstracts of the Bibliothèque des Écoles Françaises d'Athènes et de Rome, and for many in the far more complete volumes (since 1955) of the Monumenta Hispaniae Vaticana. I have cited many in my own books on crusader Valencia; but I refrain from listing the archival or published citations here, as I have tried to minimize all citations in this interpretive essay. The dating makes each letter easy to find. The translations are my own.

counterparts. Guichard objects that the Valencian crusade did not include much foreign participation. But foreign participation was irrelevant in a crusade, as Julian Bishko and others have noted. Popes had always encouraged the Spanish kings to crusade on their own borders, to their own self-interest and with their own resources, with no thought that this attitude diminished the crusading essence of the war. In any event the Valencian crusade was widely preached along the Mediterranean littoral, and in fact did attract many foreigners. In its earliest stage, at the siege of Burriana, King James feared a brawl involving not only his own people but the "*molta altra gent que y havia estranya.*" In a later phase in the late 1240s as he prepared to move against the Muslim rebels in Valencia, the king assured his council that "when the people of our realm and of other lands know and hear" his proposal to defeat and expel those Muslims, it would not be necessary to impose army service because "our people and the others" would come spontaneously.[7] Whether or not they came did not affect the international nature of the papally proclaimed crusade that followed.

King James was not only avid for formal crusade support: he actually received more than a half-dozen crusades for his own realms, and personally projected three abortive crusades overseas. His memoirs, regulations, and charters show the double preoccupation of any crusade, that is, material rewards and religiosity involving Christendom. His communications presuppose a considerable public echoing this double concern and susceptible to manipulation by it. Even minor episodes in Valencian battle were stimulated by *ad hoc* indulgences: two hundred days for breaking down some corrals near the walls of besieged Valencia, for example, or an indulgence for soldiers to build a bridge over the Guadalaviar River. Ubieto's recent acquiescence in the term "crusade," as applicable only to the pietistic Catalan contingents (who then returned home satisfied with spiritual rewards), as against the practical Aragonese who only continued their land-grabbing secular expansion as "Reconquest," does not fit the pattern of Spanish crusades in general nor of King James's crusades. Moreover, James himself could refer proudly to his "fame" throughout Christendom as a crusader, as also did the pope who sought his advice about Jerusalem in an ecumenical council as an expert on

---

[7] The two quotes are from James I, *LF*, chaps. 178 and 365.

crusades. James's invitation to lead Italy's Guelfs also rested on that public persona which mirrored his private self-image.

Another common misapprehension is that economic advantage cancels out spiritual motivation, as though the two were mutually opposed or as though the one diminished and weakened the other. The modern mind is secularist and attributes a remote purity to whatever religious motives it recognizes in the abstract. Medieval men professed an incarnationalist religion in which personal gain and self-interest were quite compatible with piety and indeed could reinforce it. A modern American might understand the analogy of an affluent alumnus who gifts his university with a building but also profits from the action in reputation (his name on the building) and from an income-tax deduction. Historians need to ponder the phenomenon of multiple motivation. In any case, this objection proves too much, since economic gain as well as power and glory were prominent even in the Eastern crusades from the beginning without jeopardizing their status as crusades. The same observation applies to objections from the Valencian crusaders' attitude toward the Muslims there—retaining them as tenants on the farms, allying with Muslims and the like. The Eastern crusader states did the same, without doubting their own crusade nature. In both East and West there were canonical distinctions between Muslim countries allied to Christian polities by treaty or understanding and those presumably hostile at a given time.

An odd objection recognizes the merely formal status of crusade in the Spanish situation but links this rather with the wider application of crusading theory to bizarre wars against Christians, heretics, or pagans. Sidestepping the recent defenses of the latter as themselves true crusades when viewed through the perspective and all-encompassing ideology of contemporaries, the sober fact is that those expressions of crusade are outside the framework of recovering Mediterranean Christian lands from the Muslims in a single yoked enterprise.

Both Ubieto and Guichard see the crusade aspect of the Valencian conquest as a single action coming late, not affecting its secular origins and early or later progress. Ubieto puts the transformation as late as 1236, and considers it ineffectual as well. This misunderstanding derives from expecting crusades to be single large enterprises. In Spain as elsewhere in that century, the popes monitored and encouraged perpetual "defensive" raids, probes, and pressure

against Muslims; they punctuated this steady activity, in times of crisis or of signal opportunity, with programs of preaching, privilege,
and slaughter as formal crusades. In modern terms, one might say
that the constant Holy War in east and west was sporadically intensified by crusades (though such a distinction would be ours, not theirs),
or that various campaigns in a long war could each (or some) be such
formal crusades.

Papal policy saw Spain and the East as two fronts in a single war
to recover from Islam the lost lands of Christendom; their attitude
dated from the twelfth-century crusades, and recurred with popes
and councils into the thirteenth century. This constant view of a
continuing and double-headed threat was a primary Christian experience, not part of the application of "crusade" to wars against all
sorts of enemies within or on the borders of Christendom. The continuum of this Spanish crusade situation was thus enlivened by a
whole series of interrelated crusades. None of this ideological framework inhibited in theory or practice, either on the Muslim or the
Christian side, alliances or clientage between Christians and Muslims,
even against rulers of one's own party.

2. *The Valencian Crusades*

Applied to King James, this international papal activity clarifies the
Valencian experience. In the wake of signal victories by Spanish
"crucesignati" in 1217, and preparations throughout the peninsula including the realms of Aragon for another such crusade, Abū Zayd
of Islamic Valencia kept attacking the borderlands of the teenage
King James. On 15 June 1222 Pope Honorius III called on all
Christians "throughout Spain" to aid James if the Muslims mounted
a full-scale war against him, and the pope offered the usual crusade
indulgences. The Muslims were attacking with such increasing fury
"that it seems hardly possible but that open warfare should break
out." Though the attacks were "frequent" from these "contiguous"
Muslims, the crusade proclamation was provisional and in the event
not carried out. Three years later, however, on 28 April 1225 the
seventeen-year-old king announced from his southern frontier at
Tortosa that "we have taken the cross to wipe out the barbarous
nations" of Valencia. He called on his barons, prelates, and citizens
to form an army, and proclaimed a general domestic Peace. Documents

show him at the siege of Islamic Peñíscola, but he eventually had to withdraw with only a negotiated acquisition of revenue "fifths" from Abū Zayd.

After that embarrassment, James became more cautious. The papal legate Cardinal Jean d'Abbeville, in Spain for church reform and crusade direction, held secret talks with Abū Zayd in August 1228, occasioned by the Muslim's expressed desire to convert to Christianity and by the civil war in Islamic Valencia which had driven Abū Zayd into the northern part of his region. Again a crusade *Cortes* was called, a domestic Peace proclaimed, and a crusade bull published from Pope Gregory IX on 12 February 1229. At the same time in April 1228, King James signed an alliance with his erstwhile enemy Abū Zayd, committing them both to war against Zayyān, the new ruler of most of Valencia. Since the barons of upland Aragon proper preferred to first mount a crusade against the Balearic Islands, the pope phrased his call to crusade with deliberate ambiguity: "if an army happens to form against the Moors in those parts," the papal legate "is to give the usual indulgences." The chronicler Bernat Desclot, a contemporary, tells how the Aragonese barons tried to turn the crusade against Valencia, and how they had the cardinal-legate attempt to persuade the king to that effect. The Catalan party prevailed, however, and King James led his crusade against the Balearics (1229–1232).

After the initial successes and enthusiasm, Pope Gregory felt it necessary to rekindle the crusade spirit and attract fresh troops. On 28 November 1229 he issued a new bull of crusade for the Balearics, to be preached through the dioceses of the metropolitans of Arles and Narbonne in southern France under the supervision of the Dominican prior of Barcelona and the great jurist Ramon de Penyafort.

King James was already pondering another Valencia crusade; on 10 March 1232 Pope Gregory commiserated with him for not having been able yet to realize his ambition of conquering Valencia. In May and June 1233 James plunged into his Valencian project by sieging and conquering the strong city of Burriana. The sixteenth-century archival historian Zurita records that the king had consulted the pope again about a Valencian crusade, had received papal bulls, and had again taken the cross. In any case, Pope Gregory IX authorized on 9 August 1233 an international crusade of serious dimension for the Valencian project; he charged the bishop of Bordeaux as papal legate to supervise the preaching of a three-year indulgence over southern France. Even now, James announced his intention of conquering Valencia city itself. With his gains consolidated in northern Valencia, the king promulgated anew in March 1235 the usual Peace and Truce which accompanied a crusade, "as we did when we went against Majorca."

James had already commissioned a much lesser mini-crusade, separately indulgenced by Rome, against Ibiza island off Valencia's coast. The king's contract of December 1234 required the archbishop-elect of Tarragona to accomplish the conquest of Ibiza with his own fleet and resources, and within a year. The archbishop and his two partners drew up their own mutual agreement in April 1235, and had conquered and divided the island among themselves by August. It is unlikely that James's Tarragona Peace and Truce had anything to do with this limited, indeed closed, enterprise. Meanwhile domestic dissent so distracted the king from his Valencian crusade, that in April 1235 the pope had to threaten yet another crusade against the Christians hindering the crusade! James's marriage agreement that December promised his new wife's future children "whatever we have acquired and are about to acquire in the kingdom of Valencia." Having lost momentum due to dissent and delays, and with the Valencian advance entering its most dangerous phase, James now felt the need to renew the general fervor and to organize the major campaign ahead into a new crusade.

He entered into a new alliance with Abū Zayd in May 1236, and at the celebrated parliament of Monzón in October called for "an army against the Moors" to undertake "the siege and capture of Valencia city." His prelates and magnates there "assumed the cross, to conquer the kingdom of Valencia, in order to exalt the Christian faith." The truce and peace of the Majorca crusade were again proclaimed, and the usual privileges for debtors taking the cross were stressed. James had several new bulls in hand, three months later, calling for a crusade to be preached over the extensive provinces of Narbonne, Arles, Auch, and Aix with the Holy Land indulgences. Another preaching schedule covered Aragon and Catalonia. The bull of 5 February 1237 directed the papal legates and crusade preachers to secure "swift and great help" with indulgences to all who gave aid according to their means, even through personal labor. The preaching was not extended to France and England which had their own crusade forming, or to Sweden or Hungary for the same reason, and Italy and Germany were too embroiled in the wars between

Frederick II and Pope Gregory with all their factions. Far from marking the start of a Valencian crusade, this activity merely refreshed it, marking instead a military turning point. The previous three to four years, preliminary to the major accomplishments, had been as much a crusade as the eight to nine years of war now starting, with their central battle of the Puig and the great sieges of Valencia, Játiva, and Biar.

Further papal bulls protected the crusade in early 1238, as James's "great army" grew, then proclaimed the joy of Christendom when Valencia city fell, and then monitored the settlement of the new kingdom. Pope Gregory on 8 January 1239 announced the glad news to the dioceses of the ecclesiastical provinces of Auch, Aix, Arles, Narbonne, and Genoa, and to "the whole world" (*"toti mundo"*). Far from ending the formal crusade, James's success led to the announcement in early 1239 of a new preaching, this time in Genoa and over to the Pyrenees, and also in James's realms, for a crusade to consolidate and defend the gains. By the time the king announced the end of his crusade in 1245, "to the great joy of the church," the pope was inviting him to duplicate his successes in the Holy Land. Instead James announced in early 1246 his plans to help Latin Byzantium by a crusade.

If the Valencian crusade was finally over for all modern historians, it ran on unchecked for the crusader king. A Muslim revolt on the scale of a counter-crusade now led to the issuance of yet another papal crusade bull and funding on 13 November 1248, setting also a program of collecting crusade tithes (actually twentieths), for the coming three years. This crusade dragged on for the better part of a decade. Pope Innocent IV followed his 1248 bull with other letters in 1250 and 1251, promoting and protecting this crusade.[8]

By 1260 James was finally able to prepare his crusade to the Holy Land; and the pope was also asking him to send vassals to the Spanish crusades in North Africa. Instead, James soon found himself embroiled in another Muslim rebellion in Murcia on his southern border, with attendant echoes in Valencia. Rome granted a crusade first to Castile in 1264, then to King James in 1265. The several

---

[8] For this crusade, dismissed by Guichard (above in note 4), see my "The Crusade against Al-Azraq: A Thirteenth-Century Mudejar Revolt in International Perspective," *American Historical Review* 93 (1988): 80–106, and its companion-piece "A Lost Crusade: Unpublished Bulls of Innocent IV on al-Azraq's Revolt in Thirteenth-Century Spain," *CHR* 74 (1988): 440–449.

papal letters show that James's role in the Murcia crusade was not peripheral or merely auxiliary. The crusade preaching was entrusted to the supervision of the archbishop of Tarragona and the bishop of Valencia as papal legates, as was the collection of the crusade "twentieths" to fund it. The close connection of the Murcian crusade with Valencia should be stressed: Murcia constituted the southern border of the Valencian kingdom; a collateral revolt broke out among Valencia's subject Muslims; and James's primary support for this crusade came from Valencia. From the king's perspective, the Murcian war can be seen as yet another Valencian crusade.[9]

This Murcian "*croata*" over, and Valencia quiescent, James began extensive preparations in 1267–1268 for a Holy Land crusade. It sailed in 1269, but soon aborted. Five years later the king was again advising an ecumenical council on crusade policy. A year after that, as James's son prepared a Holy Land crusade, the Valencian Muslims again erupted into war, which that son would make a papal crusade within a year of James's death in 1276. This final crusade in the series involved scandal in Christendom, and investigation by a commission of foreign bishops into its expenditure of the Holy Land tithe conceded by the pope. Its formal preaching was committed to the metropolitan archbishops of Arles and Narbonne as papal legates. On 2 April 1277 Pope Gregory IX granted it the new general crusade tithe that the very recent Second Ecumenical Council of Lyons had voted for the Holy Land. Eventually this Valencian crusade would absorb 15,000 pounds of Tours, an immense sum which raised a call for auditing. As late as 1279 papal and royal correspondence was concerned with charges of fraud.[10]

None of the Valencian crusades was perfunctory or merely formal. Each has its further context of supporting documentation and

---

[9] See my article in preparation "The Murcian War: A Valencian Perspective." The novel term "crusade" was coming into use (see Goñi Gaztambide, *Bula de la cruzada*, pp. 231–233) and King James's earliest use seems to be for this war: "now, when I am having a crusade [*croatam*] preached against the Saracens of Murcia" (ACA, Cancelleria, reg. 14, fol. 76v, between entries of July 14 and September 27, 1265).

[10] I have outlined this crusade in my *Islam under the Crusaders: Colonial Survival in the Thirteenth-Century Kingdom of Valencia* (Princeton, NJ, 1973), pp. 347–352. See also my essay on "The Crusade Spirit" in chapter one ("The Church and the Valencian Frontier") of my *The Crusader Kingdom of Valencia: Reconstruction on a Thirteenth-Century Frontier*, 2 vols. (Cambridge, MA, 1967); and my "The Spiritual Life of James the Conqueror, King of Arago-Catalonia, 1208–1276: Portrait and Self-Portrait," *CHR* 62 (1976): 1–35.

its context of wider crusade policies of king and pope. That wider story, minutely documented, will be told by Christopher Michael Davis in a doctoral dissertation just completed at the University of California at Los Angeles: "The Arago-Catalan Kings and Papal Crusade Policy 1196–1276." For the basic story of Valencia's many crusades, historians must rely on randomly-surviving charters. Other crusades may have entered the continuum, their documentation now lost or later to be discovered. Enough remains, however, to show the Mediterranean-wide relevance of our Valencian crusade. In an era of failed crusades, James was a hero to the pope and to crusaders elsewhere. His had been a true crusade, an enterprise of Christendom and of several popes. With no contradiction, it had also been royal, profitable, and expansionist. Neither James nor the pope nor contemporaries saw the Valencian crusade as a basically local, merely Spanish event; they were conscious instead of its universal character.

On the other hand, the word "Reconquest" can be applied to the Valencian crusade only with caution. It is useful as signalling to the reader that the subject is medieval Spain's wars against the Muslims. It is incorrect insofar as it reflects the antiquated fantasy of eight centuries of war consciously designed to recover a lost country. It is particularly misleading when suggesting a merely secular war of gain during Europe's crusade period. It is used most exactly as a substitute or substratum for crusade, as canonists did, in the sense of a just war to "recover" from Muslims the lands lost to Islam by Christendom, including the Holy Land. The evolution and fate of post-war Christians and Muslims on the Valencian frontier was deeply affected by the universal crusade history and spirit. That spirit infused not only the military adventure but also the defensive immigration later and indeed the very psyche of the settlers acting upon the now subject Mudejars. It was an aggressive, expansionist, sometimes cruel spirit. To miss its controlling presence is to miss an essential chapter of the conquest story.

THE HYBRID TREBUCHET: THE HALFWAY STEP TO THE COUNTERWEIGHT TREBUCHET

Paul E. Chevedden

Introduction

A new type of artillery—the trebuchet—had a powerful impact on world history. The trebuchet was in active service longer than any other piece of artillery. It played an important role in warfare; it contributed to the development of the centralized state; and it influenced both the development of clockwork and theoretical analyses of motion. Developed in China between the fifth and fourth centuries BCE, it reached the Mediterranean by the sixth century CE, just in time to play a critical role in one of the greatest turning points in history: the Islamic conquest movements. Thereafter it was prominently featured in siege warfare across Eurasia and North Africa and held its own until well after the coming of gunpowder ordinance. The cannon finally supplanted it during the course of the fifteenth century, but it was resurrected in the New World in the sixteenth century for one last siege of a great city, Tenochtitlan in 1521.[1]

---

[1] This study of the trebuchet has been supported by a grant from the National Endowment for the Humanities, an independent federal agency. I thank Les Eigenbrod, Vernard Foley, and Werner Soedel of Purdue University, Donald J. Kagay of Albany State University, and Theresa M. Vann of the Hill Monastic Manuscript Library for their discussions and comments on this article. On earlier forms of artillery and their replacement by the trebuchet, see Paul E. Chevedden, "Artillery in Late Antiquity: Prelude to the Middle Ages," in *The Medieval City under Siege*, eds. Ivy Corfis and Michael Wolfe (Woodbridge, Eng., 1995), pp. 131–173.
On the development of the trebuchet in China, see Herbert Frankle, "Siege and Defense of Towns in Medieval China," in *Chinese Ways in Warfare*, ed. Frank A. Keirman, Jr. and John K. Fairbank (Cambridge, MA, 1974), pp. 151–201; Joseph Needham, "China's Trebuchets, Manned and Counterweighted," in Bert S. Hall and Delno C. West, eds., *On Pre-Modern Technology and Science: Studies in Honor of Lynn White, Jr.* (Malibu, CA, 1976), pp. 107–145; Sergej A. Skoljar, "L'Artillerie de jet a l'époque Sung," *Etudes Song*, series 1, *Histoire et institutions* (Paris, 1978), 119–142; Robin D.S. Yates, "Siege Engines and Late Zhou Military Technology," in *Explorations in the History of Science and Technology in China*, ed. Li Guohao, Zhang Mehgwen, and Cao Tianqin (Shanghai, 1982), pp. 414–419; Joseph Needham and Robin D.S. Yates, *Science and Civilisation in China*, vol. 5, *Chemistry and Chemical Technology*, pt. 6,

The trebuchet replaced tension and torsion power used in artillery of classical antiquity with human and gravity power. Three major forms of this piece of artillery developed: the traction trebuchet powered by teams of people pulling on ropes (Figure 1), the counterweight trebuchet powered by the descent of a large pivoting mass (Figure 2), and an intermediate type, the hybrid trebuchet, that utilized both gravity and human power (Figure 3). The fundamental design component in all forms was a long beam fixed on a rotating axle and mounted on a framework. The axle divided the beam into two unequal sections: a long tapering arm and a broad short arm. The butt of the beam at the end of the short arm had the pulling-ropes or the counterweight attached to it. For the hybrid machine, a combination of both arrangements was used. At the extremity of the long arm, a sling was attached which held the missile. The sling was designed to open when the beam's motion and position reached

---

Military Technology: Missiles and Sieges (Cambridge, 1994); and Yang Hong, ed., *Weapons of Ancient China* (New York, 1992).

For a discussion of the historical development of the trebuchet outside of China, the following studies are of fundamental importance: Guillaume Dufour, *Mémoire sur l'artillerie des anciens et sur celle du Moyen Age* (Paris, 1840), pp. 87–112; Louis-Napoléon Bonaparte, *Études sur le passé et l'avenir de l'artillerie*, 6 vols. (Paris, 1848–1871), 2:26–61; E.N.L. Viollet-le-Duc, *Dictionnaire raisonné de l'architecture du XIe au XVIe siècles*, 10 vols. (Paris, 1854–1868), 5:218–242; Gustav Köhler, *Die Entwickelung des Kriegwesens und der Kriegführung in der Ritterzeit von Mitte des II. Jahrhunderts bis zu den Hussitenkriegen*, vol. 3 (Breslau, 1890), pp. 139–211; Rudolf Schneider, *Die Artillerie des Mittelalters* (Berlin, 1910); Henry Yule, ed., *The Book of Ser Marco Polo, the Venetian Concerning the Kingdoms and Marvels of the East*, 3rd ed., 3 vols. (London, 1926), 2:161–169; Bernhard Rathgen, *Das Geschütz im Mittelalter* (1928; reprint, Düsseldorf, 1987), pp. 578–638; Kalervo Huuri, "Zur Geschichte des mittelalterlichen Geschützwesens aus orientalischen Quellen," in *Societas Orientalia Fennica, Studia Orientalia*, 9/3 (Helsinki, 1941); Claude Cahen, "Un traité d'armurerie pour Saladin," *Bulletin d'études orientales* 12 (1947–1948): 103–163; J.-F. Finó, "Machines de jet médiévales," *Gladius* 10 (1972): 25–43, and *Forteresses de la France médiévale: construction, attaque, défense*, 3rd ed. (Paris, 1977), pp. 149–163; Donald R. Hill, "Trebuchets," *Viator* 4 (1973): 99–115; Carroll M. Gillmor, "The Introduction of the Traction Trebuchet into the Latin West," *Viator* 12 (1981): 1–8; D.J.C. King, "The Trebuchet and other Siege-Engines, *Château Gaillard* 9–10 (1982): 457–469; Paul E. Chevedden, Les Eigenbrod, Vernard Foley, and Werner Soedel, "The Trebuchet: Recent Reconstructions and Computer Simulations reveal the Operating Principles of the Most Powerful Weapon of its Time," *Scientific American* (July 1995): 66–71; and Paul E. Chevedden, "The Artillery of King James I the Conqueror," in *Iberia and the Mediterranean World of the Middle Ages: Essays in Honor of Robert I. Burns, S.J.*, vol. 2, *Proceedings from "Spain and the Western Mediterranean": A Colloquium Sponsored by The Center for Medieval and Renaissance Studies, University of California, Los Angeles, October 26–27, 1992*, edited by P.E. Chevedden, D.J. Kagay, and P.G. Padilla (Leiden: E.J. Brill, 1996), 47–94.

On the construction of a large trebuchet at the siege of Tenochtitlan, see Hugh Thomas, *Conquest: Montezuma, Cortés, and the Fall of Old Mexico* (New York, 1993), p. 520.

the desired state for discharge. In some versions of the counterweight trebuchet—those made for launching incendiary missiles—a cup for holding the projectile replaced the sling at the extremity of the long arm. The counterweight of the gravity-powered machine was either fixed immovably to the butt-end of the beam so that it would rotate with it (Figures 4 and 5), or was hung on a hinge (Figure 2). Some trebuchets even featured a combination of a fixed and a hinged counterweight (Figure 6). The first type was said to achieve greater accuracy; the second to attain greater range. The sling of the counterweighted machine was much longer than that of the traction version, making a dramatic difference in performance.

The trebuchet was far more powerful than earlier forms of artillery. Those who witnessed a display of its destructive capabilities for the first time were stunned by its effectiveness. When the Avaro-Slavs laid siege of Thessalonica in 597, the archbishop of the city was awe-struck by the devastation wrought by a battery of fifty traction trebuchets. His eyewitness account of the artillery bombardment contains the first detailed description of the traction trebuchet in an historical work. It is also the earliest unambiguous reference to the use of the traction trebuchet in the Mediterranean region:

> These [trebuchets] were tetragonal and rested on broader bases, tapering to narrower extremities. Attached to them were thick cylinders well clad in iron at the ends, and there were nailed to them timbers like beams from a large house. These timbers had the slings from the back side and from the front strong ropes, by which, pulling down and releasing the sling, they propel the stones up high and with a loud noise. And on being fired they sent up many great stones so that neither earth nor human constructions could bear the impacts. They also covered those tetragonal trebuchets with boards on three sides only, so that those inside firing them might not be wounded with arrows by those on the walls. And since one of these, with its boards, had been burned to a char by a flaming arrow, they returned, carrying away the machines. On the following day they again brought these trebuchets covered with freshly skinned hides and with the boards, and placing them closer to the walls, shooting, they hurled mountains and hills against us. For what else might one term these extremely large stones.[2]

---

[2] The translation of this passage from the *Miracula of St. Demetrius* by John I, archbishop of Thessalonica, is taken from Speros Vryonis, Jr., "The Evolution of Slavic Society and the Slavic Invasions in Greece: The First Major Slavic Attack on Thessaloniki, AD 597," *Hesperia* 50 (October–December 1981): 384, with the following change. The term "trebuchet" is used in place of "ballistrae" for the Greek

In China, the first historical work to provide a detailed description of a traction trebuchet was written more than a century and a half following the siege of Thessalonica. It appears in Li Chhüan's *Thai Po Yin Ching*, dating from 759:

> For the trebuchet [*phao chhê*] they use large baulks of wood to make the framework, fixing it on four wheels below. From this there rise up two posts [*shuang pi*] having between them a horizontal bar [*hêng kua*] which carries a single arm [*tu kan*] so that the top of the machine is like a swape [*chieh kao*]. The arm is arranged as to height, length and size, according to the city [which it is proposed to attack or defend]. At the end of the arm there is a sling [lit. nest, *kho*] which holds the stone or stones, of weight and number depending on the stoutness of the arm. Men [suddenly] pull [ropes attached to the other] end, and so shoot it forth. The carriage framework can be pushed and turned around at will. Alternatively the ends [of the beams of the framework] can be buried in the ground and so used. [But whether you use] the "Whirlwind" [*Hsüan-Fêng*] type[3] [Figure 7] or the "Four-footed" [*Ssu-Chiao*] type[4] [Figure 8] depends upon the circumstances.[5]

---

word πετροβολος (*petrobolos*). This description of traction trebuchets at the siege of Thessalonica is expertly translated by Vryonis, leaving no doubt that the machines employed were traction powered trebuchets, but Vryonis has incorrectly translated the Greek term used for these machines, leading to a serious misunderstanding of the nature and dynamic characteristics of these siege engines. The word used for these machines, πετροβολος (*petrobolos*) or "rock-thrower," is translated by Vryonis as "ballistrae" (see above) and "catapults" (p. 384 n. 23), leaving the reader with the impression that these machines are tension or torsion catapults, rather than traction trebuchets. For the Greek text of this passage, see John I, archbishop of Thessalonica, *Miracula S. Demetrii*, ed. Paul Lemerle, *Les Plus Anciens Recueils des Miracles de saint Démétrius et la Pénétration des slaves dans les Balkans*, vol. 1, *Le Text*, vol. 2, *Commentaire* (Paris, 1979), 1:154. Lynn White, Jr., was the first scholar to draw attention to this passage as a description of a traction trebuchet (Lynn White, Jr., "Technology, Western," *Dictionary of the Middle Ages*, 13 vols., ed. Joseph R. Strayer (New York, 1982–1989), 11:660. A scholarly debate still rages over the date of the Avaro-Slavic siege of Thessalonica during Maurice's reign in the sixth century, with Lemerle, Yannopoulos, and Whitby arguing for 586 and Vryonis for 597. On this dating question, see Lemerle, *S. Démétrius*, 2:50–61; P.A. Yannopoulos, "Le pénétration slave en Argolide," *Études Argiennes* = *Bulletin de Correspondance Hellénique, Suppl.* 6 (1980): 323–371; Michael Whitby, *The Emperor Maurice and his Historian: Theophylact Simocatta on Persian and Balkan Warfare* (Oxford, 1988), 117–121; and Vryonis, "Evolution."

[3] The "Whirlwind" (*Hsüan-Fêng*) type refers to the pole-framed traction trebuchet. On this machine, see Needham, "China's Trebuchets," 109, 112, 130–132; Needham and Yates, *Science and Civilisation in China*, pp. 211–213; Chevedden, "Artillery of King James I," 58–59, 61, 64–69, and figs. 1–3, and 12.

[4] The "Four-footed" (*Ssu-Chiao*) type refers to the trestle-framed traction trebuchet. On this machine, see Needham, "China's Trebuchets," 109, 133; Needham and Yates, *Science and Civilisation in China*, pp. 211–214; Chevedden, "Artillery of King James I," 59–61, 64–67, 69–71, and figs. 4–6.

[5] Needham and Yates, *Science and Civilisation in China*, 211. The earliest descrip-

The most powerful Chinese traction trebuchet had a beam of 28 *chi* in length (8.6 m). This beam, made up of seven wooden (or perhaps bamboo) spars lashed together with rope or bound with metal bands, was mounted on top of a trestle frame that stood 21 *chi* in height (6.5 m). Attached to the butt-end of the beam were 125 pulling ropes that were hauled down by a crew of 250 men. The machine was capable of throwing a stone-shot weighing between 90 and 100 catties (between 53.7 and 59.7 kg) a distance of more than 50 *pu* (77 m).[6] As impressive as this performance was, the hybrid trebuchet far surpassed the traction machine in launch capabilities.

The Hybrid Trebuchet

The transition from the traction to the counterweight trebuchet took considerable time, due to the very success of the traction machine itself, the conservatism in engineering design that prevailed in the pre-modern era, and the difficulties involved in harnessing gravity power. The idea of adding additional weight to the butt-end of the beam of a traction machine to give it more power does not appear to require great inventiveness. The butt-end itself was weighted with a framework for holding the pulling-ropes, and by experiment artillerists probably learned that a weighted butt-end enhanced the power

---

tion of a trebuchet is found in *Mozi* (Book of Master Mo), a technical treatise produced during the fourth century BCE by Mohist tacticians of the Warring States period. The fragmented and corrupt state of the surviving text of this treatise has rendered analysis and interpretation of it extremely difficult. Professor Robin Yates has painstakingly reconstructed the description of a traction trebuchet found in chapter fourteen of the treatise. A machine is described as having a rotating-beam of 30 to 35 feet in length (9.1 to 10.6 m) mounted on a horizontal axis supported upon two uprights. The uprights, which were anchored in the ground, stood 13 ft. (4.0 m) above the surface. The ratio between the short and long arms of the rotating beam was 1:3 (rotating beam: 10 m; long arm, 7.5 m; short arm, 2.5 m). Ropes were attached to the short arm of the beam and a pouch two feet 8 inches long (0.81 m) was fastened to sling cords and attached to the extremity of the long arm (Yates, "Siege Engines and Late Zhou Military Technology," 416–417; a reconstruction of the Mohist trebuchet is given in figs. 2–3, p. 417). Yates has translated the Chinese word for "pouch" (literally, "horse's jowls") in this description as "sling." This misreading has led him to conclude that the sling of the machine, consisting of a pouch and two sling cords, was only two feet 8 inches long (0.81 m). On this important text, see also Needham and Yates, *Science and Civilisation in China*, 207–210.

[6] These quantitative data, taken from the *Wu Ching Tsung Yao* of 1044, are presented in Yang Hong, *Weapons of Ancient China*, p. 266.

of the machine. Even Ibn Urunbughā's illustration of the small pole-framed traction trebuchet known as the ʿarrādah is shown with a weight on the butt-end of the beam (Figure 9). "The fixed counter-weight was such a simple idea," declared Joseph Needham, "that its development only towards the end of the + 12th century seems sur-prisingly late, especially as the ancient water-raising machine, proto-type of all *phao* [trebuchets], had always had it."[7] An opposing point of view has been offered by Donald Hill:

> At first sight, it may seem surprising that the counterweight trebuchet was not developed, as an effective engine of war, before the end of the twelfth century. After all, not only did military engineers have the example of the traction trebuchet as a spur to their inventiveness, but they could also have been inspired by watching the action of the *shādūf*—the counterweighted irrigation device. The traction trebuchet, however, is a simpler machine, while the *shādūf* does not operate at high velocity. What is in fact surprising, when one comes to consider the dynamics of the counterweight trebuchet, is that it ever became a useful engine of war at all. The engineer, Muslim or Christian, who constructed the first effective machine of this type deserves our unquali-fied respect.[8]

Even though the use of gravitational force seems simple, it took great inventiveness to proceed along a different design path and much practical skill, technical training, and experimentation to produce an effective gravity-assisted machine. There was nothing inevitable about the appearance of the hybrid or the counterweight trebuchet. The long interval of time between the emergence of these forms of artillery suggests that these machines were the product of a succession of innovations. The high performance standards achieved by the trac-tion trebuchet could even have discouraged efforts to improve the efficiency of the machine. The story of Columbus's egg may have much to tell us about the invention of the hybrid machine. Someone had to demonstrate how to accomplish the feat first before others would imitate the achievement.[9] But human inventiveness was not

---

[7] Needham and Yates, *Science and Civilisation in China*, p. 218.

[8] Hill, "Trebuchets," 108.

[9] In 1493, after Columbus had returned to Spain from his first voyage to the New World, private banquets were held in his honor. The famous episode of "Columbus's egg" presumably took place at one of these banquets. William D. Phillips, Jr., and Carla Rahn Phillips recount the story as told by Girolamo Benzoni in 1572: "Another guest at the feast challenged the importance of Columbus's voy-age by suggesting that anyone might have done the same. Columbus responded by

the only ingredient required for the development of the hybrid trebuchet. A proper social, political, technological, and economic environment had to be created that would allow such changes to occur. Such
an environment was present in South-West Asia and the Mediterranean during the period of the Islamic conquest movements.

The hybrid machine represents a critical step in the development
of the trebuchet. For the first time the force of gravity was used to
radically amplify the muscular force of the pulling crew of the machine
in order to assist in the discharge of a projectile. The next leap forward in trebuchet design came when gravity power completely replaced
the pulling crew. This innovation was prepared by many centuries of
utilization of gravitational force made possible by the hybrid machine.
Thus, the hybrid machine played an important role in the development of the counterweight trebuchet, the most powerful form of pre-
gunpowder artillery invented.

Despite more than a century and a half of research devoted to
the trebuchet, the hybrid trebuchet has escaped scholarly notice. This
machine was probably developed in the realms of Islam by the early
part of the eighth century under the impetus of the conquest movements. It can now be shown that although China invented the trebuchet, it was Islamic civilization that vastly improved the performance
of this machine. The most powerful hybrid trebuchet could launch
stone-shot more than three times heavier than that discharged by
the most powerful Chinese traction trebuchet. A comparison of the
quantitative data on the trebuchet from the region of South-West Asia
and the Mediterranean with quantitative data from China appears to
indicate that the hybrid machine was transmitted to China during

---

taking an egg and asking if anyone could make it stand on end. After various
guests had tried and failed, Columbus took the egg and set it sharply on the table,
crushing the shell slightly and leaving the egg standing in place." The moral of the
story was clear for all to see: tasks that look difficult or even impossible become
easy once someone has found the way to master them. There is no proof that the
episode of Columbus's egg ever happened, of course, but apocryphal stories have
lives of their own, precisely because they demonstrate truths that transcend the
specific event (*The Worlds of Christopher Columbus* [Cambridge, Eng., 1992], p. 190).
The truth demonstrated by the story of Columbus's egg is applicable to the development of the hybrid trebuchet: the invention of a more powerful trebuchet by utilizing the force of gravity appears simple only because someone devised a way to
do it. The hybrid machine went through centuries of development before an exclusively gravity-powered trebuchet appeared. Again, human invention showed the way.
Only in retrospect can this achievement, like Columbus's voyage, be viewed as an
ordinary or inevitable accomplishment.

the twelfth century (see below). Since it is a well-known fact that the counterweight trebuchet made its way to China during the thirteenth century from South-West Asia, the development of the trebuchet—from traction to hybrid to counterweight forms—and the diffusion of this machine across the wide expanse of Eurasia and North Africa provides one of the most dramatic illustrations of multiculturalism in the field of technology.[10]

The existence of the hybrid trebuchet has been suspected by scholars but never confirmed. Viollet-le-Duc did not believe that muscular force alone was sufficient for the successful operation of trebuchet artillery, so he reconstructed all trebuchets with counterweights. He remade every traction trebuchet he encountered in the historical sources into a hybrid machine, having a fixed counterweight and pulling-ropes.[11] Recently, Rogers has suggested that there is evidence for the existence of a "transitional device" that was "both man-pulled and possessed a fixed counterweight." Rogers is definitely referring to our hybrid machine, but the evidence he presents for the existence of this machine—a trebuchet carved in stone in the Church of Saint-Nazaire in Carcassonne (Figure 10) and the trebuchets depicted in the "Maciejowski Bible" (Figure 11)—is not conclusive. These machines may be interpreted as traction trebuchets. The best evidence for the existence of the hybrid machine is to be found in historical sources.[12]

The most detailed description of a hybrid trebuchet comes from an Arabic account of the "Fifth" Crusade that depicts a machine used

---

[10] The trebuchet, the principle artillery piece used in Eurasia and the Mediterranean world for more than a millennium, can claim an impressive multicultural legacy. Not only was it used throughout a good part of the Old World, but peoples originating outside Eurasia and North Africa also became acquainted with its use. The most striking example of this is the widespread employment of trebuchets by East African slaves in their rebellion against the 'Abbāsid Empire during the second half of the ninth century (255–269/868–882) (Muḥammad b. Jarīr al-Ṭabarī, *Ta'rīkh al-rusūl wa-al-mulūk (Annales)*, ed. M.J de Goeje et al., 15 vols. [Leiden, 1879–1901], 3:1982, 1983, 2003, 2004, 2042, 2054, 2055, 2058). The African rebels, known in Arabic sources as the Zanj (pl. Zunūj), utilized the most sophisticated military technology of the day, including trebuchets, to oppose the might of the 'Abbāsid Empire in the very heartland of its domain, southern Mesopotamia. The development of the trebuchet—from simple to more complex and powerful forms—represents one of the greatest examples of multiculturalism in the sphere of technology. Its development was the collective achievement of many civilizations across the Eurasia and North Africa.

[11] Viollet-le-Duc, *Dictionnaire raisonné*, 5:220, 233–240.

[12] Randall Rogers, *Latin Siege Warfare in the Twelfth Century* (Oxford, 1992), pp. 268–269.

by the crusaders against Damietta in 1218 having a lead box weighing two Syrian *qinṭārs* (370 kg) fixed to the butt-end of the beam. This machine employed a pulling-crew of 600 men and launched stone-shot weighing one Syrian *qinṭār* (185 kg).[13]

Such machines were used much earlier than the thirteenth century, however. Two Armenian accounts of the siege of Manzikert in 1054 by the Seljuq sultan Ṭoghrïl Beg Muḥammad describe an immense trebuchet, referred to by the term *baban*. It weighed fifteen *ʿadïls* (1,875 to 2,250 kg) and had a pulling-crew of 400 men. This machine launched stone-shot weighing between 111 and 200 kg.[14] With a pulling-crew of 400, this machine was certainly traction-powered, but its size and launch capabilities suggest that it was most likely a hybrid

---

[13] Sawīrus b. al-Muqaffaʿ, *History of the Patriarchs of the Egyptian Church*, ed. and trans. Y. ʿAbd al-Masīḥ and O.H.E. Burmester, 4 vols. (Cairo, 1942–1974), 3, pt. 2:218, 129 (Arabic text).

[14] Matthew of Edessa, *Patmutʿiwn* (Jerusalem, 1869), 142–145; and *Armenia and the Crusades, Tenth to Twelfth Centuries: The Chronicle of Matthew of Edessa* (Lanham, 1993), pp. 87–88; Aristakes Lastivertcʿi, *Patmutʿiwn Aristakisi Lastivertsʿwoy* (Erevan, 1963), pp. 92–93; and *Aristakes Lastivertcʿi's History*, trans. Robert Bedrosian (New York, 1985), pp. 103–105. Aristakes Lastivertsʿi states that the *baban* launched stone-shot weighing 60 *litra*s. If the unit of weight used by Lastivertsʿi is equivalent to the Byzantine *litra* of roughly a third of a kilogram, the weight of the stone-shot comes to about 20 kg, far too light for such an enormous piece of artillery. The *litra* employed by this author may not be a Byzantine measure of weight. The eleventh-century *litra* used by Armenians in eastern Anatolia may be related to the Arabic *raṭl*, not the Byzantine *litra*. In regions that had regular contact with Islamic lands, such as Cyprus and Trebizond, "a special *argyrike* (silver) *litra* of 12.5 *logarikai oungiai* (= 333 g) existed alongside the other units. It was apparently related to the Arab *raṭl* of 337.6 g. In the later period various 'pounds' of local circulation were in use, partly of Arab, Italian, or Turkish origin" (*Encyclopedia of Byzantium*, ed. Alexander P. Kazhdan, 3 vols. [New York, 1991], s.v. Litra). Lastivertsʿi's *litra* cannot be related to the heavier *argyrike* (silver) *litra*, since the weight of the stone-shot would still be too light (20.25 kg). It could be related to a larger Arabic *raṭl*; the Syrian *raṭl*, for example is equivalent to 1.85 kg. If it is equivalent to the Syrian *raṭl*, the weight of the 60-*litra* stone-shot would be 111 kg, a weight that a large hybrid trebuchet could manage. Ernest A.W. Budge noted in his translation of *The Chronography of Bar Hebraeus* that six *lîtrê* Syrian was equivalent to one *lîtrâ* Babylonian (Gregorius Bar Hebraeus, *The Chronography of Gregory Abū'l Faraj, the Son of Aaron, the Hebrew Physician Commonly Known as Bar Hebraeus*, ed. and trans. Ernest A.W. Budge, 2 vols. [London, 1932], 1:394). If we assume that the Syrian *lîtrê* was roughly equivalent to the Byzantine *litra* (a third of a kilogram), then a Babylonian *lîtrâ* would be roughly equivalent to a Syrian *raṭl* (1.85 kg.). An alternative interpretation is scribal or editorial error: 60 *litra*s should be read as 600 *litra*s. This is exactly how Huuri interpreted the text and came to an approximate weight of 200 kg for 600 *litra*s (Huuri, "Geschützwesen," 170). Stone-shot of such enormous weight could be launched by hybrid trebuchets. The hybrid machine used by the crusaders against Damietta in 1218 launched stone-shot weighing one Syrian *qinṭār* (185 kg).

model. Ṭoghrïl had this machine brought to Manzikert from Bitlis where it had been installed at least thirty years earlier by the Byzantine emperor Basil II (976–1025). Hence, there is little doubt that the Byzantines were familiar with the hybrid machine and probably put it to use during the military resurgence of the empire from the mid-ninth to the early eleventh century, which saw the reconquest of the Balkans, northern Syria, and Crete.

During the reconquest of Crete in 960–961, a live ass was hurled over the walls of Chandax (Heraklion) to the starving Muslim inhabitants inside.[15] The animal may not have been full-grown (an adult Asian ass can weigh up to 290 kg), but the launching of an ass of any size would seem to suggest the use of a hybrid trebuchet.

The very large trebuchet reported in the siege train of the Byzantine emperor Romanos IV Diogenes, just prior to the battle of Manzikert in 1071, is also most likely a hybrid machine. It is described as being transported in 100 carts pulled by 1,200 men and having a composite beam of eight spars. Stone-shot launched from it weighed 96 kg.[16] Each "ring" (ḥalqah) of the machine, according to Sibṭ b. al-Jawzī, weighed 200 Syrian raṭls (375 kg).[17] Such a heavy component of the trebuchet must have been used as the counterweight of the machine. It was doubtless made of iron, and its ring-shape permitted it to be fastened to the butt-end of the beam of the machine. Two such rings, utilized as counterweights, can be seen on a trebuchet illustrated in the *Cantigas de Santa Maria* (Figure 4).[18]

There is substantial evidence for the use of the hybrid machine by Islamic armies in the ninth century. At this time a new technical term is used in Arabic sources for artillery—the "big" trebuchet (*manjanīq kabīr*)—indicating the introduction of a new type of trebuchet, the hybrid model. This conjecture is supported by evidence indicating the remarkable launching capabilities of this machine. At

---

[15] Theodosios Diaconos, *Theodosii Diaconi de Creta capta*, ed. Hugo Criscuolo (Leipzig, 1979), 28, v. 718ff. Huuri, "Geschützwesen," 91, estimates the weight of the ass to be between 120 and 200 kg.

[16] Al-Fatḥ ibn ʿAlī al-Bundārī, *Ẕubdat al-nuṣrah wa-nukhbat al-ʿuṣrah*, ed. M.T. Houtsma, *Recueil de textes relatifs à l'histoire des Seljoucides*, vol. 2 (Leiden, 1889), 42.

[17] Sibṭ b. al-Jawzī, *Mirʾāt al-zamān fī taʾrīkh al-aʿyān: al-ḥawādith al-khāṣah bi-taʾrīkh al-Salājiqah bayna al-sanawāt 1056–1086* (Ankara, 1968), p. 148.

[18] This illustration shows a trebuchet with a fixed counterweight consisting of two rings mounted on the butt-end of the beam (El Escorial, Biblioteca de San Lorenzo el Real, MS T.I.1, *Cantigas de Santa Maria*, fol. 43r, cantiga 28c). The illustration is published in Gonzalo Menendez Pidal, *La España del siglo XIII: Leida en imagenes* (Madrid, 1986), p. 268; and Chevedden, "Artillery of James I," fig. 12.

the siege of Amorion in 223/838, sheep skins stuffed with earth were hurled by "big" trebuchets (*majānīq kibār*) into the ditch surrounding the town in order to fill it up so that digging-mantlets (*dabbābāt*) could be moved up to the wall.[19] The weight of these earth-filled sheep skins must have been quite heavy, probably in the range of 100 to 150 kg. Since such heavy objects are not likely to have been launched by simple traction trebuchets, the Arabic accounts of the siege of Amorion provide indirect evidence for the use of the hybrid machine by Islamic armies during the first half of the ninth century. References to trebuchets being used to fill in the ditch of a fortress or a walled city are rare. It is not until the sixteenth century that trebuchets are again mentioned as being put to such a use. In his classic treatise on technology, entitled *Le diverse et artificiose machine*, Agostino Ramelli recommends the use of counterweight trebuchets "to help fill the ditch of a fortress or other like place[s] by throwing into it various barrels or sacks full of earth, bales of wool, bundles of sticks, rocks, and other such things."[20] The successful employment of trebuchets to fill the ditch of a fortified complex required the use of machines that were capable of launching loads of great weight. Only hybrid or counterweight trebuchets had sufficient power to perform such a task.

The identification of the "big" trebuchet (*manjanīq kabīr*) with the hybrid machine is further strengthened by the connection this term has with the Armenian term for the hybrid trebuchet. Among the "big" trebuchets (*majānīq kibār*) used in the defense of Baghdad in 251/865 was one called *al-ghaḍbān* (The Furious One).[21] A corruption of this name, *baban*, is the very term used in Armenian sources to refer to the trestle-framed hybrid trebuchet.[22] Aristakes Lastiverts'i

---

[19] Ṭabarī, *Ta'rīkh*, 3:1247–1248, also 1238, 1245; and *Kitāb al-ʿuyūn wa-al-ḥadāʾiq*, ed. M.J. de Goeje (Leiden, 1871), p. 491.

[20] Agostino Ramelli, *The Various and Ingenious Machines of Agostino Ramelli: A Classic Sixteenth-Century Illustrated Treatise on Technology*, trans. Martha Teach Gnudi (New York, 1987), ch. 190 (p. 516).

[21] *Kitāb al-ʿuyūn wa-al-ḥadāʾiq*, 580; Ṭabarī, *Ta'rīkh*, 3:1541, 1551, 1552, 1559, 1560, 1561, 1578, 1579, 1583, 1584, 1597, 1621, 1626.

[22] See above n. 14 and text. For references to *baban* in Armenian historical sources, see Appendix 1 and Matthew of Edessa, *Patmutʿiwn* (Jerusalem, 1869), pp. 142–145, 177, 231, 235, 303, 306, 448, 452, 454, 465; and *Armenia and the Crusades, Tenth to Twelfth Centuries: The Chronicle of Matthew of Edessa* (Lanham, 1993), pp. 87–88, 103, 128, 131, 162, 163, 232, 233, 235, 241; Aristakes Lastivertsʿi, *Patmutʿiwn Aristakisi Lastivertsʿwoy* (Erevan, 1963), pp. 92–93; and *Aristakes Lastivertcʿi's History*, trans. Robert Bedrosian (New York, 1985), pp. 103–104.

notes that the Seljuqs also employed this term.[23] *Al-Ghaḍbān*, which had been used as a name for a particular hybrid machine, developed into a generic term for this class of artillery. At the siege of Acre in 1291, the term was still in evidence. One of the trebuchets used by the Muslims, according to Gerard de Montreal, "had the name *Haveben*, meaning furious."[24] In 1291 the term most likely referred to a counterweight, rather than a hybrid, trebuchet. If so, *al-ghaḍbān* began its life at the siege of Baghdad in 251/865 as a name for a specific hybrid trebuchet and was subsequently used as a generic term for any large trebuchet, designating first the hybrid machine and later the counterweight machine. A somewhat similar phenomenon can be seen in the Latin West. At the crusader siege of Acre in 1191, the chief trebuchet of Philip II Augustus was called Mal Voisin (Bad Neighbor).[25] This same name was used by Simon de Montfort for his chief trebuchet (*petraria*) at the siege of Minerve in 1210.[26]

There is suggestive, rather than substantial, evidence for the existence of the hybrid trebuchet prior to the ninth century. The enormous trebuchet named "The Bride," that was used with great effect in 708 during the Muslim conquest of Sind (Pakistan), may have been a hybrid model.[27] There is no direct evidence for this, but a comparison of the data available on the number of people making up the pulling crews of both traction and hybrid trebuchets indicates that large pulling crews are associated with the hybrid machine. Historical sources indicate that crews numbering as many as 400 to 600 people were used to operate hybrid machines.[28] The trebuchet called "The Bride" utilized an extremely large pulling-crew of 500

---

[23] Aristakes, *Patmutʿiwn*, p. 92; and *Aristakes Lastivertcʿi's History*, p. 103.

[24] Gerard de Montreal, *Les Gestes des Chiprois*, in *Recueil de chroniques françaises*, ed. Gaston Raynaud (Geneva, 1887); quoted in Andreas D'Souza, "The Conquest of ʿAkkā (690/1291): A Comparative Analysis of Christian and Muslim Sources," *Muslim World* 80 (July–October 1990): 242.

[25] Ambroise, *L'Estoire de la Guerre Sainte*, ed. G. Paris (Collection de Documents Inédits sur l'Histoire de la France; Paris, 1897), vv. 4,745.

[26] William of Tudela and anonymous, *La Chanson de la croisade Albigeoise*, ed. Eugène Martin-Chabot, 3 vols. (Paris, 1931–1961), 1:114–115; and *The Song of the Cathar Wars: A History of the Albigensian Crusade*, trans. Janet Shirley (Aldershot, 1996), p. 33; and Peter of Vaux-Cernay, *Historia Albigensis*, eds. P. Guébin and E. Lyon, 3 vols. (Paris, 1926–1939), 1:156. Other references are to be found in DuCange, *Glossarium*.

[27] Aḥmad b. Yaḥyá al-Balādhurī, *Futūḥ al-Buldān*, ed. Michael Jan De Goeje (Leiden, 1866), pp. 436–447.

[28] See nn. 13 and 14 above and text.

men. By comparison, the largest recorded pulling-crew for a traction trebuchet numbered 250 men. It is reasonable to suggest, therefore, that the trebuchet known as "The Bride" was a hybrid machine, and that such machines were most likely developed in the Islamic world by the early eighth century under the impetus of the conquest movements.

The Islamic conquest movements provided a great stimulus for the development of military technology. The Muslims were quick to appropriate new technologies and tactics and made extensive use of the military and engineering skills of subject peoples. They employed sophisticated artillery (the trebuchet) and quickly adopted Byzantine nautical technology and naval warfare tactics.[29] The conquests spurred innovations in weaponry and tactics by creating a social, political, technological, and economic environment that promoted military advances. Incendiary weapons, for example, were radically improved during the course of the Islamic conquests, leading to important changes in naval warfare.[30] Given the importance of artillery in the Islamic conquests, it is most likely that considerable effort was made to enhance the power of stone-projectors. Improvements in the design

---

[29] The trebuchet was known in Arabia prior to the career of the prophet Muḥammad, and the conquest movements which he began made extensive use of this formidable siege machine, utilizing the technical expertise of native Arabians— particularly Yemenīs—and that of the conquered peoples to construct and operate this new artillery. For references to the use of the trebuchet in the Islamic conquest movements, see Chevedden, "Artillery of King James I," 58 n. 27, and 60 n. 29. Foreign assistance in the construction of trebuchets is noted in the important conquest of al-Madā'in in 16/637, and such help in the construction and operation of siege machines, particularly trebuchets, was probably relied upon heavily (al-Ṭabarī, *Ta'rīkh*, 1:2428). In 97/716, a master-carpenter from Paphlagonia in Anatolia was employed to construct a large traction trebuchet used against Synnada (Theodor Nöldeke, "Zur Geschichte der Araber im 1. Jahrhundert d. H. aus syrischen Quellen," *Zeitschrift der Deutschen Morgenländischen Gesellschaft* 29 [1875], 93–94). In 128/746 al-Ṭabarī makes note of a man from Bukhāra who made and set up trebuchets (*manjanīq*) for the army of Juday' b. al-Kirmānī besieging Naṣr b. Sayyār in Marw. He established proof of his work and was promptly paid for his service (al-Ṭabarī, *Ta'rīkh*, II, 1931; Huuri, "Geschützwesen," 146). On the adoption of Byzantine nautical technology and naval warfare tactics, see V. Christides, "Naft, 2. In the Medieval Byzantine and Arab-Islamic Worlds," *EI²*, 7:884–886.

[30] A native of Syria, by the name of Kallinikos, perfected Greek fire. After accomplishing this feat, he fled the realms of Islam for the Byzantine capital where his new device was employed with devastating effect at the Muslim siege of Constantinople from 674 to 678. This weapon was quickly adopted by the Muslims who put it to use during the conquest of Sind and at the siege of Constantinople of 717–718 (Harry Turtledove, trans., *The Chronicle of Theophanes* [Philadelphia, 1982], pp. 52–53; and V. Christides, "Naft, 2. In the Medieval Byzantine and Arab-Islamic Worlds," *EI²*, 7:884–886).

of the traction trebuchet quite likely resulted in the development of the hybrid machine at this time.

The Hybrid Trebuchet in the Latin West

In 873 Charles the Bald used "new and excellent" kinds of machines (*nova et exquista machinamentorum genera applicantur*) against the Danes at the siege of Angers.[31] These machines were first interpreted as counterweight trebuchets by Viollet-le Duc, who suggested that they had been acquired from Byzantium.[32] Gillmor interpreted these machines as traction trebuchets and concluded that such machines made their first appearance in the Latin West during the ninth century.[33] Huuri had confirmed the use of the traction trebuchet by Muslim armies in the western Mediterranean during the eighth century.[34] This finding was accepted by Needham and Yates who proposed, on the basis of philological evidence examined by Huuri, that the traction trebuchet was known in realms of Byzantium during the seventh century and was diffused westward from eastern Europe.[35] Evidence now confirms that the traction trebuchet was used in the eastern Mediterranean as early as the sixth century.[36] It did not take long for this

---

[31] Regino of Prüm, *Chronicon*, ed. F. Kurze, in *Scriptores rerum germanicarum in usum scholarum ex Monumenta Germaniae Historica* (Hannover, 1890), p. 106.

[32] Viollet-le-Duc, *Dictionnaire raisonné*, 5:220. Lot and Riché also advanced the view that these machines were counterweight trebuchets (Ferdinand Lot, *L'art militaire et les armées au Moyen Âge en Europe et dans le Proche Orient*, 2 vols. [Paris, 1946], 1:222; Pierre Riché, *Daily Life in the World of Charlemagne*, trans. Jo Ann McNamara [Philadelphia, 1978], p. 80). The idea that the trebuchets used by Charles the Bald at the siege of Angers were constructed by Byzantine engineers is repeated by J.-F. Finó (Finó, "Machines de jet médiévales," 27–28). While this is certainly plausible, there is no textual evidence for this assertion.

[33] Gillmor, "Traction Trebuchet," 6.

[34] Huuri, "Geschützwesen," 54–57.

[35] Needham and Yates, *Science and Civilisation in China*, pp. 233–234. Needham and Yates also suggest that the traction trebuchet was introduced into western Europe "from Arab practice" in the late ninth century (*Science and Civilisation in China*, Table 5: "Artillery Systems in Different Ages in East and West," p. 238).

[36] See above n. 2 and text for the use of the traction trebuchet by the Avaro-Slavs at the siege of Thessalonica in 597. The Avaro-Slavs acquired the use of the traction trebuchet from a captured Byzantine soldier. In exchange for his life, this soldier constructed a traction trebuchet for the Avaro-Slavs, referred to as an *helepolis* ("city-taker"), which was instrumental in capturing the fortress of Appiaria in Moesia Inferior (in northern Bulgaria) in 587 (Theophylact Simocatta, *History*, ed. C. de Boor, re-ed. P. Wirth [Stuttgart, 1972], 2.16.1–11; and *The History of Theophylact Simocatta: An English Translation with Introduction and Notes*, trans. Michael Whitby and

machine to reach the western shores of the Mediterranean. Julian of Toledo, writing around 675, recorded the use of trebuchets (*fundibulae*) by King Wamba (672–680).[37] During the early part of the seventh

---

Mary Whitby [Oxford, 1986], pp. 65–66). Michael Whitby's dismissal of Simocattes's story regarding the acquisition of the trebuchet by the Avaro-Slavs is not convincing. He suggests that the Avars, which he describes as a cavalry nation, were responsible for introducing the traction trebuchet into Europe. This conjecture finds no historical support (Michael Whitby, *The Emperor Maurice and his Historian: Theophylact Simocatta on Persian and Balkan Warfare* [Oxford, 1988], p. 118). If the Avaro-Slavs attained knowledge of the traction trebuchet from a captured Byzantine soldier in 587, the Byzantines were doubtless making full use of this machine prior to this date. In the early seventh century, Persia's sweeping successes against the Byzantine Empire were accomplished with the aid of the traction trebuchet, and the Avaro-Slavs made use of this machine again in great numbers when they besieged Constantinople in 626. On the siege of Jerusalem, see G. Garitte, *La Prise de Jérusalem par les Perses en 614*, CSCO, vols. 202, 203, *Iber.*, 11, 12 (Louvain, 1960), VIII.3 and 5; and *Expugnationis Hierosolymae AD 614: Recensiones arabicae*, CSCO, vols. 340, 341, *Ar.*, 26–27 (Louvain, 1973), A.VIII.3–5; B.VIII.3–5; *ibid.*, CSCO, vols. 347, 348, *Ar.*, 28–29 (Louvain, 1974), C.VIII.5; V.VII.1, VIII.3–5. On the siege of Constantinople, see *Chronicon Paschale*, ed. L. Dindorf, *Corpus Scriptorum Historiae Byzantinae* (Bonn, 1832), p. 719; Theodore Syncellus, *Analecta Avarica*, ed. L. Sternberg (Cracow, 1900), pp. 306, 308, 311, 312, 313; F. Barisic, "Le siège de Constantinople par les Avares et les Slaves en 626," *Byzantion* 24 (1954): 382; A. Stratos, "The Avars' Attack on Byzantium in the Year 626," *Byzantinische Forschungen* 2 (1967): 370–376; B.C.P. Tsangadas, *The Fortifications and Defense of Constantinople*, East European Monographs, 71 (Boulder, Co., 1980), 83–94. The Byzantine counter-offensive, led by Herakleios, also made use of the trebuchet. At the siege of Tiflis in 624, according to Mousēs Dasxuranc'i, the Byzantines "surrounded the town like mountains with their four-wheeled balistra [i.e., traction trebuchets, not catapults] and divers other weapons built by Roman engineers with which they unerringly hurled enormous boulders to breach the walls" (Mousēs Dasxuranc'i, *The History of the Causasian Albanians by Movses Dasxuranci*, trans. C.J.F. Dowsett [London, 1961], p. 85).

[37] Julian of Toledo, *Historia Wambae regis*, ed. W. Levison, in *Sancti Iuliani Toletanae sedis episcopi opera, pars I*, vol. 115 of *Corpus Christianorum, Series Latina* (Turhnolt, 1976), chapt. 18, pp. 233–34. *Fundibulum* and its vernacular cognates were commonly used to refer to the trebuchet. This term is derived from *funda* ("sling") and *-bula*, the feminine substantive denoting instruments or agents. It literally means an instrument having a sling. In the Western Mediterranean, this term appears to have originally designated the trestle-framed traction trebuchet. Only later, when other terms for the trebuchet came into use, did *fundibulum* come to refer to the pole-framed traction trebuchet. A Latin-Arabic word list produced in Spain in the eleventh century gives the Latin equivalent of ʿarrādah (the pole-framed trebuchet) as *fundibalarium* (C.F. Seybold, ed., *Glossarium latino-arabicum ex unico qui exstat codice leidensi undecimo saeculo in Hispania conscripto* [Berlin, 1890], p. 208; Huuri, "Geschützwesen," 130). Albert of Aachen, writing in the mid-twelfth century, defines *fundibulum* as a small *mangenella* (*fundi-bulis aut parvis mangenellis*) (Schneider, *Artilleris des Mittelalters*, p. 59). Presumably this author is distinguishing between the two basic types of traction trebuchets: the small pole-framed machine is identified as a *fundibulum* and the larger trestle-framed machine is designated as a *mangenella*. The Catalan cognate of *fundibulum*, *fenèvol*, retained the original meaning of the Latin term and referred to a trestle-framed machine (Chevedden, "Artillery of James I," 69–71).

century, Isidore, bishop of Seville (c. 570–636), had referred to the traction trebuchet (*fundibulus*) in his *Etymologiae*.[38] Throughout the course of the eighth and ninth centuries, the traction trebuchet was used in many parts of the western Mediterranean and the Latin West: Cavadonga in 717,[39] Toulouse in 721,[40] Avignon in 737,[41] Qābis in 742,[42] Benevento in c. 750,[43] Toledo in 761,[44] Syburg in

---

[38] Isidore equated the traction trebuchet (*fundibulus*) with the two-armed stone-projecting torsion catapult (*ballista*), the most powerful artillery piece of classical antiquity (Isidore, *Etymologiarum*, ed. W.M. Lindsay, 2 vols. (Oxford, 1911), bk. 18, chapt. 10). By the fourth century this stone-projector had been replaced by the onager, and in the sixth century the onager was superseded by the traction trebuchet. By likening the *fundibulus* to the defunct ballista in terms of its "hurling and throwing" capabilities, Isidore was presenting new information on artillery to suit the realities of his own day. Medieval texts of Vegetius likewise present new information on artillery to conform to circumstances of a later period. The *fundibulus*, or traction trebuchet, was the principal artillery piece of Isidore's day. This term does not refer to the *fustibalus* (staff-sling), or to the onager, the one-armed torsion machine of late antiquity, as suggested by Bruhn de Hoffmeyer, but to the traction trebuchet (Ada Bruhn de Hoffmeyer, *Arms and Armour in Spain: A Short Survey*, vol. 1 [Madrid, 1972], pp. 95, 141).

[39] The *Chronicle of Alfonso III* states that *fundiuali* (*fundabali*) were used by the Muslims in the battle of Cavadonga in 718, by which in Asturian tradition Pelagius was able to secure a decisive victory over the army of one of the Arab governors, which effectively insured the independence of the tiny Christian kingdom (*Crónicas Asturianas*, eds. Juan Gil Fernández, José L. Moralejo, Juan Ruís de la Peña [Oviedo, 1985], pp. 128–129).

[40] The *Cronica Mozarabe de 754* records that al-Samḥ b. Mālik al-Khawlānī came to attack Toulouse and surrounded it with a siege, trying to overcome it with trebuchets and other types of machines (*fundis et diuersis generum macinis*) (*Cronica Mozarabe de 754: edición crítica y traducción*, ed. Eduardo López Pereira [Zaragoza, 1980], pp. 84–85). The term *funda* (sling), like *fundibulum*, designates here a traction trebuchet. The Greek term σφενδονη (sling), may also refer to a trebuchet (Theodosios Diaconos, *Theodosii Diaconi de Creta capta*, ed. Hugo Criscuolo [Leipzig, 1979], 28, v. 718ff.).

[41] J.T. Reinaud, *Muslim Colonies in France, Northern Italy, and Switzerland*, trans. Hāroon Khān Sherwānī (Lahore, 1954), p. 74: "Carolus urbem aggreditur, muros circumdat in modum Hierico cum strepitu hostium et sonitu tubarum cum machinis et restium funibus super muros et aedium maenia irruunt, urbem succendunt, hostes capiunt, interficiuntes trucidant." The traction trebuchets used in this siege are identified as "machines" (*machinis*) and "slings of rope" (*restium funibus*). Since the "machines" and the "slings of rope" are said to have attacked over the walls and hit houses in the city, they are doubtless artillery. I would like to thank Donald J. Kagay for translating this passage.

[42] Khalīfah ibn Khayyāt al-ʿUṣfurī, *Taʾrīkh khalīfah Ibn Khayyāt*, ed. Suhayl Zakkār, 2 vols. (Damascus, 1967), p. 531.

[43] Paul the Deacon states that the Byzantines used a *petraria* to hurl the head of a captured Lombard emissary into Benevento (Paul the Deacon, *Historia Langobardorum*, in *Monumenta Germaniae Historica: Scriptores rerum Langobardicarum* [Hannover, 1878], 5:148, and *History of the Lombards*, trans. William D. Foulke [Philadelphia, 1974], p. 221). The medieval Latin term *petraria* and its romance cognates (OF *perrier* and *perrière*, Cast. *pedrero*, It. *petriere*) are derived from the Latin *petra* or the French *pierre*

776,[45] Zaragoza in 782,[46] Narbonne in 793, Ifranjah in 793,[47] Barcelona in 802–803,[48] Tortosa in 808–809,[49] Léon in 846,[50] Soria (Sūryah) in 868,[51] Salerno in 871,[52] and Syracuse in 877–887.[53] The machines

---

and refer to a "rock-thrower." This term is analogous to the Greek terms βετροβολος (petrobolos) and τετραρέα (tetrarea), which both mean "rock-thrower," and designates the trestle-framed trebuchet.

[44] Ibn al-Athīr, al-Kāmil fī al-taʾrīkh, ed. C.J. Tornberg, 13 vols. (Beirut, 1965), 5:528; Aḥmad ibn ʿAbd al-Wahhāb al-Nuwayrī, Nihāyāt al-ʿarab fī funūn al-adab, ed. Muḥammad Abū al-Faḍl Ibrāhīm, 31 vols. to date (Cairo, 1964–), 23:340.

[45] In the siege of the castle of Syburg, the Saxons, we are told, did more damage to themselves with their trebuchets (petrariae) than they did to those inside the castle (Annales regni Francorum, 741–829, ed. F. Kurze, Scriptores rerum germanicarum in usum scholarum ex MGH [Hannover, 1895], p. 44; Bernhard W. Scholz, trans., Carolingian Chronicles: Royal Frankish Annals and Nithard's Histories [Ann Arbor, 1970], p. 53).

[46] Akhbār majmūʿah fī fatḥ al-Andalus, in Colleccion de Obras Arábigas de Historia y Geografía, vol. 1 (Madrid, 1867), 1:115; Ibn al-Athīr, al-Kāmil, 6:68; al-Nuwayrī, Nihāyāt al-ʿarab, 23:348.

[47] Abū al-ʿAbbās Aḥmad b. Muḥammad Ibn ʿIdhārī al-Marrākushī, al-Bayān al-mughrib fī akhbār al-Andalus wa-al-Maghrib, ed. G.S. Colin and Lévi-Provençal, 3 vols. (Leiden, 1948–1951), 2:64.

[48] Prior to the expedition against Barcelona in 802–803 conducted by Charlemagne's son Louis, Charlemagne issued a capitulary which listed the equipment to be transported by the army on a siege campaign. The equipment included fundibulae, as well as ammunition for the artillery: stone-shot transported by twenty pack-horses (Capitularia regum Francorum, ed. Alfred Boertius and Victor Krasue, MGH Leges 2.1, no. 77 [Hannover, 1883], chs. 9, 10). On this important capitulary, see Bernard S. Bachrach, "Military Organization in Aquitaine under the Early Carolingians," Speculum 49 (January 1974): 28.

[49] The account of this siege in the biography of Louis the Pious entitled, Vita Hludowici, introduces a new term for the trebuchet, manganum (Vita Hludowici, in MGH SS, 2:615; A. Cabaniss, trans., Son of Charlemagne: A Contemporary Life of Louis the Pious (Syracuse, 1961), p. 48; Huuri, "Geschützwesen," 54; Gillmor, "Traction Trebuchet," 6). Manganum is derived from the Greek μαγγανον. Before counterweight trebuchets were introduced, manganum was used by some authors to refer to the trestle-framed traction trebuchet and by other authors to indicate the single pole-framed traction trebuchet. In the fifteenth century manganum was used by some authors to refer to various types of counterweight trebuchets. The term appears as mangonibus in the Vita Hludowici and is listed along with rams, sheds, and other engines used by Louis in his successful siege of Tortosa in 808–809.

[50] Ibn ʿIdhārī, Bayān, 2:88; Ibn al-Athīr, al-Kāmil, 7:24; al-Nuwayrī, Nihāyāt al-ʿarab, 23:385.

[51] Ibn ʿIdhārī, Bayān, 2:100.

[52] The Chronicon Salernitanum, written around 980, records that a Muslim petraria destroyed a tower on the city walls of Salerno during the siege of 871 (Chronicon Salernitatum, ed. Ulla Westerbergh [Stockholm, 1956], pp. 169–170, ch. 164).

[53] The letter of Theodosius to Leo the Deacon describes the 877–887 siege of Syracuse by the Muslims. Trebuchets, identified anachronistically as catapults (catapultarum), launched exceptionally large stones and destroyed a tower located next to one of the city gates. After five days of bombardment these trebuchets destroyed the city wall adjoining this tower (De expugnatione Syracusarum, ed. L.A. Muratori, Rerum italicarum scriptores 1.2 [Milan, 1725], pp. 259–260).

used at Angers, identified as both "new" and "excellent," cannot be simple traction trebuchets, which had been used in western Europe since the seventh century. The new evidence for the existence of the hybrid trebuchet suggests that the *machinae* employed at Angers were hybrid models. Their use at Angers on the Loire river in northern France in 873 indicates that knowledge of advanced artillery spread quickly throughout the Mediterranean and Europe during the ninth century.

Abbo of Saint-Germain-des-Prés was the first to provide a description of the hybrid trebuchet in the Latin West. This description is found in *De bello parisiaco*, Abbo's long Latin poem about the Norse siege of Paris in 885–886. Abbo was an eyewitness to the siege, and his description of the hybrid trebuchet identifies the basic component parts of the machine. During the siege, Abbo relates that the Franks prepared beams for machines identified as *mangana*. Each beam had a big weight and from the extremity of the beam extended an iron "tooth" or prong, required for the release of the sling. These beams were mounted on trestle frames appropriately described as "a pair of upright frames of equal length." The full account reads:

> Our men prepared for action beams each with a great weight and each having an iron prong at its topmost extremity, so as to knock out the machines of the Danes more quickly. With a pair of upright frames of equal length (*longis aeque lignis geminatis*) they built machines which are called in the vernacular *manganum* from which they threw huge stones, and in throwing them, they crushed the low mantlets (*humiles scaenas*) of the savage people. They often shattered the skulls of these unfortunate men, and they destroyed many Danes and many of their shields.[54]

This brief description has elicited many interpretations, but the most plausible one is that the *manganum* described here is a trestle-framed

---

[54] Abbo, *Le Siège de Paris par les Normands*, ed. and trans. Henri Waquet (Paris, 1942), 1.360–367 [pp. 42–43]): "Magno cum pondere nostri/ Tigna parant, quorum calibis dens summa peragrat,/ Machina quo citius Danum quisset terebrari/ Conficiunt longis aeque lignis geminatis/ Mangana quae proprio vulgi libitu vocitantur;/ Saxa quibus jaciunt ingentia, sed jaculando/ Allidunt humiles scaenas gentis truculentae. Sepe quidem cerebrum cervice trahunt elegorum,/ Vah! multosque terunt Danos, plures quoque peltas." The English translation was provided by Donald J. Kagay. Waquet's translation of this passage, cited above, is translated into English and discussed by David Hill in his article, "Siege-craft from the Sixth to the Tenth Century," in *De Rebus Bellicis*, pt. 1, *Aspects of the "De Rebus Bellicis"*, ed. M.W.C. Hassall (Oxford, 1979), p. 115. For a discussion of this passage, see Gillmor, "Traction Trebuchet," 2–5.

hybrid trebuchet. The beam of the machine is described as having a huge weight, indicating the use of gravitational force. Both Waquet and Hill have interpreted the phrase, *magno cum pondere . . . tigna*, as referring to heavy pieces of wood.[55] Gillmor has translated the phrase literally as "beams with a heavy weight" but has failed to see the implications of this interpretation for the existence of the hybrid trebuchet. She has conjectured that "Abbo may have indicated that a crew was lifting the rock to be hurled into a sling," or he "could have referred to the act of loading with rocks or other heavy materials the receptacle which functioned as the counterweight."[56] Köhler thought the machine was torsion powered, while Schneider contended that it was a trebuchet. Waquet and Lot interpreted the machine as a counterweight trebuchet.[57] Because of an error in translation, Schneider attributed the use of the *manganum* to the Norse and suggested that the Danes first introduced the trebuchet to the Latin West.[58]

Finó did not believe the account offered sufficient information to verify the existence of trebuchet artillery in the ninth century, but he equated the phrase, *conficiunt longis aeque lignis geminatis*, with wooden beams of equal length joined together.[59] Rogers, likewise, concluded that "Abbo's eyewitness account cannot be used to confirm any specific form of artillery at the siege of Paris."[60] Gillmor, however, maintained that the machine was a simple traction trebuchet. She translated the phrase, *conficiunt longis aeque lignis geminatis*, as "double beams of equal length," and concluded that it referred to "a single composite beam resting on a fulcrum."[61] Similarly, Contamine rendered this phrase as, "beams of equal length bound together."[62] The interpretation of *lignis geminatis* as a composite beam composed of two spars dates at least as far back as Dufour's study of artillery

---

[55] Abbo, *Le Siège de Paris*, p. 43; Hill, "Siege-craft from the Sixth to the Tenth Century," 115.

[56] Gillmor, "Traction Trebuchet," 3.

[57] Abbo, *De bello parisiaco*, p. 43; Lot, *L'art militaire*, 1:222.

[58] Köhler, *Entwickelung*, pp. 154–155; Schneider, *Die Artillerie des Mittelalters*, pp. 60–62.

[59] Finó, "Machines de jet médiévales," 28.

[60] Rogers, *Latin Siege Warfare*, p. 255, uses Abbo's description of the hybrid trebuchet to illustrate "the source problems involved in ascertaining precisely which kind of artillery was used in the early and the central Middle Ages."

[61] Gillmor, "Traction Trebuchet," 3.

[62] Contamine, *War in the Middle Ages*, p. 105.

published in 1840.[63] The use of the word *geminatis*, meaning "twofold," "double," "twin," or "coupled," to qualify *lignis* suggests that the author is referring to the two uprights of a trestle frame which are paired together to support the axle of the trebuchet on which the throwing arm of the machine is mounted. In such a brief description, it would be unusual for a medieval author to focus on a secondary detail of the machine (e.g., the composite throwing arm) and ignore the basic structural configuration of the engine. It seems fair to conclude that Abbo has provided a description of the machine by indicating its main components: a vertically pivoted beam with a fixed counterweight mounted on a trestle frame.[64]

The evidence indicating the employment of the traction trebuchet as early as the seventh century in the Latin West, and the use of the hybrid trebuchet during the ninth century undermines Schneider's conjecture that there was a period from the fifth to the ninth century during which artillery was not used in western Europe.[65] This evidence also demolishes a view held by other scholars that the transition from ancient to medieval artillery was delayed in the Latin West until the ninth century.[66] The new evidence also refutes a popular, and prevailing scholarly, notion that the artillery employed during the early Middle Ages was primitive and ineffective.

Technical Terminology of the Traction and Hybrid Trebuchets

When the traction trebuchet was introduced to South-West Asia and the Mediterranean in the sixth century, the nomenclature for the

---

[63] Dufour, *Mémoire sur l'artillerie*, pp. 96–97.

[64] Needham and Yates interpreted *lingnis geminatis* as referring to "two high posts between which presumably swung the trebuchet arm" and hence considered this component of the machine to be a trestle frame (Needham and Yates, *Science and Civilisation in China*, 233).

[65] Schneider, *Artilleris des Mittelalters*, pp. 1–26.

[66] Gillmor and other scholars contend that there is a chronological gap in the evidence for the existence of the trebuchet in the Latin West. Gillmor does indicate, however, that this gap is philological in nature (Gillmor, "Traction Trebuchet," 1–2, 7). A philological gap, however, does not necessarily indicate a real gap. There are definitely gaps with regard to the appearance of specific terms for the trebuchet in the Latin West during the early Middle Ages. There are no gaps in Western European sources with respect to references to the trebuchet during this period. Many terms were used to designate the trebuchet, such as: *ingenium, fundibulum, funda balearis, machina, manganum, manganellum, petraria*, and *tormentum*. On these terms, see Huuri, "Geschützwesen," 53–62.

machine was established on the basis of its framework, reflecting Chinese practice.[67] The nomenclature denotes the most obvious design feature of the machine: its framework. This component consisted either of a single pole (fixed to a cruciform base or set in the ground) or a trestle.

In Arabic, the term ʿarrādah (pl. ʿarrādāt) was used to designate the small pole-framed trebuchet, while the term manjanīq (pl. majāniq, manājīq, manājanīq, and majanīqāt) was used to identify the larger trestle-framed machine. The Arabic technical literature on the trebuchet provides further evidence to support the thesis that the technical terminology of the trebuchet is related to the configuration of the machine's frame. Al-Ṭarsūsī identified three trestle-framed traction trebuchets (sing. manjanīq) in his military manual, all differentiated on the basis of each machine's distinctive trestle frame. The Arab trebuchet (al-manjanīq al-ʿarabī) had a trapezoidal trestle frame, the Persian or Turkish trebuchet (al-manjanīq al-fārisī wa-huwa al-turkī) a triangular frame shaped in the form of the Greek letter lambda, and the Christian or Frankish trebuchet (al-manjanīq al-rūmī wa-huwa al-ifranjī) a trestle frame in the shape of an isosceles triangle.[68]

In Greek, the nomenclature of the trebuchet was also related to the machine's frame. The Strategikon of Maurice, dating from the early seventh century, employed μηχανη (mēchanē) as a generic term to refer to heavy artillery or to siege engines of any type,[69] μαγγανον (manganon) to refer to the pole-framed trebuchet,[70] and πετροβολος (petrobolos) to

---

[67] See nn. 3 and 4 and text.

[68] See Chevedden, "Artillery of James I," 61 and figs. 4, 5, and 6. The lambda-shaped, trestle-framed trebuchet is identified in Chinese sources as the "crouching-tiger" trebuchet (hu tun phao). On this machine, see Needham, Gunpowder Epic, pp. 21–22, 277–278, and fig. 74.

[69] George T. Dennis and Ernst Gamillscheg, eds., Das Strategikon des Maurikios (Vienna, 1981), 10.1.11 (p. 336). The word mēchanē is a very loose term. Campbell has studied the many and varied meanings given to it in classical antiquity, which include artillery of all types, cranes, scaling ladders, battering rams, mobile siege towers, flame-throwers, and mantlets (Duncan B. Campbell, "Auxiliary Artillery Revisited," Bonner Jahrbücher, 186 [1986]: 126–128). To this long list of devices which the term mēchanē encompasses can now be added the crossbow (see Chevedden, "Artillery in Late Antiquity," 143–144).

[70] Manganon, from which manganikón is derived (see below), originally meant a means for charming or bewitching others and came to be applied to the trebuchet, a device which bewitched others by its power or was deemed to have magical properties because of its power (Henry G. Liddell and Robert Scott, A Greek-English Lexicon [Oxford, 1968], s.v., μαγγαν-ov; Yule, Marco Polo, 2:164). The term is not derived from μοναγκων (monangkōn), or "one-arm," the name given to the one-armed

refer to the trestle-framed trebuchet.[71] The *Taktika* of Leo VI, compiled in c. 905, used μαγγανικον (*manganikon*) as a generic term for heavy artillery,[72] αλακατιον (*alakation*) to designate the pole-framed machine,[73] and τετραρεα (*tetrarea*) to refer to the trestle-framed machine.[74] The tenth-century treatise of Constantine VII Porphyrogennetos, *De ceremoniis*, employed two terms to designate the pole-framed trebuchet—μαγγανικον (*manganikon*) and ειλακ[α]τιῶν (*eilak[a]tiōn*)—and two terms to refer to the trestle-framed machine—τετραρεα (*tetrarea*) and λαβδαρεα (*labdarea*).[75] The *tetrarea* had a trestle frame in the shape of an equilateral or isosceles triangle, while the *labdarea* had a frame in the shape of the Greek letter *lambda*.

In the Latin West, a variety of terms were used to refer to the trebuchet in both Latin and the European vernaculars, but a clear terminological dichotomy is evident prior to the advent of the counterweight trebuchet, based upon the configuration of the machine's frame. The differences in terminology for artillery in medieval European sources reflect a pluralism of language, not a pluralism of forms of artillery. Medieval authors utilized vocabulary of classical and later Latin, vernacular terminology, and foreign loan words to desig-

---

torsion machine of classical antiquity, the onager, as was suggested by Jähns and recently advocated by Schmidtchen (Max Jähns, *Handbuch einer Geschichte des Kriegswesens* [Leipzig/Berlin, 1878–1880], p. 472; Volker Schmidtchen, "Militärische Technik zwischen Tradition und Innovation am Beispiel des Antwerks: Ein Beitrag zur Geschichte des mittelalterlichen Kriegswesens," in *Gelêrter der arzenîe, ouch apotêker: Beiträge zur Wissenschaftsgeschichte. Festschrift zum 70. Geburtstag von Willem F. Daems*, ed. Gundolf Keil [= *Würzburger medizinhistorische Forschungen*, 24], [Pattensen, Hannover, 1982], 120). *Manganon* passed into medieval Latin as *manganum* (dim., *manganellum*), from which numerous European venacular cognates were spawned, and from the form *manganikón*, this term passed into Arabic via Aramaic as *manjanīq* (Franz Blatt, ed., *Novum glossarium mediae latinitatis ab anno DCCC usque ad annum MCC*, s.v., *manganum* and *manganellum*; *Oxford English Dictionary*, s.v., *mangonel*; *EI²*, new ed., s.v., *mandjanīq*). The term μαγγανον (*manganon*) is used three times in the *Strategikon* of Maurice to designate devices which may be interpreted as machines used for siege warfare other than artillery (*Strategikon* 10.3.8 [p. 342]; 10.3.15 [p. 344]; 10.4.8 [p. 346]); it is twice used to refer to artillery advanced by besiegers against a city (*Strategikon* 10.3.40 [p. 346], 10.3.23–24 [p. 344]); and, in one case it is used to refer to artillery used defensively on the top of towers (*Strategikon* 10.3.21 [p. 344]).

[71] *Strategikon* 10.1.52 (p. 430), 10.1.55 (p. 340), and 10.3.8–9 (pp. 342–344).

[72] Leo VI, *Leonis imperatoris tactica*, in *Patrologiae cursus completus, series graeco-latina*, ed. J.-P. Migne, vol. 107, 669–1120 (Paris, 1848), 5.7, 5.8, 6.27, 14.83, 15.27; Huuri, "Geschützwesen," 84–86 n. 3.

[73] Leo VI, *Tactica*, 5.7, 6.27, 14.83, 15.27; Huuri, "Geschützwesen," 84–86 n. 3.

[74] Leo VI, *Tactica*, 15.27; Huuri, "Geschützwesen," 84–86 n. 3.

[75] Constantine VII Porphyrogenniti, *Constantini Porphyrogeniti imperatoris De ceremoniis aulae byzantinae*, ed. J.J. Reiske, 2 vols. (Bonn, 1829–1830), 1:670, 671, 672; Huuri, "Geschützwesen," 77 n. 4, 86.

ILLUSTRATIONS
1–11

1. The city of Naples, defended by Richard, count of Acerra, is besieged by King Henry VI of Germany in 1191. Henry's army bombards the city with stone-shot launched from a pole-framed traction trebuchet. The machine is operated by a pulling-crew of eight knights and a "shooter" holding the sling. The defenders prepare to launch stone-shot from a similar machine mounted on a tower. Peter of Eboli, *Liber ad honorem Augusti*. Bern, Burgerbibliotek, cod. 120 II, fol. 109r.

2. A hinged counterweight trebuchet from *Bellifortis*, a treatise by Conrad Kyeser of Eichstätt which was left incomplete at his death in 1405. The main beam, counterweight box, sling, projectile, windlass and framework are all clearly visible. The machine has some of its dimensions numbered; the long arm of the beam is forty-six feet, and the short arm eight. The prong at the end of the long arm, which is essential for the release of the sling, is not depicted. Instead, both cords of the sling are incorrectly shown as being attached to a ring at the extremity of the long arm. This massive machine used a simple peg-and-hole catch-and-trigger device to retain and release the beam. A hole is drilled in the base of one of the triangular trestles of the machine, shown in the foreground, for the insertion of the peg. A restraining rope, attached to the base of the other triangular trestle is drawn over the long arm of the beam at a point just above the windlass and is looped over the bottom end of the peg. When the peg is lifted out of its socket, the looped end is released, and the beam flies free. Trebuchet beams were often banded circumferentially with iron (as shown in the illustration), or lashed with rope, to help withstand splitting. This type of machine was identified in Arabic historical sources as the Western Islamic trebuchet (*manjaniq maghribi*). Germany, Göttingen, Niedersächsische Staats- und Universtätsbibliothek, Cod. MS philos. 63, fol. 30r.

3. A pole-framed hybrid trebuchet bombarding a fortification. It has a fixed counterweight on the butt end of its beam and is operated by a single man. From *Avis aus Roys*, an anonymous manual of instruction for kings and princes written and illuminated in France (probably Paris) about the middle of the fourteenth century. New York, The Pierpont Morgan Library, MS M.456, fol. 127r.

4. Muslim siege of Constantinople as depicted in the *Cantigas de Santa Maria* (c. 1280). Figures 4 and 5 form a narrative sequence. This illustration shows a trebuchet (foreground L.) in the process of assembly. Its rotating beam with a fixed counterweight is being mounted on the trestle frame of the machine. The chief engineer is guiding the axle bearings of the rotating beam onto the journal blocks surmounting the two trestles. Behind the counterweight trebuchet is a "hand-trebuchet," operated by a single man. This traction machine consists of a forked beam, pivoted on a horizontal axis that is supported by a single pole-frame. The pulling rope, attached to the frame of the machine, passes around a pulley affixed to the forked end of the beam, giving the puller a mechanical advantage. *Cantigas de Santa Maria*, 28c. Escorial, MS T.I.1, fol. 43r.

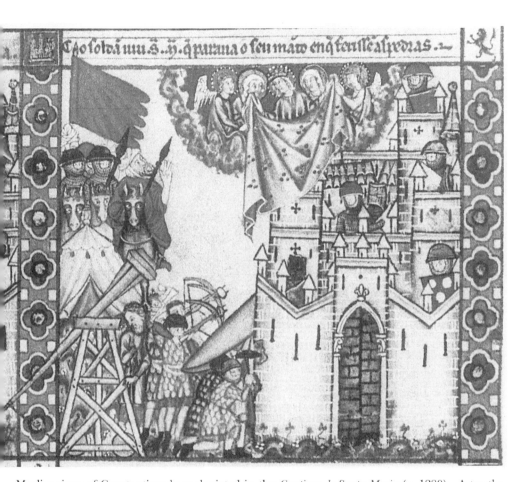

. Muslim siege of Constantinople as depicted in the *Cantigas de Santa Maria* (c. 1280). A trestle-framed counterweight trebuchet (foreground L.) is being prepared for discharge while massed crossbowmen are about to unleash a barrage of bolts to clear the battlements of defenders. Under mantlet, sappers, wearing close-fitting *cervellières* and scale cuirasses, dislodge stones from the city wall. The tent encampment (shown above the trebuchet as a form of perspective) has "behind" it heavy armored cavalry in European-style equipment, led by two Muslim commanders in turbans. Mary intervenes in the siege and uses her mantle, held by two saints and two angels, to protect the city from bombardment. Protective screens, suspended from the battlements of city walls and castles, were widely used in the pre-gunpowder era throughout Eurasia and North Africa to shield fortifications from bombardment. *Cantigas de Santa Maria*, 28d. Escorial, MS T.I.1, fol. 43r.

6. A trestle-framed counterweight trebuchet having a fixed and a hinged counterweight. In front of the trebuchet is a cat-castle (*chat-chastel*), a combination of a "cat" or mantlet (here equipped with a ram) and a "castle" or mobile siege-tower. From Paolo Santini's *Tractatus*, 1470-75. Paris, Bibliothèque Nationale, Codex Latinus 7239, fol. 109r.

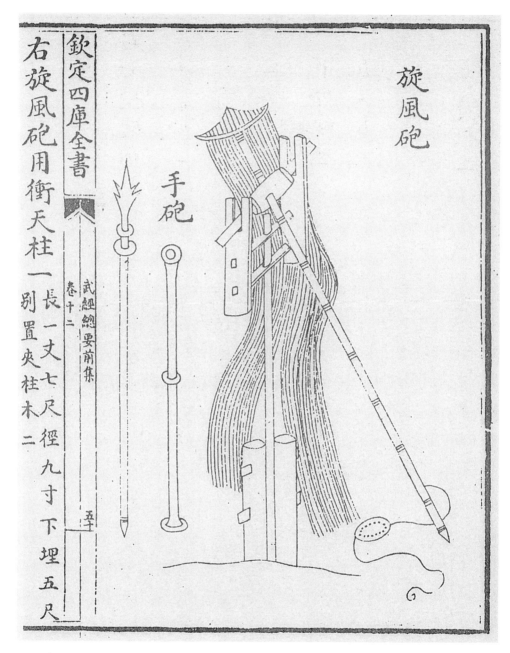

旋風砲

手砲

欽定四庫全書

武經總要前集

卷十二

五十

右旋風砲用衝天柱一長一丈七尺徑九寸下埋五尺別置夾柱木二

7. *Center*: The Chinese pole-framed trebuchet called a "Whirlwind" (*hsüan-kêng*) machine because it could be turned to face any direction. According to the Chinese military treatise *Wu Ching Tsung Yao* ("Collection of the Most Important Military Techniques"), completed in 1044, this trebuchet had a beam of 5.5 m in length mounted on top of a pole-frame that stood 5.2 m in height. Attached to the butt-end of the beam were forty pulling ropes that were hauled down by a crew of fifty men. The machine was capable of throwing a stone-shot weighing 1.8 kg a distance of more than 77m. *Left*: The Chinese "hand-trebuchet," operated by a single man. A pole, fixed in the ground, carried a pin at its topmost extremity which acted as a fulcrum for the arm of the machine. Tsêng Kung-Liang, ed., *Wu Ching Tsung Yao (Chhien Chi)*, ch. 12, p. 50a.

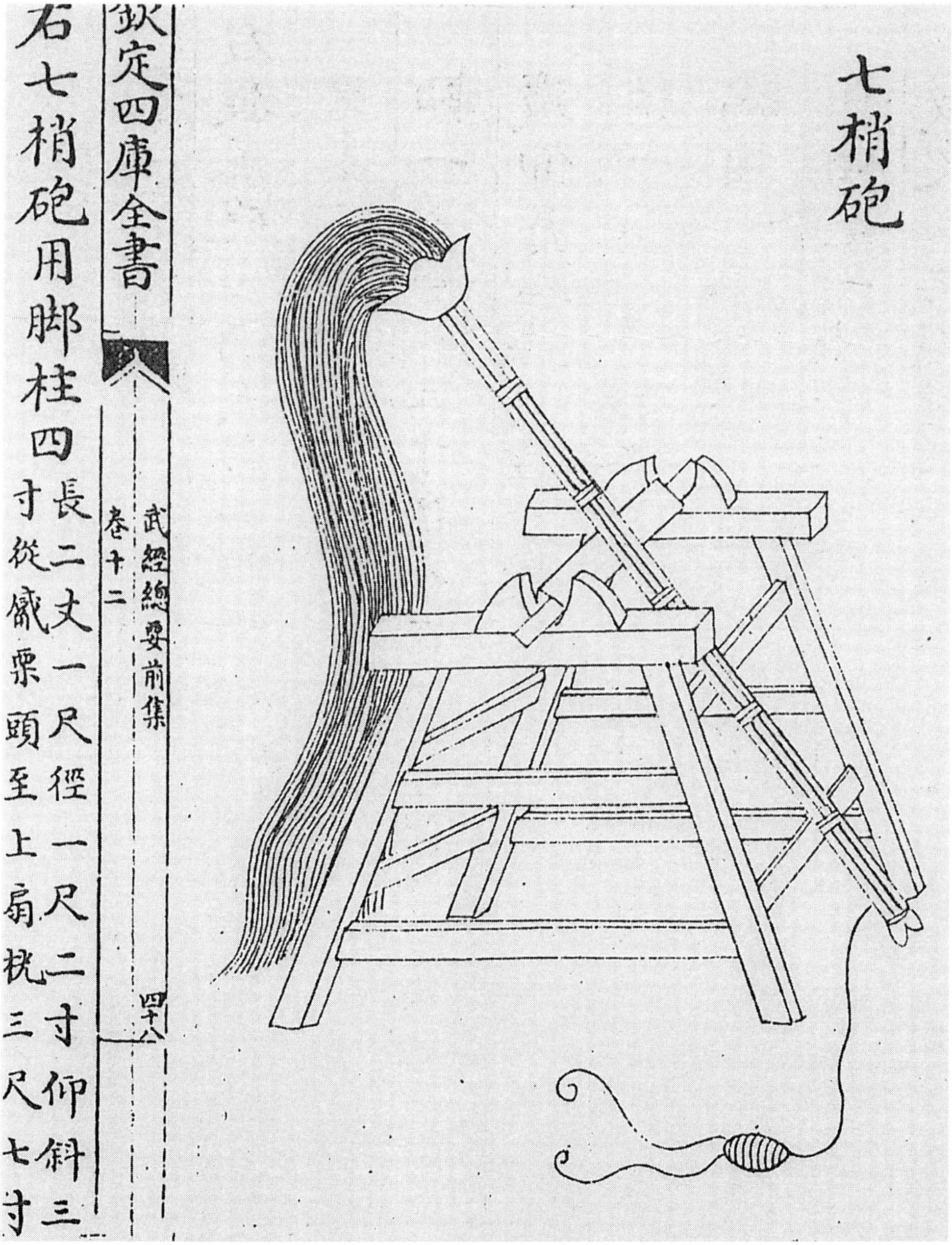
七梢砲
欽定四庫全書
武經總要前集
卷十二
四十八
右七梢砲用脚柱四
長二丈一尺徑一尺二寸仰斜三
寸從
栗頭至上扇枕三尺七寸

8. The Chinese "four-footed," or trestle-framed, trebuchet with a composite beam of 8.6 m made up of seven wooden (or perhaps bamboo) spars lashed together with rope or bound with metal bands. The beam was mounted on a trestle frame that rose to a height of 6.5 m. The butt-end of the beam had 125 pulling ropes attached to it that were hauled down by a crew of 250 men. This machine was capable of throwing a stone-shot weighing between 53.7 and 59.7 kg a distance of more than 77 m. Tsêng Kung-Liang, ed., *Wu Ching Tsung Yao (Chhien Chi)*, ch. 12, p. 48a.

The Pole-framed Trebuchet

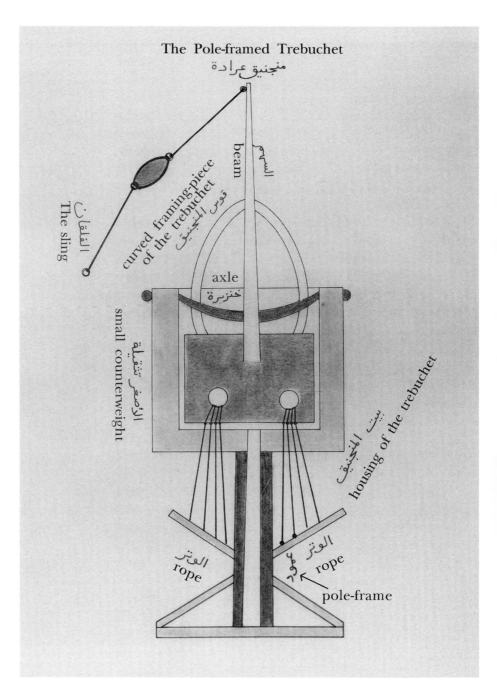

منجنيق عرّادة

beam السهم

The sling القلطة

curved framing-piece of the trebuchet قوس المجنيق

axle خنزيرة

small counterweight الثقل الصغير

housing of the trebuchet بيت المجنيق

rope الوتر

rope الوتر

pole-frame

9. The single pole-framed traction trebuchet (*manjanīq ʿarrādah*), illustrated in Ibn Urunbughā al-Zaradkāsh's *Kitāb anīq fī al-manājanīq* (867/1462-63). A small counterweight is fixed to the butt-end of the rotating beam of this machine to enhance its power. After *Kitāb anīq fī al-manājanīq*, MS 3469/1, Ahmet III Collection, Topkapı Sarayı Müzesi Kütüphanesi, Istanbul, fol. 44r.

10. Detail of a stone fragment with a relief carving on its outer face depicting a siege. This fragment, mounted on a wall in the Church of Saint-Nazaire in Carcassonne, France, dates from the early thirteenth century. Some scholars believe it depicts the siege of Toulouse in 1218 in which Simon de Montfort was killed by a stone-shot hurled from a trestle-framed trebuchet. The relief carving shows a trestle-framed traction machine being prepared for discharge. Pulling ropes are attached to six rings affixed to the butt-end of the beam, and a six-member pulling-crew is set to launch a rounded stone-shot which is being placed in the pouch of the sling by the operator of the machine. This trebuchet has a curved axle, a feature which it shares with the pole-framed traction trebuchet illustrated in Ibn Urunbughā al-Zaradkāsh's *Kitāb anīq fī al-manājanīq* shown in Figure 9.

11. A trestle-framed traction trebuchet as it is about to discharge a stone-shot from its sling. The pulling crew—obscured by a scene of galloping knights in the foreground—is in the process of hauling down the ropes attached to the butt-end of the beam. The traction power of the pulling-crew swings the throwing arm of the beam upward, sending the operator of the machine aloft. By holding onto the sling for a moment and then releasing it, the operator increases the efficiency of the machine by utilizing the force generated by the flexion of the beam. From the "Maciejowski Bible" produced in Paris around 1250. New York, The Pierpont Morgan Library, MS M.638, fol. 23v.

nate the trebuchet. Scholars who have examined the terminological variations exhibited in the sources have erroneously concluded that the diversity of terms reflects differences in the size of a particular projectile-launcher, or in the weight of the projectile discharged from it, or even fundamental differences in the kind of artillery employed (e.g., tension, torsion, or traction varieties).[76] Despite the perplexing nature of the terminological pluralism of medieval artillery, a binary nomenclature for the trebuchet is evident in the Latin West. This binary nomenclature prevailed until the coming of the counterweight trebuchet. The most commonly used term to denote the pole-framed trebuchet was *manganellus*, while the heavier trestle-framed machine was usually identified by the term *petraria*.[77]

When the hybrid machine appeared, the terminology for the trebuchet was already established, and this terminology was related to the configuration of the frame of the machine, a component that remained unchanged regardless of whether the machine was a traction or a hybrid model. This fact may explain why the hybrid machine finds only scant representation in the nomenclature of the trebuchet in the region of Western Asia and the Mediterranean. The machine was simply subsumed under the existing nomenclature. The ninth-century Arabic references to the hybrid machine, for example, refer to it as a "big" trestle-framed trebuchet (*manjanīq kabīr*). This technical term appears only in two siege accounts of the ninth century (Amorion in 223/838 and Baghdad in 251/865) and does not reemerge until the twelfth century, at which time it most likely designates the latest artillery innovation of the day: the counterweight trebuchet.[78] While Arabic chroniclers largely ignored the hybrid trebuchet, Arabic oral culture did not. The fact that the Arabic

---

[76] Various interpretations of the differences in terminology are discussed in Rogers, *Latin Siege Warfare*, pp. 254–266.

[77] Huuri was the first scholar to determine that a binary nomenclature was being used for medieval artillery, but he failed to identify the machines correctly (Huuri, "Geschützwesen," 57–62, 91, 93, 127, 140, 179, 212, 218–219).

[78] During the twelfth century, trebuchets are again referred to as "big" in narrative accounts of sieges, doubtless denoting the counterweight trebuchet. In Syriac, Arabic, and Greek accounts, trebuchets are identified as "big," "great," and "immense" or "frightful" (sieges of Tyre in 1124, 'Azāz in 1125, Shayzar in 1138, Baghdad in 1157, Alexandria in 1174, Maṣyāf in 1176, Āmid in 1183, Kerak in 1184, Thessalonica in 1185, Jerusalem and Tyre in 1187, and Acre in 1190). A component associated only with the counterweight trebuchet—the windlass—is first mentioned in a description of a trebuchet used by the Byzantine army at the siege of Zevgminon in 1165. Nicetas Choniates records that the Byzantine emperor

term *al-ghaḍbān* was used by both Seljuq Turks and Armenians to refer to the hybrid trebuchet indicates that this term was derived from a lively Arabic oral tradition, which went unrecorded by the literary classes. The elusiveness of the hybrid trebuchet in the domain of terminology does not reflect its meager usage in operations of mechanized siegecraft. During the ascendancy of the hybrid trebuchet in Western Asia and the Mediterranean world (eighth to the middle of the twelfth century), this machine was widely used, but it was identified by terms that formerly denoted the trestle-framed traction trebuchet. Hence, a clear technological change—the introduction of the hybrid machine—was not generally reflected in terminological changes. Despite this terminological gap, a few languages developed a distinct nomenclature for the hybrid trebuchet: Armenian, Syriac, Latin, French, and Occitan.

The Hybrid Trebuchet in Armenian Sources: Baban

Four different terms were used in Armenian to refer to the trebuchet: *mekʿenay, manghion, pʿilipan,* and *baban*. *Mekʿenay* and *manghion* are both derived from Greek: *mekʿenay* from μηχανάς (*mēchanás*) and *manghion* from μάγγανον (*mánganon*). Both terms designated the trestle-framed traction trebuchet.[79] The term *pʿilipan* (also *pʿilikhan,* and *pʿilikuan* or *pʿilikuann*) and the Georgian term *pʿilekavani* are derived from the Persian *pīlvār-afkan* or its abbreviated form *pol(o)kan*.[80] The Persian

---

Andronikos I Comnenos "took charge of a trebuchet and by using the sling, the windlass, and the rotating beam, shook . . . the wall . . . violently" (Nicetas Choniates, *Nicetae Choniatae Historia*, ed. J. van Dieten, *Corpus fontium historiae byzantinae*, vol. 11, pt. 1 [Berlin, 1975], p. 134).

[79] Hübschmann and Huuri considered both terms to be derived from μηχανάς (*mēchanás*) (Heinrich Hübschmann, *Armenische Grammatik,* vol. 1, *Armenische Etymologie* [Hildesheim, 1962], p. 363; Huuri, "Geschützwesen," 82). For *mekʿenay,* see Sebēos, *Patmutʿiwn Sebēosi* [*History of Sebēos*] (Evevan, 1979), pp. 170–171; and *Sebēos' History,* trans. Robert Bedrosian (New York, 1985), pp. 169–170; Matthew of Edessa, *Patmutʿiwn,* trans. Ara E. Dostourian (Jerusalem, 1869), pp. 69, 445, 462, 505; Matthew of Edessa, *Armenia and the Crusades, Tenth to Twelfth Centuries: The Chronicle of Matthew of Edessa,* trans. Ara E. Dostourian (Lanham, 1993), pp. 53, 230, 238, 259. On *manghion,* see Sebēos, *Patmutʿiwn,* p. 171, and *Sebēos' History,* p. 170.

[80] *Pʿilikan* is used by Matthew of Edessa and Aristakes Lastivertsʿi (Matthew of Edessa, *Patmutʿiwn,* pp. 231, 235, 203, 452; and *Armenia and the Crusades, Tenth to Twelfth Centuries: The Chronicle of Matthew of Edessa,* pp. 128, 131, 162, 233; Aristakes Lastivertsʿi, *Patmutʿiwn Aristakisi Lastivertsʿwoy,* ed. K. Juzbashjan [Erevan, 1963], p. 91; and *Aristakes Lastivertcʿi's History,* trans. Robert Bedrosian [New York, 1985], p. 103).

term means "a thrower of elephant-size objects." This was probably the original term given to the trestle-framed traction trebuchet when it was introduced into Iran sometime during the sixth century. Following the Islamic conquest of Iran, Arabic terminology for the trebuchet predominated, and the trestle-framed traction machine was referred to as the *manjanīq*. The original Persian term for the trestle-framed traction trebuchet survived however in Armenian and Georgian. Scholars have translated *pʿilipan* as "war machine", "ballista", and "catapult." Persian lexicography links this machine with the *manjanīq*, the trestle-framed traction trebuchet.[81]

The term *baban*, as we have seen, is a corruption of the Arabic *al-ghaḍbān* (The Furious One) and refers to the hybrid model of the trestle-framed traction trebuchet. Two Armenian historians of the twelfth century, Matthew of Edessa and Aristakes Lastivivertsʿi, both note the use of this machine at a number of sieges during the eleventh and twelfth centuries (see Appendix 1).[82] At the siege of Manzikert in 1054, the Seljuq sultan Ṭoghrïl Beg bombarded the city with a *baban* that discharged huge stones weighing between 111 and 200 kg. The machine opened a breach in the city wall before the defenders destroyed it by setting it on fire.[83] In 1064 Alp Arslan bombarded Ani with a *baban* which demolished a portion of the city wall.[84] In 1068 Emperor Romanos IV Diogenes laid siege to Manbij

---

I would like to thank Ara Ghazarian, the Armenian bibliographer at the Wiedner Library at Harvard University for directing me to the above references and assisting me in connecting *pʿilikan* to its Persian root. The Georgian term *pʿilekavani* is used twice in the Georgian version of Antiochus Strategos' account of the siege of Jerusalem by the Persians in 614 to denote the artillery used by the besiegers (G. Garitte, ed., *La prise de Jérusalem*, CSCO, vol. 202, Iber. 11, pp. 19–20). I would like to thank Paul Crego, Georgian bibliographer at the Wiedner Library at Harvard University, for transliterating the Georgian term for this word.

[81] For translations of this term as "war machine," see Matthew of Edessa, *Chronicle of Matthew of Edessa*, pp. 128, 131, 162, 233; as "ballista," see Aristakes Lastivertsʿi, *Récit des malheurs de la nation Arménienne*, trans. Marius Canard and Haig Berbérian (Brussels, 1973), pp. 83–84; and as "catapult," see Aristakes Lastivertsʿi, *History*, p. 103. On *pīlvār-afkan* and its abbreviated form, see ʿAlī Akhbar Dihkhudā, *Lughat Namah-i Dihkhudā* (Tehran, 1958–1966), s.v. pol(o)kan; Mohammad Moʿīn, *An Intermediate Persian Dictionary* (Tehran, 1983), s.v. pol(o)kan.

[82] Matthew of Edessa, *Patmutʿiwn*, pp. 142–145, 177, 231, 235, 203, 306, 448, 452, 454, 465; and *Chronicle of Matthew of Edessa*, pp. 87–88, 103, 128, 131, 162, 163, 232, 233, 235, 241; Aristakes Lastivertsʿi, *Patmutʿiwn*, pp. 92–93; and *History*, pp. 103–104.

[83] See n. 14 above and text.

[84] Matthew of Edessa, *Patmutʿiwn*, p. 177; and *Chronicle of Matthew of Edessa*, p. 103.

and bombarded the city with a number of *baban*s until it finally capitulated. These machines hurled large stones which "caused sections of the town to collapse."[85] Alp Arslan besieged Edessa in the spring of 1071 for fifty days and subjected the city to violent bombardment from *baban*s and *p'ilipan*s.[86] Edessa was besieged again in 1095–1096 by the Artuqid Sökmen of Sarūj and Balduq, the ruler of Samosata. After sixty-five days of bombardment, *baban*s made breaches in the city wall. Although the besiegers rushed the wall through the gaps, the defenders successfully fought them off.[87] The Rūm Seljuq ruler Qïlïch Arslan besieged Melitene with *baban*s in 1096–1097.[88] In 1124, the Artuqid ruler Nūr al-Dawlah Balak subjected Manbij to artillery assault using *baban*s,[89] and the crusaders battered the walls of Tyre with *baban*s and *p'ilipan*s.[90] During the following year Aq Sunqur al-Bursuqī and Ṭughtigin laid siege to ʿAzāz and bombarded the city with a dozen *baban*s.[91] In 1137 John II Komnenos besieged Anavarza (ʿAyn Zarbah) for thirty-seven days and battered its walls with his *baban*s.[92] These accounts provide graphic testimony of the destructive power of the hybrid trebuchet (see Appendix 1).

The Hybrid Trebuchet in Syriac Sources: Qalqûmê

Syriac sources also allow us to trace the use of the hybrid trebuchet, due to the fact that this language employed a specific term for this machine: *qalqûmê*. The Syriac term *qalqûmê* was derived from the Greek word χαράκωμα (*charakōma*). The Greek term originally referred to a palisade, and Syriac accounts of the siege of Nisibis in 573 describe a palisade (*qalqûmê*) constructed around the city.[93] By the

---

[85] Matthew of Edessa, *Patmutʿiwn*, p. 231; and *Chronicle of Matthew of Edessa*, p. 128.

[86] Matthew of Edessa, *Patmutʿiwn*, p. 235; idem, *Chronicle of Matthew of Edessa*, p. 131; Judah B. Segal, Segal, *Edessa: "The Blessed City"* (Oxford, 1970), pp. 220–221.

[87] Matthew of Edessa, *Patmutʿiwn*, p. 303; and *Chronicle of Matthew of Edessa*, p. 162; Segal, *Edessa*, p. 225.

[88] Matthew of Edessa, *Patmutʿiwn*, p. 306; and *Chronicle of Matthew of Edessa*, p. 163.

[89] Matthew of Edessa, *Patmutʿiwn*, p. 448; and *Chronicle of Matthew of Edessa*, p. 232.

[90] Matthew of Edessa, *Patmutʿiwn*, p. 452; and *Chronicle of Matthew of Edessa*, p. 233.

[91] Matthew of Edessa, *Patmutʿiwn*, p. 454; and *Chronicle of Matthew of Edessa*, p. 235.

[92] Matthew of Edessa, *Patmutʿiwn*, p. 465; and *Chronicle of Matthew of Edessa*, p. 241.

[93] John of Ephesus, *Iohannis Ephesini Historiae Ecclesiasticae pars tertia*, ed. and trans. E.W. Brooks, *CSCO*, vol. 105, *Scri. Syri* 54 (Paris, 1953), p. 278; and *Ecclesiastical History*, p. 367; Gregorius Bar Hebraeus, *Makhtebhânûth Zabhnê*, ed. Paul Bedjan

ninth century, however, the term had taken on an entirely new meaning. According to Bar Bahlul, *qalqûmê* may refer to a "tower," "the
platform of a trebuchet or a tower," or "a tower (*manār*) similar to
a trebuchet."[94] None of these definitions, however, appear to match
the operations of the *qalqûmê* as described in siege accounts from the
ninth to the twelfth century. These machines are described as functioning in the same way as trebuchets (*manganîqê*) and "great" trebuchets (*manganîqê rawrbê*): they are "set up" before cities and castles,
just as *manganîqê* are;[95] they throw stones, as do the *manganîqê*;[96] and
they batter or strike the walls of cities and castles.[97]

Bar Hebraeus recounts that 'Abd Allāh ibn Ṭāhir used *qalqûmê*
in 824 at the siege of Keysun (Kaysūm). According to him, these
machines hurled stones equivalent to a load borne by an ass.[98] Huuri
estimated the weight of these stones to be between 50 and 100 kg.[99]
Both Michael the Syrian and the *Chronicle of AD 1234* mention that
qalqûmê were used at the siege of Amorion in 223/838.[100] This information corroborates Arabic accounts which indicate that the hybrid
machine was employed at this siege and strongly suggests that the
term *qalqûmê* refers to this machine.[101] The *Chronicle of AD 1234* further notes that these machine hurled large stones against the city.
The *qalqûmê* employed by Zangī in his siege of Edessa in 1144 are
credited with breaking down the city walls on all sides, destroying
seven towers, and making breaches in the wall.[102] During the siege

---

(Paris, 1890), p. 83; and *Chronography*, 1:77. I would like to thank Wheeler Thackston
of Harvard University for his help on the Syriac terms referring to artillery. Any
errors are mine, not his.

[94] Hassano Bar Bahlul, *Lexicon Syriacum*, 3 vols. (Paris, 1901), 2:1797.

[95] Nöldeke, "Zur Geschichte der Araber," 93–94; Bar Hebraeus, *Makhtebhânûth
Zabhnê*, pp. 111, 141, 270, 285, 305, 319, 364, 375, 386, 460, 467, 578; *Anonymi
auctoris Chronicon ad annum Christi 1234 pertinens* (hereafter cited as *Anon. Syriac Chron.*)
in *CSCO*, vol. 82, *Scr. Syri*, ser. 3, vol. 15 (Paris, 1916), pp. 92, 94, 120, 126, 140,
155, 160–161, 190.

[96] Nöldeke, "Zur Geschichte der Araber," 93–94; *Anon. Syriac Chron.*, *CSCO*, vol.
109, *Scr. syri* 56 (Paris, 1952), p. 235; *Anon. Syriac Chron.*, *CSCO*, *Scr. Syri*, ser. 3, vol.
15 (Paris, 1916), pp. 14, 34, 190; Bar Hebraeus, *Makhtebhânûth Zabhnê*, pp. 104, 138,
141, 149.

[97] *Anon. Syriac Chron.*, *CSCO*, *Scr. Syri*, ser. 3, vol. 15 (Paris, 1916), pp. 92, 94, 120.

[98] Bar Hebraeus, *Makhtebhânûth Zabhnê*, p. 141.

[99] Huuri, "Geschützwesen," 150.

[100] Michael the Syrian, *Chronique de Michel le Syrien, patriarche jacobite d'Antioche
(1166–1199)*, ed. and trans. Jean B. Chabot, 4 vols. (Paris, 1899–1924), 4:535; *Anon.
Syriac Chron.*, *CSCO*, *Scr. Syri*, ser. 3, vol. 15 (Paris, 1916), p. 34.

[101] See n. 19 and text.

[102] *Anon. Syriac Chron.*, *CSCO*, *Scr. Syri*, ser. 3, vol. 15 (Paris, 1916), pp. 121, 132.

of Ascalon by Baldwin III in 1153 a single *qalqûmê* was mounted on a mobile siege tower, and this machine discharged small stone-shot.[103]

The above information on the operation of the *qalqûmê* indicates that this machine is a trebuchet. Its connection with hybrid trebuchets used at Amorion confirms that the *qalqûmê* is a hybrid model. Scholars have used a variety of terms to translate *qalqûmê*, thereby obscuring its meaning. J.-B. Chabot employed both "retranchement" and "machines."[104] E.A. Wallis Budge used "engines,"[105] "engines of war,"[106] and "battering rams."[107] A.S. Tritton usually utilized "engines"[108] or "great engines."[109] He often translated both *qalqûmê* and *manganîqê* simply as "engines"[110] or, in the case of "great" *manganîqê* and *qalqûmê*, he used "great engines."[111] Albert Abouna favored an array of terms for *qalqûmê*: "retranchements,"[112] "machines de siège,"[113] "béliers,"[114] "baliste,"[115] and "mangonneaux."[116]

The technical terms for trebuchet used in medieval Syriac texts— *qalqûmê*, *manganîqê*, and *manganîqê rawrbê*—apparently do not correspond with Arabic pre-thirteenth-century nomenclature for artillery: *ʿarrādah* for the pole-framed traction trebuchet; *manjanīq* for the trestle-framed traction trebuchet; *manjanīq kabīr* (during the ninth century) for the hybrid trebuchet; and "big trebuchet" (*manjanīq kabīr*), "great trebuchet" (*manjanīq ʿazīm*), and "immense" or "frightful trebuchet" (*manjanīq hāʾil*) during the twelfth century for the counterweight trebuchet. Syriac sources may easily have used *ʿarrâdê* to refer to the pole-framed trebuchet, since the Arabic term for this machine, *ʿarrādah*,

---

[103] *Anon. Syriac Chron.*, CSCO, Scr. Syri, ser. 3, vol. 15 (Paris, 1916), p. 155. The fact that the *qalqûmê* of Baldwin III discharged small stone-shot does not invalidate our contention that the term *qalqūmē* designates the hybrid trebuchet. Obviously, there were big hybrid machines, as well as small ones.

[104] Michael the Syrian, *Chronique*, 3:97, 192.

[105] Bar Hebraeus, *Chronography*, 1:219.

[106] Bar Hebraeus, *Chronography*, 1:77, 129.

[107] Bar Hebraeus, *Chronography*, 1:239.

[108] Anon., "The First and Second Crusade from an Anonymous Syriac Chronicle," trans. Arthur S. Tritton with notes by Hamilton A.R. Gibb, *Journal of the Royal Asiatic Society* (1933): 286, 289, 293, 301.

[109] Ibid., 93.

[110] Ibid., 97, 282, 283.

[111] Ibid., 95.

[112] *Anon. Syriac Chron.*, CSCO, vol. 354, Scr. syri 154 (Paris, 1974), 68.

[113] Ibid., 24, 71, 74.

[114] Ibid., 90, 91, 95, 100, 105.

[115] Ibid., 117.

[116] Ibid., 143.

is a loan word, borrowed from Aramaic-Syriac. The Aramaic-Syriac term refers to a wild ass. During the fourth century this term was used to refer to artillery, namely the one-armed torsion catapult of late antiquity known as the onager, from the Greek term οναγρος (*onagros*), or wild ass.[117] Later, when Arabic borrowed the Aramaic-Syriac term *'arrâdê* to identify a new type of artillery (the pole-framed traction trebuchet), Syriac authors did not follow suit, even though they were obviously familiar with the meaning of the Arabic term.[118] The reason Syriac nomenclature for artillery does not recognize the pole-framed trebuchet is not due to its absence in siege operations. This machine was used in great numbers, but because it was small, it was not deemed worthy of mention in brief accounts of sieges that concentrated on the most significant machines of war. Siege accounts for the reigns of Saladin (1169–1193) or King James I the Conqueror (1208–1276), for example, rarely mention the pole-framed trebuchet.

It is apparent, therefore, that Syriac terminology for artillery makes reference only to trestle-framed trebuchets. *Manganîqê*, which is found in siege accounts in Syriac sources from the sixth to the thirteenth century, denotes the trestle-framed traction machine. *Qalqûmê* refers to the hybrid trebuchet, and the "great trebuchet" (*manganîqê rawrbê*), which only appears in twelfth-century siege accounts, refers to the trestle-framed counterweight trebuchet (see Appendix 2).

The Hybrid Trebuchet in the Latin West: The "Balearic" Trebuchet

During the ascendancy of the hybrid trebuchet in the Latin West (from the ninth to the thirteenth century), terms that had been used to identify the trestle-framed traction trebuchet—such as *ingenium, machina, manganum, petraria, tormentum*—were also used to designate the hybrid machine. Although the hybrid machine was subsumed under such

---

[117] T.J. Lamy, ed., *Sancti Ephraem Syri hymni et sermones*, 4 vols. (Mechlin, 1882–1902), 2:17: *aqîm 'law(hi) 'arrâdê w ballestôs* ("He set up on it an onager and a ballista."); Huuri, "Geschützwesen," 81 n. 4; R. Payne Smith, *Thesaurus syriacus*, 2 vols. (Oxford, 1879–1927), 2:2988; Siegmund Fraenkel, *Die aramäischen Fremdwörter im Arabischen* (Leiden, 1886), p. 243; Carl Brockelmann, *Lexicon syriacum*, 2nd ed. (Halle, 1928), p. 547.

[118] For the definition of *'arrâdê* as wild ass, not a piece of artillery, see Bar Bahlul, *Lexicon Syriacum*, 2:1461.

terms, medieval authors writing in Latin did introduce a new term for the hybrid machine—the "Balearic" trebuchet. Due to the prestige of Balearic slingers in antiquity, the term "Balearic" (L. *Baliaris*, ML. *Balearis*) became a stock epithet in the Latin West for the most powerful trebuchet in the medieval siege arsenal.[119] "Balearic" was applied first to the hybrid machine and later to the counterweight trebuchet. The shortened form of *Balearis*, *balea*, became *biblia* (dim. *biblieta*) in medieval Latin. Its cognate in Old French appeared most commonly as *bible*, and in German as *blida* or *blide* (also *bleide, bidda, pleiden, pleyde, plaid, plijde,* and *pleite*). The assimilation *b* > *v* explains its form in northern France as both *bivle* and *blive*. In Wales, *bible* took the form of *blif*. In Occitania, the term appeared as *bride*, reflecting the influence of the German form *blide*. The correspondence *b* > *f* explains its form in Italian, *biffa* (also *biffe* and *buffa*). The vernacular forms of *balea* do not appear until the thirteenth century when the counterweight machine was the most powerful trebuchet used. It is therefore most likely that these vernacular forms designate the counterweight, not the hybrid, machine. Giles of Rome, for example, identifies the *biffa* as a hinged-counterweight trebuchet, and Conrad Kyeser of Eichstätt designates one of the large hinged-counterweight trebuchets illustrated in his famous treatise *Bellifortis* (1402–1405) as a *blida grandis*.[120]

De Poerck suggested that all of the cognates of *balea* were derived from the Latin *bubalus* ("wild ox" or "buffalo").[121] This etymological error has been compounded by disagreement regarding the structural configuration of the machine. Accepting Viollet-le-Duc's conclusion that all traction trebuchets were hybrid machines, Enlart suggested that the *bible* was identical to the mangonel (*mangonneau*), a machine he believed utilized both traction and gravity power. Gay

---

[119] Flavius Vegetius Renatus, *Epitoma Rei Militaris*, ed. and trans. Leo F. Stelten (New York, 1990), 1.16; A.V.M. Hubrecht, "The Use of the Sling in the Balearic Isles," *Bulletin van de vereeninging tot bevordering der kennis van de antike beschaving* 39 (1964): 92–93; Manfred Korfmann, "The Sling as a Weapon," *Scientific American* 229 (April 1973): 34–42.

[120] For the description of the *biffa* by Gilles of Rome, see Schneider, *Die Artillerie des Mittelalters*, pp. 163–164. For Kyeser's *blida grandis*, see Conrad Kyeser aus Eichstätt, *Bellifortis: Facsimile-Ausgabe der Pergamenthandschrift, Cod. MS philos. 63 der Universitätsbibliothek, Gottingen*, ed. and trans. Götz Quarg, 2 vols. (Düsseldorf, 1967), 1: fol. 48r; 2:32.

[121] G. De Poerck, "L'Artillerie à ressorts médiévale: Notes Lexicologiques et étymologiques," *Bulletin Du Cange* 18 (1945): 35–49. For the development of the cognate forms of *balea*, De Poerck's study is essential. His etymology of *balea*, however, appears to be in error.

proposed that the *bible* was a counterweight trebuchet with the counterweight attached rigidly to the butt-end of the beam. Greimas suggested that the *bible* was a stone-projecting siege engine in the form of a horn.[122]

Machines identified by chroniclers of the "First" Crusade as *fundae Baleares, instrumenta Balearia, arcus Baleares,* and *Balearis* are probably all hybrid trebuchets.[123] The most detailed description of the "Balearic" trebuchet is found in *The Conquest of Lisbon,* an account of the crusader siege of Lisbon in 1147. In the first major assault on the city during early August, the Germans and Flemings "undertook to shatter the walls and the towers of the enemy with five Balearic [trebuchets]." The fact that these machines were capable of destroying fortifications indicates that they were large artillery pieces. The Anglo-Norman forces erected two "Balearic" trebuchets (*due funde Balearice*) against the walls of Lisbon between the Porta del Ferro and the south-western corner tower. These machines, operated by pulling crews organized in shifts of 100 men each, discharged 5,000 stone projectiles in ten hours. Since each machine hurled 250 missiles in an hour, the sequence of discharge for both machines was slightly better than four shots per minute.[124] This account confirms that the hybrid trebuchet could achieve an extremely rapid rate of discharge. Köhler argued that the "Balearic" artillery used at Lisbon was traction powered, while Schneider maintained that the propulsive force was supplied by a counterweight.[125] The existence of the hybrid machine proves that both scholars were right.

---

[122] Camille Enlart, *Manuel d'archéologie française depuis les temps mérovingiens jusqu'a la Renaissance,* pt. 2, 2nd ed. (Paris, 1932), pp. 491, 492, fig. 211; Victor Gay, *Glossaire archéologique du moyen age et de la Rennaissance,* vol. 1 (Paris, 1887), p. 154; A.J. Greimas, *Dictionnaire de l'ancien français uusqu'au milieu du XIVe siècle,* 2nd ed. (Paris, 1980), p. 70.

[123] *Recueil des historiens des croisades: Historiens occidentaux,* 5 vols. (Paris, 1844–1896), 3:221, 674, 691, 692; 4:157, 253, 263, 324, 367, 471, 475, 602, 678. For other references to the hybrid trebuchet under these terms, see Suger, abbot of St. Denis, *Vie de Luis VI le Gros,* ed. and trans. Henri Waquet (Paris, 1929), pp. 124–125; Richard of Devizes, *The Chronicle of Richard of Devizes of the Time of King Richard the First,* ed. John T. Appleby (London, 1963), pp. 38–39; R.E. Latham, *Dictionary of Medieval Latin from British Sources* (London, 1975), pp. 177, 1029, 1031; and Huuri, "Geschichte," 43 n. 1, 44 n. 2, 52 n. 1, 59 n. 1, 66, 67 n. 1, 175.

[124] *De expugnatione Lyxbonensi,* ed. and trans. Charles W. David (New York, 1936), pp. 134–137, 142–143. Rogers, *Latin Siege Warfare,* p. 185, suggests that the 5,000 stone missiles discharged from the Anglo-Norman "Balearic" trebuchets were "doubtless of relatively small size." This conjecture clashes with the historical evidence. Only large stone-shot would have been capable of destroying fortifications.

[125] Köhler, *Entwickelung,* pp. 164–165; Schneider, *Die Artillerie des Mittelalters,* pp. 12–14.

The Hybrid Trebuchet in the Latin West: Chaable *and* Calabre

The Old French term *chaable* (also *cheable, caable,* and *chadable*) and its medieval Latin cognates (*cabulus, chaablis, chaablum,* and *chadabula*) were most likely used to refer to the hybrid trebuchet.[126] In his account of the siege of Château-Gaillard by Philip Augustus in 1203–1204, William the Breton mentions that a section of wall that remained standing, despite being mined, was brought down by the blows of three stones launched from a large *petraria,* identified by the term *chadabula.*[127] By designating this machine as a big trestle-framed trebuchet (*magna petraria*), William the Breton refers to it in the same way as do ninth-century Arabic authors, who employ the technical term "big trestle-framed trebuchet" (*manjanīq kabīr*). Since *chaable* and its cognates are derived from the French word used to denote cable, rope, or hoisting tackle (*chable*), it is clear that this machine makes use of traction power. The machine probably became known by its pulling-ropes because a great many ropes were attached to the butt-end of the beam to accommodate a large pulling-crew. This conjecture is in accord with our earlier supposition that large pulling-crews are associated with the hybrid machine. In an inventory of the arms and equipment of Philip Augustus stored at the castle of Chinon, a large and a small *chaablum* are listed.[128] The machine is even featured in the *Song of Roland.*[129]

Contamine and Nicolle have linked *chaable* with the Occitan term *calabre.*[130] Corominas, likewise, has argued that *calabre* is derived from Old French *caable* and hence refers to ropes or cables and the siege machine by this name.[131] The Occitan term, however, is derived from

---

[126] DuCange, *Glossarium,* s.v. *cabulus, chaablis, chaablum;* Edouard Audouin, *Essai sur l'armée royale au temps de Philippe Auguste* (Paris, 1913), pp. 101–102. Violett-le-Duc suggested that the term *chaable* designated the onager (Viollet-le-Duc, *Dictionnaire raisonné,* 5:219–221, 240–241, and figs. 7 and 8 [pp. 222–223]).

[127] William the Breton, *Gesta Philippi Augusti,* in *Oeuvres de Rigord et de Guillaume le Breton,* ed. H.-F. Delaborde, vol. 1 (Paris, 1882), p. 219: "Magna petraria, que Chadabula vocabatur."

[128] Reg. A, MS. Vatican, Ottoboni lat. 2796, fol. 90v: "I magnum chaablum et I parvum." Published in Audouin, *Essai sur l'armée royale,* pp. 190–191.

[129] *La Chanson de Roland,* ed. T. Atkinson Jenkins, rev. ed. (Boston, 1924), lines 98 and 237.

[130] Philippe Contamine, *War in the Middle Ages,* trans. Michael Jones (Oxford, 1984), p. 103; David C. Nicolle, *Arms and Armour of the Crusading Era, 1050–1350,* 2 vols. (New York, 1988), 2:590.

[131] Joan Corominas with José A. Pascual, eds. *Diccionario crítico etimológico Castellano e Hispánico,* 6 vols. (Madrid, 1980–1991), 1:748.

the Catalan word *algarrada*, which is itself a loan-word borrowed from the Arabic term for the pole-framed trebuchet, *ʿarrādah* (pl. *ʿarrādāt*).[132] *Calabre* may have initially referred to the pole-framed trebuchet, but descriptions of the *calabre* indicate that it was a piece of heavy artillery, not a small pole-framed trebuchet designed for anti-personnel use. In the Albigensian crusade, the *calabre* is equated with the *petraria*, the trestle-framed trebuchet.[133] At Simon de Montfort's siege of Beaucaire in 1216, a *calabre* broke down one the city gates and its forewall.[134] At his siege of Toulouse in 1218, *calabres* bombarded a tower in the middle of the Garonne River on the western side of the city. These machines discharged "squared stones and rounded boulders" and unleashed such devastating blows that "the whole rampart was shattered and its motar knocked out, wall, gateways, vaults, quoins and all."[135] The ability of this machine to destroy fortifications suggests that it is a hybrid trebuchet. It is unlikely that the term *calabre* was ever used to identify the counterweight trebuchet, since this machine was designated under its own name (*trabuquet*) in accounts of the Albigensian crusade.[136]

The Hybrid Trebuchet in Spain

The hybrid trebuchet doubtless was used in Castile and the realms of Aragon during the ascendancy of the hybrid machine, but it remains difficult to identify because a distinct nomenclature was not developed for it. The machine was subsumed under generic terms for artillery or under terms which formerly designated the traction trebuchet. In Alfonso X's most detailed discussion of artillery in the

---

[132] The *Gran Conquesta de Ultramar* provides the key to solving the etymology of *calabre*. In the account of the crusader siege of Jerusalem in 1099, it mentions that, "the Christians built a large *algarrada*, which is called a *colafre* in French" (*La Gran Conquista de Ultramar*, ed. Pascual de Gayangos [Madrid, 1877], 3.42 [p. 344]). This reference confirms that the two terms are synonymous and refer to the single pole-framed traction trebuchet. This term is cited elsewhere in the *Gran Conquista* as *calabra* (p. 654) and *calabre* (pp. 343 and 491).

[133] William of Tudela, *Chanson*, 1:114–115; and *Song*, p. 33.

[134] William of Tudela, *Chanson*, 2:148–149, 152–153, 168–169; and *Song*, pp. 95, 96, 99.

[135] William of Tudela, *Chanson*, 3:130–131, 136–137; and *Song*, pp. 156–157.

[136] William of Tudela, *Chanson*, 1:238–239; 3:58–59, 62–63, 156–157, 178–179, 182–183, 186–187, 300–301.

Siete partidas, artillery is divided into two categories: trebuchets activated by a counterweight and other trebuchets which discharge their missiles using traction power.[137] In the Latin West, the historical work that provides the greatest amount of information on medieval artillery is the *Book of Deeds* of James I the Conqueror, count-king of the realms of Aragon (1208–1276). This remarkable text is especially rich in information on siege-warfare and heavy artillery, because it was composed by an experienced artillerist.[138] Most of the deeds that are recounted pertain to the establishment of the crusader kingdom of Valencia, one of the greatest military and political achievements of the thirteenth century. This achievement was accomplished by "a war of maneuver, bluff, and relatively bloodless surrender,"[139] but the critical factor that facilitated such success was James's ability to conduct effective siege-warfare. Although he made use of the counterweight trebuchet in his conquest of the cities of Majorca and Valencia, in most siege operations James used a machine designated by the term *fenèvol*. This machine is mentioned by James sixty-two times in his *Book of Deeds*, more than any other piece of artillery, and it was employed by him in sixteen siege operations.[140] Only one or two of these machines were utilized in most of James's sieges. The presence of such a limited number of heavy artillery pieces suggests that these machines were hybrid trebuchets.[141]

---

[137] Alfonso X, *Las Siete Partidas del Rey Don Alfonso el Sabio*, ed. Real Academia de la Historia, 3 vols. (Madrid, 1801), 2.23.24.

[138] James I, count and king, Realms of Aragon, *Llibre dels fets del rei En Jaume*, ed. Jordi Bruguera, 2 vols. (Barcelona, 1991). The earlier edition of the *Llibre* by Ferran Soldevila, with extensive historical notes, may also be consulted (*Llibre dels feits*, in *Les quatre grans cròniques, Jaume I, Bernat Desclot, Ramon Muntaner, Pere III*, ed. Ferran Soldevila [Barcelona, 1971]). On the authorship, authenticity, and peculiar structure of the *Llibre*, see R.I. Burns, S.J., "The King's Autobiography: The Islamic Connection," in his *Muslims, Christians, and Jews in the Crusader Kingdom of Valencia* (Cambridge, Eng., 1984), pp. 285–288, with bibliographical notes.

[139] Robert I. Burns, S.J., and Paul E. Chevedden, "al-Azraq's Surrender Treaty with Jaume I and Prince Alfonso in 1245: Arabic Text and Valencian Context," *Der Islam* 66, no. 1 (1989): 2.

[140] James I, *Llibre dels fets*, 15.17, 15.19, 15.25, 15.25, 15.31, 15.32, 15.37, 15.38, 16.8, 16.32, 16.37, 40.2, 41.2, 41.10, 41.22, 41.28, 69.12, 69.14, 69.43, 125.11, 126.4, 126.6, 130.15, 156.5, 159.6, 159.8, 159.10, 162.2, 163.10, 163.12, 174.4, 175.7, 176.17, 192.9, 192.11, 193.2, 193.10, 193.11, 194.7, 197.4, 197.6, 202.5, 202.7, 202.11, 202.12, 203.3, 203.6, 203.10, 262.5, 263.1, 311.7, 315.3, 357.5, 401.11, 401.13, 460.1, 461.1, 461.8, 462.1, 462.2, 462.3, 463.1.

[141] See Chevedden, "Artillery of James I."

The Hybrid Trebuchet in China and the Diffusion of
Artillery Technology across Eurasia

Seventh-century Chinese data on the trebuchet analyzed by Needham and Yates indicate that a traction trebuchet could discharge a 66-lb (30 kg) stone-shot some 150 yards (137 m). A century later, in 755, trebuchets were employed during the An Lu-shan rebellion that required pulling-crews of 200 men each. Between the eighth and the eleventh century there appears to have been no noticeable increase in the size of pulling-crews for Chinese traction trebuchets. The Chinese military treatise, *Wu Ching Tsung Yao* ("Collection of the Most Important Military Techniques"), completed in 1044, provides the following quantitative data on a number of different types of traction trebuchets:[142]

Type of trebuchet	Ht. of frame	Length of beam	No. of ropes	No. of pullers	No. of loaders	Wt. of stone-shot	Range
Hand-trebuchet	n/a	2.5 m	n/a	1	2	0.3 kg	n/a
Pole-framed "Whirlwind"	5.2 m	5.5 m	40	50	1	1.8 kg	77 m +
Lambda-framed "Crouching Tiger"	5.3 m (front) 4.9 m (rear)	7.7 m	40	70	1	7.2 kg	77 m +
Trestle-framed with one-component beam (version no. 1)	5.3 m (front) 4.9 m (rear)	7.7 m	40	40	1	1.2 kg	77 m +
Trestle-framed with one-component beam (version no. 2)	3.1 m	8.0 m	45	40	1	1.2 kg	77 m +
Trestle-framed with two-component beam	6.1 m	8.0 m	50	100	1	15.0 kg	92 m +
Trestle-framed with five-component beam	3.1 m	3.2 m	80	157	2	41.8–47.7 kg	77 m +
Trestle-framed with seven-component beam	6.5 m	8.6 m	125	250	2	53.7–59.7 kg	77 m +

---

[142] Yang Hong, *Weapons of Ancient China*, p. 266. The metric equivalencies of the Chinese weights and measurements in *Wu Ching Tsung Yao* have been established according to the equivalencies in Sung Ying-Hsing, *T'ien'Kung K'ai-Wu: Chinese*

The most powerful Chinese traction trebuchet, with a pulling-crew of 250 men, could throw a stone-shot weighing between 53.7 and 59.7 kg a distance of more than 77 m. A pulling-crew of 250 is not substantially larger than a pulling-crew of 200, recorded in the eighth century. If the size of the pulling-crew can be used as a rough indicator of the capabilities of a traction trebuchet, it appears that there was no marked improvement in the performance of the Chinese traction trebuchet from the eighth to the eleventh century.

In the twelfth century, however, the range of Chinese trebuchets increases dramatically, reflecting perhaps the incorporation of innovations from the West. For example, Chhên Kuei (first half of twelfth century) records the following data on trebuchets in his *Shou Chhêng Lu* ("Guide to the Defense of Cities"):[143]

Type of trebuchet	Range in *pu*	Range in meters
Third-class trebuchet	250 *pu*	384 m
Second-class trebuchet	260 *pu*	399 m
First-class trebuchet	270 *pu*	415 m
"Far-reaching" trebuchet	350 *pu*	538 m

It appears that before the twelfth century, China made no substantial design changes on the traction trebuchet to dramatically improve its performance. The improved performance of Chinese trebuchets in the twelfth century probably reflects the incorporation of design changes brought about by the diffusion of the hybrid machine to China from South-West Asia. If this interpretation is accepted, a more complex pattern of artillery development and diffusion emerges. Historians of artillery have commonly argued that the traction trebuchet was developed in China and was transmitted to Europe and the Mediterranean World during the early Middle Ages. The next advance in artillery technology is considered to be the introduction of the counterweight trebuchet. This machine has been assumed by many to be a European invention which did not appear until the

---

Technology in the Seventh Century, trans. E-Tu Zen Sun and Shiou-Chuan Sun (University Park, PA, 1966), pp. 362–363.

[143] Frankle, "Siege and Defense of Towns in Medieval China," 167–168.

early thirteenth century. During the course of the thirteenth century, the Mongols, using Muslim engineers, introduced the counterweight trebuchet to China, bringing the most powerful version of this machine back to the land of its birth.

Our analysis suggests a more complex schema of artillery development and diffusion across Eurasia and North Africa, summarized below:

1. Traction trebuchet developed in China between the fifth and the fourth centuries BCE
2. Transmission of the Chinese traction trebuchet to South-West Asia and the Eastern Mediterranean by the sixth century
3. Transmission of the traction trebuchet to the Western Mediterranean by the seventh century
4. Hybrid trebuchet developed most likely in the realms of Islam under the impetus of the conquest movements by the early part of the eighth century
5. Transmission of the hybrid machine back to China in the twelfth century
6. Development of the counterweight trebuchet in the region of South-West Asia or the Mediterranean during the twelfth century
7. Transmission of the counterweight machine to China during the thirteenth century.

One significant result of the discovery of the hybrid trebuchet is renewed confidence in quantitative data on the trebuchet from historical sources originating in South-West Asia and the Mediterranean. Scholars have been very skeptical about data from this region pertaining to weights of projectiles of trebuchets when the weights recorded greatly exceed what has been noted in Chinese sources for the traction trebuchet. Scholars have attempted to explain away heavy projectile weights by arguing that these weights may be exaggerated or that there may be doubt about the units of weight used.[144] Huuri, for example, underestimated trebuchet performance during the period of hybrid ascendancy. He calculated that trebuchets used during this period normally launched projectiles weighing between 50 and 75 kg.[145] Finó discounted William the Breton's testimony that a *petraria* employed by Philip Augustus at the siege of Boves in 1185 discharged stone-shot so heavy scarcely four men could lift the

---

[144] Huuri, "Geschützwesen," 90, 91, 149, 150; Needham and Yates, *Science and Civilisation in China*, 217 n. *h*.
[145] Huuri, "Geschützwesen," 64, 160, 186.

projectiles. After estimating that the missiles would have weighed at least 200 kg, Finó dismissed the account as widely exaggerated.[146] With the discovery of the hybrid trebuchet, there is now good reason to place greater trust in the quantitative data on the trebuchet found in historical sources. This discovery helps to undermine a common misconception shared by many scholars that the artillery employed during the period between classical antiquity and the modern era was primitive and ineffective.

The great leap forward in launch capabilities of the trebuchet began with the development of the hybrid machine. Once engineers became familiar with the use of gravitational force, the way was prepared for the next advance in artillery technology: the development of a fully mechanized trebuchet powered exclusively by the force of gravity. This machine could launch projectiles up to a common maximum of 300 kg, and a few reportedly threw stones weighing between 900 and 1,260 kg. The emergence of the counterweight trebuchet led to an increase in the scale of warfare and produced revolutionary changes in military architecture. Fortifications were transformed in order both to withstand the impact of the new artillery and to make full defensive use of the new artillery to prevent enemy machines from getting within effective range. The major breakthrough that led to these innovations was the invention of the hybrid trebuchet, the essential half-way step in the development of true gravity-powered artillery.

---

[146] William the Breton, *Philippidos*, in *Oeuvres de Rigord et de Guillaume le Breton*, ed. H.-F. Delaborde, vol. 2 (Paris, 1885), 54; Finó, "Machines de jet médiévales," 35–36.

APPENDIX 1

*Armenian Terms for Trebuchets in the Chronicles of
Matthew of Edessa and Aristakes Lastivertsʻi*

Abbreviations

ME   Matthew of Edessa. *Patmutʻiwn.* Jerusalem, 1869.

ME [E]   Matthew of Edessa. *Armenia and the Crusades, Tenth to Twelfth
          Centuries: The Chronicle of Matthew of Edessa.* Translated by
          Ara E. Dostourian. Lanham, 1993.

AL   Aristakēs Lastivertsʻi. *Patmutʻiwn Aristakisi Lastivertsʻwoy.* Edited
          by K.N. Juzbashan. Erevan, 1963.

AL [E]   Aristakes Lastivertsʻi. *Aristakes Lastivertcʻi's History.* Translated
          by Robert Bedrosian. New York, 1985.

Year	Place	Besieger	Armenian term	Source
1031–1032	Edessa	Naṣr al-Dawlah	1 *mknay* (*mekena*)	ME, 69 ME [E], 53
1054	Manzikert	Ṭoghrïl Beg	*baban* *pʻilipan*	ME, 142–145 ME [E], 87–88 AL, 92–93 AL [E], 103–104
1064	Ani	Alp Arslan	*baban*	ME, 177 ME [E], 103
1068	Manbij	Romanos IV Diogenes	*baban* *pʻilipan*	ME, 231 ME [E], 128
1071	Edessa	Alp Arslan	*baban* *pʻilipan*	ME, 235 ME [E], 131
1095–1096	Edessa	Sökmen of Sarūj and Balduq, ruler of Samosata	*baban* *pʻilipan*	ME, 303 ME [E], 162
1096–1097	Melitene (Malatya)	Qïlïch Arslan	*baban*	ME, 306 ME [E], 163

Table cont.:

Year	Place	Besieger	Armenian term	Source
1123–1124	Kharput (Ḥiṣn Ziyād)	Nūr al-Dawlah Balak	*mknay* (*mekenay*)	ME, 445 ME [E], 230
1124	Manbij	Nūr al-Dawlah Balak	*baban*	ME, 448 ME [E], 232
1124	Tyre	Crusaders	*baban* *pʻilipan*	ME, 452 ME [E], 233
1125	ʻAzāz	Aq Sunqur al-Bursuqī and Ṭughtigin	12 *baban*	ME, 454 ME [E], 235
1136–1137	Keysun	Muḥammad b. Amīr Ghāzī	No *mekenay*	ME, 462 ME [E], 238
1137	Anavarza	John II Komnenos	*baban*	ME, 465 ME [E], 241
1150–1151 (?)	Tell Bashir	Masʻūd I b. Qïlïch Arslan	*mekenay*	ME, 505 ME [E], 259

APPENDIX 2

Syriac Terms for Trebuchets

Abbreviations

A.1   Anon. *Chronicon AD 1234 pertinens*. Vol. 1, edited by J.B.
            Chabot, *CSCO* 81, *Scr. Syri* 36 (Paris, 1953).

A.1 [L]   Anon. *Chronicon AD 1234 pertinens*. Vol. 1, edited by J.B.
            Chabot, *CSCO* 109, *Scr. Syri* 56 (Paris, 1952).

A.2   Anon. *Anonymi auctoris chronicon AD 1234 pertinens*. Vol. 2,
            edited by J.B. Chabot, *CSCO, Scr. Syri*, ser. 3, vol. 15
            (Paris, 1916).

A.2 [E]   Anon. "The First and Second Crusade from an Anony-
            mous Syriac Chronicle." Translated by Arthur S. Tritton
            with notes by Hamilton A.R. Gibb, *Journal of the Royal
            Asiatic Society* (1933), 69–101; 273–305.

A.2 [F]   Anon., *Anonymi auctoris chronicon AD 1234 pertinens*. Vol. 2,
            translated by Albert Abouna, *CSCO* 354, *Scr. Syri* 154
            (Paris, 1974).

BH   Bar Hebraeus, *Makhtebhânûth Zabhnê*. Edited by Paul Bedjan.
            Paris, 1890.

BH [E]   Bar Hebraeus. *The Chronography of Gregory Abū'l Faraj,
            the Son of Aaron, the Hebrew Physician Commonly Known as
            Bar Hebraeus*. Vol. 1. Translated by Ernest A.W. Budge.
            London, 1932.

CSCO,   *Corpus Scriptorum Christianorum Orientalium, Scriptores Syri*
Scr. Syri

J Eph   John of Ephesus, *Iohannis Ephesini Historiae Ecclesiasticae
            pars tertia*. Edited by E.W. Brooks, *CSCO* 105, *Scr. Syri*
            54 (Paris, 1953).

J Eph [E]   John of Ephesus. *The Third Part of the Ecclesiastical History
            of John of Ephesus*. Translated by R. Payne-Smith. Oxford,
            1860.

J Eph [L]   John of Ephesus, *Iohannis Ephesini Historiae Ecclesiasticae
            pars tertia*. Translated by E.W. Brooks, *CSCO* 106, *Scr.
            Syri* 55 (Paris, 1953).

M   Michael the Syrian. *Chronique de Michel le Syrien, patriarche
            jacobite d'Antioche (1166–1199)*. Edited and translated by
            Jean B. Chabot. 4 vols. Paris, 1899–1924.

N   Nöldeke, Theodor. "Zur Geschichte der Araber im 1. Jahrhundert d. H. aus syrischen Quellen." *Zeitschrift der Deutschen Morgenländischen Gesellschaft* 29 (1875), 76–98.

WSC   Palmer, Andrew, Sebastian Brock, and Robert Hoyland. *The Seventh Century in the West-Syrian Chronicles.* Translated Texts for Historians, vol. 15. Liverpool, 1993.

Year	Place	Syriac term	Translation
573	Nisibis	qalqûmê (J Eph, 278) qalqûmê (BH, 83)	χαράκωμα (J Eph [L], 210) palisade (J Eph [L], 367) engines of war (BH [E], 77)
573	Dara	mankanemata (J Eph, 287) manganon (J Eph, 287) manganîqê (A.1, 203) manganîqê (A.1, 204) manganîqê (A.1, 209)	machinamenta (J Eph [L], 218) μηχανήματα engines (J Eph [E], 379) ballistas (μάγγανόν) (J Eph [L], ?18) machines (J Eph [E], 379) machinas (A.1 [L], 160) machinas (A.1 [L], 161) ballistarum (A.1 [L], 165)
628	Edessa	manganîqê (A.1, 235)	ballistarum (A.1 [L], 184) catapults (WSC, 139)
640	Caesarea	72 manganîqê (BH, 104)	engines of war (BH [E], 97)
663 or 668	Constantinople	balistrae (N, 92)	ballistae (N, 97) catapults (WSC, 33)
664	Synnada	manganîqê (N, 93–94)	maschines (N, 98) catapult (WSC, 33–34)
692	Mecca	manganîqê (A.1, 293) manganîqê (BH, 111)	ballistas (A.1 [L], 228) catapults (WSC, 201) engines of war (BH [E], 103)
717–718	Constantinople	manganîqê (A.1, 301) manganîqê (BH, 116)	ballistis (A.1 [L], 234) catapults (WSC, 212) engines of war (BH [E], 107)
812–813	Baghdad	manganîqê (BH, 138)	engines of war (BH [E], 126)
824	Keysun	30 manganîqê (A.2, 14) qalqûmê (BH, 141)	30 mangonneaux (A.2 [F], 10) engines of war (BH [E], 129)
838	Amorion	qalqûmê (M, 4:535) manganîqê (M, 4:535) qalqûmê (A.2, 34) manganîqê (BH, 149–150)	retranchement (M, 3:97) balistes (M, 3:97) machines de siège (A.2 [F], 24) engines of war (BH [E], 136–137)

Table cont.:

Year	Place	Syriac term	Translation
1071	Edessa	qalqûmê (BH, 246) manganîqê (BH, 246)	engines (BH [E], 219) machines for siege attack (BH [E], 219)
1106	Melitene (Malatya)	qalqûmê (M, 4:591) qalqûmê (BH, 270)	machines (M, 3:192) battering rams (BH [E], 239)
1124	Kharput (Ḥiṣn Ziyād)	4 manganîqê (M, 4:603) qalqûmê (A.2, 92) manganîqê (BH, 285)	balistes (M, 3:211) beaucoup de retranchements (A.2 [F], 68) great engines (A.2 [E], 93) engines of war (BH [E], 251)
1124	Tyre	manganîqê rawrbê and qalqûmê sagī'ē (A.2, 94)	gros mangonneaux et des machines de siège numbreuses (A.2 [F], 71) great engines (A.2 [E], 95)
1125	ʿAzāz	manganîqê rawrbê (A.2, 98) qalqûmê (A.2, 99) manganîqê (A.2, 99)	grands mangonneaux (A.2 [F], 73) engines (A.2 [E], 97) machines de siège et aux mangonneaux (A.2 [F], 74) engines (A.2 [E], 97)
1137	Shayzar	manganîqê (M, 4:621) manganîqê (BH, 301)	balistes (M, 3:245) engines of war (BH [E], 264)
1139	Baalbek	manganîqê (A.2, 105)	mangonneaux (A.2 [F], 79) engines (A.2 [E], 273)
1144	Edessa	qalqûmê (A.2, 120) manganîqê (A.2, 120) manganîqê (A.2, 121) qalqûmê (A.2, 121) manganîqê (BH, 305)	béliers (A.2 [F], 90) mangonneaux (A.2 [F], 90) engines (A.2 [E], 282) mangonneaux (A.2 [F], 91) béliers (A.2 [F], 91) engines (A.2 [E], 283) engines of war (BH [E], 268)
1145	Bira/Birta	10 qalqûmê (A.2, 126)	béliers (A.2 [F], 95) engines (A.2 [E], 286)
1144	Edessa	qalqûmê (A.2, 132)	béliers (A.2 [F], 100) engines (A.2 [E], 289)
1146	Edessa	qalqûmê (A.2, 140) qalqûmê (A.2, 140)	béliers (A.2 [F], 105) béliers (A.2 [F], 105) engines (A.2 [E], 293)
1153	Ascalon	qalqûmê (A.2, 155) manganîqê (BH, 319)	baliste (A.2 [F], 117) engine (A.2 [E], 301) engines of war (BH [E], 280)

Table cont.:

Year	Place	Syriac term	Translation
1164	Ḥārim	*manganîqê* (A.2, 161)	mangonneaux (A.2 [F], 121) engines (A.2 [E], 303)
1178	Ḥārim	*qalqûmê* (A.2, 190)	mangonneaux (A.2 [F], 143)
1184	Kerak	*manganîqê* (BH, 364)	engines of war (BH [E], 317)
1187	Jerusalem	*manganîqê rawrbê* (BH, 375)	mighty engines of war (BH [E], 325)
1187	Tyre	*manganîqê* (BH, 378)	engines of war (BH [E], 328)
1189–1192	Acre	7 *manganîqê* (BH, 386)	engines of war (BH [E], 334)
1229	Khilāt	20 *manganîqê* (BH, 460)	engines of war (BH [E], 394)
1234	Kharput (Ḥiṣn Ziyād)	*manganîqê* (BH, 467)	engines of war (BH [E], 400)
1243	Caesarea	*manganîqê* (BH, 476)	engines of war (BH [E], 407)
1289	Tripoli	*manganîqê* (BH, 566)	engines of war (BH [E], 482)
1291	Acre	300 *manganîqê* (BH, 578)	engines of war (BH [E], 493)

THE EMERGENCE OF "PARLIAMENT" IN THE THIRTEENTH-CENTURY CROWN OF ARAGON: A VIEW FROM THE GALLERY

Donald J. Kagay

As Joseph Strayer has so aptly pointed out, "political representation was one of the great discoveries of medieval government".[1] By this process, the major elements of European societies in the late twelfth and thirteenth centuries could be consulted, asked for money, or summoned for military service by sovereigns who also acted as feudal suzerains. The people called to a royal assembly actually and figuratively represented the entire realm while simultaneously "offering the prince . . . the rights and privileges recognized and conceded to him."[2] Despite the importance of the people in this parliamentary equation, we have few opportunities to look through their eyes at the inner workings of the representative assembly. Most of the popular accounts of such parliamentary machinery are restricted to England. In the Crown of Aragon, which was every bit as politically innovative as England, the narratives of the assembly describes it from the royal point of view. It is the intention of this paper to broaden the perspective of such assemblies by comparing royal and popular accounts of one Catalan assembly that took place at Barcelona in 1228. With such new evidence, it is hoped that a more balanced understanding of the early public meetings of eastern Spain can be attained. A careful assessment of such evidence, however, can lead to new questions centering on the real understanding of and accountability to the parliamentary process by the majority of the assembly members who, like the rest of their societies, were "unlettered".

The baserock of all European parliaments was the royal court, that ever-shifting group of illiterate noble retainers who accompanied the peripatetic and under-funded sovereign on his constant journeying. When the king was in need of money, manpower or simply

[1] Joseph R. Strayer, *On the Medieval Origins of the Modern State* (Princeton, NJ, 1970), p. 64.
[2] Antonio Marongiu, *Medieval Parliaments*, trans. S.J. Woolf (London, 1968), p. 51.

advice, he could expand the proportions of the royal court by summoning all of his great men to meet him on a specified day and place.
The king's men, tied to him by feudal bonds of varying strength,
all had to assist and counsel their lord whenever he requested it.[3]
These vassalic obligations and the afforcement of the royal court
they brought about made such great advisory councils a common
feature of the European political landscape from the twelfth century
onward. Though these meetings proved increasingly important to
the king, they attained only the faintest of institutional outlines until
the beginning of the thirteenth century.[4] The ephemeral nature of
such meetings is perhaps best expressed in the myriad of names
applied to them in the official records from the late twelfth century.
This nomenclature varied from a "full and specious deliberation,"[5]
to a "distinguished," "praiseworthy," "solemn," or "full court."[6] By
the thirteenth century, however, curial terminology had been greatly
clarified as the great assembly was almost always called a "general court" (*curia generalis*) or a *cort general* (to use the Catalan or the
Aragonese).[7] By and large, then, the variety of names for the extraordinary meetings reflect their close connections to the royal court.
The emergence of terminological precision demonstrates that in the
view of the royal chancery, at least, the extraordinary assembly was
becoming, if not yet an institution, a recognizable and common political event. A milestone in this journey toward institutional status was
the Barcelona assembly of 1228. To gain a wider perspective of this
crucial assembly, we must balance the official version against the
recollections of the men who attended the meeting and saw it from
a different vantage point—namely, from the audience.

Until now, knowledge of the Barcelona assembly has been derived
solely from the laws it issued and a remarkably full account of it
in the autobiographical royal chronicle, the *Liber del Feyts*, or "Book

---

[3] Thomas N. Bisson, "The Problem of Feudal Monarchy: Aragon, Catalonia,
and France," *Speculum* 53 (1978): 464–470.

[4] Marongiu, p. 51; Evelyn S. Procter, "The Development of the Catalan *Corts*
in the Thirteenth Century," *Estudis Universitaris Catalans* 22 (1936): 525–528; A.R.
Myers, *Parliaments and Estates in Europe to 1789* (New York, 1975), pp. 64–65.

[5] *Arxiu de la Corona de Aragó, Colección de Ripoll*, no. 23, f. 17v; *Liber feudorum maior*,
ed. Francisco Miguel Rosell, 2 vols. (Barcelona, 1945), 1: doc. 483, p. 513.

[6] Procter, 536.

[7] See Appendix II. For the title of *curia* and *corte* in Castile, see Evelyn Procter,
Curia and Cortes in León and Castile 1072–1295 (Cambridge, 1980), pp. 7–9; Joseph F.
O'Callaghan, *The Cortes of Castile and León, 1188–1350* (Philadelphia, 1989), pp. 14–19.

of Deeds."[8] After a tumultuous year enforcing his authority in the Pyrenean county of Urgel, the twenty-year-old king of Aragon and count of Barcelona, James I, spent November of 1228 in the seaside city of Tarragona.[9] According to the sovereign, some of the Catalan nobles and townsmen present at Tarragona proposed to him the idea for the invasion of Majorca. Relishing the prospect of expanding his realms, the young sovereign promised he would summon a "general court at Barcelona."[10] True to his word, James called together a large body of Catalan nobles, clergy, and townsmen to the port city on 18 December 1228. On the next day, the summoned parties came before the sovereign in the palace. After reviewing the troubled record of his early life when his realms were overwhelmed by civil war, James turned to the Balearic project, not only asking the members of the assembly for their advice and help concerning the expedition but also about how he could "best put his realms at peace." Initially, the three groups were in favor of the expedition, but they indicated that no final decision could be made until they had "deliberated apart." Two days later, on 20 December, James received the major nobles "in secret council" and was pleased to find that they were overwhelmingly in favor of the project. Overjoyed, the king determined to summon another full session of the *Corts* on the next morning, which he would orchestrate even down to arranging the speaking order of its participants. Receiving concrete pledges of money, ships, and military support in this meeting, the king proceeded to pacify his realms by issuing a peace and truce for all the Catalans. It is almost certain that the townsmen were dismissed at this point, and yet the *Corts* did not come to an end until two days later. The king kept his great clergy and nobles with him until Christmas Eve, and issued important directives for the government of Catalonia during his absence and a plan for the division of Majorcan lands that might be conquered. The first of these last sessions—on December 23—was referred to as a *curia solempnis* ("solemn court").[11]

---

[8] *Llibre dels Feyts del Rei En Jaume* [*LF*], ed. Jordi Bruguera, 2 vols. (Barcelona, 1991).

[9] Diego Monfor y Sors, *Historia de los condes de Urgel*, 2 vols. in *Colección de documentos inéditos del Archivo General de la Corona de Aragón* [*CDACA*], ed. Prospero de Bofarull y Moscaró, 42 vols. (Barcelona, 1850–1856) 9:463–464.

[10] *LF*, 28, chap. 47.

[11] *LF*, caps. 48–55, pp. 98–106; *Biblioteca de San Lorenzo de Escorial*, Sección de manuscritos, Ms. d, ii, 12, ff. 57–58; *Colección de los cortes de los antiguos reinos de Aragón*

Normally, the view we have of such proceedings comes from the Crown, through the literate servants who recorded them. By a twist of irony that only history can fashion, it was from the very activity of this emerging bureaucracy that the testimony from the audience of the 1228 assembly can be heard. This obscure window to the past originates in a set of lawsuits which endured for almost twenty years (1255–1271) and pitted the count of Urgel, Alvar II de Cabrera, against his two aggrieved wives, Constanza de Montcada and Cecilia de Foix.[12] The records of this litigation are preserved in the section of *procesos* (lawsuits) of the royal chancery still housed in the *Arxiu de la Corona de Aragó* at Barcelona. At the end of eighty parchment files or *legajos*, all carefully numbered from one to eighty, two other un-numbered *legajos* are attached.[13] In these files, claims to castles and lands contested by Alvar's wives and their bigamous husband are discussed. The most important of these for our purposes are those articles of complaint that touched on conflicting rights to lands in Majorca, which referred to the *Corts* of 1228 that dealt with the land division principle, or *repartamiento*, of the island.[14] Though hard pressed to find any witnesses to an event so long past, the judges of the 1271 case eventually found six men with firsthand knowledge of the assembly—five participants and one person with acquaintances who had served in the meeting. Though of different ranks (one was a petty nobleman and the other five, townsmen or villagers), the accounts they give us of the 1228 meeting are remarkably consistent and differ in some important ways from the royal version of the same events. To ascertain these different aspects, several questions have to be asked of our witnesses and then compared with James's remembrance.

Firstly, how was the meeting summoned? The king simply says that he had the *curia generalis* convened. One of the urban witnesses, however, claimed that he had been in Tarragona in the fall of 1228 and had seen the king order his Jewish scribe to write letters of summons for the Christmas assembly.

---

y de Valencia y el principado de Cataluña [*CAVC*], ed. Fidel Fita y Colomé and Bienvenido Oliver, 26 vols. (Madrid, 1895–1922), 1, pt 1:120–122.

[12] Monfar y Sors, 1:542–559; T.N. Bisson, *The Medieval Crown of Aragon* (Oxford, 1986), p. 251.

[13] *Arxiu de la Corona de Aragó*, Cancillería real, Procesos, no. 518; Federico Udina Martorell, *Guia historica y descriptiva del Archivo de la Corona de Aragón* (Madrid, 1986), p. 251. I would like to thank Elena Lourie of Ben Gurion University for first pointing out this *proceso* to me.

[14] ACA, Pergaminos de Jaime I, no. 597; *CDACA*, 6:95–98, doc. 16.

Secondly, what did the witnesses call the assembly and how did this differ from the royal terminology? On only three occasions did the witnesses refer to the meeting as a *curia*. In one of these instances, they called the assembly a "full court," a term used to describe extraordinary assemblies in the Crown of Aragon from the mid-twelfth century. By far, the more popular label applied by the witnesses, however, was *parlamentum*, a parley or discussion.

Thirdly, can any of the internal workings of the Barcelona assembly be gleaned from the testimony of the witnesses? The evidence in this regard is both sketchy and revealing. James leaves an account of his moving opening speech to the *Corts* but all the witnesses could recall of this *praepositio*, or proposal, was that the king spent a good deal of verbiage in justifying a Balearic invasion. He did this by recalling an incident of piracy by agents of the Muslim ruler of Majorca perpetrated on Catalan merchantmen some months before the assembly. No matter what the subject of the royal oration, at least one of our informants who heard the king's words could not understand them and could not find any member of the noble estate who was able to enlighten him on the matter. As far as the other sessions and private deliberations of the Barcelona assembly, our authorities are silent.

It must be clear from the above that the scholar must rely on the royal view to trace the course of the parliaments in the Crown of Aragon. Even when systematic study of these assemblies began in the sixteenth century at the behest of the Hapsburg and Bourbon monarchs, the parliamentary manuals this research produced could only proceed from the barely-breathing parliamentary institutions themselves and the vast corpus of law they had produced.[15] To peer inside the emerging organization, we must rely on the remarkable series of Catalan chronicles of the thirteenth and fourteenth centuries commencing with the *Liber dels Feyts*. No journals or treatises emanated from the participants of the *Corts* as with the medieval English parliament.[16] Thus these sketchy remembrances of the 1228

---

[15] Antonio Campmany y Montpalau, *Practica y estilo de celebrar cortes en el reino de Aragón, principado de Cataluña, y reinado de Valencia* (Madrid, 1821); Jeronimo de Blancas y Tomas, *Modo de proceder en cortes de Aragón* (Zaragoza, 1641); Lúis Peguera, *Practica, forma, y estila de celebrar corts generals en Catalunya* (Barcelona, 1701).

[16] Ronald Butt, *A History of Parliament: The Middle Ages* (London, 1989), pp. 219–220, 573–577; T.F. Tout, "The English Parliament and Public Opinion, 1376–1388," *Historical Studies of the English Parliament*, ed. E.B. Fryde and Edward Miller, 2 vols. (Cambridge, 1970), 1:303.

assembly must serve to give us a clearer understanding of what stage
the Catalan *Corts* had attained by the time it reached this milestone.

From the records of our informants, it is clear that the Catalan
general assembly was generally called together through the issuance
of letters in Latin from the royal chancery. According to the witness who saw them being written, these summonses were sent only
to the Catalan nobles. How the other ranks were congregated is not
mentioned but they, too, were presumably notified by a member of
the burgeoning corps of royal messengers. Remarkably, the first extant
summons of any parliamentary estate in Catalonia dates from the
last decade of James I's life.[17]

The difference in nomenclature used by the king on one hand
and his people on the other is an intriguing one. The king always
refers to the meeting as a "general" or "solemn court." The participants also call the Barcelona meeting a court but vary this description with the title "parliament." For a British audience of the thirteenth
century, calling a great assembly a parliament seemed not only log-
ical but downright necessary.[18] In France and Italy, the "parliament"
was any kind of political meeting but also a parley between warring
parties or the truce or agreement which emanated from such parleys.[19]
In Italian communes, the word connoted the entire citizen body,
whether gathered for political or military ends.[20] In the medieval Crown
of Aragon, however, such an appellation for an extraordinary assembly does not make its appearance in political and literary parlance
until the mid-fourteenth century, and then only with the very limited usage of a joint public assembly of Catalonia, Valencia, and
Aragon.[21] In the urban arena, *parlamentum* referred to Barcelona's

---

[17] *ACA*, Cancillería real, R. 23, ff. 33r–v; Donald J. Kagay, "The Development
of the *Cortes* in the Crown of Aragon, 1064–1327" (Ph.D. diss., Fordham University,
1981), pp. 403–415.

[18] George O. Sayles, *The King's Parliament of England* (New York, 1974), pp. 33–34,
73; Butt, pp. 79–80.

[19] Marongiu, pp. 27, 78; *The Song of Roland*, trans. Glyn Burgess (London, 1990),
119, stanza 202, in 2836, p. 119.

[20] J.C.L. de Sismondi, *A History of the Italian Republics, Being a View of the Origin,
Progress and Fall of Italian Freedom* (London, 1907), p. 20.

[21] The application of the term parliament to the general court of the Crown of
Aragon has long sown seeds of confusion. The difference between these seemingly-
identical institutions has brought a great number of conflicting explanations. From
the late thirteenth century, writers such as Ramón Lull referred to the parliament
as a general assembly of king and great men of the realm which addressed some
pressing national issue. Such a literary understanding of the term mirrored politi-

town council which ruled the city in conjunction with a royal vicar.[22] With these contemporary meanings in mind, what precisely could our informants mean by parliament? One of the articles of complaint of the 1271 lawsuit may hold the answer. In it, a dispute between the townsmen of Vich and the village's lord Gaston de Foix was settled "after a parliament had been publicly announced." This form of arbitration contained most of the features of an eighteenth-century town meeting in which disputes of all sorts were settled directly.[23] Perhaps then our witnesses use the term parliament to describe only the first public session of the *Corts* when the king "explained his case and asked . . . [the people] to help and stand by me."[24]

No matter what the witnesses called the 1228 assembly, however, they revealed some important facts about it in their depositions. The statement that few of the nobles queried fully understood what the king had said in his opening speech is especially interesting. Despite the compact nature of most of the *Cortes* meeting sites, acoustics played a real part in the success or failure of such meetings by either clarifying or muting the words of the sovereign and the other speakers. Even when participants could hear what was being said, they increasingly could not comprehend it since Latin remained the official language of the Catalan parliament until the mid-fourteenth century, when it was not widely known outside of the royal bureaucracy and the clergy. Such a language gap would eventually lead to the formal adoption of Catalan for parliamentary proceedings. With this in

---

cal reality when such kings as Alfonso IV summoned a *colloquium seu parlamentum* at Tarragona with the Catalan clerics in 1329. Pedro IV, on the other hand, applied the same terms to several general meetings of all the Catalan estates. Even when no king was present, as during the interregnum of 1410–1412, the elective assembly of Caspe with representatives from all three realms of the Crown of Aragon also referred to itself as a parliament. Even the early modern experts on the eastern Spanish great assemblies could not entirely agree on what the term parliament meant in the matrix of the Crown of Aragon, some saying it was a meeting of one or more estates of the Catalan *Corts* "for some need or use of the king or the Republic" while others insisted it was a gathering of representatives of all three states of the Crown of Aragon (*ACA*, Cancillería real, R. 539, ff. 4–12v; Peguera, pp. 114–115; *Glossari general Lul.lia*, ed. Miguel Colom Mateu, 10 vols. [Mallorca, 1985], 4:84; Lúis Garcia de Valdeavellano y Arcimus, *Curso de historia de los instituciónes españoles de los orígenes al final de la edad media* [Madrid, 1968], 436; *CAVC*, I, pt. 2:459; 11:465).

[22] *ACA*, Cancillería real, R. 9, f. 11; R. 19, f. 192; *CDACA*, 8:120–122, 143–146, docs. 46, 58.

[23] Myers, p. 22.

[24] *LF*, ed. Soldevila, chap. 387, 143.

mind, is it not possible that some of our informants did not understood the king's words because they had been uttered in a language
they did not speak? Even after the change to the vernacular in the
late fourteenth century, such royal classical scholars as Martin I
(1395–1410) could not resist littering his opening speeches to the
Corts with Latin erudition, which he was then dutifully bound to
translate for the unlettered in his audience.[25] The words of our young-
est witness, who had not actually attended the 1228 meeting, allow
us to focus on another facet of the parliament's inner workings. The
statement that he could have gone "to see and hear" the assembly,
though not officially summoned to it, demonstrates that at least the
public sessions of the *Corts* were not the closeted affairs portrayed in
thirteenth- and fourteenth-century manuscript miniatures. They rather
had more in common with eastern Spanish assemblies of the eleventh
century in which great groups of the local population would crowd
into the only sizeable building of the district—whether church,
monastery, or castle—and stand as an audience for the rendering of
justice by their secular or ecclesiastical betters.[26]

Despite the possibility that participants in parliamentary proceedings might misunderstand their full import, the general impact of
the *Corts* was to implant a sharp image, which in the case under
consideration had not faded from the minds of those who had
attended the Barcelona assembly even after forty-three years had
passed. The curial ceremonies were thus much better remembered
than the meeting's substantive work. Thus, the glittering array of
great churchmen and nobles were largely remembered by name, as
were the details of the final enthusiastic ovation of the *Cortes*'s work.
In a way, then, the parliament acted very much as a "memory
palace" for even its unlettered members by, in some sense, tying
image to content in a way not unlike that of the educational edifices
of Hugh of St. Victor and Thomas Aquinas.[27]

---

[25] *Parlaments a les corts catalanes*, ed. Ricard Albert and Joan Gassitot (Barcelona, 1928), pp. 64–65.

[26] Archibald Lewis, *The Development of Southern French and Catalan Society, 718–1050* (Austin, 1965), pp. 364–365, 373–375.

[27] Patrick J. Geary, *Phantoms of Remembrance: Memory and Oblivion at the End of the First Millennium* (Princeton, NJ, 1994), pp. 124–128; Ivan Illich, *In the Vineyard of the Text: A Commentary to Hugh's Didascalion* (Chicago, 1993), pp. 44–45; Frances A. Yates, *The Art of Memory* (Chicago, 1966), pp. 65–79.

Though the frustratingly incomplete testimony I have discussed here is seldom as clear as the royal version of the same event, it yet retains an impartiality which the king's account, motivated by any number of agenda, does not and, indeed, could not always possess. The addition of this new strain of evidence to the account that James I has already provided of the 1228 meeting casts some flickering light on the great assembly's inner recesses. But it does not serve to transform the early thirteenth-century *Corts* into a full-fledged institution. Instead, it confirms that it was still in a larval stage and like its contemporary counterpart, the English Parliament, was to remain for some time "an occurrence, an occasion, but not yet a separate court."[28]

In a wider sense, this testimony is crucial for understanding the development of all royal, Latin-based institutions in a vernacular-speaking Catalonia.[29] James I, like his ancestor Peter IV, looked on Catalonia (at least compared with Aragon) as a "blessed land, peopled with loyalty."[30] Even so, James I, though *illiteratus* by any standard,[31] was canny enough to utilize the university graduates streaming back into Catalonia from Bologna and Montpellier to help build a new administrative superstructure founded on "learned Latin" and Roman law which comprised much of the higher education of the day.[32] Despite a barrage of complaints by noble and commoner alike that twice forced James I to outlaw the use of Roman law in his courts,

---

[28] H.G. Richardson and G.O. Sayles, *Parliaments and Great Councils in Medieval England* (London, 1961), p. 9.

[29] For the spread of the vernacular in the last decades of the Carolingian empire, see Kenneth Levine, *The Social Context of Literacy* (London, 1986), p. 55; Michael T. Clanchy, *From Memory to Written Record* (Cambridge, MA, 1986), p. 274; Rosamond McKitterick, *The Carolingians and the Written Word* (Cambridge, 1989), pp. 31–32; Brian Stock, *The Implications of Literacy: Written Language and Models of Interpretation in the Eleventh and Twelfth Centuries* (Princeton, NJ, 1983), p. 52; Paul Saenger, "Literacy, Western European," *Dictionary of the Middle Ages*, ed. Joseph R. Strayer et al., 13 vols. (New York, 1982–1989), 7:600–601.

[30] Pere III of Catalonia, *Chronicle*, trans. M. Hillgarth and J.N. Hillgarth, 2 vols. (Toronto, 1980), 2:419; Helene Wieruskowski, "The Rise of the Catalan Language in the Thirteenth Century," in *Politics and Culture in Medieval Spain and Italy, Storia e Litteratura, Raccolta de studi e testi* (Rome, 1971), p. 115.

[31] For discussion of *literati* and *illiterati*, see Robert E. Lerner, "Literacy and Learning," *One Thousand Years: Western Europe in the Middle Ages* (Boston, 1974), p. 214; Franz Bäuml, "Varities and Consequences of Medieval Literacy and Illiteracy," *Speculum* 55 (1982): 246–247.

[32] Walter J. Ong, *Orality and Literacy: The Technologizing of the Word* (London, 1986), pp. 112–113; Clanchy, pp. 213–214.

the complex of Latin learning held sway over parliament and court-room until the fifteenth century, when the first editions of Catalan law appeared in Catalan.[33]

In reality, then, our informants of 1271 were called on to cast their memories back to an era that witnessed profound changes in the way royal government was conducted in Catalonia and across Europe. A gap had been inserted between Crown and people—it was, at once, linguistic, legal, and procedural. Written texts, which could only be understood by "lettered" professionals, held a verifiable precedence over unwritten custom.[34] Yet ultimately, government must return to people and what they have seen, heard, and experienced. It thus must have afforded our informants some consolation that, no matter how sophisticated and complex the royal estate grew, there was a limit to its text-based knowledge and still a place, albeit small, for the imperfect and fleeting memory of man.[35]

---

[33] *The Usatges of Barcelona: The Fundamental Law of Catalonia*, trans. Donald J. Kagay (Philadephia, 1994), p. 48.

[34] Brian Stock, *Listening for the Text. On the Uses of the Past* (Baltimore, 1990), pp. 7–8; idem, *Implications*, pp. 30–31; Bäuml, p. 249; Lerner, p. 214; Levine, p. 52; Carole Lansing, epilogue to Joseph Strayer, *The Albigansian Crusade* (Ann Arbor, MI, 1971), pp. 182–183.

[35] Clancy, pp. 214–215, 218, 232–233.

APPENDIX I

Arxiu de la Corona de Aragó
Procesos, no. 518 (First Part)[36]

TESTIMONY OF BERENGUER DE SAN VINCENTE

(fol. 2v) Item interogatus super **XXIX**// et similiter **XXX** articulis, respondit que dominus Jacobus nunc Rex Aragonum quondam// tempore bene sunt primum que audivit dicti xl anni mandavit curia in civitatem// Barchinone et vidit que fuerunt apud Barchinonam plures nobiles, scilicet dominus// Comes Empuriarum tunc istis Ugueti Comitis que nunc est Berengarius de Sancta Eugenia, dominus de Turricella,// dominus Nono Jaufredus de Rocabertino et G. de Montecatheno et iste B. et plurii// alii nobiles, milites et clerici et burgenses indixit et fecit eos// congregari in palatio suo. Et ibi proposuit que proponebat in insulas majoricas.// Et rogavit omnes que sequerent eum. Et [***] omnes tenendas has per bono// exiverunt inde et inciperunt se parare ad dictum exercitum.

Item interogatus, dixit que// curia ista fuit mandata ad festum Nativitate domini. Et haec fuit in dictis festis// Natalis domini.

Item dixit que in illa curia et in diem Natalis domini dictus B. fuit// respondendum per dictum dominum G. de Montecatheno.

Item dixit que sequente festo// Sancte Marie mensis Septembri dictus dominus Rex cum exercitu suo cepit terram per capiendam// civitatem Maioricam in loco que vocatur Sancta Polomia. Et postmodum// in sequentibus festivitatibus Nativitatis domini, fuit capta dicta civitas Maioricarum,// {scilicet festum [***] Sancti Silvestri et Sancte Columbe}.

//Item interogatus, dixit que dictus G. in tempore deillo que dicta curia fuit celebrata,// et etaim audiverat loqui de dicto exercitu Maioricarum. Nec scit nec audivit que dictus dominus Rex deliberavisset// in alio loco de predicto exercitu Maioricarum. Immo credit que tunc// dictus dominus Rex in dicta curia deliberavit primo [***]

---

[36] Signa: // end of manuscript line
        [***] illegible text
        { } written above line
        [//] words scratched out

cum exercitu suo insulas Ma// (fol. 3)   ioricarum. Aliud nescit super predictis articulis et super aliis articulis et non fuit// interogatus qualiter tum fuit productus super predictis articulis et petitione domini Gastone.//

TESTIMONY OF R. RASTRI

R. Rastri cives Barchinone juratus et interogatus super **XXIX** articulo et super **XXX**, respondit// que dominus Jacobus nunc Rex Aragonum et plures nobiles Catalonie quorum nomina nescit,// plures episcopi et prelati ecclesiarum et plures cives et burgenses diversorum locorum fu// erunt congregati in civitate Barchinone in quondam festo Nativitatis domini secundum pro huc iste// R. tunc vidit et audivit. Et tunc dictus Rex in presencia hominum predictorum in palatio eiusdem// domini Regis, id est Barchinone, fecit parlamentum et dixit que ipse dominus Rex praeponit// de Barchinone ad capiendam civitatem Maioricarum. Iste tamen R. non inde interfuit// ipsi parlamento. Set audivit tunc dici publice per civitatem Barchinone que dictus// dominus Rex praeposuerat et dixerat in parlamento que volebat ire captum Maioricas. Et// que nobiles et prelati Ecclesiarum responderant sibi que sequerent ipsum. Dixit que iste R. que post dictum parlamentum, vidit et audivit que plures nobiles et milites// de Catalonia et cives Barchinoneet prelati eccleisiarum fecerunt preparere se// ad eundum Maioricas faciendo fieri {in Barchinona arma} tribus galeas, taurides, et lenys// et alia eis necesaria per ipso viatico.

Item dixit in seqente mense julii sequente per// sibi videtur dominus Rex cum exercitu suo recessit de litore Barchinone iuxta insulas maior// icas. Et que in sequente mense Augusti secundum que credit appulerit apud Maioricas, scilicet apud// Palomiam. Et existerant in terram apud Sanctam Ponciam. Et in sequentibus festi// vitatibus Nativitatis domini, scilicet in vigiliam circumcisionis domini vel in crastinum eiusdem circumcisionis vel in cratinum// eiusdem circumcisionis cepit dominus Rex cum exercitu suo civitatem Maioricarum.// (fol. 3v)   Et iste R. interfuit ipsi capcione. Et recessit Barchinonam quondam dominus Rex inde recessit// post predam dictae civitatis Maioricarum.

Interogatus si {scit que} dominus qualiter deliberavit et dixit// in palatio suo quod est Barchinone que volebat ire Maioricas deliberaverat et dixerat// in aliquo alio loco que vellet ire Maioricas, respondit se nescire nec audivisse dici.//

Item interogatus quot anni sunt a dicto festo Nativitatis domini que dominus Rex incepit deliberare// de dicta capcione Maioricarum, respondit se non recordari,

Item interogatus de nominibus// illorum que interfuerunt dicto parlamento, respondit se nescire quare non interfuit// licet esset Barchinone. Aliud nescit super predictis articulis et super aliis articulis non fuit// interogatus qualiter tum fuit productus super predictis articulis a petitione domini Gastonis.

TESTIMONY OF BERENGUER DE SALANO DE SAN PERE DE RELINARES

G. Berenguer de Salano de Sancti Petri de Relinares de termino de Castri de Vequarisses// juratus et interogatus super XXIX et super XXX articulis, respondit// que quondam tempore in festo Omnium Sanctorum iste B. {per duos dies ante per duos vel post} fuit in Barchinonam cum// Inculphi de Minorisa avunculo suo et fuit ibi similiter dominus Jacobus// Dei gratia nunc Rex Aragone et erat ibi similiter Nuno Sancii, G.// de Montecatheno et Comes Impuriarum et aliis istius Comitis interest et// tunc vidit et audivit iste G. que dictus dominus Rex// existens in palatio suo veteri Barchinone vocavit quondom nepotem domini// Rabassa que vocabatur Berenguer et mandavit ei que scriberet litteras per sua// quibusdam nobilibus Cathalonie que tunc presentes non erat in festo// Nativitatis domini subsequenti essent Barchinone per facto Maioricarum// quod scribatur dominus Berenguer habito dicto mandato incepit scribere litteras// predictas set tamen iste G. ignorat quibus fuit scriptum et// (fol. 4) ignori ipsarum litterarum. Item G. dixit que dicto festo Nativitatis// domini subsequenti sic per v dies ante ipsum festum vel post// vidit iste G. et audivit que dictus dominus Rex et plures Nobiles Cath// alonie et plures prelati ecclesiarum et cives et burgenses diversorum locorum// fuerunt in civitate Barchinone et dominus Rex fecit parlamentum in dicto// palatio veteri iste G. presente et audiente set nescit iste G. nec// potuit intelligere que visa exposuit ibi dictus dominus rex nec que fuerunt// que impenderunt ei nobilis predicta nec scit esset quis primo incepit// verbi loqui set parlamento finito vidit et audivit iste G. que omnes// diversi clamabant tantam bonitatem

qualiter dominus Rex et nobiles et alii homines con// venierunt que
adeant insulas Maioricas. Postmodum in eodem anno in mense//
Septembri subsequenti vidit dictus G. que dominus Rex et alii que
ibat insulas Maioricas// recesserunt de Barchinona et in eodem
mensem Septembri in die festi// Sancte Michaelis frangerunt portum sine appulerunt apud Palomaria. Et in vigiliam// festi Circumcisionis domini subsequentis que erat festum Sancti Silvesti// et
Sancte Columbe intraverunt et ceperunt civitatem Maioricarum.

Interogatus// si scit que dominus Rex deliberavisset in alio loco
per iret Maio// ricas ante dictum festum Omnium Sanctorum, respondit se nescit.//

Interogatus quot annos sunt a dicti tempore citatio, respondit que
fuit in// anno que currebat annus MCCXXIX. [//Alius nescit]
Item// dixit que ipse G. [//fuit presens] fuit cum dicto domino Rege
in dicto// exercitu Maioricarum et fuit in capcione Maioricarum.
Aliud nescit// super aliis articulis non fuit interogatus que tum fuit
productus// (9 fol. 4v)   super predictis articulis et peticione domini
Gastonis.

TESTIMONY OF G. DE RONDONO

G. de Rondono civis Barchinone juratus et interogatus super XXIX
et super// XXX° articulis, respondit que quondam tempore citra
festum Nativitatis domini sequentem [***]// sibi videtur que fuit
dominus Rex Aragone que nunc est in civitate Barchinone et//
fuerunt ibi plures nobiles Cathalonie et plures prelati Ecclesiarum et
episcopi et alii// plures cives et burgenses diversorum locorum. Et
tunc dictus dominus Rex cum predictis// prelati fecit parlamentum
et deliberavit in palatio suo veteri Barchinone// que iret {apud}
Maioricas set non recordantur iste G. licet pluribus dictibus fuis-
sent// presentes in dicto parlamento et deliberacione quis primo
locutus fuit// nec recordatur et de verbis que fuerunt inter eos super
dicto parlamento// et deliberacione. Dixit et que essent in (h)estatem
{tunc} proxime ventura post dictum// festum sequentem in mensem
julii et augusti totum navigium que erat Barchinone recessit. Inde
[***] ivit usque portum de Salodio et cum essent omnes ibi congre-
gari// recesserunt dicto portu de Salodio omnes. Inetenim similiter
in mense Septembri// subsequenti post festum Nativitatis domini et in
eodem mensem appulerunt// ad [//portum] terram Maioricarum et in

sequenti festo Sancti Silvestri et Sancte// Columbe que post festum
Nativitatis domini intraverunt et ceperunt dictam// civitatem Maioricarum, nescit tum iste G. si dominus Rex tempore que// incepit
deliberare in civitatem Barchinone citra dictum festum Nativita-
tis// domini deliberaverat et tractaverat iam in alio loco de dicto exercitu Maio// ricarum. Item dixit que iste G. et fuit in dicto exercitu
Maioricarum et fuit// donec dicta civitas fuit capta. Interogatus quot
annis fuerunt a dicto festo// Nativitatis domini citato que dominus
Rex habuit deliberacionem super predicto exercitu// in Barchinona,
respondit se credere que in festo Nativitatis domini erunt XLIII// anni.

   Item interogatus que fuerunt presentes in dicto parlamento, res-
pondit// que dominus Nuño et G. de Montecatheno et Comes Im-
pariarum, R. Berengario// Bernardo de Sancta Eugenia dominus
de Turricello de Montigno et plures alii et qualiter quasi omnes//
boni barones de Cathalonia erunt ibi. Aliud nescit super predictis//
articulis.

TESTIMONY OF P. DE CASTRONOLO

P. de Castronolo cives Barchone juratus et interogatus super XXIX
et XXX articulis,// respondit que quondam tempore citra festum
Nativitatis domini ipsi per aliquot dies ante ipsum// festum dominus Rex Aragone que nunc est et plures nobiles Cathalonie et plures//
episcopi et alii prelati Ecclesiarum fuerunt congregati in civitate
Barchinone qualiter dominus// Rex per litteras suas mandaverat ibi
curia celebrari et quadam die cum essent// omnes congregati in
palatio veteri Barchinone predictus dominus Rex interissent// et audi-
vissent proposuit et dixit in plena curia que rex Maioricarum cepit
sibi// quandam navem que erat hominum suorum et quod ipse mit-
tat ad dictum Regem// Maioricarum Jasquium scriptorem suum ut
restitueret sibi dictam navem quod doctus Rex Maioricarum noluerit
eam sibi restituerit et que dictus// Jasquius ex parte ipsius domini
Regis acunydaverit ipsum Regem Maioricarum et que ipse dominus
Rex Aragoni// volebat habere ab ipsis nobilibus consilium qualib-
iter procedere super predicto negocio// et tandem in dictam curiam
fuit deliberatum per dominus Rex cum exercitu suo// (fol. 5v) ire
ad capiendum civitatem et terram Maioricarum set nescit nec recordatur iste P. que supra non respondit hiis que dominus Rex pro-
posuerat. Item dixit que iste P. fuit [***]// cum domino Rege in

dicto exercitu Maioricarum et que ipsa civitas fuit capta// in festo circumcisionis domini secundum que firmiter credit in festum circumcisionis// [//domini fuit ab illo festo] et non scilicet in illo festo quinquicionis circumcisionis// domini que fuit post dictum festum circumcisionis domini set in alio subsequenti.// Dixit et que post celebracionem dicte curie in qua fuit deliberatum// de exercitu Maioricarum in subsequenti mense augusti recessit {f} totam navigium// fuerat apud portum de Saladio congregatum de dicto portu// apud Palomiam.

Interogatus si scit que dominus Rex ante predictam curiam que// celebravit in dictam civitatem Barchinone de predicto exercitu Maioricarum deliberavisset// in Barchinone vel alibi super predicto exercitu, respondit se nescire nec audisse// dici.

Item interogatus quot annis sunt a celebracione dicte curie citato, respondit// se credere que in festo Nativitatis domini erunt xlii anni fuerunt.//

Et interogatus que sunt presentes in celebracione dicto curie, respondit que dominus Nuno et G. de Montecatheno et Comes Impuriarum et Episcopi// Gerund-ensis et Barchinone et plures alii nobiles et prelati.

TESTIMONY OF A. O., TOWNSMAN OF BARCELONA

(fol. 8) A. O. civis {Barchinone comorans subtus patatium Domini Regis} juratus et interogatus super XXIX et XXX articulis// respondit que quondam tempore citra festum Nativitatis domini aut paulo ante ipsum festum// aut paulo post vidit et audivit iste A. que dominus Rex celebravit curiam// in Barchinona et fuerunt ibi plures Nobiles de Cathalonia et tunc fuit// deliberatum in ipsam curiam secundum que a pluribus publice audivit dici in// ipsam civitatem que dominus Rex cum exercitu suo iret captum civitatem// Maioricarum set iste A. non interfuit celebrationem ipsius Curie {que recordit} qualiter tunc// temporis iste A. erat juvenis et non curabant se intromittere que inter// essent celebrationi ipsius Curie et sic iste A. non audivit de que// fuerunt proposita et dicta in ipsam Curiam nec quis primo locutus fuit.

Item// dixit iste A. que se vidisset et audivisset in (h)estatem subsequenti scilicet in// mensem Septembri subsequenti. Secundum que firmiter credit que dominus Rex cum// exercitu et navigio suo recessit de portu Salodii ubi erat ipsum navigium// congregatum et iverunt insulas Maioricas et appulerunt in eodem// mensem apud Palomiam citra festum Sancte Michaelis Septembri// sicut sibi videtur et in subsequenti festo sancti Silvestri et sancti Columbe// dominus Rex cum exercitu suo in que existit iste A. destruit et cepit civi// tatem Maioricarum.

Interogatus quot annis fuit [***] dicto tempore post vel// ante dictum festum, dixit iste A. non recordari.

Item interogatus si scit que// dominus Rex ante dictam temporem deliberavisset Barchinone vel aliquo loco super predicto exercitu// Maioricarum, responidt se nescire.

Item interogatus quot annis fuit a dicto tempore citato// que dominus Rex deliberavit in Barchinonam ire Maiorici. Item respondit se credere// que suntquadreginta et duo annos et amplius. Aliud nescit super predictis.//

TESTIMONY OF BERENGUER, KNIGHT

(Second Part, fol. 7)   Item interogatus super iiii articulo, respondit se nescire usque que predictum Castrum habeat ipsos terminos.// Credit tamen que habeat terminos et per villam sit de termino ipsius Castri// et hac credit per eo qualiter vidit que homines ipsius ville veniunt ad parlamentum// ad dictum Castrum quando mandatur eis ex parte domini Gastonis. Et exercuit// ad sonum quando bailus domini Gastonis emitit sonum.

Item interogatus super// VI articulo, respondit que fama est in villa Vici que Castrum// domini Gastonis teste ex castro. Nam iste audivit dici ab omnibus// et etiam quando ex parte domini Gastonis preconizat parlamentum publice mandat// hominibus ville Vici secundum que iste B. et plures audivit ut veniat ad// Castrum ad parlamentum. Dixit que audivit precone preconizante// publice quando expectabat vinum vel alia victualia que essent aliquarum como// rantium iuxta castrum predictum que notabat et dicebat que morabatur iuxta Castrum.

APPENDIX II

ASSEMBLIES OF JAMES I THE CONQUEROR (1213–1276)

DATE OF MEETING	PLACE OF MEETING	TITLE
June 16, 1169	Zaragoza	*plena curia*
June, 1188	Huesca	*solempnis curia*
November, 1192	Barcelona	*celebris curia*
May, 1208	Huesca	*general cort*
August, 1214	Lerida	*cort*
September 5–8, 1218	Lerida	—
September, 1219	Huesca	*cort general*
March 18, 1223	Daroca	—
April 28, 1225	Tortosa	*corts*
April 1, 1227	Alcalá	—
June 2, 1227	Almudevar	*cort*
February 6, 1228	Daroca	*curia generalis*
December 18–23, 1228	Barcelona	*curia generalis* *curia solemnis*
December 17, 1232	Monzón	*cort general*
March 16, 1235	Tarragona	*curia generalis*
March 15, 1236	Zaragoza	*cort general*
October 15, 1236	Monzón	*curia generalis*
1239	Valencia	—
1243	Daroca	*curia*
January 21, 1244	Barcelona	—
January 7, 1247	Huesca	*cort general*

Table cont.:

DATE OF MEETING	PLACE OF MEETING	TITLE
February, 1250	Alcañiz	*curia generalis*
April 11, 1261	Valencia	—
December 6, 1262	Valencia	*corts*
November 12, 1264	Barcelona	*cort*
December, 1264	Zaragoza	*cort*
April 26, 1265	Exea de los Caballeros	—
April 13, 1266	Valencia	—
March 20, 1271	Valencia	—
March 20, 1272	Lerida	—
December 7, 1275	Alcira	—
January 26, 1275	Lerida	*cort*
November 1, 1275	Lerida	—

THE COUNCIL OF PEÑAFIEL 1302:
THE CASTILIAN CHURCH'S REASSERTION OF ITS
LIBERTAS ECCLESIASTICA

Paulette L. Pepin

Though Fernando IV of Castile-León (1295–1302) is a rather obscure and inconspicuous historical figure, his reign symbolizes the Castilian Church's necessity for reasserting possession of its *libertas ecclesiastica*. Liberties, meaning clerical rights, privileges and immunities such as exemption from royal taxation, the right to judgement in ecclesiastical courts, protection of ecclesiastical property and payment of tithes, apparently were only of minor concern for the Castilian clergy in the thirteenth century.[1] Then, clergy did not find it necessary to protect their liberties by regularly holding provincial and diocesan church councils, but instead relied upon their prerogative to demand the redress of their grievances in the *Cortes*.[2]

During the first half of the thirteenth century, until the death of Fernando III in 1252, church-state relations were relatively harmonious since they shared a "common Christian Mission," the reconquest.[3] The Castilian Church supported the reconquest militarily, spiritually, and, especially, financially.[4] The Spanish victory at Las Navas de Tolosa in 1212 would cost the Castilian clergy half their year's income.[5] Later, in 1215 at the Fourth Lateran Council, the papacy

---

[1] Joseph F. O'Callaghan, "The Ecclesiastical Estate in the Cortes of León-Castile," *CHR* 67 (1981): 187.

[2] Ibid., 185, 191–197. O'Callaghan's article deals substantively with the Castilian clergy's active participation in the *cortes* of Castile in the thirteenth century. He states that when these churchmen, ". . . saw their interests threatened they were quick to demand redress." This is evident in the *Cortes* of 1255, 1272, and 1275. Peter Linehan, *The Spanish Church and the Papacy in the Thirteenth Century* (Cambridge, 1971), pp. 20–35, discusses in depth the Castilian clergy's lack of enthusiasm for holding councils or for reforming themselves, but does not address their use of the *Cortes* to demand redress of their grievances or the resulting actions of the king. His discussion primarily concerns the Castilian clergy's total disregard for their *libertas ecclesiastica*.

[3] Linehan, p. 108.

[4] Ibid., pp. 101, 102.

[5] Ibid., p. 5, fn. 5; *Chronique latine inédite des Rois de Castile (1236)*, ed. Georges

demanded that the Spanish clergy be taxed for the projected Fifth Crusade.[6] This outraged the Castilian prelates who felt that they should not be expected to pay for a foreign war when they were already paying for their own crusade. For this reason, and the reforming zeal of the papacy, the relationship between the Castilian Church and the papacy was strained throughout the thirteenth century.[7]

While the Castilian clergy vigorously objected to the papacy's increased fiscal demands, they were also reluctant to oppose the Castilian monarch's demands for additional tax revenue. Even after Pope Innocent IV granted Fernando III the use of the *tercias reales* (the third part of the ecclesiastical tithe destined for the upkeep of the churches) in 1247, in order to continue the reconquest, the Castilian clergy remained compliant.[8] This obliging behavior was due, in part, to the nationalistic nature of the reconquest, but a more fundamental reason for their docility was the potential wealth which they believed would be gained after the completion of the reconquest. Willingly they accepted Fernando III's interference in their business, to the point of subordinating the defense of their liberties and immunities, for the expected windfall which never fully materialized. Indeed, most of the Castilian clergy did not share bountifully in the spoils of the reconquest.

Cirot, *BH* 14 (1912): 355; and Demetrio Mansilla, *Iglesia-castellano-leonesa y curia romana en los tiempos del rey San Fernando* (Madrid, 1945), p. 51.

[6] J.D. Mansi, *Sacrorum conciliorum nova et amplissima collectio* (Florence and Venice, 1759–1798), Canon no. 71; Hubert Jedin and John Dolan, eds., *Handbook of Church History* (New York, 1968), 4:170; Joseph F. Donavan, *Pelagius and the Fifth Crusade* (Philadelphia, 1950), p. 28.

[7] Linehan, pp. 1–35, discusses in depth the papal legate John of Abbeville's zealous attempts during his sojourn in the Iberian peninsula (1228–1229) to implement the reforming canons of the Fourth Lateran Council upon the Spanish clergy, in particular the elimination of clerical concubinage, and the necessity for promoting the calling of provincial and diocesan councils. For their part the Spanish prelates strove fervently to thwart John of Abbeville's endeavors, which they considered to be a personal mission on his part to compel the Spanish Church to become subservient to the papacy; see Mansi, 22:991, 1003, canons nos. 6, 14.

[8] Linehan, pp. 108, 111–112; O'Callaghan, "The Ecclesiastical Estate," 191; *Les registres de Innocent IV*, ed. Elie Berger (Paris, 1884–1921), 1:377, no. 2538. This is the first papal bull (1247) specifically authorizing the king the use of the *tercias reales* for the reconquest. Ironically, the Castilian clergy had in all probability lost control over the *tercias* when they acknowledged the king's right to collect the tax at the Council of Palencia in 1129, and they continued to allow succeeding kings to continue to do so, apparently without ever asking the consent of the clergy. See *ES* 20:482–486.

An analysis of the *repartimiento* shows that the more generous donations were restricted to the churchmen who were royal favorites. From 1250–1253, the Bishop of Segovia, Raimundo, a royal secretary, was granted donations amounting to a sizeable number of oxen and sheep, crops, churches, and estates with their accompanying rents.[9] Moreover, Raimundo's allegiance to the crown enabled him to be appointed as the first Archbishop of Seville in 1259.[10] The Bishops of Palencia, Cuenca, Avila and Coria were granted only a small share of Seville's rewards: a few sheep and oxen, orchards of figs and olives, and perhaps a church or house.[11]

Linehan sharply disagrees with this assessment regarding Bishops Pedro of Coria and Mateo of Cuenca, since he classified them as "well-heeled prelates" who received relatively generous treatment.[12] Though these bishops did receive a share of the spoils, the evidence does not indicate generous royal donations.[13]

Nevertheless, it was not until the accession of his son Alfonso X (1252–1284), with his imperial ambitions and the outbreak of civil war which placed even heavier fiscal burdens[14] on the clergy, that their relationship became openly antagonistic.[15] In their desire to achieve freedom from secular control and arrest the king's fiscal demands, the prelates, under the guidance of Sancho, Archbishop

[9] Linehan, p. 113; Julio González, *Repartimiento de Sevilla*, 2 vols. (Madrid, 1951), 2:28, 175, 231, 266, 300, 309, 320; Joseph F. O'Callaghan, *The Learned King: The Reign of Alfonso X of Castile* (Philadelphia, 1993), p. 51; Antonio Ballesteros Beretta, *Alfonso X* (Barcelona-Madrid, 1963), pp. 89–100, 322.

[10] Linehan, p. 113; Antonio Ballesteros Beretta, *Sevilla en el siglo XIII* (Madrid, 1913); O'Callaghan, *The Learned King*, p. 51; Ballesteros Beretta, *Alfonso X*, p. 320.

[11] González, *Repartimiento*, 2:29, 297–298, 305.

[12] Linehan, pp. 113–114.

[13] González, *Repartimiento*, 2:28–29, 300.

[14] O'Callaghan, "The Ecclesiastical Estate," 191–192; idem, *The Learned King*, pp. 53–54; Linehan, pp. 121–123; Ballesteros Beretta, *Alfonso X*, pp. 199–207, 1071–1072, nos. 244, 262, 264, 269, 272. At the inception of Alfonso X's reign the prelates hoped to recover the *tercias reales*, and the king told them at his first *cortes* held in Seville in 1252 that he would not alter the extraction until he had surveyed his kingdom. However, three years later, Alfonso X found it necessary to demand the *tercias reales*. This continual exaction prompted the bishops to declare their disapproval at an assembly that the king had summoned to Valladolid in the summer and fall of 1255. Alfonso X did not support the return of the *tercias reales*, but the bishops did find him more amenable in defending certain other rights of the Church, in particular the collection of the tithe.

[15] Linehan, pp. 124–127; Joseph F. O'Callaghan, *A History of Medieval Spain* (Ithaca, New York, 1975), p. 362; Jofré de Loaysa, *Crónica de los Reyes de Castilla, Fernando III, Alfonso X, Sancho IV y Fernando IV, 1284–1305*, Antonio García Martínez, trans. and ed. (Murcia, 1961; rept. 1982), p. 81.

of Toledo, convoked a council at Alcalá de Henares in 1257, where they attempted to establish a tradition of regular councils.[16] This important step, which was taken in accordance with the precepts set forth at the Fourth Lateran Council, stressed the responsibility of the episcopate to summon provincial councils, and in many respects might be considered a call for political action. Not only could this council strengthen the Castilian prelates ability to affect a nascent movement of independence from monarchical control, but it could also provide the church with a political forum and the prescription for advocating Christian reform and renewal.[17]

At this meeting, however, the bishops of Palencia, Osma, Sigüenza and Cuenca never put their good intentions into action, probably because neither the bishops of the provinces of Compostela nor those of Toledo were ever sincerely zealous in carrying out their program. The lack of initiative on the part of the Alcalá bishops may be explained by examining some of these episcopal participants. Sancho, the Archbishop of Toledo, was the brother of Alfonso X, and is depicted by Linehan as a political opportunist, who took advantage of Alfonso X's worsening political position, "making ecclesiastical discontent serve his own ends."[18] Though this criticism probably had some validity, the archbishop's energy and devotion to the Church's cause does not completely support Linehan's rather disapproving statement.[19] On the other hand, several of the council's attendants, among them Raimundo of Segovia and Mateo Reinal of Cuenca, were extremely loyal to Alfonso X, and this may account for the fact that at the close of the council the prelates declared their allegience to Alfonso X, who was attempting to secure territory in

---

[16] Linehan, pp. 166–169; Fidel Fita, "Concilio de Alcalá de Henares (15 enero 1257)" *BRAH* 10 (1887): 152–154, "... ad dei gloriam et honorem statuimus quod nos dicti comprovinciales Episcopi annis singulis bis in anno ad celebrandum provinciale concilium in dei nomine congregemur."; José Sánchez Herrero, *Concilios provinciales y Sinodos Toledo de los de siglos XIV y XV* (Seville, 1976), p. 29, only mentions the existence of the council.

[17] Linehan, p. 166; Mansi, 22:982, canon no. 1, *De fide Catholica*.

[18] Luis Suárez Fernández, "Evolutión histórica de hermandades castellanos," *CHE* 16 (1951): 5, 7, refers to the formation of *hermandades* amongst the lower clergy in order to protect their rights against encroachments by their prelates, at a time when Alfonso X was preoccupied with his quest to become Holy Roman Emperor and the outbreak of Moorish revolts and invasions in Andalusia.

[19] Fita, 153–154; Linehan, p. 166; José Manuel Nieto Soria, *Las relaciónes monarquia-episcopado castellano como sistema de poder (1252–1312)* 2 vols. (Madrid, 1983), 1:690.

Murcia.[20] The Alcalá council appears to have awakened some sense of political consciousness, but no previous foundation had been laid to assure the continuation of such congregations; therefore, as Linehan states, "the Alcalá meeting stands in a void."[21] Subsequent councils, like that of Burgos in 1261,[22] Brihuega in 1267,[23] and possibly others of uncertain dates, did not encourage radical independent action against the king as the Alcalá council had attempted. Instead, the bishops appear to have called these other councils principally to insure the protection of their prerogatives, and prevent such abuses as royal seizure of church property during episcopal vacancies.[24]

Neither the clergy's use of the *Cortes* to express their grievances against the king, nor the calling of church councils, persuaded Alfonso X from continually encroaching on the Church's liberties. His abusive behavior forced the bishops in 1277 to appeal to Pope Nicholas III.[25] Not even this action prevented the king from altering his policies toward the Church. Later, Alfonso's son, Sancho (later Sancho IV, 1284–1295), revolted against him and actively sought support from the Castilian clergy for his cause. Many of the indignant and exasperated Castilian clergy, including the bishops of Astorga, Zamora,

---

[20] Fita, 153–154: "Hoc autem statuendum decrevimus, salvo iure et domino domini Regis, quod nos in omnibus et per omnia conservare semper intendium fideliter et devote"; Nieto Sorio, 1:690.

[21] Linehan, p. 173.

[22] Fita, 153–154.

[23] Nieto Soria, 1:690, 721, no. 208, never refers to this meeting as a council but states that it was a reunion of the bishops of Osma, Cuenca, Palencia, Segovia, Sigüenza, and Segorbe, and representatives of the bishops of Jaén and Córdoba, who did not attend the Alcalá meeting. Based upon the age and fragile condition of the original document in the Palencian archives, he insists that it was held in 1266, not on 7 March 1267.

[24] O'Callaghan, *The Learned King*, p. 53; Fidel Fita, "Concilios españoles inéditos, provincial de Burgos de 1261 y nacional de Sevilla 1478," *BRAH* 22 (1893): 209–257; Linehan, pp. 175–176; Ballesteros Beretta, *Alfonso X*, 445.

[25] O'Callaghan, "The Ecclesiastical Estate," 196; Linehan, pp. 218–220; L*es registres de Nicholas III (1277–1280)*, ed. by Jules Gay (Paris, 1938), 341–344, no. 743. Most of the Castilian clergy's grievances dealt with Alfonso X's subjection of the Church. First and foremost was king's continual exaction of the *tercias*, which he had tended to treat as permanent source of revenue. The bishops also complained about many other abuses by the crown, including royal interference in episcopal elections, the extortion of subsidies from the clergy and their vassals, royal prohibitions forbidding prelates to impose ecclesiastical censures except in certain cases (the violation of churches, assault upon the clergy, and failure to pay tithes), and forbidding the clergy to assemble to treat of their grievances or to report them to the Holy See.

Mondeñedo, Túy, Badajoz, and Coria,[26] saw Sancho as a liberator
and enthusiastically supported him against his father, with the understanding that he would guarantee their liberties.[27]

However, Sancho's subsequent reign did not foster the renewal of
the once intimate relationship between the Castilian Church and the
monarchy. A few of Sancho's policies provoked controversy with the
Castilian prelates. In particular, as O'Callaghan stresses, Sancho was
determined to regain all sources of potential revenue, which included
all royal lands that had passed under the control of the Church.
The importance of increasing his treasury also had encouraged the
king to reform tax collection. In 1287, Sancho contracted with a
Catalan Jew, Abraham el Barchelón, to collect taxes. This action
aroused such opposition, especially from the townspeople, that he
was forced at the *Cortes* of Haro in 1288 to abandon Jewish tax
farming.[28] At the same *Cortes*, Sancho promised the Castilian churchmen that he would stop seizing certain Church monies which Pope
Gregory X had granted to his father in 1275 to aid in the wars
against the Muslims. Though, as Linehan states, it was "hardly a
generous concession since the six-year grant had been made thirteen
years before."[29]

Indeed, Sancho IV's reign was marked by continual concessions
to and compromises with the Church. This was especially evident
in regard to Sancho's confirmation of the Church's established privileges, liberties and customs to specific prelates at the insistence of
their bishop.[30] Sancho IV even made further concessions and promises
to the Castilian clergy in his desire to maintain their support. This
was especially true in regard to the Bishop of Cartagena, Diego
Martínez Magez. During the very early months of the rebellion of
the *Infante* Sancho, Diego confirmed his support of this prince, espe-

---

[26] Linehan, p. 220; Ballesteros Beretta, *Alfonso X*, p. 972; *ES*, 26:243–244.

[27] O'Callaghan, "The Ecclesiastical Estate," 197; *MHE* (Madrid, 1851–1948),
2:94–97, no. 220.

[28] O'Callaghan, "The Ecclesiastical Estate," 198; Evelyn S. Procter, *Curia and
Cortes in León and Castile 1072–1295* (Cambridge, 1980), pp. 150, 200; Mercedes
Gaibrois de Ballesteros, *Historia del reinado de Sancho IV de Castilla* (Madrid, 1922),
1:194; *Cortes* 1:103.

[29] Linehan, p. 243; Ballesteros Beretta, *Alfonso X*, p. 728; *Cortes*, 1:103.

[30] Juan Loperráez Corvalán, *Descripción histórica de Obispado de Osma* (Madrid, 1788),
1:262–263, 2:221, 225–227, nos. 82, 84; Prudencio de Sandoval, *Antigüedad de la
ciudad y iglesia catedral de Túy* (Braga, 1610; reprt. Barcelona, 1974), 160; José María
Fernández Catón, *Catálogo del archivo histórico diocesano de León*, 2 vols. (León, 1978),
1:24–25, no. 32.

cially after he had been guaranteed his rights and privileges.[31] Diego's loyalty and service to Sancho during his rebellion had been so apparent and advantageous, in contrast to the fidelity that the city of Murcia showed to Alfonso X,[32] that Sancho conferred privileges to Diego in March 1283, extending the boundaries of his bishopric.[33] Soon after the death of Alfonso X, to repay the loyalty of the bishop and his church and chapter, Sancho IV ordered the municipal councils, nobles, knights, and town officials of the kingdom of Murcia not to interfere in the tax exemptions of the diocese of Cartagena.[34] Not only was Diego a useful bishop for the Church, but he was undoubtedly useful to the king. Moreover, during the waning years of Sancho IV's reign, the Castilian prelates were willing to work with the crown to protect their rights, and would not tolerate royal oppression.

Sancho IV died in Toledo on 25 April 1295, and was succeeded by his nine-year old son, Fernando IV. Fernando's kingship was preserved by the devotion and determination of his ingenious mother, María de Molina, who protected her son from the constant political upheavals that beset his reign.[35] Ironically, once Fernando reached his majority he failed to recognize what his mother had done to secure the throne, and instead showed a complete indifference toward her. He even accepted malicious accusations from his nefarious uncle, the *Infante* Juan and his cohort, Juán Núñez de Lara, that she had committed malfeasance during her tenure as regent.[36]

Initially, Fernando IV dealt with the Castilian clergy cautiously, under the guidance of his regents, his mother and unscrupulous grand-uncle, Enrique.[37] Beginning in August 1295, however, the Castilian prelates were refused access to the deliberations of the *Cortes* by

---

[31] Juan Torres Fontes, "El Obispado de Cartagena en el siglo XIII," *Hispania* 13 (1953): 516.

[32] Ibid., 517–525.

[33] Ibid., 518, 562.

[34] Ibid., 520; Gaibrois de Ballesteros, *Sancho IV*, 3:2, no. 4.

[35] Cayetano Rosell y López, ed., *Crónica del rey don Sancho IV*, in *BAE* 66:89, chap. 12; Antonio Ballesteros Beretta, *Historia de España: su influencia en la historia universal* (Barcelona, 1922), 3:35; Loperráez Corvalán, 1:265.

[36] *CFIV* 1:88, 97–98; César González Mínguez, *Fernando IV de Castilla (1295–1312): La guerra civil y el predominio de la nobleza* (Valladolid, 1976), pp. 125–132; Ballesteros, *Historia*, 3:39; Mercedes Gaibrois de Ballesteros, *María de Molina* (Madrid, 1936), p. 139.

[37] Fernando IV granted and confirmed privileges to these bishops during the early sessions of his first *cortes* from late July to mid-August, 1295. *ES*, 17:110, 41:89;

the forceful demands of the townspeople.[38] María de Molina had
allied with them to preserve her son's throne[39] against the aggressive behavior of her brothers-in-law, the Infantes Juan and Jaime,
and Denis of Portugal.[40] This action denied the Castilian Church its
only access to a political forum, the *Cortes*. The clergy were defiant
and obstinate in their protest, but they were soon appeased by the
guarantee of specific liberties and privileges which had been disre-
garded in previous years.[41]

In the *ordenamiento de prelados*, enacted by the Valladolid *Cortes* on
16 August, the king guaranteed the clergy that he would not despoil
the goods of a vacant diocese, interfere in episcopal elections, impose
taxes on the prelates and their churches,[42] and finally, he would not
seize the *jus spolii*, the goods of the deceased prelate, "but would
allow the cathedral chapter to use the goods of a deceased prelate
to pay his debts, and carry out his bequests, and provide him with
an honorable burial."[43] These were largely the same assurances
Alfonso X gave to the clergy in 1255 and 1275.[44]

The regents, in particular María, were willing to do almost anything even to the point of redressing the grievances of the prelates
to secure the throne for Fernando IV.[45] This latest ordinance was
issued to pacify the disgruntled prelates who, having failed to become
part of the power structure, might support one of the many candidates to the throne. From their past history, the bishops were known
as feeble and indecisive, but this was the first time that they had
been excluded from the *Cortes*. Perhaps this crisis, which had left the

---

Loperráez, 3:233, no. 90; Prudencio de Sandoval, p. 161; Santos García Larragueta,
Catálogo de los pergaminos de la Catedral de Oviedo (Oviedo, 1957), p. 181, no. 516;
Angel Barrios García, *Documentación medieval de la Catedral de Avila* (Salamanca, 1981),
pp. 156–57, no. 162; Catón Fernández, 1:24–25, no. 32; Nieto Soria, 2:225–229,
nos. 534–541; Antonio Ubieto Arteta, *Colección diplomática de Cuéllar* (Segovia, 1961),
p. 102, no. 45; Antonio García y García, et al., eds., *Catálogo de los manuscriptos e
incunables de la Catedral de Córdoba* 6 vols. (Salamanca, 1976), 6:223, no. 53.

[38] *CFIV*, 10; *MFIV* 2:40–41, no. 22; González Mínguez, *Fernando IV*, 37; Wladimiro
Piskorski, *Las cortes de Castilla* (Barcelona, 1977), p. 98.

[39] Procter, pp. 186–195.

[40] *CFIV*, chaps. 10 and 11; González Mínguez, 4.

[41] *Cortes*, 1:133–135; O'Callaghan, "The Ecclesiastical Estate," 199.

[42] *Cortes*, 1:133–134.

[43] O'Callaghan, "The Ecclesiastical Estate," 199.

[44] Ibid., 192, 195; Loperráez Corvalán, 3:81–83, no. 58; Ballesteros Beretta, *Alfonso
X*, pp. 737–738, 1071–1072, 1107, nos. 256–257, 259–261, 263, 265, 270, 276,
278, 977–983; Pedro Fernández del Pulgar, *Historia secular y ecclesiástica de Palencia*
(Madrid, 1679–1680), 2:336–338.

[45] *Cortes*, 1:133.

clergy politically isolated, would provoke them to make a concerted effort. For example, Gonzalo, Archbishop of Toledo, had lacked courage and fortitude in the past, and Maria had no idea how he would react to this new challenge. She and Enrique would find out shortly.

Within two days of the enactment of this ordinance on 16 August, the representatives of the *concejos* of Extremadura and those of the Archdiocese of Toledo issued a letter affirming that they would not interfere with the vassals of Archbishop Gonzalo and of their other lords, as long as the townspeople's rights were preserved.[46] This was a precautionary measure, taken by the *hermandad* to avert any possible abusive action the archbishop and the other lords might take against such *concejos* under their jurisdiction as Alcalá, Brihuega, Uceda and Salamanca. The *hermandad* also wished to assure the archbishop and the other lords that its primary concern was the safekeeping of the townspeople's rights.[47] Though the *hermandad* perhaps thought this was a prudent action, this letter provoked the archbishop to issue his protest of 16 August 1295.[48]

The language of the protest exhibits anger, resentment, exasperation and outrage. In the opening paragraph, Gonzalo, acting as spokesman for the rejected prelates, not only declared his disapproval of the townspeople's action, but his outrage at their arrogance and disregard for the Church's rights.[49] He knew from the *ordenamiento general* (8 August 1295) that the ecclesiastical estate had been excluded from the king's entourage, from control of royal estates, and from civic positions, like the collection of taxes.[50]

The primate indignantly claimed that the *Cortes* itself was illegal. The archbishop purposely avoided the use of the word *Cortes*, and instead periphrastically referred to the convocation as a gathering.[51] Because the prelates, as traditional counsellors of the monarch, were not permitted to consult on the townspeople's petitions, the enactment of the *ordenamiento general* could not be considered legal. The

---

[46] *MFIV*, 2:38.

[47] Luis García de Valdeavellano, "Carta de hermandad entre los concejos de la extremadura castellana y del arzobispado de Toledo in 1295," *Revista Portugesa de Historia* 7 (1969): 59.

[48] *MFIV*, 2:40–41, no. 22.

[49] Ibid.

[50] *Cortes*, 1:131.

[51] *MFIV*, 2:40–41, no. 22; Piskorski, p. 40.

townspeople had gained control of the government without the participation of either the prelates or the nobility.[52]

The prelates condemned the treachery of the *concejos* concerning specific privileges granted to the vassals of the archbishop and certain lords in Extremadura. These privileges, the archbishop argued, were not legal, because only the archbishop and the other lords could consent to the privileges made to their vassals and, furthermore, the clergy would never consent to such an infringement on their rights.[53] The *concejos* had overstepped their bounds, and had extended unwarranted and excessive authority over the vassals of the archbishop and the other lords of Extremadura.[54]

This document was notarized and made public on 16 August 1295. What was the reaction of the king, the regents, or the townspeople? The chronicle mentions only the ecclesiastical protest, but records no other reaction. According to González Mínguez, several prelates who did not specifically witness the document agreed with it and, in fact, had expressed concern that their rights would be damaged or diminished by the townspeople's domination of the *Cortes*.[55] Many of these prelates, including the bishops of Avila, León, Oviedo, Orense, Mondoñedo, Osma, Túy and Lugo had their privileges, liberties, customs and rights reaffirmed by Fernando IV.[56] These ecclesiastical charters were a reiteration of many of the same rights guaranteed by the ordinance of 12 August. María and Enrique knew that the archbishop and the other bishops who had been excluded from the deliberations would probably protest. They also knew that they had to answer the prelate's petitions and protests favorably, in order to convince him to remain neutral.

However, as the civil war, which had begun with Fernando IV's reign, intensified, María de Molina continually found it necessary to pay for the nobles' loyalty (the Haros alone received 30,000 *maravedís*), and to restore all their possessions to them, in return for their recognition of Fernando as the true king.[57] On the other hand, the

---

[52] *MFIV*, 2:40, no. 22.

[53] Ibid.

[54] Ibid.

[55] González Mínguez, *Fernando IV*, p. 39.

[56] *MFIV*, 2:32–35, nos. 15–16; *ES*, 17:110, 18:168, 22:157; Loperráez, 3:233, no. 90; Sondoval, 161; García Larragueta, p. 181, no. 516; Barrios García, p. 157, no. 163; Fernández Catón, p. 53, no. 77; González Mínguez, *Fernando IV*, p. 40.

[57] *CFIV*, 1:12–13; *MFIV*, 2:42, no. 23; González Mínguez, *Fernando IV*, pp. 42–43.

Church was in a less secure position. The regents seem to have sensed this. Not wanting any of the prelates to advocate support for the rebel, the king, like his father, took further conciliatory actions. For example, Fernando IV granted to Juan Alvarez, Bishop of Osma, a donation of half the income owed to him by the bishop's vassals as compensation for providing military assistance against the rebels. Two years later, in 1298, while still in the midst of the civil war, the king once again acknowledged Juan Alvarez's services to him by bestowing honors on him.[58] Similar concessions were made to Sancho, Bishop of Avila, who was a personal advisor to the queen mother. In 1296, Fernando IV granted the vassals of this bishop exemption from certain taxes. Later in 1298, the king exempted the bishop and the cathedral clergy from paying the *yantar*.[59] Royal favors such as these confirmed the Bishop of Avila's support of Fernando IV, even until the king's death in 1312.[60]

Though the monarchy granted many prelates favors, it abused and neglected many others. This is seen in the assemblies which met between August 1297 and May 1302, when anarchy caused María to summon six *Cortes*.[61] In each of these meeting, the townspeople attempted to enhance their power by demanding that the king prohibit certain rights and privileges claimed by the clergy. One immunity that continually provoked the townspeople was clerical tax exemption on royal property that the Church acquired. This exemption limited the crown's revenue at a time when the perpetual need for additional funds to fight the rebels drained the treasury. This forced the king and his regents to request *servicios* from the townspeople at each of these *Cortes*.[62] By 1301 the cost of fighting the civil war had escalated to the point that the king had to ask the townspeople at

---

[58] *MFIV*, 2:171–172, no. 124.

[59] Procter, p. xvi, defines the *yantar* as "a lord's right to hospitality at the expense of his tenants or a money payment in lieu thereof; taken by the king, the queen, the heir to the throne, certain royal officials acting for the king and by other lords."

[60] Gaibrois de Ballesteros, *María*, p. 187; Nieto Sorio, 1:411, no. 131; AHN carpeta 23, no. 13; Barrios García, pp. 171–172, no. 175.

[61] *CFIV*, 72–73, chap. 4; *Cortes*, Manuel Colmeiro's *Introducción*, 1:192–193; González Mínguez, *Fernando IV*, pp. 90–91. The existence of this *cortes* was not fully recognized until Joseph F. O'Callaghan, "Las cortes de Fernando IV: Cuadernos inéditos de Valladolid 1300 y Burgos 1308," *Historia, Instituciones, Documentos* 13 (1987): 6–9, published its *cuadernos*.

[62] *CFIV*, 44, 53, 81, chaps. 2, 3, 7; "And then everyone in the entire kingdom agreed that the king should render his *servicio* in order to pay his knights."; Colmeiro, 1:199–197.

both *Cortes* of Burgos and Zamora for five *servicios*.[63] The townspeople
agreed to support the king and to pay the additional taxes, but at
the same time they demanded that the clergy pay taxes on all property acquired from the crown.

As early as 1199, Alfonso VIII of Castile had conceded a privilege to the Bishop of Cuenca, giving him the right to acquire royal
property, and he made a similar grant to the Archbishop of Toledo
in 1207. However, these were exceptions, for at the *Cortes* of Nájera,
probably held in 1185, Alfonso VIII had imposed a ban on such
acquisitions by the church, probably due to the clergy's excessive
use of the king's royal licenses. Alfonso VIII died in 1214 and the
execution of such a law was probably weakened by his death.[64]
Possibly that is one of the reasons why Sancho IV attempted to limit
the church's right to acquire royal estates at his *Cortes* of Haro in
1288.[65] Nevertheless, the townspeople complained at the Cuéllar
Cortes of 1297 that the Castilian clergy had been acquiring royal property, especially since 1288, and were not taxed or not sufficiently
taxed as their neighbors were.[66] In the later *Cortes* of Valladolid in
1298 and 1299, and at the *Cortes* of Zamora in 1301, the townspeople once again challenged the Church's right to gain control over
royal domains.[67] At Zamora, these townspeople further demanded
that any property acquired since the *Cortes* of Haro in 1288 should
be returned to the crown's jurisdiction.[68] Later that year, at Burgos,
this prohibition was modified so that only those clerics who had
acquired royal property since 1288 should pay taxes on it.[69] This
desire to tax the clergy appears to be a violation of Boniface VIII's
Clericis laicos and the 1295 ordinance protecting ecclesiastical rights,
but there were no protests, nor was there even an appeal to Rome.

It was not only the Church's immunity from paying certain taxes
which the townspeople resented, but the clergy's claim to jurisdiction over secular affairs. Townspeople objected to summons before
ecclesiastical courts for secular violations and crimes, and to excommunication for temporal offenses. At the meetings of the *Cortes*, the

---

[63] Ibid., 81; *Cortes*, 1:152; Colmeiro, *Introducción*, 1:196–197.
[64] Julio González, "Sobre la fecha de las Cortes de Nájera," *CHE* 74 (1975): 358.
[65] Gaibrois de Ballesteros, *Sancho IV*, 3:126, no. 208.
[66] *Cortes*, 1:135, art. 3.
[67] *Cortes*, 1:138, 141, 144, arts. 7, 9, 13; González Mínguez, *Fernando IV*, p. 147;
O'Callaghan, "The Ecclesiastical Estate," 201.
[68] *Cortes*, 1:144, art. 13; O'Callaghan, "The Ecclesiastical Estate," 201.
[69] *Cortes*, 1:146, art. 6; O'Callaghan, "The Ecclesiastical Estate," 201.

townspeople complained to the king that the Church was acting contrary to the royal *fueros*. In 1299, at the Valladolid *Cortes*, the king acknowledged the townspeople's grievances by decreeing that "no one should be summoned before ecclesiastical judges in lawsuits that concern their landed estates, since they should be summoned before secular judges according to their *fueros*."[70] With regard to the townspeople's complaint in the *Cortes* in 1299 that the Church abused its right of excommunication, the king responded favorably that "neither bishops nor deans nor chaplains nor vicars should impose the sentence of excommunication upon the laity concerning temporal cases."[71]

From 1297 until 1302, the relationship between church and state deteriorated to the point that the Castilian prelates were forced to defy Fernando's sovereignty. The cause of this open defiance was apparent in the actions of the king. Faced with the almost insurmountable difficulty of preserving the Castilian throne intact for her son, María ignored the Church's rights. As she tried to curb the power of the rebels, she held on firmly to her trusted allies, the townspeople. The politically astute queen knew she could only extend support to the Church when she needed it.

After seven years of regency, Fernando IV, entered his majority on his sixteenth birthday, 6 December 1301.[72] While there are obviously many circumstances prior to 1301 which could have provoked the Castilian prelates to seditious action, Fernando's majority seems to have initiated a climactic series of events which would result in the summoning of the first provincial church council in forty-five years.

What exactly pushed complacent prelates to do this? The intrigues of Juan and the other nobles who sought to separate Fernando from his mother's influence, and so to control his government, had continually caused the prelates great alarm.[73] If the magnates succeeded in gaining the young king's ear, the prelates would be effectively excluded from his council. This is probably what motivated the newly-installed Archbishop of Toledo, Gonzalo Díaz Palomeque, to initiate the summoning of a provincial church council.[74] How ironic

---

[70] *Cortes*, 1:141, art. 8.
[71] Ibid., 1:144, art. 9.
[72] *CFIV*, 84.
[73] Jofré de Loaysa, *Crónica*, p. 181; *Cortes*, 1:84–98; González Mínguez, *Fernando IV*, pp. 121–130.
[74] *MFIV*, 2:183–184, no. 132; Nieto Sorio, 2:246, no. 582; Gonzalo Daíz Palomeque was the nephew of the former Archbishop, Gonzalo García Gudiel, who had been

that this prelate should encourage such a radical plan of action. For Gonzalo Díaz, as Bishop of Cuenca in 1282, was one of four prelates who had crowned Sancho IV and María de Molina. Later, in 1300, he aided María in her negotiations to end hostilities with Juan.[75]

The prelates agreed with the archbishop that the only method which would assure that their rights, liberties and immunities would be protected was to summon a church council.[76] Here the prelates could act and let all the estates of the kingdom know where they stood. They would no longer allow the king flagrantly to disregard the privileges which he conceded to them in the *Cortes* of Valladolid in 1295.[77] For so long they had been denied the right of free assembly, and they now proceeded to claim it. For this action Fernando would call them traitors.[78]

On 1 April 1302, the Archbishop of Toledo presided over this provincial Church Council at Peñafiel.[79] Those assembled, along with the archbishop, were his suffragan bishops, Alvaro of Palencia, Fernando of Segovia, Simon of Sigüenza, Juan of Osma, Pascasio of Córdoba, and Pascual of Cuenca.[80] Fernando Gutierrez, Bishop of Córdoba, is named in the preamble, and in the list of confirmers, but the Bishop of Jaén is not mentioned at all. Though the bishopric of Jaén was a suffragan see of the province of Toledo, so were Oviedo and Cartagena (though vacant and still under Aragonese control), and their bishops were not participants. Therefore, it would seem that Jaén's bishop was not present.[81]

Those prelates who did participate came to Peñafiel, not to defy or to challenge the power of the king openly, but to defend their

---

elevated in 1299 as Cardinal of Albano at the Roman *curia*. Gonzalo Díaz was installed as Archbishop of Toledo in 1299, and remained archbishop until his death in 1310.

[75] *Crónica de Rey don Sancho IV*, in *BAE* 66:69, 117, chaps. 1, 7.

[76] J. Tejada y Ramiro, *Colección de canones y de todos los concilios de iglesia de España y de America*, 7 vols. (Madrid, 1859–1863), 3:433.

[77] Ibid.; *Cortes*, 1:133; *MFIV*, 2:40–41, no. 22.

[78] Linehan, pp. 20–53.

[79] Tejada y Ramiro, 3:433.

[80] Vicente de Lafuente, *Historia ecclesiastica de España* (Madrid, 1873), 4:407; Tejada y Ramiro, 3:433, 455; Sánchez Herrero, p. 29.

[81] Lafuente, 4:294; Tejada y Ramiro, 3:433–445; Sánchez Herrero, p. 29. Tejada y Ramiro believes that the Bishops of Jaén and Córdoba also participated, and Sánchez Herrero agrees with this assertion. Pedor Pascual, Bishop of Jaén, who had been held captive by the Muslims, died in 1300. The new Bishop of Jaén, García Pérez, was installed as bishop in March, 1301 (*MFIV*, 2:242, no. 177).

long-neglected *libertas ecclesiastica*. They would function as a defensive coalition which, outraged at the indifference of the monarchy toward their prerogatives, intended to defend their rights. They were not being seditious, although that was how the king interpreted their actions.[82] After a long period of complacency, they would now raise their voices against the clamor of the anti-clerical *Cortes*.

Before examining the significance of the fifteen canons these fathers decreed at Peñafiel, it is imperative to note the length of the deliberations. Though many sessions of the *Cortes* could conceivably have met a few weeks longer, the fact that these prelates did not treat this meeting capriciously is indicated by its six-week duration, closing on 13 May 1302. During these six weeks they unequivocally stated what their ecclesiastical immunities were and what their doctrine and regulations were.[83] The reform of church discipline was of primary concern to these prelates, as expressed in the council's preface: "we have gathered in common agreement for the purpose of establishing wholesale rules, for the good members of our flock, the salvation of their souls, the reform of the customs of our church."[84]

A strong vital church had to have a foundation based on renewed and effective discipline. The first five canons, which are summarized below, all dealt with the rules and regulations for all clerics and laymen to follow, subject to appropriate punishment:

I. That at all times clerics should recite the canonical hours.
II. That no cleric may have a mistress publicly.
III. That clerics should administer to the sick the sacraments of penance and the Eucharist, and not allow these people to die without them.
IV. That no one should receive the sacrament of the Eucharist before he has confessed; that priests should deny communion to those who they do not know for certain have been to confession.
V. That priests should maintain the inviolable secrecy of the confessional, which complies with the Fourth Lateran Council, canon 21; that laymen should confess with their own priests.[85]

---

[82] Linehan, p. 244; Lafuente, 4:407–408, a royalist, states that their actions were seditious.

[83] Tejada y Ramiro, 3:443, 445.

[84] Ibid.: ". . . pro subditorum commodo, aninarumque salute, morum reformatione, et ecclesiarum nostrarum, inde de communi consensu salubriter duximus statuendum."

[85] Tejada y Ramiro, 3:434–438; Sánchez Herrero, p. 30, in summarizing the canons of the Peñafiel Council, divides the first five canons into the following categories: *Clerigios* (canons nos. 1, 2); *Pastoral Sacramental (Eucaristia)* (canons nos. 4, 5); and *Viatico* (canon no. 3).

In briefly discussing the more notable canons of this council, the historian Tejada y Ramiro states that the second canon is one that necessitates more consideration, since it prohibited ecclesiastics from having mistresses publicly.[86] How ironic that the one "peculiar institution"[87] the Castilian clergy would not relinquish to Innocentian reform,[88] to the point of yielding their *libertas ecclesiastica* to the monarchy in return for their protection from papal reformists, should be found in this declaration. The tenacious efforts of the legate, John of Abbeville, had finally come to fruition. Their condemnation of their despised and wayward brothers was incontrovertible. If anyone should violate this constitution and did not heed a warning from his superiors, then he would be deprived of the revenues of his benefice. And if the cleric in question should not have a benefice and should continue to sin, he should be suspended from office, and punished accordingly.[89]

The Archbishop of Toledo, along with his suffragans, realized how significant discipline was to their cause of *libertas ecclesiastica*, but of equal importance were the long-disregarded privileges conceded to them by previous kings. *Libertas ecclesiastica* meant securing, even demanding, what was rightfully theirs. This included the right of the Church to collect the tithe (*decima* or *diezmo*),[90] and to oppose the monarchy's interference in episcopal elections, its violation of the goods and property of a vacant sees, and its confiscation of the *jus spolii*, the goods of the deceased prelates.[91] Since these abuses were damaging to the financial well-being of all churches, the prelates decreed that all Christians should pay the tithe under penalty of excommunication.[92] This was the severest castigation, but an effective weapon

---

[86] Tejada y Ramiro, 3:433; Sánchez Herrero, p. 30.

[87] Linehan uses this expression to refer to the Spanish clergy's obstinacy in maintaining their custom of clerical marriage and concubinage. Henry Charles Lea, *History of Sacerdotal Celibacy in the Christian Church* (New Hyde Park, NY, 1966), pp. 259–261, discusses the Castilian clergy's lack of initiative in enforcing clerical celibacy and their desire, despite papal directive against marriage and concubinage, to maintain their prerogative.

[88] Mansi, 22:1003, canon no. 14; Jedin, 4:167: "The bull of convocation, *Vineam domini sabaoth*, clearly outlined the council's program. It would deal with the welfare of all of Christendom; vices were to be uprooted, virtues planted, abuses eliminated, morals renewed. . . ."

[89] Tejada y Ramiro, pp. 435–436. This prohibition was not only directed at subordinate clerics, but to all clerics, especially higher clergy, who were to set an example.

[90] Ibid., pp. 439–440; Sánchez Herrero, p. 30.

[91] *Cortes*, 1:133–135.

[92] Tejada y Ramiro, pp. 439–440, canon no. 7.

in a society where one's religion was the foundation of one's life. If one was excommunicated, one was a damned outcast in a sea of Christian souls.

Canon 8 decreed that the ministers of Christ should prepare the dough for the host using only wheat and water, without any other elements emphasizing the sacredness and spiritual purity of the Eucharist.[93] This was also designed to strengthen the authority of priests since medieval piety "considered the Eucharist as the possession of the priest and defined his priesthood in terms of the power to consecrate."[94]

Furthermore, this canon reaffirms the Church's traditional doctrines, established at the Fourth Lateran Council in 1215, concerning the communion host's miraculous change into the living body of Jesus Christ, "*transsubstantiatio*."[95] In the introductory profession of faith (Canon 1) of this extraordinary council, the Doctrine of the Eucharist was enunciated. It was the first official use of the term "*transsubstantiatio*," a theological precept that had caused considerable controversy amongst the early scholastics, among them, Berengar of Tours (1010–1088) and Lanfranc of Bec (1010–1089). Yet with the emergence in the twelfth century of Aristotelian dialectical procedure, and the concept that universals were in particulars (the belief that Jesus' risen body was really in the bread and wine), the Doctrine of the Eucharist became solidified.[96]

Three canons (9, 10, 11) are concerned with ecclesiastical difficulties. Canon 9, while not referring to a unique difficulty, appears to address a very troublesome problem within the Province of Toledo; usurers and those individuals who did business with such voracious layman.[97] Each bishop was ordered to punish individuals who violated this prohibition.[98]

---

[93] Ibid., p. 440, canon no. 8.

[94] Joseph M. Powers, *Eucharistic Theology* (New York and London, 1967), p. 31.

[95] Ibid.; Jedin, 4:170; Leonard Elliott Binns, *Innocent III* (London, 1931), p. 172; Mansi, 22:1007, canon no. 22.

[96] Powers, pp. 22–31; Richard W. Southern, "Lanfranc of Bec and Berengar of Tours," in *Studies in Medieval History presented to F.M. Powicke* (Oxford, 1948), pp. 27–48; Steven Ozment, *The Age of Reform 1250–1550* (New Haven, 1980), pp. 6, 90.

[97] Though canon no. 9 does not specifically mention the Jews as usurers, more than likely, this is the group to whom the Peñafiel fathers are referring. O'Callaghan, *Cortes*, p. 181, affirms that "The area of greatest friction between Christians and Jews was commerce, especially moneylending."

[98] Tejada y Ramiro, pp. 440–441, canon no. 9; Sánchez Herrero, p. 30.

The canon that follows relates to another unique situation, not only in the Province of Toledo, but throughout the Iberian Peninsula, namely, the conversion of Jews and Muslims to Christianity. In order to protect these converts to the Christian faith, the Peñafiel fathers acknowledged that converts' baptism should not be a sign for losing all their goods. They were Christians and they must be protected by Christians. As the historian Sánchez Herrero indicates, this action was "an imitation of what King James II of Aragon (1291–1327) had ordered for his kingdoms on November 17, 1297."[99]

What intensified and aggravated the relations between church and state in 1302 were the provisions in Canons 6, 13, 14 and 15. The king viewed these measures, moreover, as promoting further disorder and rebellion. But the assembled prelates believed they were justified in their actions. Their first action was the promulgation of Pope Boniface VIII's bull, *Clericis laicos* (24 February 1296).[100] The bull's purpose was the prohibition of illegal taxation of the clergy, an abuse that the thirteenth-century Castilian monarchs had deliberately committed. From 1295 to 1302, relations between Fernando IV and his Castilian churchmen were often strained in regard to taxation, and when they could no longer tolerate his indifference, they registered their grievances openly. Since ancient times, the law had protected clerics and their goods from taxation, and Boniface's bull defended this prerogative against the enemies of the Church. Though Boniface originally directed this bull at the French king, Philip IV, its prohibitions also applied to Castile.[101] The bishops exercised their prerogative and ordered that each one of them should publish the bull in his diocese. If anybody violated this constitution, then he would be subject to excommunication.[102]

This coalition of bishops, provoked by the monarchy's insensitivity and neglect of their rights, demanded in Canon 13 civil immunity for imprisoned clerics[103] and the discontinuation of the monarchy's policies of unlawful seizure of ecclesiastical goods and property, as well as its abuse of their liberties and customs. If these prerogatives, assured by previous kings, were not affirmed, they threatened to

---

[99] Tejada y Ramiro, p. 441, canon no. 10; Sánchez Herrero, p. 30.

[100] Brian Tierney, *The Crisis of Church and State 1050–1300* (Englewood Cliffs, NJ, 1964), pp. 172–176; Sánchez Herrero, p. 31.

[101] Tierney, pp. 172–176.

[102] Tejada y Ramiro, pp. 442–443, canon no. 6; Sánchez Herrero, p. 31.

[103] Tejada y Ramiro, pp. 444–445, canon no. 14; Sánchez Herrero, p. 31.

excommunicate all those individuals who continued to abuse their rights. The threats they made were not idle ones, but were meant to affect control over the Church's jurisdiction. If the queen and the *infantes* should illegally seize church property, an interdict would be declared in the diocese; if they failed to restore the property within one month, they were to be excommunicated.[104] Members of the military orders who committed these transgressions would also face similar measures. Also, specifically included in this directive, were the king, his brothers and sisters, *alcaldes, merinos* and other town officials, as well as the town councils, who were all subject to canonical penalties if they violated the Church's immunities.[105] The canon likewise stated that neither soldiers nor court favorites could purchase ecclesiastical possessions. If they purchased these goods, and they were not restored to the church within two months, then the violators would suffer excommunication.[106]

While these canons were being deliberated, an additional statement was issued on 10 April 1302,[107] directed at the king's abusive treatment of the Castilian clergy. The king was accused of violating the privileges conceded to the Church and harassing its clergy by unjustly demanding tribute from them and arresting clerics and trying them in secular courts. If these violations persisted, the prelates threatened him with an interdict, to be imposed on any place he happened to be visiting. And, if he did not comply with the provisions of this declaration, then the interdict would be imposed throughout the ecclesiastical province.[108] These words could be judged as being inflammatory, but the prelates, led by Archbishop Gonzalo, had formed this coalition to defend and secure what was theirs, the *libertas ecclesiastica*.[109]

Unfortunately the strength and confidence which the Castilian prelates exhibited at Peñafiel soon dissipated, and they succumbed to Fernando's cajolery and to his promises not to ignore their rights and privileges or to treat them abusively. Only after Pope Clement V insisted forcefully that the Order of the Knights Templar be dissolved

---

[104] Tejada y Ramiro, pp. 442–443, canon no. 13; Sánchez Herrero, p. 31.
[105] Ibid.
[106] Tejada y Ramiro, p. 445, canon no. 15; Sánchez Herrero, p. 32.
[107] *MFIV*, 2:283, no. 200; Diego de Colmenares, *Historia de ciudad de Segovia y compendio de las historias de Castilla* (Madrid, 1640; reprt., 2 vols., Segovia, 1969), pp. 443–444.
[108] Ibid.
[109] Sánchez Herrero, p. 32.

did these mercurial prelates again become imbued with the spirit of defiance that they had shown at Peñafiel. This papal pronouncement and Fernando's continued harassment prompted the Castilian prelates to call four additional church councils to defend their liberties and to protect their immunities. Certainly Fernando IV's reign can be judged a successful attempt by the Castilian clergy to reassert possession of their *libertas ecclesiastica*. However, one may also conclude that the bishops' contradictory behavior, which ranged from strong and forceful demands to total submission to the king, did not enable them to establish a position of strength, and nor allow them to confirm the perpetual possession of their *libertas ecclesiastica*.

DEFEAT FROM THE JAWS OF VICTORY: STEPHEN OF BLOIS IN ENGLAND

Steven Isaac

When Stephen of Blois rushed across the English Channel in 1135 to claim his uncle's throne, the speed of his action bought him several years of relative security. His opponents found their position severely undermined within the space of a few weeks. However valid Matilda's claims might have been to her father's English crown, Stephen had the benefit of being the anointed king. His acquisition of the duchy of Normandy left her with Anjou as her only base of support, and the long-standing animosity between Normans and Angevins only precluded her attracting large number of sympathizers within the duchy. Yet it was only a matter of time before the business of kingship meant that Stephen was going to anger certain of his subjects. Matilda naturally attracted these, like Baldwin de Redvers or Eustace fitzJohn, who suffered losses under the new monarch.[1] Her cause received its greatest boost in the spring of 1138 when Matilda's half-brother Robert, earl of Gloucester, renounced his fealty to Stephen and officially joined her cause. With him Matilda gained a capable military leader and, through his properties, a necessary foothold in England itself.[2] And with Robert of Gloucester's defection, the incidence of rebellion picked up its pace.

The conflict between Stephen and Matilda has naturally attracted much attention from historians. Starting with John Horace Round's dominating picture of Geoffrey de Mandeville as a professional traitor, always ready to sell himself for an ever-growing list of powers, privileges, and immunities, interpretations of Stephen's reign have

---

[1] *GS*, pp. 30–45, Redvers fled to the Angevin court after Stephen crushed his 1136 revolt and gave his castles to his own supporters; according to Richard of Hexham, *Church Historians of England*, trans. Joseph Stevenson (London, 1856), p. 46, fitzJohn joined the Scottish invasion of 1138 and apparently lost his castle of Alnwick after the Battle of the Standard.

[2] William of Malmesbury, *HN*, p. 23, who is usually reliable with dates, puts Robert's *diffidatio* immediately after Whitsuntide, or Pentecost.

often focused on the role of the independent-minded magnates. It was the heyday of the infamous adulterine castle:

> For every great man built him castles and held them against the king; and they filled the whole land with these castles. They sorely burdened the unhappy people of the country with forced labour on the castles; and when the castles were built, they filled them with devils and wicked men.[3]

Even accounting for clerical hyperbole, this picture from the *Anglo-Saxon Chronicle* shows why the explosion of private fortifications has garnered so much attention. Frank Stenton, after noting that accurate perceptions of the castle's role have been skewed by too much attention to baronial castles, cannot himself avoid discussing them.[4] The result has been a portrayal of Stephen as an ineffectual king hamstrung by countless barons holed up in their castles. Such an interpretation has its merits, especially for the warfare that followed Matilda's arrival in England in 1139. But for the year-and-a-half following the earl of Gloucester's defiance, the chronicles show a different view of the king.

Before Matilda and Robert landed at Arundel, Stephen vigorously quelled the revolts that sprung up, especially around Gloucestershire, Herefordshire, and Wiltshire. More so than at any other point in his reign, in 1139 Stephen was influencing the course of events in England, rather than just reacting to circumstances. During that time, castles figured prominently in Stephen's strategy. Nor were they adulterine castles, but instead such fortresses that had become an integral part of the feudal landscape in the seven decades since the Conquest. Stenton noticed their importance even though he gave more attention to the adulterine castles. He wrote that "It is highly significant that the castles which determined the general course of the war . . . were castles which are known to have been in existence before the troubles began."[5] The role of these fortresses in Stephen's strategy was typically determined by location, formidability of the defenses, and the estimated loyalty of the owner (or castellan in the case of royal castles). Stephen's assessment of these factors influenced his campaigning throughout 1138 and 1139. Until 30 September

---

[3] *ASC*, p. 264.

[4] Frank Stenton, *The First Century of English Feudalism, 1066–1166* (Oxford, 1961), pp. 192–209.

[5] Stenton, p. 202.

1139, the king had his greatest opportunity to secure his position, to collect as many ardent supporters as possible and to arrange matters so that wavering barons would at least not defect.

To better understand the events of 1139, the developments of the previous year must be assessed. Stephen had faced a number of rebellious magnates already, but their revolts had been sporadic and more or less independent. Neither the *Gesta Stephani* nor the *Historia Novella*, the most partisan accounts from Stephen's reign, attribute earlier rebellions to any loyalty to King Henry's daughter.[6] But with Robert of Gloucester's formal repudiation of Stephen's lordship, the king had to deal with a flurry of revolts as Robert's vassals tried to honor his change of loyalty. The situation was quite serious since a number of Robert's supporters held English ports. Walchelin Maminot held Dover and Robert of Lincoln, Wareham castle. Moreover, Robert was a major landholder in Kent; besides Dover he also held castles at Canterbury and Leeds.[7] Neither was an inconsequential threat since the former likely had a stone keep by this time and the latter, located as it was on islands in a lake, would be hard to reduce. Kent was important to the king as a link to his supply of Flemish stipendiaries. Stephen reacted quickly to bring military and political pressure against his new opponents. While his queen enforced a naval blockade of Dover, the newly appointed earl of Derby, Robert of Ferrers, influenced Maminot, his son-in-law, to surrender. Another earl, Gilbert de Clare (whom Stephen had just made earl of Pembroke), captured Leeds at about the same time.[8] While Stephen's supporters secured southeastern England for him, he had already penetrated Robert's real base of support. Moving from a popular

---

[6] *GS*, p. 28–32. Baldwin de Redvers, although he never recognized Stephen as king, seems at first to have been more concerned about losing Henry I's gifts to him than about Matilda's own disinheritance. Likewise, Robert of Bampton was stirred to action by the change in patronage caused by Henry I's death. In the north, King David of Scotland was openly partisan to Matilda, but he attracted no English magnates to his side until 1138. See *OV*, 6:511, for Stephen's Christmas siege of Bedford, which was triggered by the Beauchamp resentment of Stephen's gifts to the Beaumont clan.

[7] *OV*, 6:516–518.

[8] *OV*, 6:518. On the composition of the castles, see Plantagenet Somerset Fry, *Castles* (Newton Abbot, Devon, 1980), pp. 201, 252. The date of the tower at Canterbury is still an open question, although Fry leans towards sometime during Henry I's reign. Since the tower was dressed with Caen stone, and none of Henry II's Pipe Rolls have figures commensurate with transporting such material, Fry's assessment seems reasonable.

reception at Gloucester in mid-May, Stephen went north to sup-
press the revolt at Hereford of Geoffrey Talbot, who had anticipated
Robert's defiance by several weeks. The king stayed outside Hereford
for approximately a month, apparently blockading the garrison into
submission. In the interest of a peaceful surrender, Stephen agreed to
let Geoffrey Talbot go free once royal troops had been installed in
the castle.[9] The king had made such an arrangement in 1136 with
costly results; Talbot gave him another opportunity to learn a lesson
in the politics of warfare. Stephen had hardly moved his forces out
of Hereford when Talbot returned to burn much of the town beyond
the River Wye. Moving quickly ahead of the king to Bristol, he then
energized that garrison to plague Stephen's supporters at Bath.[10]

While besieging Hereford, Stephen had used the time there to
summon the feudal levies. After a brief foray against Ludlow, Stephen
then turned against Bristol, the heart of Robert's earldom and the
center of the only enclave (except Wareham) still holding out against
the king. Virtually nothing remains of this castle today, but at the
time Stephen approached, it was already an imposing fortress. It
occupied the peninsula where the Avon and Frome rivers meet. To
augment the castle's strong site, Robert had raised a substantial keep
surrounded by stone curtain walls.[11] The strength of the castle occasioned a council in which no suggested a direct assault. One plan
called for the damming of the Avon so that it would flood the city
and cut off the castle. That, combined with the construction of two
siege castles on the sides of the roads into Bristol, should have starved
the garrison into submission. But Stephen never got to implement
this tactic. One drawback to summoning all his manpower reserves
was that it pulled lukewarm supporters directly into the conflict, supporters whose views could not be discounted without the risk of
alienating them. So when a faction within Stephen's host began to
voice reservations about the planned siege, the king soon realized
he would only harm his cause by doing nothing before Bristol's
walls.[12] He had experienced the same situation in 1136 when men
whose counsel he could not ignore had vitiated the results of the

---

[9] *OV*, 6:520; and John of Worcester, pp. 259–260.
[10] *GS*, pp. 58–60.
[11] Fry, pp. 194–195. R.A. Brown, H.M. Colvin, and A.J. Taylor, *The History of the King's Works*, 4 vols. (London, 1963–1982), 2:577–578.
[12] *GS*, pp. 64–66. John of Worcester, pp. 261–262.

long, arduous siege of Exeter. And it seems that only a month before, similar advice had let Geoffrey Talbot loose again.

Although unable to capture Bristol, Stephen used the rest of the summer to reduce the territories under the control of Robert and his supporters. He left a daring garrison at Bath, which he had just strengthened, to contain and harass Bristol. Meanwhile, the outposts the king came upon felt the brunt of his frustration. At Cary, "his engine scattered fire and showers of stones among the besieged and the pressure went on until their rations ran short."[13] Finding Harptree under-garrisoned, "he ordered some to set fire to the gates, others to put engines and scaling ladders against the walls, all to make eager and strenuous efforts to break in...."[14] Turning back to the north, he then moved against Shrewsbury, held by yet another marital relation of the earl of Gloucester.[15] By this time Stephen had probably dismissed many of his feudal levies and was campaigning with his household troops and stipendiaries. The siege was as sharp as those at Cary and Harptree, culminating in the hanging of ninety-three defenders. Neither John of Worcester or Orderic Vitalis record any dissent from Stephen's forces at this harshness. The act reaped other dividends as professions of allegiance poured in from a number of minor lords in the region.[16] By the end of August, only Wareham (outside of Bristol) remained open to pro-Matilda forces. The castellan at Wareham, Ralph Paganel, had already been chastised by Stephen at Dudley Castle, and he agreed to a truce when Stephen approached Wareham.[17] If we accept William of Malmesbury's assertion that only Bristol was left to Robert of Gloucester,[18] then Stephen must have exacted quite favorable terms.

By 1139 Stephen was in an enviably strong position: the Battle of the Standard had quelled the threat from Scotland; he had hemmed in his active opponents at Bristol or stranded them on the continent; and he controlled the southern coast of England and its ports.

---

[13] *GS*, pp. 66–68: "Sed rex percitus illuc adventans valide et infesse castellum Cari obsedit, balistisque ignem et lapidum imbres inter inclusos, adempta cessatione, discutientibus, usque ad escarum indigentiam vexatos...."

[14] Ibid., "...vacuumque paene reperiens, istos portis ignem apponere, illos muris machinas et scalas aptare, omnes vero ad ingrediendum sedule et feruenter jussit insudare...."

[15] John of Worcester, pp. 262–263.

[16] *OV*, 6:252.

[17] John of Worcester, p. 263.

[18] *HN*, p. 24.

Stephen's strategy in 1139 had two simple objectives: to consolidate his preeminence, thus giving wavering barons reason to pause before defecting, and to prevent Matilda from landing in England. He was reasonably assured of the former so long as he kept his rival on the continent. Should she land, however, then he hoped his dominance would continue to keep some of his magnates "on the fence." Stephen had also begun to learn how much or how little he could rely on parts of the feudal structure. His closest advisors were undoubtedly those who urged him to decisive action, such as the plans for taking Bristol. Diluting this group with advice from numerous magnates had only tended to hamstring the king's projects. Not only did Stephen need to avoid an irresolute appearance in 1139, he began to take steps that signalled that lukewarm support would no longer suffice.

The major event of 1139, aside from the Empress Matilda's landing at Arundel, was Stephen's arrest of the bishops of Salisbury, Lincoln, and Ely. Roger of Salisbury had been the second most powerful man in England under Henry I. As the head of the Exchequer, he still remained a powerful figure in Stephen's reign and incurred the envy of Waleran of Meulan's faction. William of Malmesbury explicitly blames the great building projects of Bishop Roger and Alexander of Lincoln as the cause; he wrote that certain laymen, "vexed that they would be surpassed by clerks in the amassing of wealth and the size of their castles, nourished within their hearts an unseen grudge of envy."[19] Stephen held out against his advisors' wishes for some time, but their arguments began to tell. Specifically, they said that the bishops had "built castles of great renown, raised up towers and buildings of great strength" in order to aid Matilda.[20] William of Malmesbury records the same argument, that the bishops were awaiting the Empress in order to hand over their castles.[21]

The rumors of the impending arrival of Matilda and Robert of Gloucester were flying through England, and Stephen eventually concluded that the arrest of the priests outweighed the risks of Matilda seizing such fortresses as Devizes, Salisbury, Sherborne and Malmesbury. William of Newburgh described Devizes and Sherborne as

---

[19] Ibid., p. 25: "His moti quidam po tentes laici, qui se a clericis et opum congerie et municipiorum magnitudine speratum iri dolerent, cecum intra pectora vulnus alebant invidie."

[20] *GS*, p. 74: ". . . castella nominatissima construxisse, turres et aedificia munitissima subvexisse. . . ."

[21] *HN*, p. 26.

castles of the "costliest workmanship."[22] William of Malmesbury went into more detail: "masses of masonry, surmounted by towers . . . over a great extent of ground."[23] Such imposing structures would undoubtedly have required Stephen's full resources to capture, and he already knew he could not rely on all his levies, especially if the fortresses in question were not openly in rebellion. A quick stroke was also necessary so that the Roger's vassals in Wiltshire could not act against Stephen while he occupied each castle. Three months after the intrigues that gave Stephen possession of all their citadels, he was nonetheless brought back to Wiltshire to invest Marlborough.[24]

Stephen had other compelling reasons for taking the castles of Roger and his nephews. For years he had been a peer of the Anglo-Norman magnates; now as king, he had to remind many of his dominant position. In a culture where visible symbols held such importance, castles made a powerful impression. The acquisition of eight castles (Devizes, Sherborne, Salisbury, Malmesbury, Newark, Sleaford, Banbury, and Ely) could not help but raise Stephen's prestige. The question he had to face was whether that increase in prestige would be offset by the "public relations" damage of arresting bishops. He took the gamble and won, managing by a mixture of veiled threats and obfuscation to avoid censure by the English episcopacy.[25]

R.H.C. Davis has rightly pointed out that a castle did not ensure control of an area; later in the Anarchy both Stephen and the earl of Gloucester often crossed areas nominally under the control of the other.[26] But castles did exercise a measure of political control. Stenton has demonstrated how the majority of castles, both royal and private, were garrisoned by vassals drawn from conglomerations of baronies.[27] As Stephen tightened his control over more castles, his influence likely grew among the lesser vassals of his greater tenants who thus served the king directly for part of the year. As for the castles confiscated from Roger of Salisbury, Sidney Painter has shown that Devizes had a permanent garrison of twenty in the days of King

---

[22] William of Newburgh, *The History of English Affairs, Book I*, ed. and trans. P.G. Walsh and M.J. Kennedy (Warminster, 1988), p. 58.

[23] *HN*, p. 25: "Apud Scireburnam et apud Divisas multum terrarum edificiis amplexus, turritas moles erexerat."

[24] John of Worcester, p. 268. Stephen was besieging John the Marshal when Matilda landed three days' march away at Arundel.

[25] *HN*, pp. 30–34.

[26] Davis, p. 73.

[27] Stenton, pp. 212–215.

John.[28] It was doubtless a much larger number during the Anarchy when its military significance was greater.

The fact that Matilda was able to land at Arundel cannot be taken as a signal that Stephen's policies failed. Rather, 1139 saw a marked decrease in baronial rebellion. Beginning in May, Stephen and his allies suppressed eleven outbreaks in 1138 that were connected to Matilda's claim to the throne. Over a longer span of time in 1139, he conducted only three such operations. Obviously, the real test of Stephen's consolidation of his position came once his rival was on English soil. Had he achieved enough of a reputation to prevent a stampede of discontented barons from joining the Empress's party? William of Malmesbury noted the disappointment of Robert of Gloucester when he "found in England that the nobles were either hostile or gave no help, apart from a very few who had not forgotten the faith they once swore."[29] Only two great landed lords immediately gave themselves to her cause: Miles of Gloucester and Brien fitzCount of Wallingford. As for the rest, the monk of Malmesbury complained that "the castellans, keeping safe within their fortifications, were watching how things would turn out."[30]

Stephen had created the conditions for such reluctance. By 1139 the king had achieved a position that was relatively secure by feudal standards. He had shown himself a skillful, and successful, campaigner, capable of reducing strongholds through patient blockade or vigorous assault. He had captured both wooden and stone fortifications. He had tightened the military and political screws on his magnates, reasserting his control over royal castellans and even dispossessing his mightiest ecclesiastical vassals.

The inescapable question then must be: why did Stephen blunder so terribly at Arundel? How could he possibly grant Matilda safe passage to Bristol when he had her completely encircled at Arundel? Had the experiences with Baldwin de Redvers and Geoffrey Talbot served to teach him nothing? The *Gesta Stephani* makes it clear that after surprising Matilda at Arundel, Stephen fully intended to assault the castle. His brother Henry, bishop of Winchester, then arrived to dissuade him from the attempt. He argued that Robert

---

[28] Sidney Painter, "Castle-Guard," *AHR* 40 (1935): 450–459.

[29] *HN*, p. 35: "iste, preter paucissimos qui fidei quondam iurate non immemores erant, in Anglia optimates vel adversantes vel nichil adivuantes expertus est."

[30] Ibid., p. 36: "Aliquanti castellanorum, intra munitiones suas se contutantes, exitum rerum speculabantur."

of Gloucester would wreak havoc elsewhere while Stephen was tied down besieging Matilda. The *Gesta Stephani* and other sources have accepted that Henry's logic persuaded his brother. But this stance ignores how Stephen later would not abandon his siege of Matilda at Oxford despite the nearby ravages of her supporters. Nor does the argument carry much weight that Stephen feared the "public relations" backlash that would supposedly attend his attack on Matilda. The *Gesta Stephani* reveals no hesitation, however, on his part to actually assault Arundel. Stephen knew that the danger posed by Matilda was that she was a magnet for the disaffected. She was a focal point for otherwise isolated opposition. Confident of his position, Stephen may have seen in Matilda's release a chance to flush out any remaining resentment of his reign. Also, given the relative quiet of 1139, Stephen may have felt Matilda would have been disheartened like her half-brother by the lack of support. Stephen understood that success bred more success; his ploy was meant to be the magnanimous act of an unassailable monarch. Unfortunately for the peace of Stephen's reign, Miles of Gloucester completely undermined that reputation within a few weeks of Matilda's release.

POLITICS MAKES UNEASY BEDFELLOWS:
HENRY I OF ENGLAND AND THEOBALD OF BLOIS

Jean A. Truax

At intervals during his thirty-five year reign, King Henry I of England engaged in a struggle for control of Normandy that sometimes became so desperate that it threatened to topple him from his hard-won throne. At first, his opponent was his elder brother, Duke Robert Curthose, and later Henry continued the contest with Robert's son William Clito. Henry's nephews Theobald and Stephen of Blois, the sons of his sister Adela, usually have been seen as his most important allies in this contest. Sir Richard Southern wrote:

> In this sea of troubles it was essential to keep at least one ally, and Henry's policy until the Angevin marriage of 1128 was based on friendship with the count of Blois: The price and guarantee of this was the reception of the count's brother Stephen into the highest circle of the Anglo-Norman nobility.[1]

On the other hand, C. Warren Hollister sounded a note of caution, stating: "My own reading of the evidence persuades me that Theobald needed Henry more than Henry needed Theobald. . . ."[2] In any case, Henry I and his nephews clearly discovered common interests in the turbulent world of twelfth-century politics. However, a close inspection of the sources reveals that Theobald's policies underwent several major shifts during the course of his uncle's reign in England, and particularly after 1120, his goals seem to have diverged more and more from those of his royal uncle.

During the early part of Henry I's reign, as he struggled to wrest Normandy from his brother Robert Curthose, the king's nephews Theobald and Stephen were still young, and Henry's sister Adela governed Blois-Chartres. During these years, Adela seems to have replaced her family's traditional hostility toward the Capetians with

---

[1] Sir Richard Southern, "The Place of Henry I in English History," *Proceedings of the British Academy* 48 (1962): 135.

[2] C. Warren Hollister, "Henry I and the Anglo-Norman Magnates," *Monarchy, Magnates and Institutions in the Anglo-Norman World* (London, 1986), p. 186.

a policy of cautious cooperation.[3] It was only when Adela's son
Theobald began to take an active role in the government of the
duchy that the house of Blois-Chartres adopted a more aggressive
attitude toward the Capetian monarchy and moved into a close
alliance with the English monarch. Theobald first appears in the
sources as an independent player in 1107, fighting in alliance with
Guy de Rochefort to lift Prince Louis's siege of Gournay-sur-Marne.
De Rochefort's son, Hugh de Pomponne, who was the castellan of
Gournay-sur-Marne, had precipitated the quarrel by an attack on
some traveling merchants.[4] However, the conflict had larger political implications, and Theobald's intervention placed him squarely in
the camp of the enemies of the heir to the French throne. The
Rochefort family had allied itself to the party of Bertrada de Montfort
and her sons in opposition to Prince Louis. The betrothal of Prince
Louis to Lucienne de Rochefort had been intended to heal the breach
within the family, but when the Council of Troyes annulled the
agreement in May 1107, relations between the parties were soured
once more.[5] At least according to Suger, an ardent royalist, Theobald
did not perform well in his first recorded military engagement. As
the abbot wrote: "To avoid capture, the count himself preferred to
be found among the first rather than the last to flee. He abandoned
his host and hurried back home."[6]

Despite the initial hostility between the young Count Theobald
and the Capetians, the rupture was not complete. In fact, when open
hostility between Henry I and the newly crowned Louis VI began
in 1108 with Henry's capture of the castle at Gisors, Theobald sided
with the French king, his feudal lord.[7] Sometime in the fall of 1109,
Theobald's mother Adela visited the French king in Paris, where her
presence was recorded in a charter granted by Louis to the abbey
of Saint-Pére-de-Chartres.[8] Although Henry returned to England in

---

[3] *La Chronique de Morigny (1095–1152)*, ed. Léon Mirot (Paris, 1912), p. 22; Suger,
Vie de Louis VI Le Gros, ed. & trans. Henry Waquet (Paris, 1964), pp. 14–18, 46–48;
OV 6:70, 156–158.

[4] Suger, pp. 68–76.

[5] Achille Luchaire, *Louis VI Le Gros, Annales de sa vie et de son Régne (1081–1137)*
(Paris, 1890), nos. 50, 51; idem, "Louis le Gros et ses Palatins (1100–1137)," *Revue
Historique* 37 (1888): 242–249; H. d'Arbois de Jubainville, *Histoire des ducs et des comtes
de Champagne*, 2 vols. (Paris, 1860), 2:176–179.

[6] Suger, p. 76.

[7] Ibid., pp. 102–104.

[8] Luchaire, no. 86; *Cartulaire de l'Abbaye de Saint-Père de Chartres*, 2 vols., ed.
M. Guerard (Paris, 1840), 2, no. 66.

the early summer of 1109, hostilities with the French continued, as evidenced by Louis's siege of the castle of Meulan, held by Henry's chief supporter, Robert of Meulan.[9] Nevertheless, members of the house of Blois-Chartres continued to appear regularly at the French king's court. On 14 September 1110 at Étampes, Louis took the abbey of Bonneval under his special protection and confirmed the charter in which Adela of Blois had relinquished certain rights over the abbey. Her sons Theobald and Stephen both consented to the grant.[10] Early in the following year, Louis again visited Étampes, where Count Theobald witnessed his charter in favor of the monks of Saint-Jean-en-Vallée, a monastery also patronized by the house of Blois-Chartres.[11] However, during the same period, the correspondence of Bishop Ivo of Chartres hints at a possible dispute between King Louis and Theobald of Blois. The count tried to intercede with the bishop of Chartres on behalf of Geoffrey Borel, whom Bishop Ivo had excommunicated for appropriating goods belonging to the abbey of Notre-Dame-de-Bonne-Nouvelle d'Orleans. The bishop was caught between count and king, for at the same time King Louis was urging Bishop Ivo to deal severely with the offender.[12] The disagreement over Borel's actions is the only hint of a possible conflict between Theobald and his overlord at this date.

During the same year, the house of Blois-Chartres was forced to appeal to King Louis for help against their marauding vassal Hugh le Puiset. Suger wrote that "... accompanied by his very noble mother, who had always served the king nobly, ... [Count Theobald] hurried into the royal presence and begged the king with many pleas to give aid, showing how he had merited it for his great service."[13] The king met with his barons at Melun on 12 March 1111 to discuss the actions of Hugh le Puiset[14] and subsequently laid siege to Hugh's stronghold at Le Puiset. Theobald naturally participated in the attack, but once again Suger implied that he fought poorly. The

---

[9] Luchaire, no. 103.

[10] Ibid., no. 102.

[11] *Cartulaire de Saint-Jean-en-Vallée de Chartres*, ed. René Merlet (Chartres, 1906), p. 9, no. 13.

[12] *Epistolae Ivonis Carnotensis Episcopi*, eds. M. Bouquet et al., *Recueil des historiens des Gaules et de la France*, ed. Leopold Delisle (Paris, 1869–1904), 15:152–154, nos. 125–130; D'Arbois de Jubainville, pp. 185–186.

[13] Suger, p. 130.

[14] Ibid., p. 134; Luchaire, no. 110; Ivo of Chartres *Ep* no. 111 in *PL*, vol. 162, cols. 129–130.

abbot gave most of the credit for the success of the operation to a bald priest who rallied the attackers and led them in storming the walls of the castle, thus accomplishing "what had been impossible for an armed count and his followers."[15] Suger's account, written with the knowledge of Theobald's later defection, betrays his hostility toward the young count, even though Theobald actually sided with Louis VI during the events being described. In any case, their joint victory may have set the stage for future discord, for when the fortress was taken, King Louis took charge, ordering the castle razed to the ground and carrying Hugh le Puiset off to prison. The king's actions at Le Puiset are an early example of his general policy of strengthening his control over the French magnates, which Theobald may well have viewed as an encroachment upon his own rights as Hugh le Puiset's immediate overlord.

While the members of the house of Blois-Chartres were occupied with their own affairs, Henry I's struggle for control of Normandy began anew as another nephew, William Clito, the son of the imprisoned Robert Curthose, began his prolonged effort to wrest control of the duchy from his uncle.[16] Perhaps in response to the renewed conflict in Normandy, the year 1111 saw the first open alliance between Theobald of Blois and Henry I. Theobald sought his uncle's support in a new dispute with Louis VI, which began when Theobald sought to re-assert his own authority over the lordship of Le Puiset by erecting an unauthorized castle in the district on an estate called Allaines.[17] Suger wrote that the count "threw the land into confusion ... [and] drew the barons into his party with promises and gifts."[18] Orderic asserted that Count Theobald protected his unruly vassals as they terrorized the countryside, and noted that some of them, "as the record of their deeds openly proclaims, revered neither God nor men as they should have done."[19] Theobald openly allied himself with Louis's enemies during this period by marrying his sister Lithuise to Milo de Montlhéry, a nephew of Guy de Rochefort.[20]

---

[15] Suger, p. 138.

[16] *OV* 6:164; *Chronica Monasterii de Hida, RS* 45:308; Sandy Burton Hicks, "The Impact of William Clito Upon the Continental Policies of Henry I of England," *Viator* 10 (1979): 1–21; Southern, 135.

[17] Suger, pp. 140–142; D'Arbois de Jubainville, p. 196.

[18] Suger, p. 142.

[19] *OV* 6:160.

[20] D'Arbois de Jubainville, p. 199; Suger, p. 172; Luchaire, "Louis le Gros et ses Palatins," 242–249; Ivo of Chartres, *Ep* 238 in *PL* vol. 162, col. 246.

Suger made it plain that Henry I vigorously supported his nephew when he wrote: ". . . the abundant resources of both England and Normandy allowed . . . [Louis] no rest when the illustrious King Henry expended all his effort and all his energy in raiding his land."[21] Theobald's initial efforts against King Louis were unsuccessful. Orderic wrote that when the count's forces engaged those of the king near the river Torcy, "the count and his companions were chased to the gates of Lagny; many who hid in vineyards and behind hedges were captured."[22] Later the same year, however, Theobald defeated the French king in a battle at Meux.[23] In August 1111 Henry I crossed the channel to Normandy to take part in the conflict in person.[24]

Theobald and his family acquired an additional motive for conflict with the Capetians in 1112, when Count Odo of Corbeil died. Suger wrote that after his death, Count Theobald and his mother tried to take possession of his castle at Corbeil "by giving every gift, present and promise possible."[25] To prevent the castle from falling into Theobald's hands, Louis decided to negotiate directly with Theobald's vassal, the imprisoned Hugh le Puiset, who was the dead count's nephew and heir. In return for his freedom, Hugh gave up the disputed castle to the king and promised not to re-fortify his seat at Le Puiset.[26] Shortly after his release from prison, in the presence of Countess Adela and at her suggestion, Hugh signed a charter making reparation for his past offenses against the abbey of St.-Jean-en-Vallée, a house long patronized by the countess and her family.[27] It would be interesting to know what conversation passed between Adela and Hugh on this occasion, for soon afterward Hugh allied himself with his feudal overlord, Count Theobald, and Henry I and began to rebuild his fortifications at Le Puiset, breaking his recent promise to King Louis.[28] Then Hugh and Theobald launched an attack on the French king's army at Toury, scattering the royal troops and

---

[21] Suger, pp. 142, 148.

[22] *OV* 6:160.

[23] Ibid., 6:160–162.

[24] W. Farrer, "An Outline Itinerary of King Henry the First," *EHR* 34 (1919): 351.

[25] Suger, p. 150.

[26] Ibid., p. 152.

[27] *Cartulaire de Saint-Jean-en-Vallée de Chartres*, p. 9, no. 14.

[28] Suger, pp. 142–144; Kimberley A. LoPrete, "The Anglo-Norman Card of Adela of Blois," *Albion* 22 (1990): 584–586.

putting them to flight.[29] However, Louis later engaged and defeated Theobald at Janville, forcing him to take refuge in Le Puiset.[30] Finally Theobald seized upon the pretext of a wound suffered at Janville to beg the French king to allow him to return to Chartres. Suger wrote that the king, "being more kind and gentle than people thought possible," granted Theobald's humble petition, although many men, and the reader suspects that the abbot was one of them, attempted to talk him out of "letting loose an enemy who was trapped by a lack of foodstuffs."[31] After this major defeat, hostilities between Count Theobald and the French king tapered off.

In the meantime, King Henry took steps to put down the rebellion in his own lands and to win a crucial new ally to his cause. Fulk of Anjou met with Henry I at Alençon in February 1113 and concluded an alliance with him that was sealed by the betrothal of his daughter to Henry's son William Adelin. Then Henry made peace with his rebellious barons, Amaury de Montfort and William Crispin, and restored Évreux to Count William, who had been in exile in Anjou. In March the two monarchs met at Gisors and concluded their own peace treaty, in which Louis, outmaneuvered, outnumbered and surrounded by Henry's allies, ceded Bellême, Maine and Brittany to the English king.[32] Significantly, in his brief discussion of the agreement, Suger recognized Count Theobald as an equal party in the pact with the two monarchs, writing: "The magnates of the kingdom and the monastic clergy worked together for an alliance of peace between the king of England, the king of Gaul, and Count Theobald."[33]

Both the count and his younger brother Stephen were present in Henry's entourage during this period, for Orderic noted their presence with the king when Henry visited St.-Évroul in February 1113.[34] After the peace treaty was concluded at Gisors, King Henry undertook the task of subduing the counties he had gained by the agreement. Although he had imprisoned his arch-enemy Robert of Bellême in November of the preceding year,[35] Robert's vassals continued to

---

[29] Suger, pp. 154–162.

[30] Ibid., pp. 166–168.

[31] Ibid., p. 168.

[32] *OV* 6:180.

[33] Suger, p. 170.

[34] *OV* 6:174.

[35] Ibid., 6:178; Florence of Worcester, *Chronicon ex Chronicis*, 2 vols. (London,

hold out against the king in the stronghold of Bellême. Count Theobald took a leading part in the final attack on the fortress, which surrendered on 3 May 1113.[36]

Orderic's statement that Theobald and his younger brother Stephen were part of Henry's entourage during the royal visit to St.-Évroul in 1113 is our first indication that Stephen had joined his uncle's court. Orderic stated that Stephen was knighted by the king and received the lands of Count William of Mortain after the count was captured at the battle of Tinchebrai (1106).[37] These early favors granted to Stephen of Blois suggest that Henry I and his nephews had discovered some common interests in the turbulent years since 1111 when Theobald's troubles with King Louis over control of Le Puiset had begun.

The new alliance between Henry and Theobald is also illustrated by an incident that took place during the following years of nominal peace. In 1115 King Louis led a military force to punish his rebellious vassal Thomas of Marle.[38] Count Theobald himself did not respond to King Louis' appeal for support,[39] and to make matters worse, one of the count's vassals, Hugh le Manceau, captured one of the king's supporters, Count William of Nevers, as he was returning from the expedition. Theobald placed William in prison, where he remained until at least 1120.[40] The papal legate, Cardinal Cono of Praeneste, excommunicated Hugh and his men and threatened to do the same to Count Theobald. According to a letter that Bishop Ivo of Chartres wrote to the papal legate, Theobald offered to present himself before the judges of the Peace of God for their decision. The bishop felt that Theobald had been justified and asked the legate not to carry out his threat.[41] Bishop Ivo's intervention was unsuccessful, and Theobald was excommunicated for his actions.[42]

1964), 2:66; *ASC* 1112 AD; Simeon of Durham, *Historia Regum*, RS 75, 2:247; Henry of Huntingdon, *Henrici Archidiaconi Huntendunensis Historia Anglorum*, RS 74, p. 238; Robert of Torigny, *Chronicle*, RS 82, 4:93.

[36] *OV* 6:182.

[37] Ibid., 6:42; *Regesta Regum Anglo-Normannorum*, C. Johnson and H.A. Cronne, eds. (Oxford, 1956), vol. 2, no. 1102.

[38] Suger, pp. 172–180.

[39] D'Arbois de Jubainville, p. 217.

[40] Ivo of Chartres, *Ep* no. 275, in *PL* vol. 162, cols. 277–278; *OV* 6:288–290; *Chronica Monasterii de Hida*, p. 310.

[41] D'Arbois de Jubainville, p. 217.

[42] *Chronica Monasterii de Hida*, p. 310.

Theobald's attack on William of Nevers can be interpreted as a protest against King Louis' efforts to impose his own authority on vassals who were accustomed to exercising their own independence. It can also be seen as a well-considered step in King Henry's campaign to retain possession of Normandy, for William of Nevers and his mother, Countess Helwise of Évreux, were both leading supporters of William Clito.[43]

Theobald's conflict with King Louis during the years of so-called peace between 1113 and 1116 illustrates the fragility of the treaty concluded at Gisors. In 1116, hostilities broke out anew between Henry I and Louis VI.[44] In addition, Baldwin VII of Flanders went to war against Henry on William Clito's behalf.[45] Theobald and his brother Stephen loyally supported their uncle during these dark days. Suger wrote: "With help from his nephew, the palatine count Theobald, and from many disaffected men of the kingdom of the French, . . . [Henry] strove to unsettle the realm and disturb its king, for he wished to withdraw from his lordship."[46] Henry and Theobald sent the young count of Mortain at the head of an army into Brie to keep Theobald's vassals there from joining the rebellion while their lord was absent. Henry also gave Séez, Alençon and the other lands of Robert of Bellême in that region to Theobald, who in turn presented them to his younger brother.[47] The first two years of the campaign did not go well for Henry and his allies, and his fortunes had reached a low point by the fall of 1118.[48]

In the second week of November 1118, Henry attacked L'Aigle. In the ferocious fighting, Theobald was unhorsed and captured, but the king and his brother Stephen managed to rescue him.[49] Then, to make matters worse, the town of Alençon rebelled against Stephen. Orderic wrote that when Stephen first took over Alençon he "fortified the castles by filling them with arms and his own troops, imposed heavy corvées and taxes on the inhabitants, and by changing the

[43] Ibid., p. 309; Hicks, 8.
[44] *ASC* 1116 AD; William of Malmesbury, *Gesta Regum Anglorum* (London, 1964), p. 633; *Chronica Monasterii de Hida*, p. 309; Florence of Worcester 2:71; Simeon of Durham, *Gesta Regum*, p. 252; Robert of Torigny, *Chronicle*, p. 99; *OV* 6:184–188.
[45] *OV* 6:190; William of Malmesbury, *Gesta Regum*, pp. 629–631; *Chronica Monasterii de Hida*, p. 314.
[46] Suger, p. 184.
[47] *OV* 6:196.
[48] Suger, pp. 190–192; *OV* 6:194–200; *Chronica Monasterii de Hida*, pp. 311–313.
[49] *OV* 6:204.

customs they had enjoyed under the king made himself hated and his men disloyal."[50] By late 1118, Stephen had decided that the men of the town were disloyal to him, so he demanded members of their families as hostages to insure their good behavior. After one woman was raped by her guards, the citizens approached Count Fulk of Anjou for help.[51] Despite the fact that his daughter was betrothed to Henry's son William Adelin, Fulk immediately came and laid siege to Alençon. Theobald and Stephen rushed to the relief of their forces in the town but were unable to raise the siege.[52]

As the spring of 1119 continued, more and more Norman nobles rushed to join the rebellion against King Henry.[53] However, as spring turned into summer, the tide began to turn in the king's favor. Henry succeeded in winning Fulk of Anjou back to his side, as evidenced by the celebration of the marriage between the count's daughter and his own son in June 1119.[54] Baldwin of Flanders died in the same month, and thus another enemy was removed from the scene.[55]

In July, Henry launched a major offensive in the Évrecin. Unable to get the garrison of Évreux to surrender, he consulted the noblemen present, including his nephew Stephen, about setting fire to the town. Although the king expressed concern about destroying churches in the conflagration, those present finally decided to go ahead because it was the only way that they could deliver the town from the traitors, and they could rebuild the churches afterwards.[56] After the burning of Évreux, fierce fighting continued in the region until finally the two royal armies faced one another at Bremulé on 20 August 1119.[57] The major supporters of both kings were present, but the

---

[50] Ibid., 6:196.

[51] Ibid., 6:206; *Ex Gestis Consulum Andegavensium Auctore Monacho Majoris Monasterii*, Bouquet 12:499–500.

[52] *OV* 6:206–208. See also Suger, p. 192; Louis Halphen and René Poupardin, *Chroniques des Comtes d'Anjou* (Paris, 1913), pp. 155–160; Josèphe Chartrou, *L'Anjou de 1109 à 1151: Foulque de Jérusalem et Geoffroi Plantagenet* (Paris, 1928), pp. 11–12.

[53] *OV* 6:214–222.

[54] Ibid., 6:224; Suger, pp. 194–196; *ASC* 1119 AD; Florence of Worcester, 2:72; William of Malmesbury, *Gesta Regum*, pp. 634, 652; *Chronica Monasterii de Hida*, p. 319.

[55] *OV* 6:224; Suger, p. 194; *ASC* 1119 AD; Simeon of Durham, *Gesta Regum*, p. 248; *Chronica Monasterii de Hida*, p. 315; Robert of Torigny, *Chronicle*, p. 103.

[56] *OV* 6:228.

[57] Suger, pp. 196–198; *OV* 6:234–242; *ASC* 1119 AD; Henry of Huntingdon, pp. 241–242; Robert of Torigny, *Chronicle*, pp. 102–103; *Chronica Monasterii de Hida*, pp. 317–318.

sources do not specifically mention the presence of either Theobald
or Stephen of Blois. King Henry won a great victory at Bremulé,
but it was only temporary, and by September King Louis was back
in Normandy, where he captured and burned the castle at Ivry.[58]
According to Orderic's account, Henry and his loyal knights succeeded in driving Louis away.[59] Abbot Suger, however, maintained
that Louis turned back after a time because he could not locate the
English army. On his way back to France, Louis made a detour to
Chartres, intending to take revenge on Count Theobald by burning
the town. He was persuaded to spare the city when the citizens and
the clergy came out to him in a procession, bearing their most precious relic, the tunic of the Virgin, and begged him "not to take
revenge on them for a wrong committed by others."[60] The *Chronicle
of Morigny*, however, stated that King Louis did burn the town of
Chartres.[61] D'Arbois de Jubainville, seeking to reconcile the two
accounts, maintained that the king did actually attack Chartres with
burning missiles, but was persuaded to end the assault by the citizens' appeal.[62]

In view of what happened soon afterwards, it is possible that this
dramatic story conceals something more mundane. Perhaps King
Louis met with Count Theobald or his mother Countess Adela at
this time, and laid the foundations for the peace negotiations that
were soon to begin. D'Arbois de Jubainville stated that Theobald's
absence left Chartres defenseless at this time,[63] but there is nothing
in the sources to indicate where the count was between the battle of
Bremulé and the attack on his capital city. In any case, in view of
Countess Adela's continuing active role in the politics of her family
and her history of support for the Capetians, the king may have preferred to negotiate with the count's mother.

Additional evidence in support of this supposition is offered by a
close examination of the activities of another key player in the peace
negotiations, Thurstan, the archbishop-elect of York. Thurstan, previously one of the clerks of King Henry's household,[64] had been

---

[58] Suger, p. 198.
[59] *OV* 6:246–248.
[60] Suger, p. 198.
[61] *Chronicle of Morigny*, p. 31.
[62] D'Arbois de Jubainville, pp. 241–242.
[63] Ibid., p. 241.
[64] Donald Nicholl, *Thurstan, Archbishop of York (1114–1140)* (York, 1964), pp. 1–14.

elected archbishop in August 1114.[65] The new archbishop had never been consecrated, however, because he refused to make the profession of obedience that Archbishop Ralph d'Escures of Canterbury demanded of him.[66] Thurstan had begged Henry on several occasions to allow him to go to Rome to appeal to the pope, but Henry had always refused to let him go, fearing further papal intervention in his kingdom and especially the possibility that the pope might consecrate Thurstan himself.[67] Thurstan accompanied Henry to Normandy in April 1116, concerned with protecting his own interests and hoping that he might be permitted to go on from there to Rome.[68] He returned to York only briefly in February 1118 before rejoining Henry on the continent.[69]

In the first months of 1118 it appeared that Thurstan's problem might be resolved without the long journey to Rome, for the new pope, Gelasius II, was already on his way to France.[70] Even without a personal visit, Thurstan obtained a letter from the new pope demanding his consecration, but Ralph d'Escures refused to honor it because by the time that Thurstan presented it to him Pope Gelasius was already dead, at Cluny in January 1119.[71] The new pope, Calixtus II, continued his predecessor's journey, and as he drew closer to France, Hugh the Chanter recorded that King Henry and Archbishop Ralph, afraid that Thurstan would find a way to approach the pope, urged him to return to his see in England. Thurstan temporized, saying that he did not want to visit his see at Easter time, when he would not be able to consecrate the chrism and perform the other duties of archbishop. Shortly after this, a letter from Pope Calixtus II arrived, summoning Thurstan and the

---

See *Regesta*, vol. 2, nos. 652, 681, 817, 939, 1000 and 1075, for charters that Thurstan witnessed before his election. Hugh the Chanter stated that King Henry "had full confidence in him" and used him "both in England and in Normandy to make arrangements and payments, and do business of all kinds." *The History of the Church of York 1066–1127*, ed. Charles Johnson (Oxford, 1990), p. 56.

[65] Hugh the Chanter, p. 56; *ASC* 1114 AD; Florence of Worcester, 2:67; Simeon of Durham, *Gesta Regum*, p. 248; Henry of Huntingdon, pp. 238–239; Robert of Torigny, *Chronicle*, p. 94.

[66] Hugh the Chanter, p. 56; Florence of Worcester, 2:67.

[67] Hugh the Chanter, pp. 62–64, 76, 84–86.

[68] Ibid., p. 76; Florence of Worcester, 2:69; Simeon of Durham, *Gesta Regum*, pp. 250–251.

[69] Hugh the Chanter, p. 94; Eadmer, *Historia Novorum in Anglia*, RS 81:244.

[70] Hugh the Chanter, p. 94.

[71] Ibid., p. 100.

other bishops to a general council to be held at Rheims in October.[72]

Thurstan finally left Henry's entourage to travel to the council in September 1119, and at this point, his adventures became intertwined with the larger political scene and particularly with the house of Blois-Chartres. A close inspection of Thurstan's itinerary reveals several visits to Blois and Chartres, and suggests that Thurstan sought to use the influence of Count Theobald and his mother Adela to resolve his own problems and perhaps also to bring peace to Normandy. When he left King Henry's court, Thurstan traveled first to Chartres to meet the rest of his party, which had gone on ahead.[73] He met the pope at Tours on September 22, and returned with him to visit the town of Blois. Hugh the Chanter, almost our only source for these events, does not mention a meeting with Count Theobald or Countess Adela, but it is not reasonable to think that Thurstan did not stop to pay his respects upon entering their lands, or that when Pope Calixtus came to Blois, his visit escaped the notice of the ruling family.

Thurstan and Pope Calixtus then traveled together to Rheims for the council. Thurstan's presence with the papal party was recorded on October 3 at Morigny, where the pope dedicated a new church. Cardinal Cono of Praeneste, the papal legate, who was also to play a large part in the peace negotiations, attended the ceremonies. Bishop Geoffrey of Chartres and Étienne, the abbot of St.-Jean-en-Vallée, also attended, along with both King Louis and Queen Adelaide.[74] It is possible that the presence of the two churchmen from the Chartres area at this gathering, along with Thurstan of York, the king of France and the papal legate, provided an opportunity for further negotiations. The pope and his entourage arrived in Rheims on 18 October, and the following day, Calixtus II consecrated Thurstan archbishop of York.[75] When the news was brought to King Henry, he swore that Thurstan would never enter any part of England as long as he lived, unless he first made his profession to the archbishop of Canterbury.[76]

Hugh the Chanter of York naturally focused his narrative on the consecration of his archbishop, but other accounts make it plain that

[72] Ibid., p. 108.
[73] Ibid., p. 114.
[74] *Chronicle of Morigny*, pp. 31–33.
[75] Hugh the Chanter, pp. 118–120; *OV* 6:252; Simeon of Durham, *Gesta Regum*, p. 254.
[76] Hugh the Chanter, p. 120.

the most noteworthy event of the council was the papal effort to make peace between the English and French kings. King Louis appeared before the council on 20–21 October, and the speech that Orderic wrote for him indicates that the claims of William Clito to the duchy of Normandy lay at the root of the long-standing quarrel. Orderic also pointed out Count Theobald's commanding role in the conflict and had King Louis complain to the council about his activities:

> Count Theobald is my vassal, but at his uncle's prompting he has iniquitously risen against me. Grown above himself through his wealth and power, he rebelled against me and violating his fealty, waged bitter war on me, so causing turmoil and great suffering in my kingdom.[77]

Out of all the crimes that the count of Blois had committed against the French king, Orderic singled out for inclusion in his speech Theobald's imprisonment of Count William of Nevers, which had occurred in 1115.[78] Upon hearing the French king's petition, Pope Calixtus announced that he would meet with King Henry and Count Theobald to make peace.[79]

In the meantime, Henry continued his military operations against his rebellious magnates by laying siege to Breteuil. One of the baronial leaders was Amaury de Montfort, who had rebelled because King Henry had denied him the county of Évreux after the death of his uncle, Count William, in April 1118.[80] Suddenly Count Theobald appeared in a new and unusual role, acting as the peacemaker in Orderic's account. He attempted to pacify the rebels, and finally brought Amaury de Montfort to meet with Henry. De Montfort surrendered the castle to the king, and was given the entire county of Évreux in return. De Montfort's capitulation, and perhaps Henry's generosity, convinced some of the other rebel barons to surrender, including Eustace of Breteuil, Hugh of Gournay and Robert of Neubourg. King Henry then assembled an army to march against Stephen of Aumale, who also surrendered when he learned that the king was coming to attack him.[81] At this point, King Henry seemed

---

[77] *OV* 6:256–258.
[78] Ibid., 6:258.
[79] Ibid., 6:264.
[80] D'Arbois de Jubainville, p. 245. See André Rhein, *La Seigneurie de Montfort en Iveline, Mémoires de la Société Archéologique de Rambouillet* (Versailles, 1910), 21:38–57, for a summary of this baron's long-standing quarrel with Henry I.
[81] *OV* 6:276–280.

to be in a good position; he had cemented his alliance with Anjou, Baldwin of Flanders was dead, he had kept Louis VI out of Normandy, and he had largely pacified Louis' allies, his own rebel barons.

However, despite Henry's rising fortunes, Orderic painted the English king as a humble suppliant when he met with Pope Calixtus II at Gisors on November 23–24. According to Orderic, the pope began his appeal for peace by begging Henry to release Robert Curthose. Henry responded that the duke's bad government of Normandy and the resulting deplorable condition of the Church had forced him to invade in the first place.[82] Henry also stated that he had always been kindly disposed toward William Clito and had invited him to his court on several occasions. According to Orderic, Henry even implied that he would at some point turn the government of Normandy over to Clito, stating that he had placed the young boy under the guardianship of Helias of Saint-Sens in the hope that "by developing his judgment and all his moral qualities and talents . . . [he] might make him the equal in every way to . . . [Henry's] own son."[83] The king also suggested that he had invited Clito to "become a participator with my son in the riches of the kingdom."[84] Most remarkably, Orderic reported that Henry had offered Clito three counties in England to rule, so that the nobles of his court might see how he would govern. Sadly, however, Helias of Saint-Sens had turned the boy against Henry and used him to stir up trouble for the king. Finally Henry renewed his offer of friendship to his nephew. In Orderic's words, Henry said:

> I urge him to make peace and offer him still through your holiness the same terms that I have often offered through others, for I both desire to give you complete satisfaction and wish to further the general tranquillity of the people and the advancement of my nephew as if he were my own son.[85]

Similarly, although Hugh the Chanter emphasized the struggle over the archbishopric of York rather than the peace negotiations with France, even his brief account emphasized Henry's humility and desire to make peace:

---

[82] Ibid., 6:284–286.
[83] Ibid., 6:286–288.
[84] Ibid., 6:288.
[85] Ibid., 6:290.

Our king set forth the wrong done by the king of France and his own righteousness, and answered quietly and humbly, like a wise and modest man: "I am sorry about the quarrel, I want peace; as always, I am anxious to do willingly whatever the duke of Normandy owes to the king of France."[86]

The Hyde chronicler suggested that Clito met with Henry I in person at some time after the battle of Bremulé and begged him to release Robert Curthose and allow the two of them to go away to the Holy Land and never bother him again.[87] It seems unlikely that a face-to-face meeting between the two antagonists would have gone unnoticed by the other chroniclers, but perhaps the Hyde chronicler's statement does reflect a offer made through intermediaries as part of the ongoing negotiations. In any case, none of the accounts of the peace talks in late 1119 portrays Henry I bargaining from the position of strength that he clearly enjoyed as a result of his recent successes against his enemies. Instead, he is depicted as anxious, even desperate, to make peace.

Orderic's account may hint at the reason for Henry's dilemma, for the author made it clear that the king did not exercise absolute control over his most important ally, Count Theobald of Blois. At Gisors, the pope also complained about the count's unjustified imprisonment of William of Nevers, but in this case Henry seems to have brushed his complaint aside with vague assurances: "I will put my nephew Theobald, who is a true lover of justice, under your guidance for the general good."[88]

In any case, the meeting at Gisors broke up without definite results. When the English king and the pope parted company, Archbishop Thurstan remained with the papal party because of Henry's continued antagonism. The king had not only refused to admit the archbishop to England unless he made the required profession to Canterbury, he had also sent men to England to confiscate Thurstan's possessions.[89] Hugh the Chanter recorded that his archbishop occupied a position of great esteem among the pope's followers.[90] On 30 November, King Louis met the pope at Ferriers. On this occasion, the king, obviously seeking to stir up more trouble for his English rival, took

---

[86] Hugh the Chanter, p. 128.
[87] *Chronica Monasterii de Hida*, pp. 320–321.
[88] *OV* 6:290.
[89] Hugh the Chanter, pp. 130–132.
[90] Ibid., pp. 134, 138.

Thurstan's side in the archiepiscopal controversy. According to Hugh the Chanter, Louis told the pope:

> In the conference with the king of England on behalf of the arch-
> bishop, a man consecrated by your hands, as it were by the hands of
> St. Peter, and on this account exiled as though accursed, the matter
> was handled with too little severity, too little justice.[91]

While King Henry remained in Normandy, visiting Bayeux and Arganchy, Thurstan traveled with the papal party.[92] On 10 March 1120 Thurstan participated in the consecration of the bishop of Geneva at Gap. Bishop Bernard of St. David's in Wales was also present,[93] and in view of this cleric's long and active career in King Henry's government, it is likely that he was acting at this time as the king's representative in the continuing negotiations between the papacy and the two kings. At this time, the pope gave Thurstan let-ters to the king demanding that he be allowed to occupy his see, and also granted him the unusual privilege of wearing his pallium outside his own province.[94] The archbishop then took his leave of the pope, and embarked upon a period of what Hollister has described as "shuttle diplomacy."[95] First, Thurstan traveled to Chartres, where he visited Count Theobald and Countess Adela. Hugh the Chanter reported that the two "were less well disposed to their brother and uncle réspectively on account of... [Thurstan's] exile." Hinting at a role for Theobald and Adela in the upcoming negotiations, the author wrote that Thurstan "did not entirely conceal from them what he had done and what he carried."[96] The Chanter's cryptic statement undoubtedly referred to Thurstan's archiepiscopal pallium and to the letters from the pope on his behalf. The archbishop's biographer also noted that Thurstan avoided going to the king of France at this time because "there was still serious strife between him and our king."[97] In late March or early April, Thurstan trav-

---

[91] Ibid., p. 134.

[92] Farrer, 511–512.

[93] Hugh the Chanter, p. 148.

[94] Ibid., p. 150; Mary B. Cheney, "Some Observations on a Papal Privilege of 1120 for the Archbishops of York," *Journal of Ecclesiastical History* 31 (1980): 429–439. For the text of the privilege, see *The Historians of the Church of York and Its Archbishops, RS* 71, 3:41–44, no. 23.

[95] C. Warren Hollister, "War and Diplomacy in the Anglo-Norman World: The Reign of Henry I," *Monarchy, Magnates and Institutions*, p. 276.

[96] Hugh the Chanter, p. 152.

[97] Ibid.

eled to Soissons, where he met with the papal legate Cardinal Cono. They decided that Cono would go to King Louis's Easter court at Senlis to recruit the archbishop of Tours and the bishop of Beauvais to deliver the letters from the pope to King Henry.[98] Still unwilling to visit Louis' court because of the conflict between the two monarchs, Thurstan went back to visit Countess Adela, where the two discussed her proposed entry into the convent at Marcigny. Thurstan spent Easter at Coulombs and met with Cardinal Cono at Dammartin on 20 April. Since the two bishops had proved unable, or perhaps unwilling, to deliver the papal letters, the two agreed to send the correspondence with two unnamed lesser clerics. In the early part of May Thurstan returned to Chartres to escort Countess Adela to the convent at Marcigny.[99] On 30 May, King Henry met with Cardinal Cono at Vernon and agreed to restore Thurstan to his see, but he asked that the archbishop remain out of England for the time being.[100] After the meeting, Thurstan returned to France, where peace was finally concluded between the two monarchs. As part of the agreement, Henry's son William did homage to King Louis of France for the duchy of Normandy.[101] William of Malmesbury placed Theobald and Adela at the center of the peace negotiations, writing that ". . . by the exertions of his father-in-law [Fulk of Anjou] and of Theobald, the son of Stephen, and of his aunt Adela, Louis king of France conceded the legal possession of Normandy to the boy, on his doing him homage."[102] Simeon of Durham added that the nobles of Normandy also did homage for their lands to Prince William at that time.[103] Hugh the Chanter naturally highlighted the role of his hero in the peace negotiations:

> For the archbishop took great pains to procure a peace between the two kings by means of Cardinal Cono and the archbishops, bishops, and nobles of France. And this by the grace of God was brought to a good end not long afterwards after much bargaining on both sides, mainly by his diplomacy and mediation, he being the man on the Norman side in whom the king of the French had the most confidence.[104]

---

[98] Ibid., p. 152. Easter in 1119 was on April 18.
[99] Ibid., pp. 152–154.
[100] Ibid., p. 158.
[101] Ibid., p. 160; Florence of Worcester, 2:72; William of Malmesbury, *Gesta Regum*, p. 634; *Chronica Monasterii de Hida*, p. 319.
[102] William of Malmesbury, *Gesta Regum*, p. 652.
[103] Simeon of Durham, *Gesta Regum*, p. 258.
[104] Hugh the Chanter, p. 160.

Simeon of Durham also noted that Thurstan had been "vigilant and diligent" in arranging the agreement between the two kings.[105] After this, Thurstan seems to have acted as Henry's liaison with the papal legate, and perhaps also with Count Theobald, for as Henry was about to depart for England in the fall of 1120, he sent Thurstan to meet with Cardinal Cono one final time—significantly, at Chartres.[106]

To this point in the reign of Henry I, Theobald of Blois was the English king's most crucial ally, the one neighboring magnate whom he could not afford to alienate. Nothing illustrates this point better than the negotiations that led to the peace of 1120. It appears that King Louis of France made his initial approach to the count of Blois in the fall of 1119, immediately after the battle of Bremulé. Theobald's influence was such that once he himself had decided on peace, he was able in a relatively short time to reconcile the rebellious Norman magnates with King Henry. Archbishop Thurstan of York's strenuous round of shuttle diplomacy in 1119 and 1120 and the prominence of Blois-Chartres in his itinerary surely indicates that no peace could have been made without Theobald's cooperation and agreement.

Accustomed as we are to believing that peace is always better than war, modern readers readily assume that Henry I must have been a satisfied, happy ruler as he prepared to set sail across the English Channel in the fall of 1120. However, the evidence suggests that Henry may have been nagged by the thought that he should have continued the fight a little longer. After all, he had quelled the rebellion against him, and with Baldwin VII of Flanders dead and a new pact with Fulk of Anjou in place, Louis VI stood isolated as his only remaining enemy. If Henry had persevered, he might have captured William Clito himself and thrown him into prison with his father, thus solving his problem permanently. Perhaps Theobald of Blois had decided to make an independent peace in 1120, and Henry I came unwillingly to the bargaining table, knowing that he could not continue the struggle without his nephew Theobald, who had emerged from the conflict of 1111–1120 as one of the key magnates of northern Europe, a power broker among kings, dukes, archbishops and popes. We will never know the truth, and what happened immediately afterward has forever obscured the question.

---

[105] Simeon of Durham, *Gesta Regum*, p. 258.
[106] Hugh the Chanter, p. 164.

The politics of the Anglo-Norman world changed drastically and irrevocably on 20 November 1120. As Henry was preparing for his voyage across the channel to England, a proud sea captain approached the king and asked him to make the crossing in his fine vessel, the White Ship.[107] Henry declined, saying that he would not change his own plans at the last minute, but that he would gladly entrust other members of his party, including his son and heir William Adelin, to the captain. The prince and his companions gave the delighted sailors wine, and the entire party soon became quite drunk.[108] Orderic noted that Count Stephen of Mortain and several others disembarked, "realizing that there was too great a crowd of wild and headstrong young men on board."[109] Elsewhere, he remarked that Count Stephen left the ship because he was suffering from diarrhea.[110] The Hyde chronicler placed Count Theobald at the scene of embarkation, but the manuscript ends just at that point.[111] The tipsy sailors paid little attention to their duty as the merry party set sail, and the White Ship struck a rock in the harbor and sank without warning. Everyone perished except a butcher from Rouen, who survived by clinging to a spar until he was rescued the next morning.[112] When the news came to King Henry's court, everyone was afraid to tell the king about the disaster. Finally, Count Theobald of Blois hit upon a plan. The next day, by prearrangement, a young boy flung himself at Henry's feet, and between sobs, announced the dreadful news to the king. Henry was so overcome by the news that he fell to the floor in anguish.[113] Hugh the Chanter also stated that Count Theobald consoled his bereaved uncle,[114] while Henry of Huntingdon recorded the count's presence at King Henry's Christmas court.[115] Henry's personal grief over the loss of his only son was undoubtedly made even worse by the knowledge that he now had no heir to follow him as ruler of England and Normandy, the prizes that he had labored so long and hard to secure.

---

[107] *ASC* 1120 AD; Florence of Worcester, 2:72; Henry of Huntingdon, pp. 242–243; Simeon of Durham, *Gesta Regum*, p. 259.

[108] *OV* 6:296; William of Malmesbury, *Gesta Regum*, p. 653.

[109] *OV* 6:296.

[110] Ibid., 6:306.

[111] *Chronica Monasterii de Hida*, p. 321.

[112] *OV* 6:298; William of Malmesbury, *Gesta Regum*, p. 654.

[113] *OV* 6:300.

[114] Hugh the Chanter, p. 164.

[115] Henry of Huntingdon, p. 243.

Both Theobald and Stephen remained with their bereaved uncle during January 1121, the first time that the charter record indicates that either man took part in the daily business of the royal court.[116] The modern reader wonders what thoughts were going through their minds during their stay at court. Before 1120, Theobald and Stephen could have expected to play major roles in a cousin's kingdom. After the disaster of the White Ship, perhaps both men hoped for something more. By this time, Theobald enjoyed a strong continental power base, which, if united to Normandy, would make him the master of a vast medieval empire. Stephen, for his part, may have hoped to profit from a growing Anglo-Norman tradition by which younger sons inherited their families' new lands in England, while their elder brothers retained the continental patrimony.[117]

However, if Theobald and Stephen hoped that one of them would be named Henry's heir at once, they were disappointed, for almost immediately, Henry I began to look for a new bride, since his first wife Edith Matilda had died in 1118.[118] On 29 January 1121, about two months after the disaster of the White Ship, Henry married Adeliza of Louvain.[119] As the months went by and Adeliza showed no signs of becoming pregnant, the possibility of a renewed challenge from William Clito hung over the king like a threatening storm cloud.[120] Furthermore, as Hicks has noted, Henry's foreign policy was left in a shambles by the loss of his heir, for Prince William had been the cornerstone of his alliances with Louis VI and Fulk of Anjou. The alliance with Louis VI had been confirmed by Prince William's homage to the French king for Normandy, while the English heir's marriage had sealed Henry's pact with Anjou.[121] Henry's

---

[116] Stephen witnessed two charters on 7 January 1121; the first was a notification of the election of Bishop Richard of Hereford (*Regesta 2*, no. 1243), and the second a charter confirming gifts made to the abbey of Shrewsbury (*Regesta 2*, no. 1245). During the same period, Theobald witnessed a charter to Peterborough Abbey (*Regesta 2*, no. 1244) and two to Westminster Abbey (*Regesta 2*, nos. 1247 & 1249).

[117] Emily Z. Tabuteau, "The Role of Law in the Succession to Normandy and England, 1087," *The Haskins Society Journal* 3 (1991): 155–169.

[118] *OV* 6:188; *ASC* 1118 AD; Henry of Huntingdon, pp. 240–241; Florence of Worcester, 2:71; Simeon of Durham, *Gesta Regum*, p. 252; Robert of Torigny, *Chronicle*, pp. 101–102.

[119] *OV* 6:308; William of Malmesbury, *Gesta Regum*, p. 654; Florence of Worcester 2:75; Henry of Huntingdon, p. 243; Robert of Torigny, *Chronicle*, p. 104.

[120] *OV* 6:328.

[121] Hicks, pp. 8–9.

dilemma became even worse in 1121–1122, when the disgruntled
Count Amaury of Évreux induced Count Fulk of Anjou to arrange
an alliance with the pretender by marrying his daughter Sibyl to
William Clito. As his daughter's marriage portion, Count Fulk gave
Clito the county of Maine "until he could recover his lawful inher-
itance."[122]

After this, Count Amaury schemed to entice the Norman nobles
to join his party, and by 1123, Waleran of Meulan, William of
Roumare and many other Norman magnates were once again in
rebellion.[123] Henry moved swiftly against the rebels, and aided by a
timely invasion of French territory by the Holy Roman Emperor[124]
and a papal annulment of Clito's marriage,[125] he brought the conflict to an end in 1124. As before, the evidence shows that Stephen
of Blois loyally supported his uncle in the conflict. Late in October,
Pain of Gisors rebelled and treacherously attacked Robert of Candos,
the king's castellan. Robert set fire to the town to drive out the
rebels, and King Henry himself hurried to the scene, hoping to
confront his enemies in battle. But when they heard of the king's
approach, the rebels fled, leaving Henry to annex all their lands. He
granted the lands of Pain of Gisors to the traitor's son Hugh, who
"was at that time with Stephen, count of Mortain, and having no
knowledge of his father's crimes, was in the king's service."[126] The
statement verifies Stephen's loyalty to Henry at this time, and may
even imply his presence with the king during these campaigns. Orderic
also noted that the charter appointing Warin as abbot of St.-Évroul
given at York on 6 December 1122 was addressed to Stephen as
count of Mortain.[127] At the same time, Stephen also attested Henry's
charter confirming the monks of Charleval in their possession of the
English lands that Count William of Évreux had given them.[128] It

---

[122] *OV* 6:332; also William of Malmesbury, *Gesta Regum*, pp. 654–655.

[123] *OV* 6:332–354; *Chrono Rotomagensi*, Bouquet 12:784; Simeon of Durham, *Gesta Regum*, pp. 274–275; *ASC* 1123–1124.

[124] Suger, pp. 218–232; Ekkehard, *Chronicon Universale*, MGH SS 6:262; Otto of Freising, *The Two Cities: A Chronicle of Universal History to the Year 1146 AD*, ed. and trans. Christopher Mierow (New York, 1966), p. 243; Hollister, "War and Diplomacy", pp. 286–287.

[125] *OV* 6:164–166; Sandy Burton Hicks, "The Anglo-Papal Bargain of 1125: The Legatine Mission of John of Crema," *Albion* 8 (1976): 301–310; Chartrou, pp. 17–18; Schieffer, p. 215; *Epistolae Calixti II Papae*, Bouquet 15:251.

[126] *OV* 6:342–344.

[127] Ibid., 6:324; *Regesta 2*, no. 1337.

[128] *Regesta 2*, no. 1338.

appears that Henry deeply appreciated his nephew's loyalty, for during this period, he consented to, and perhaps arranged, Stephen's splendid marriage to Matilda, the daughter of Count Eustace III of Boulogne.[129]

On the other hand, Theobald seems to have taken no part in the hostilities.[130] He may have visited his uncle's court at least once during this period, for his attestation appears on a charter issued in 1123 by Archbishop Geoffrey of Rouen.[131] King Henry crossed from England to Normandy on 11 June 1123, and was at Rouen in October and November, so it is possible that Theobald visited his uncle at this time.[132]

However, French sources reveal that Theobald also acted in cooperation with King Louis VI during this period. The charter evidence records that Theobald, perhaps asserting his own authority over his vassal Hugh le Puiset, helped Louis VI negotiate an agreement between Hugh and the monks of Bonneval.[133] Most remarkably, when the Emperor Henry V invaded France in the summer of 1124 and kept King Louis from supporting the Norman rebels, Count Theobald and his forces came to the aid of the Capetian monarch. Abbot Suger was apparently unable to accept Theobald's possible change of heart, so he made the curious accusation that the count fought on both sides of the conflict at the same time:

> The palatine count Theobald replied to the earnest request of France, and arrived there in the company of his uncle Hugh, the noble count of Troyes, even though he was waging war on the king with another uncle, the English king.[134]

However, Suger failed to give the details of any hostile actions that Theobald took against his overlord during the wars of 1122–1124, while the help that the count gave Louis VI against the emperor could be interpreted as a failure to support Henry I, who clearly benefited from the emperor's timely invasion. Theobald probably placed his own interests above those of either monarch on this occasion, for had the emperor's invasion been successful, his own lands

---

[129] J.H. Round, *Calendar of Documents Preserved in France Illustrative of the History of Great Britain and Ireland, Vol. I, 918–1206* (London, 1899), no. 1385.

[130] D'Arbois de Jubainville, p. 265.

[131] Bouquet 15:322 n. B.

[132] Farrer, 531.

[133] Luchaire, no. 323.

[134] Suger, p. 224.

would have been engulfed in the struggle. Furthermore, Theobald's decision may have been dictated by his alliance with his other uncle, Hugh of Troyes, a pact which bore fruit shortly thereafter, in 1125, when Hugh retired to a monastery, leaving the county of Champagne in the hands of his nephew Theobald.[135] It is possible that Theobald decided in 1124 to cooperate with King Louis, his feudal overlord, in opposing the German invasion in the hope of insuring the king's tacit acceptance of his eventual succession in Champagne. In any case, his failure to support King Henry on this occasion is the first indication that Theobald's interests were beginning to diverge from those of his uncle.

After this struggle with his barons, Henry I was able to enjoy only two years of peace before the specter of William Clito returned to haunt him once more. At his Christmas court in 1126, perhaps seeking to capitalize on possible Anglo-Norman dissatisfaction with Henry's nomination of his daughter Matilda to succeed him, King Louis of France "addressed the nobles of the realm . . . and asked them urgently to give sympathy and help to William the Norman."[136] On this occasion, Louis sealed his renewed alliance with Clito by giving him Jeanne de Montferrat, the sister of his own Queen Adelaide, as a bride. As a wedding present, he granted the bridegroom Pontoise, Chaumont, Mantes and the Vexin. Shortly thereafter William Clito arrived at Gisors at the head of an army, intending to claim Normandy for himself.[137]

However, Clito's attention was soon diverted elsewhere, for on 2 March 1127 Duke Charles the Good of Flanders was murdered by rebellious vassals.[138] The conspirators immediately attempted to raise William of Ypres, the illegitimate son of Philip of Loo and therefore a grandson of Robert the Frisian, to the comital throne.[139] Opposition to William of Ypres soon emerged, for he was suspected of having conspired with the murderers, and soon Flanders stood on

---

[135] D'Arbois de Jubainville, pp. 275–276.

[136] *OV* 6:368.

[137] Ibid., 6:370.

[138] Ibid., 6:370; Suger., pp. 240–244; *ASC* 1127 AD; Henry of Huntingdon, p. 247; Hermann of Tournai, *Liber de Restauratione S. Martini Tornacensis, MGH SS* 14:285; Walter of Therouanne, *Vita Karoli Comitis Flandriae, MGH SS* 12:549–550, chapt. 27; Galbert of Bruges, *Histoire du Meurte de Charles Le Bon, Comte De Flandre (1127–1128)*, ed. Henri Pirenne (Paris, 1891), pp. 24–36; David Nicholas, *Medieval Flanders* (London, 1992), pp. 62–66.

[139] Galbert of Bruges, pp. 35, 42–45.

the brink of civil war. In an unprecedented display of royal authority, Louis VI intervened, ordering the barons of Flanders to come to his court to elect a new count. On 23 March, at the king's instructions, the barons elected William Clito count of Flanders. King Louis and William Clito then traveled together to Flanders to punish the murderers and install the new count in his domain.[140]

It seems likely that Louis VI established Clito in this crucial position in order to give him a base from which to further harass his English uncle. Although in the spring of 1127 there was peace in western Europe, both between Henry I and Louis VI and between the latter and Theobald of Blois, thoughts of renewed conflict were never far from the French king's mind. Suger wrote that when Louis rushed to avenge the murder of Charles the Good, "warfare with the English king and Count Theobald did not hold him back."[141] On 14 April 1127, Louis VI and William Clito made an agreement with the citizens of Saint-Omer regarding taxes and trade duties. The king and the count-elect promised that the same concessions would be granted in the territories of Theobald of Blois and Henry I when peace was concluded with those parties.[142] Clearly, in order to make the promised concessions, Louis VI and William Clito would have to fight, and win, a new war against Henry I and Theobald of Blois.

True to the French king's expectations, Henry I moved at once to counter the renewed threat of William Clito. A later chronicler, Matthew of Paris, wrote that Clito claimed the English throne in his own right at this time.[143] Henry met this challenge by claiming the Flemish throne for himself.[144] On the diplomatic front, Henry cemented a crucial alliance with Fulk of Anjou on 22 May 1127, when the betrothal of Henry's daughter the Empress Matilda to Fulk's son Geoffrey was announced.[145] The marriage was celebrated slightly over a year later, on 17 June 1128.

According to Galbert of Bruges, it was reported on 24 March 1127 that William of Ypres had received "an enormous sum of

---

[140] Ibid., pp. 81–84; Suger, pp. 244–250; Hermann of Tournai, p. 288; Walter of Therouanne, p. 557, chapt. 44; *OV* 6:370; Henry of Huntingdon, p. 247; *ASC* 1127 AD.

[141] Suger, p. 244.

[142] Luchaire, no. 384.

[143] Matthew of Paris, *Chronica Majora*, RS 57, 2:153–154; *Historia Anglorum*, RS 44, 1:239.

[144] Simeon of Durham, *Gesta Regum*, p. 282; Walter of Therouanne, pp. 557–558, chapt. 45; Ganshof, "Roi de France," 210.

[145] *ASC* 1126 AD; Henry of Huntingdon, p. 247.

money and three hundred knights" from the English king.[146] Galbert stated that the rumor was false, and that William of Ypres had obtained five hundred pounds in English currency from the treasure of Charles the Good and had used it to hire mercenaries. The story that the money came from Henry I was concocted to conceal the fact that William had actually received the money from the count's murderers. However, in the following year, Galbert reported that two of William Clito's rebellious vassals, Ivan and William, "had received many gifts from the king of England and were about to receive more in return for the expulsion of his nephew."[147] The author also noted that Henry I and his father-in-law Godfrey of Lorraine planned at that time to marry one of Godfrey's daughters to another of William's rivals for the comital office, Arnold of Denmark.[148] Henry of Huntingdon gave Henry I credit for inducing Thierry of Alsace to lay claim to Flanders for himself.[149] On the economic front, Henry instituted an embargo on English trade with Flanders, and relied upon his father-in-law to reduce traffic between that country and the mainland.[150] During this period, William Clito wrote to Louis VI asking for his help against Henry I, whom he accused of trying to turn the Flemings against him "by arms and immoderate amounts of money."[151] Although Henry I did not immediately take up arms against his troublesome nephew, he used every other means available to hinder Clito's latest venture.

Stephen of Blois became directly involved in the war with William Clito when the latter invaded Boulogne, "lay[ing] waste his lands relentlessly with fire and sword."[152] The invasion came to nothing, however, because Thierry of Alsace, asserting his own claim to the comital throne, captured Lille, Furnes and Ghent. Unable to fight a war on two fronts, William Clito then concluded a three-year truce with Stephen.[153]

---

[146] Galbert of Bruges, pp. 78–79.

[147] Ibid., p. 277.

[148] Ibid., p. 147. However, according to Orderic's account, Godfrey of Lorraine was on the other side of the struggle, for the Norman chronicler wrote that Clito received help from the duke of Lorraine when he laid siege to the town of Aalst in the summer of 1128, *OV* 6:372.

[149] Henry of Huntingdon, p. 249. See also *Ex Chronico Turonensi*, Bouquet 12:470.

[150] Hicks, "Impact of William Clito," 18; Ganshof, "Les origines du concept de souverainete nationale en Flandre," p. 144.

[151] *Epistolae Ludovici VI, Regis Francorum*, Bouquet 15:341.

[152] *OV* 6:372; Walter of Therouanne, pp. 557–558, chapt. 45.

[153] *OV* 6:372.

By contrast, Theobald of Blois seems to have taken little part in the conflict.[154] Relations between uncle and nephew were at least cordial during this period, since in 1127 Bernard of Clairvaux wrote to Theobald asking him for a letter of recommendation for a cleric of his acquaintance who was traveling to King Henry's court.[155] It is possible that Theobald did meet with Henry I during this period, for his attestation appears on a charter granting a fair to the church of St. Mary of Glastonbury that dates between 1126 and 1129.[156] But there is also evidence that the count carefully maintained his ties with the Capetians during this conflict. As late as August 1127, the French abbeys of Saint-Étienne de Sens and Saint-Jean de Sens made an agreement ceding the church and cemetery of Saint-Sauveur to Saint Jean in the presence of Louis VI and at his request. Theobald's seneschal, André de Baudement, was also present.[157] At some time before June 1128, Louis VI wrote to Pope Honorius regarding the reform of the monastery of Saint-Martin au Val, near Chartres. He noted that he had given the Church of Saint-Martin to the monks of Marmoutier at the insistence of Count Theobald.[158] These two events seem to indicate that, far from being at war with Louis VI, Theobald was remaining quietly in the background, seeking to cultivate renewed ties with his overlord.

In June or July 1128, Henry launched an invasion of France. Although he remained at Épernon for only eight days, his timely intervention prevented Louis VI from going to the aid of the embattled Clito.[159] The French king was also distracted at this time by events within his own household. His long-time favorite, Étienne de Garlande, who held the offices of both seneschal and chancellor, overstepped his bounds by attempting to marry his niece to Amaury de Montfort and to pass his office of seneschal on to de Montfort. This proved too much for Louis VI, who deprived Garlande of his offices and his property.[160] The result was a small armed rebellion by Étienne de Garlande and Amaury de Montfort. Suger maintained

---

[154] D'Arbois de Jubainville, p. 285.
[155] Bernard of Clairvaux *Ep* no. 41 in *PL* 182, col. 148.
[156] *Regesta 2*, no. 1590.
[157] Luchaire, no. 393.
[158] Ibid., no. 413; D'Arbois de Jubainville, pp. 289–290.
[159] Luchaire, no. 414; Henry of Huntingdon, pp. 247–248; Robert of Torigny, *Chronicle*, pp. 112–113.
[160] Luchaire, "Louis VI et ses Palatins," 262–265; D'Arbois de Jubainville, p. 287.

that the position of the rebels, particularly de Montfort, "had been strengthened by aid from the English king and Count Theobald."[161] It is significant that on the one occasion that Theobald of Blois may have chosen to intervene in French affairs, it was on the side of de Montfort, the count of Évreux, whose lands in western Normandy posed a major threat to the king of France, and a man with whom Theobald had forged a crucial alliance in 1119. However, once again, the sources are silent regarding any concrete assistance that Theobald may have given the rebels.

Although the rebellion of Garlande and de Montfort dragged on until 1130, the war in Flanders came to an abrupt end in July 1128 when Clito was wounded in the hand at the siege of Aalst and died of gangrene several days later.[162] It is perhaps a sign of Louis' weakness at the time that he recognized Thierry of Alsace, whom Henry I had earlier supported, as the new count of Flanders.[163]

Once again Theobald had remained in the background but had emerged a winner. In 1128, King Louis' weakness insured his own independence, his uncle's candidate was safely installed in Flanders, and he enjoyed a renewed alliance with Amaury de Montfort. Once peace had returned, Theobald found it possible to pursue his relationship with his uncle more openly and to communicate with him on a more regular basis. Henry and Theobald met again in 1129, when Theobald witnessed a royal charter issued at Havering which recorded a grant of lands to Robert of Leicester.[164] In 1130, the monks of the abbey of Rebais went back on a promise to the monastery of St.-Évroul to return some relics of the latter's patron saint, saying that they would not do so unless Count Theobald approved the transfer. Odo of Montreuil, a monk of St.-Évroul, went to King Henry at Vernon and asked him to intercede with his nephew for them. Orderic stated that the king spoke to his nephew and obtained his consent, so we may assume that they were together at the time.[165] The two men met again on 13 January 1131, when Henry visited Pope Innocent II at Chartres.[166] Theobald's presence is confirmed by his attestation of a charter in favor of the abbey of

---

[161] Suger, p. 254.
[162] *OV* 6:374–378; Galbert of Bruges, pp. 170–172.
[163] Galbert of Bruges, p. 176; see also Hermann of Tournai, p. 289.
[164] *Regesta 2*, no. 1607.
[165] *OV* 6:340.
[166] Suger, p. 260; *OV* 6:420; Robert of Torigny, *Chronicle*, p. 119.

Fontevrault issued during the papal visit,[167] but others seem to have taken charge of the festivities. Orderic notes that Henry was entertained at Chartres in the home of the vidamesse Helisende, the wife of Bartholomew Boel.[168] It seems strange that Count Theobald remained unmentioned, unlike prior papal visits, when his mother Adela took the leading role in the festivities. Theobald was also in his uncle's entourage in July or August 1131 at Arques, where he witnessed a charter in favor of the abbey of Holy Trinity at Caen.[169]

Relations between Count Theobald and King Louis VI worsened at this time, but hostilities never reached the level of the years before 1120. At the beginning of 1130, William of Nevers and Theobald's vassal, Hugh le Manceau, went to war over a fief held from Count Theobald. William of Nevers resorted to force of arms rather than answer a summons to his former captor's court to settle the matter. Louis VI and the bishop of Autun supported William, and when they besieged the castle at Cosne, Hugh le Manceau called on his lord for help. As soon as Theobald approached, accompanied by Geoffrey of Anjou, King Louis abandoned the siege. Geoffrey of Anjou played the leading role in the confrontation, and going in hot pursuit, captured William of Nevers and returned him to Theobald's prison once more.[170] It should be noted that Hugh le Manceau was a vassal and a long-time supporter, undoubtedly someone, like Amaury de Montfort, whom Theobald felt obliged to help as a matter of honor. In these cases, the count appears have acted in order to help old continental allies and to further establish his own independence rather than to support any plans of the English king.

One further small conflict between Theobald and the Capetians occurred in the realm of ecclesiastical politics. In 1131, a quarrel arose between the bishop of Paris, Stephen of Senlis, and the canons of the cathedral chapter, over the bishop's efforts at reform, which had infringed upon some of the chapter's rights.[171] Bishop Geoffrey of Chartres wrote to his fellow bishop, urging him to appear before the king's court to answer the charges that had been made against him. The exiled bishop instead took refuge at Lagny, within the

---

[167] *Regesta 2*, no. 1687.
[168] *OV* 6:420.
[169] *Regesta 2*, no. 1692.
[170] Halphen and Poupardin, *Chroniques des Comtes d'Anjou*, pp. 200–201; D'Arbois de Jubainville, pp. 291–292.
[171] Bernard of Clairvaux, *Ep* nos. 46–47 in *PL* vol. 182 cols. 153–154.

lands of Theobald of Blois.[172] It is possible to interpret this extension of hospitality to a cleric who had fallen out of favor with the
Capetian court as part of a mediation attempt by the bishop of
Chartres. At most, the count could be accused of turning a blind
eye to the presence of a fugitive within his territory.

However, even though Theobald's activities during the latter part
of the reign of Louis VI were benign by comparison with previous
years, Louis attempted to continue the conflict with the count of
Blois until the very end of his life. By 1132, the king's health was
failing. Suger wrote: "The weight of his body weakened him to the
point where he had become very stiff in bed; but he did not slacken
his struggle against the king of England and Count Theobald and
all others."[173] It is significant that of the king's many enemies, Suger
singled out Henry and Theobald, and seems to have regarded Theobald as second only to the king of England. Louis attacked Theobald's
town of Bonneval and burned it to the ground, sparing only the
cloisters of the monks, who were under his special protection.[174] On
another occasion, he sent his men to destroy Theobald's property at
Château-Renard. It is perhaps fitting that the last towns that Louis VI
ravaged belonged to his life-long enemy, Theobald of Blois. However, by the end of his life, King Louis had reconciled himself with
the count of Blois-Chartres. Orderic recorded that when the king
lay ill with a severe bout of diarrhea in 1135, he called Theobald
of Blois and Ralph of Vermandois to him and made peace between
them.[175] The incident is not recorded in Suger's history, perhaps
because once again the abbot could not bear to write anything favorable about his favorite villain. However, Suger did note that in 1137,
Louis sent the counts of Blois and Vermandois to Aquitaine with his
son Louis for the prince's marriage to the heiress Eleanor.[176] Thus,
although their quarrel had endured for a lifetime, by the time that
Louis VI died in 1137, he and his greatest enemy, Count Theobald
of Blois, were at peace.

Theobald's career after 1120 stands in marked contrast to the preceding years. From 1111 until the wreck of the White Ship in 1120,
Theobald was King Henry I's most steadfast ally, earning in the

---

[172] *Epistolae Stephani Parisiensis Episcopi*, Bouquet 15:334–335, no. 10.
[173] Suger, p. 270.
[174] Ibid., p. 272.
[175] *OV* 6:446.
[176] Suger, p. 280; *OV* 6:490.

process the undying hatred of his own feudal overlord, Louis VI. However, after 1120, the count became much more circumspect and generally abstained from the quarrel between the two monarchs, acting only to support crucial allies and to safeguard his own independence from his overlord.

The reasons for Theobald's change of heart can never be fully known, but the historian can offer a few educated guesses. Perhaps Theobald was simply tired of the fight. D'Arbois de Jubainville suggested that Theobald experienced a sudden burst of religious feeling as a result of seeing so many members of his family perish so suddenly in the wreck of the White Ship in 1120.[177] According to the life of St. Norbert, Theobald approached the holy founder of the abbey of Prémontré about becoming a monk of his house. However, the saint dissuaded him, saying that the abbey, as beneficiary of Theobald's vast lands, could never perform the feudal services owed to the king, and that furthermore, the count's vassals would be deprived of his protection.[178] Shortly thereafter, at Norbert's suggestion, Theobald married Mathilde, the granddaughter of the marquis of Istry, a family with which St. Norbert enjoyed a close friendship.[179]

However, while Theobald and many other Anglo-Norman families must have been grief-stricken at the loss of their relatives in the wreck of the White Ship, it is unlikely that the count abandoned the quest for power and independence that he had pursued with single-minded dedication over the past decade. By 1120, Theobald was the master of two counties and he may have looked forward to someday acquiring Champagne from one uncle and Normandy from the other. Uniting Blois, Chartres, Champagne and Normandy would make Theobald the greatest magnate in northern Europe, far more powerful than his nominal overlord, the king of France. But, as Luchaire pointed out with respect to Normandy, in order to assume the ducal throne, Theobald would have to gain the support of Normandy's overlord, the king of France.[180] It appears that Theobald may have viewed temporary cooperation with Louis VI as the price of inheriting Champagne in 1125, and it is likely that he hoped to win the

---

[177] D'Arbois de Jubainville, p. 250.
[178] *Ex Vita S. Norberti Archiepiscopi Magdeburg*, Bouquet 14:229.
[179] Ibid., pp. 229–230; D'Arbois de Jubainville, p. 263.
[180] Luchaire, "Louis le Gros et ses Palatins," 274.

Capetian's consent to his eventual accession in Normandy by mini-
mizing his confrontations with the latter during the years between
1120 and 1135.

There is no direct evidence that Count Theobald had his eyes on
Normandy, but in 1135 as King Henry's body was being carried
across the channel for burial at Reading Abbey, Theobald met with
Robert of Gloucester and a group of Norman magnates at Neubourg
to discuss the possibility of his assuming control of the duchy of
Normandy.[181] The discussions ended when word arrived that Stephen
had been crowned in England. Orderic wrote that Theobald ". . . [was]
offended at not getting the kingdom though he was the elder, [and]
hurried away to see to important affairs which demanded his attention in France, and heedlessly allowed Normandy to be battered for
a long time. . . ."[182]

It is difficult to tell whether Orderic overstated his case in describing Theobald's resentment of his brother's success, since the
evidence that Theobald's subsequent behavior provides is mixed. Immediately after he received the news of Stephen's coronation, Theobald
negotiated a six-month truce with Geoffrey of Anjou in Normandy.[183]
His action can be interpreted either as an effort to buy his brother
valuable time to consolidate his hold on England, or as an attempt
to forge an alliance against him. In any case, shortly afterwards,
Waleran of Meulan and Robert of Leicester had to pay Theobald
one hundred marks of silver to get his help in an attack on Roger
of Tosny.[184] In 1137, Stephen promised Theobald an annual payment of two thousand marks of silver in order to get him to permanently renounce his claims to England and Normandy. Robert of
Torigny said that Stephen was forced to take this action because
"Count Theobald was angry because Stephen had obtained possession of the crown, which he said belonged to him."[185] Theobald was
as good as his word, however, for soon afterwards he helped obtain
a papal bull from Innocent II approving Stephen's election.[186] In

---

[181] *OV* 6:42, 454, 548. Earlier, Orderic stated that Theobald had actually ruled
the duchy for a period of time. Theobald was also offered the crown of England
and the duchy of Normandy after Stephen was captured at the battle of Lincoln
in 1141.

[182] *OV* 6:454.

[183] Ibid., 6:458.

[184] Ibid., 6:464.

[185] Robert of Torigny, *Chronicle*, p. 132.

[186] Bouquet 13:84n, 15:391–392; Richard of Hexham, *Historia de gestis regis Stephani*

1141, when Stephen lay in prison after his capture at Lincoln, Theobald refused to accept the crown from the barons of Normandy, offering to resign his rights to Geoffrey of Anjou. In return, Theobald asked for the city of Tours for himself, and requested that Geoffrey and Matilda release Stephen from prison and allow him and his sons to retain possessions of their family lands, conditions which Geoffrey refused to accept.[187] Abbot Suger described a golden crucifix that he had made for St.-Denis, which was ornamented with precious gems that the donors had obtained as alms from Count Theobald. The count had been given the jewels by his brother Stephen, who in turn had gotten them from the treasures amassed by King Henry.[188] The jewels may have been part of a continuing series of payments that Stephen made to his elder brother in order to insure his neutrality and occasional assistance during the civil war. The evidence suggests that Theobald had hoped to inherit Normandy from his uncle, and perhaps these expectations determined Theobald's policies in the years after 1120.

But if Theobald failed to create a medieval empire for himself in northern Europe by joining the duchy of Normandy to his other continental possessions, he did achieve the one goal that had driven his actions since he became count of Blois and Chartres in 1107— the preservation of his own independence in the face of the expanding authority of the Capetian dynasty of France. Long before the wreck of the White Ship opened up vast new possibilities in his calculations, Theobald had fought to maintain the traditional independence of his house in the face of persistent encroachments by the French king. Before 1120, this goal was best served by maintaining a vigorous alliance with his uncle Henry I. After 1120, Theobald played a more cautious game, remaining in the background and confronting his overlord only when his immediate interests were threatened. Theobald was equally skillful in both roles, and although he failed to win Normandy, the peaceful acquisition of Champagne in 1125 must stand as a tribute to his political wisdom.

---

et de bello de Standardii (1135–1139), RS 82, 3:147–148; D'Arbois de Jubainville, p. 326.

[187] OV 6:548.

[188] Suger, De Rebus in Administratione Sua Gestis, Oeuvres complétes de Suger, ed. A. Lecoy de la Marche (Paris, 1867), p. 195.

RULERS OF MEDIEVAL SPAIN

Navarre (Pamplona)

Iñigo Iñiquez Arista (810–851)
|
Garcìa Iñiguez (851–870)
|
Fortún Garcés (870–905)
|
Sancho I Garcés (905–926)
|
García I Sánchez (926–970)
|
Sancho II Garcés (Navarre, Aragon) (970–994)
|
García II Sànchez (Navarre, Aragon) (994–1000)
|
Sancho III Garcés "The Great" (Navarre, Aragon) (1000–1035)
|
García IV (1035–1054)
|
Sancho IV (1054–1076)
|
Sancho V (Navarre, Aragon) (1076–1094)
|
Pedro I (Navarre, Aragon) (1094–1104)
|
Alfonso I "the Battler" (Aragon, Navarre) (1104–1134)
|
García V "the Restorer" (1134–1150)
|
Sancho VI "the Wise" (1150–1194)
|
Sancho VII "the Strong" (1194–1234)

Commencement of French Rule

Castile/León

Sancho II (Castile) (1066–1072)
|
Alfonso VI (Léon) (1065–1109)/(Castile) (1072–1109)
|
Urraca (Castile/Léon) (1109–1126)
|
Alfonso VII (Castile, Léon, Galicia) (1126–1157)

Sancho III (Castile) (1157–1158)
|
Alfonso VIII (Castile) (1158–1214)
|
Enrique I (Castile) (1214–1217)

Fernando II (Léon) (1157–1188)
|
Alfonso IX (Léon) (1188–1230)

Castile

Fernando III (Castile) (1217–1252)
(Léon) (1230–1252)
|
Alfonso X "the Wise" (1252–1284)
|
Fernando IV (1295–1312)
|
Alfonso XI (1312–1350)
|
Pedro I "the Cruel" (1350–1369)
|
Enrique II (1369–1379)
|
Juan I (1379–1390)
|
Enrique III (1390–1406)
|
Juan II (1406–1454)
|
Enrique IV (1454–1474)
|
Isabella I "the Catholic" (1474–1516)

Aragon

Sancho III Garcés "the Great" (Navarre/Aragon) (1000–1035)
|
Ramiro I (1035–1063)
|
Sancho I (1063–1094)
|
Pedro I (Aragon, Navarre) (1094–1104)
|
Alfonso I "the Battler" (Aragon, Navarre) (1104–1134)

Ramiro II "the Monk" (Aragon) (1134–1137)
|
Petronilla (1137–1173)
[Married to Ramón Berenguer, count of Barcelona]

Barcelona

Wilfred "the Hairy" (873–914)
|
Borrell I (898–914)
|
Sunyer (914–940)
|
Borrell II (940–992)
|
Ramón Berenguer I "the Old" (1035–1076)
|
Ramón Berenguer II "Tow Head" (1076–1082)
|
Berenguer Ramón "the Fratricide" (1076–1097)
|
Ramón Berenguer III "the Great" (1097–1131)
|
Ramón Berenguer IV (1131–1162)

Crown of Aragon

Alfonso II "the Chaste" (1163–1196)
|
Pedro II "the Catholic" (1196–1213)
|
Jaime I "the Conqueror" (1213–1276)
|
Pedro III "the Great" (1276–1285)
|
Alfonso III "the Generous" (1285–1291)
|
Jaime II "the Justiciar" (1291–1327)
|
Alfonso IV "the Benign" (1327–1336)
|
Pedro IV "the Ceremonious" (1336–1387)
|
Juan I "the Hunter" (1387–1395)
|
Martin I "the Humane" (1395–1412)
|
Fernando I "de Antequera" (1412–1416)
|
Alfonso V "the Magnanimous" (1416–1458)

Juan II (Navarre, Crown of Aragon) (1458–1479)
|
Fernando II "the Catholic" (1479–1516)

Nasrid Kingdom of Granada

Muhammad I (1232–1273)
|
Muhammad II (1273–1302)
|
Muhammad III (1302–1309)
|
Nasr (1309–1314)
|
Ismail I (1314–1325)
|
Muhammad IV (1325–1333)
|
Yūsuf I (1333–1354)
|
Muhammad V (1354–1359; 1362–1391)
|
Ismail II (1359–1360)
|
Muhammad VI (1360–1362)
|
Yūsuf II (1391–1392)

Muhammad VII (1392–1408)
|
Yūsuf III (1408–1417)

(continued on next page)

Nasrid Kingdom of Granada
(continued from previous page)

|
Muhammad VIII (1417–1419; 1427–1429)
|
Muhammad IX (1419–1427; 1429–1445; 1447–1453)
|
Yūsuf IV (1430–1432)
|
Muhammad XI (1448–1454)
|
Yūsuf V (1445, 1450, 1462–1463)
|
Said (1454–1464)
|
Abu al-Hasan Ali {Muley Hacén} (1464–1485)
|
Muhammad XIII (1485–1487)
|
Muhammad XII {Boabdil} (1482–1492)

BIBLIOGRAPHY

Actas de las Primeras Jornadas Luso-Españolas de Historia Medieval (IX–72). *A pobreza e a assistencia aos pobres na Peninsula Iberica durante a Idade Media*. 2 vols. Lisbon, 1973.

Aguado de Cordoba, Antonio Francisco. *Bullarium Equestris Ordinis S. Iacobi de Spatha per annorum seriem nonnullis*. Madrid, 1719.

[Alarcón, Maximiliano A.] "Documento arabígo del monasterio de Poblet." *Memorial Hisórico Español* 6 (1853): 111–119.

Albert, Ricard, and Joan Gassitot, eds. *Parlaments a les corts catalanes*. Barcelona, 1928.

Altisent, Agustí, ed. *Diplomatari de Santi Maria de Poblet: I (960–1177)*. Barcelona, 1993.

———. *Historia de Poblet*. Poblet, 1974.

Anales Toledanos I, II, III. In *ES* 23:381–423.

Antuña, M. "Abenjátima de Almería y su tratado de la peste." *Religión y Cultura* 1 (1928): 68–90.

Arie, Rachel. "Un opuscule grenadin sur la Peste Noire de 1348: La 'Naisha' de Muhammad al Saquiri." *Boletín de la Asociacion Española de Orientalistas* 3 (1967): 189–199.

Arjona Castro, Antonio. "Las epidemias de peste bubónica en Andalucía en el siglo XIV." *B.R.A. Córdoba* 56 (1985): 49–58.

Arrizabalaga, Jon. "Facing the Black Death: Perceptions and Reactions of University Medical Practioners." In *Practical Medicine from Salerno to The Black Death*, edited by Luis Garcí-Ballester et al. (Cambridge, 1994), pp. 237–288.

Asheri, Judah. *Zikhron Yehuda, ve-hu sefer she'elot u-teshuvot*. Berlin, 1846.

Bakrî, Abû 'Ubayd Abd Allah Ibn abd al-Azzin al. *Kitab mu'jam mâ ista 'jam*. Edited by F. Wustenfeld. 2 vols. Gottingen and Paris, 1876–1877.

Baer, Yitzhak. *A History of the Jews in Christian Spain*. 2 vols. Translated by Louis Schoffman. Philadelphia, 1961; reprint ed., 1978.

———, ed. *Die Juden im Christlichen Spanien: Urkunden und Regesten*. 2 vols. Berlin, 1970 (1929–1936).

Balaguer, Victor. *Las ruinas de Poblet*. Madrid, 1885.

Ballesteros Beretta, Antonio. *Alfonso X el Sabio*. Barcelona, 1984.

———. *Historia de España y su influencia en la historia universal*. 11 vols. Barcelona, 1922.

Ballesteros Gaibrois, Manuel. *Don Rodrigo Jiménez de Rada*. Madrid, 1943.

Baquero Moreno, Humberto Carlos. "A Peste Negra e os legados a igreja." *Revista de Ciencias Historicas* 6 (Porto, 1991): 133–143.

Barber, Malcolm. *The New Knighthood: A History of the Order of the Temple*. Cambridge, 1994.

———. "The Order of Saint Lazarus and the Crusades." *CHR* 80 (1994): 439–456.

Barrios García, Angel. *Documentación medieval de la Catedral de Avila*. Salamanca, 1981.

———. *Estructuras agrarias y de poder en Castilla. El ejemplo de Avila (1085–1320)*. Salamanca, 1983.

Bat Ye'or [Yahudiya Masriya]. *The Dhimmi. Jews and Christians Under Islam*. Revised and Enlarged English Edition. Author's text translated by David Maisel. Document section translated by Paul Fenton. Translated by David Littman. Rutherford, NJ, 1985.

Batlle Gallart, Carmen. *L'assistència als pobres a la Barcelona medieval (s. XIII)*. Barcelona, 1987.

——. *La Seu d'Urgell medieval: La ciutat i els seus habitants.* Barcelona, 1985.
——. "La ayuda a los pobres en la parroquia de San Justo de Barcelona." In *A pobreza.*
Batlle Gallart, Carmen and Casas, C. "La caritat privada i les institucions benèfiques de Barcelona (segle XIII)." In *La pobreza y la asistencia a los pobres en la Cataluña medieval,* edited by Manuel Riu. 2 vols. (Barcelona, 1980–1982), 1: ?
Baudot, Marcel. "La Gestation d'une léprosarie du XIVᵉ siècle: La maladrerie Saint-Lazare de Montpellier." In *Actes du 110ᵉ Congrès national des sociétés savants,* 1:411. Paris, 1987.
Bäuml, Franz. "Varities and Consequences of Medieval Literacy and Illiteracy." *Speculum* 55 (1980): 237–265.
Behar, Ruth. *Santa María del Monte. The Presence of the Past in a Spanish Village.* Princeton, NJ, 1986.
Beraud-Villars, Jean Marcel. *Les Touareg au pays du Cid: Les invasions almoravides en Espagne aux XIᵉ et XIIᵉ siècles.* Paris, 1946.
Berceo, Gonzalo de. *Milagros de Nuestra Señora.* Madrid, 1982.
Beriac, Françoise. *Histoire des lépreux au moyen âge, une société d'exclus.* Paris, 1988.
Bernard of Clairvaux. "Liber ad Milites Templi: de laude novae militiae." In *S. Bernardi opera,* eds. J. LeClercq and H.M. Rochais, 3:312–339. Rome, 1963.
Berthe, Maurice M. "Famines et épidémies dans le monde paysan de Navarre aux XIVᵉ et XV siècles." *Académie des Inscriptions et Belles Lettres. Comptes rendus des seánces* 2 (Paris, 1983), 299–314.
Biraben, Jean Noël. *Les hommes et la peste en France et dans les pays européens et mediterranéens.* Paris, 1975–1976.
Bisson, Thomas N. *The Medieval Crown of Aragon: A Short History.* Oxford, 1986.
——. "The Problem of Feudal Monarchy: Aragon, Catalonia, and France." *Speculum* 53 (1978): 464–470.
Blancas y Tomas, Jeronimo de. *Modo de proceder en cortes de Aragón.* Zaragoza, 1641.
Bloch, Marc. *Feudal Society.* Translated by L.A. Manyon. 2 vols. Chicago, 1964.
Bonaparte, Louis-Napoléon. *Études sur le passé et l'avenir de l'artillerie.* 6 vols. Paris, 1848–1871.
Bonnassie, Pierre. *La Catalogne du milieu du Xᵉ a la fin du XIᵉ siècle: croissance et mutations d'une société.* 2 vols. Toulouse, 1975–1976.
Bosch Vila, Jacinto. *El oriente arabé en el desarallo de la cultura de la marca superior.* Madrid, 1954.
Bowsky, William M., ed. *The Black Death: A Turning Point in History?* Huntingdon, NY, 1978.
Braudel, Fernand. *The Mediterranean and the Mediterranean World in the Age of Philip II.* Translated by Siân Reynolds. New York, 1992.
Bridbury, A.R. "The Black Death." *Economic History Review* 2nd ser., 24 (1973): 577–592.
Brodman, James W. *Ransoming Captives in Crusader Spain.* Philadelphia, 1986.
——. "What is a Soul Worth? Pro Anima Bequests in the Municipal Legislation of Reconquest Spain." *Medievalia et Humanistica* n.s. 20 (1993): 15–24.
Brown, R.A., H.M. Colvin, and A.J. Taylor. *The History of the King's Works.* 4 vols. London, 1963–1982.
Brundage, James A. *Medieval Canon Law.* London, 1996.
Burgess, Glyn, trans. *The Song of Roland.* London, 1974.
Burns, Robert I. "The Crusade Against Al-Azraq: A Thirteenth-Century Mudejar Revolt in International Perspective." *AHR* 93 (1988): 80–106.
——. *The Crusader Kingdom of Valencia: Reconstruction on a Thirteenth-Century Frontier.* 2 vols. Cambridge, MA, 1967.
——. *Diplomatarium of the Crusader Kingdom of Valencia: The Registered Charters of Its Conqueror, Jaume I, 1257–1276.* 2 vols. Princeton, 1985–.

——. "The Guidaticum Safe-Conduct in Medieval Arago-Catalonia: Mini-Institution for Muslims, Christians, and Jews." *Medieval Encounters* 1 (1995): 51–113.
——. *Islam Under the Crusaders: Colonial Survival in the Thirteenth-Century Kingdom of Valencia.* Princeton, NJ, 1973.
——. "A Lost Crusade: Unpublished Bulls of Innocent IV on Al-Azraq's Revolt in Thirteenth-Century Spain." *CHR* 74 (1988): 440–449.
——. *Muslims, Christians, and Jews in the Crusader Kingdom of Valencia: Societies in Symbiosis.* Cambridge, MA, 1984.
——. "The Spiritual Life of James the Conqueror, King of Arago-Catalonia, 1208–1276: Portrait and Self-Portrait." *CHR* 62 (1976): 1–35.
Cabrillana, Nicolás. "La crisis del siglo XIV en Castilla: La Peste Negra en el Obispado de Palencia." *Hispania* 28 (1968): 245–258.
——. "Los despoblados en Castilla la Vieja." *Hispania* 28 (1971; 1972): 450–550; 5–60.
Cahen, Claude. "Un traité d'armurerie pour Saladin." *Bulletin d'études orientales* 12 (1947–1948): 103–163.
Campmany y Montpalau, Antonio. *Practica y estilo de celebrar cortes en el reino de Aragón, principado de Cataluña, y reinado de Valencia.* Madrid, 1821.
Camps i Arboix, Joaquim de. *La Masia Catalana: Historia-arquitectura-sociologia.* Barcelona, 1969.
Carlé, María del Carmen. "El precio de la vida en Castilla del rey Sabio al emplazado." *CHE* 15 (1951): 132–156.
Carmichael, Ann G. *Plague and the Poor in Renaissance Florence.* Cambridge, 1986.
Carmona García, Juan Ignacio. *El sistema de hospitalidad publica en la Sevilla del antiguo Regimen.* Seville, 1979.
Caro de Torres, Francisco. *Historia de las ordenes militares de Santiago, Calatrava y Alcántara.* Madrid, 1629.
Carpenter, Dwayne Eugene. *Alfonso X and the Jews: An Edition of and Commentary on Siete Partidas 7.24 "De los Judíos".* Berkeley, 1986.
Carpentier, Elisabeth. "Autour de la Peste Noire, famines et épidémies dans l'histoire du 14ᵉ siècle." *Annales Economies Societés Civilisations* 17 (1962): 1062–1090.
Cartulaire de l'Abbaye de Saint-Père de Chartres. Edited by M. Guerard. 2 vols. Paris, 1840.
Cartulaire de Saint-Jean-en-Vallée de Chartres. Edited by René Merlet. Chartres, 1906.
Carvalho, Sérgio Luís P. "A peste de 1348 em Sintra." In *1383–1385 e a crise geral dos seculos XIV/XV: Actas* (Lisbon, 1985), pp. 129–135.
Casado Alonso, Hilario. *Señores, mercaderes y campesinos. La comarca de Burgos a fines de la edad media.* Valladolid, 1987.
Casiri, Miguel. *Bibliotheca arabico-hispanica escurialensis.* 2 vols. Madrid, 1760–1770.
Charlo Brea, Luis, ed. and trans. *Cronica latina de los reyes de Castilla.* Cadiz, 1984.
Chartrou, Josèphe. *L'Anjou de 1109 à 1151: Foulque de Jerusalem et Geoffroi Plantagenet.* Paris, 1928.
Chaves, Bernabé de. *Apuntamiento legal sobre el dominio solar de la Orden de Santiago en todos sus pueblos.* Facsimile Ed. Barcelona (Madrid), 1975 (1740).
Chejne, Anwar G. *Muslim Spain, Its History and Culture.* Minneapolis, 1974.
Chevedden, Paul E. "Artillery in Late Antiquity: Prelude to the Middle Ages." In *The Medieval City under Siege,* edited by Ivy Corfis and Micheal Wolfe (Woodbridge, England, 1995), pp. 131–173.
——. "The Artillery of King James I the Conqueror." In *Iberia and the Mediterranean World of the Middle Ages: Essays in Honor of Robert I. Burns, S.J.,* vol. 2, edited by P.E. Chevedden, D.J. Kagay, and P.G. Padilla (Leiden, 1996), pp. 47–97.
——, Les Eigenbrod, Vernard Foley, and Werner Soedel. "The Trebuchet: Recent Reconstructions and Computer Simulations reveal the Operating Principles of the Most Powerful Weapon of its Time." *Scientific American* (July 1995): 66–71.
Christian Jr., William A. *Local Religion in Sixteenth-Century Spain.* Princeton, NJ, 1981.
La Chronique de Morigny. Edited by Léon Mirot. Paris, 1912.

Cirot, Georges, ed. "Crónica latina de los reyes de Castilla." *BH* 14 (1912): 30–46, 109–118, 244–274, 353–374; 15 (1913): 18–37, 70–187, 268–283, 411–427.

Clanchy, Michael T. *From Memory to Written Record.* Cambridge, MA, 1986.

Los códigos españoles concordados y anotados. Edited by M. Rivadeneyra. 12 vols. Madrid, 1847–1851.

Coelho, Maria Helena da Cruz. "Um testamento redigido em Coimbra no tempo da Peste Negra." In *Homens, espaços e poderes (séculos XI–XVI): Notas do Viver Social.* 2 vols. (Lisbon, 1990), 1:60–77.

Cohen, Jeremy. *The Friars and the Jews: The Evolution of Medieval Anti-Judaism.* Ithaca, 1982.

Cohn, Samuel Kline. *The Cult of Remembrance and the Black Death: Six Renaissance Cities in Central Italy.* Baltimore, 1992.

Colección diplomática de las colegiatas de Albelda y Logroño, I, 924–1399. Edited by E. Saínz Ripa. Logroño, 1981.

Colmeiro, Manuel. *Cortes de los antiguos reinos de León y Castilla.* 2 vols. Madrid, 1883–1903.

Colmenares, Diego de. *Historia de la insigne ciudad de Segovia y compendio de las historias de Castilla.* 3 vols. Segovia, 1969 (1640).

Colom Mateu, Miguel, ed. *Glossari general Lullia.* 10 vols. Mallorca, 1985.

Conde, José Antonio. *História de la dominación de los árabes en España.* 3 vols. Madrid, 1820–1821.

Conrad, Lawrence I. "TÄ'ÜN and WABÄ: Conceptions of Plague and Pestilence in Early Islam." *Journal of the Economic and Social History of the Orient* 25 (1982): 268–307.

Contreras Mas, Antonio. *La asistencia publica a los leprosos en Mallorca; siglos XIV al XIX.* Mallorca, 1990.

Crónicas de los reyes de Castilla desde Don Alfonso el Sabio, hasta los católicos Don Fernando y Doña Isabel. Edited by Cayetano Rosell y López. Madrid, 1875.

Cuesta Gutiérrez, Luisa. *Formulario notarial castellano del siglo XV.* Madrid, 1947.

Curchin, Leonard. *The Local Magistrates in Roman Spain.* Toronto, 1990.

Cuvillier, Jean Pierre. "La population catalane au XIVe siècle. Comportements sociaux et niveaux de vie d'aprés les actes privés." *Mélanges de la Casa de Velázquez* (1969): 159–187.

d'Arbois de Jubainville, H. *Histoire des ducs et des comtes de Champagne.* 2 vols. Paris, 1860.

Danon, Josep. *Visió histórica de L'Hospital General de Santa Creu de Barcelona.* Barcelona, 1985.

Davis, Natalie Z. "Poor Relief, Humanism, and Heresy. The Case of Lyon." *Studies in Medieval and Renaissance History* 5 (1968): 215–275.

de Sismondi, J.C.L. *A History of the Italian Republics, Being a View of the Origin, Progress and Fall of Italian Freedom.* London, 1907.

de Soto, Domingo. *Deliberación en la causa de los pobres.* Madrid, 1965.

Diago, Francscio. *Historia de los victoriosissimos antiguos Condes de Barcelona.* Reprint. Biblioteca Hispanica Puvill. Valencia (Barcelona), 1974 (1603).

Dinanah, Taha. "Die Schrift von Abï Djafar Ahmed b. 'Alí b. Mohammed b. 'Alí b. Hátima aus Almerian über die Pest." *Archiv Für Geschichte der Medizin* 19 (1927): 37–81.

Dols, Michael. *The Black Death in the Middle East.* Princeton, NJ, 1977.

Domenech y Montaner, Luis. *Historía y arquitectura del monasterio de Poblet.* Barcelona, 1927.

Donovan, Joseph P. *Pelagius and the Fifth Crusade.* Philadelphia, 1950.

Doñate Sebastia, José M. "Datos negativos referidos a la Plana de Castellón, en relación con la peste negra de 1348." In *VIII Congreso de Historia de la Corona de Aragón.* 2 vols. (Valencia, 1967), 2:27–43.

Dozy, Reinhardt. *Recherches sur l'histoire et la littérature des l'Espagne pendant de Moyen Age*. 2 vols. Leiden, 1860.

Duby, Georges. *The Knight, The Lady, and The Priest: The Making of Modern Marriage in Medieval France*. Translated by Barbara Bray. New York, 1983.

———. *Medieval Marriage: Two Models from Twelfth-Century France*. Translated by Elborg Forster. Baltimore, 1978.

Dufour, Guillaume. *Mémoire sur l'artillerie des anciens et sur celle du Moyen Age*. Paris, 1840.

Duran i Sanpere, Agustí. *Llibre de Cervera*. Barcelona, 1977.

Eadmer. *Historia Novorum in Anglia*. Vol. 81 of *RS*.

Ekkehard. *Chronicon Universale*. Vol. 6 of *MGH SS*.

Elias, Norbert. *The Civilizing Process*. 2 vols. New York, 1982.

Elliott, John H. *The Count-Duke of Olivares. The Statesman in an Age of Decline*. London, 1986.

———. *Imperial Spain 1469–1716*. Harmonsworth, Eng. 1970.

Elliott-Binns, Leonard. *Innocent III*. London, 1931.

Emery, Richard W. "The Black Death of 1348 in Perpignan." *Speculum* 62 (1967): 611–623.

Estepa, Carlos, and et al. *Burgos en la Edad Media*. Valladolid, 1984.

Estow, Clara. "The Economic Development of the Order of Calatrava, 1158–1366." *Speculum* 57 (1982): 267–291.

Études sur l'histoire de la pauvreté (moyen âge–XVIᵉ siècle). Edited by Michel Mollat. 2 vols. Paris, 1974.

Faes, J. Tolivar. *Hospitales de leprosos en Asturias durante las edades media y moderna*. Oviedo, 1966.

Fernández Armesto, Felipe. *Before Columbus: Exploration and Colonization from the Mediterranean to the Atlantic, 1229–1492*. Philadelphia, 1987.

Fernández Catón, José María. *Catálogo del archivo histórico diocesano de León*. 2 vols. León, 1978.

Fernández Llamazares, J. *Historia compendiata de las cuatro ordenes militares de Santiago, Calatrava, Alcántara y Montesa*. Madrid, 1862.

Ferotin, Marius. *Recueil de chartes de l'abbaye de Silos*. Paris, 1897.

Ferrer i Mallol, María-Teresa. "La redacció de l'instrument notarial a Catalunya. Cèdules, manuals, llibres i cartes." *Estudios Históricos y Documentos de los Archivos de Protocolos* 4 (1974): 29–192.

Ferrer-Chivite, Manuel. "El factor judeo-converso en el proceso de consolidación del título 'Don'." *Sefarad* 45 (1985): 131–173.

Finestres y de Monsalvo, Jaime. *Historia del real monasterio de Poblet*. 6 vols. Barcelona, 1947–1955 (1746).

Finó, J.-F. *Forteresses de la France médiévale: construction, attaque, défense*. 3rd ed. Paris, 1977.

———. "Machines de jet médiévales." *Gladius* 10 (1972): 25–43.

Fita y Colomé, Fidel, and Bienvenido Oliver, eds. *Colección de los cortes de los antiguos reinos de Aragón y de Valencia y el principado de Cataluña*. 26 vols. Madrid, 1895–1922.

Fita, Fidel. "Bula inédita de Honorio II." *BRAH* 7 (1885): 335–346.

———. "Concilio de Alcalá de Henares (15 enero 1257)." *BRAH* 10 (1887): 151–159.

———. "Concilios españoles inéditos, provincial de Burgos de 1261 y nacional de Sevilla 1478." *BRAH* 22 (1893): 209–257.

Florence of Worcester. *Chronicon ex Chronicis*. 2 vols. London, 1964.

Font Rius, José María. *Cartas de población y franquicia de Cataluña. I. Textos*. 2 vols. Madrid-Barcelona, 1969.

Forey, Alan J. *The Templars in the Corona de Aragón*. London, 1973.

———. *The Military Orders from the Twelfth to the Early Fourteenth Centuries*. Toronto, 1992.

Forteza, Patricia de. "Yermos y despoblados: Problemas de terminología." In *Estudios en Homenaje a Don Claudio Sánchez Albornoz en sus 90 Años.* 6 vols. (Buenos Aires, 1985), 3:73–85.

Monumenta iuris canonici, corpus glossatorum. Edited by Gérard Fransen and Stephen Kuttner. Vatican City, 1969–1990.

Frankle, Herbert. "Siege and Defense of Towns in Medieval China." In *Chinese Ways in Warfare,* edited by Frank A. Keirman Jr. and John K. Fairbank (Cambridge, MA, 1974), pp. 151–201.

Frazer, James G. *The Golden Bough: A Study in Magic and Religion.* Abridged Ed. New York, 1927.

Freedman, Paul. *The Origins of Peasant Servitude in Medieval Catalonia.* Cambridge, 1991.

Fry, Plantagenet Somerset. *Castles.* Newton Abbot, Devon, 1980.

Gaibrois de Ballesteros, Mercedes. *Historia del reinado de Sancho IV de Castilla.* 3 vols. Madrid, 1922.

——. *María de Molina.* Madrid, 1936.

Galbert of Bruges. *Histoire de Meurte de Charles Le Bon, Comte de Flandre (1127–1128).* Edited by Henri Pirenne. Paris, 1891.

Gallego Blanco, Enrique. *The Rule of the Spanish Military Order of Saint James.* Leiden, 1971.

García de Valdeavellano, Luis. "Carta de hermandad entre los concejos de la extremadura castellana y del arzobispado de Toledo in 1295." *Revista Portugesa de Historia* 7 (1965): 57–76.

——. *Curso de historia de los instituciónes españoles. De los orígenes al final de la Edad Media.* Madrid, 1968.

García del Moral, Antonio. *El Hospital Mayor de San Sebustian de Córdoba: Cinco siglos de asistencia médico sanitaria instituctional (1363–1816).* Córdoba, 1984.

García Edo, Vicente. "Actitud de Jaime I en relación con los musulmanes del reino de Valencia durante los años de la conquista (1232–1245): Notas para su estudio." In *Ibn al-Abbar, polític i escriptor àrab valencià (1199–1260): Actes del Congres internacional "Ibn al-Abbar i el seu temps," Onda, 20–22 febrer, 1989.* Valencia, 1990.

García González, Juan José. *Vida económica de los monasterios benedictinos en el siglo XIV.* Valladolid, 1972.

García Larragueta, Santos Agustin. *Catálogo de los pergaminos de la Catedral de Oviedo.* Oviedo, 1957.

García Luján, José Antonio. *Privilegios reales de la catedral de Toledo (1086–1462).* 2 vols. Toledo, 1982.

García y García, Antonio, Francisco Cantelar Rodriguez, and Manuel Nieto Cumplido, eds. *Catálogo de los manuscriptos e incunables de la Catedral de Córdoba.* 6 vols. Salamanca, 1976.

Garmonsway, G.N., ed. and trans. *The Anglo-Saxon Chronicle.* London, 1972.

Garrad, K. *The Causes of the Second Rebellion of the Alpujarras.* Ph.D. Dissertation, 1955.

Garrido Garrido, José M., ed. *Documentación de la Catedral de Burgos (804–1183). Fuentes medievales castellano-leonesas.* Burgos, 1983.

Gautier de Sibert, Pierre Edme. *Histoire de l'ordre militaire et hospitalier de Saint-Lazare de Jérusalem.* Paris, 1983 (1772).

Gautier-Dalché, J. "La peste noire dans les états de la Couronne d'Aragon." *BH* 64 (1962): 65–80.

——. "Sepúlveda a la fin du Moyen Age; evolution d'une ville castillane de la meseta." *Le Moyen Âge* 69 (1963): 805–828.

Gillmor, Carroll M. "The Introduction of the Traction Trebuchet into the Latin West." *Viator* 12 (1981): 1–8.

Girouard, Mark. *Life in the English Country House. A Social and Architectural History.* Harmondsworth, Eng. 1980.

Glick, Thomas F. *Irrigation and Society in Medieval Valencia.* Cambridge, MA, 1970.

——. *Islamic and Christian Spain in the Early Middle Ages.* Princeton, NJ, 1979.
Godoy Alcántara, José. *Ensayo histórico etimológico filológico sobre los apellidos castellanos.* Barcelona, 1975 (Madrid, 1871).
Goitein, S.D. *A Mediterranean Society: The Jewish Communities of the Arab World as Portrayed in the Documents of the Cairo Geniza.* 5 vols. Berkeley, 1967–1988.
González de Fauve, María Estela. "Testimonios de la crisis del siglo XIV en Aguilar de Campoo." In *Estudios en Homenaje a Don Claudio Sánchez Albornoz en sus 90 Años.* 6 vols. (Buenos Aires, 1986), 4:25–33.
González Mínguez, César. *Fernando IV de Castilla (1295–1312): La guerra civil y el predominio de la nobleza.* Valladolid, 1976.
González Palencia, Angel. *Los mozárabes de Toledo en los siglos XII y XIII.* 4 vols. Madrid, 1926–1930.
——. "Noticias sobre don Raimundo, arzobispo de Toledo." *Spanische Forschungen der Görresgesellschaft* 6 (1937): 90–141.
González, Julio. *Alfonso IX.* Madrid, 1944.
——. *Regesta de Fernando II.* Madrid, 1943.
——. *Reinado y diplomas de Fernando III.* 3 vols. Cordoba, 1980–1986.
——. *El reino de Castilla en la época de Alfonso VIII.* 3 vols. Madrid, 1960.
——. *Repartimiento de Sevilla.* 2 vols. Madrid, 1951.
——. *Repoblación de Castilla la Nueva.* 2 vols. Madrid, 1975.
——. "Sobre la fecha de las Cortes de Nájera." *CHE* 74 (1975): 357–361.
Goñi Gaztambide, José. *Historia de la bula de la cruzada en España.* Vitoria, 1958.
Gorosterratzu, Javier. *Don Rodrigo Jiménez de Rada.* Pamplona, 1925.
Grabois, Aryeh. "Militia and Malitia: The Bernardine Vision of Chivalry." In *The Second Crusade and the Cistercians,* edited by Michael Gervers (New York, 1992), pp. 49–56.
Grassotti, Hilda. "Don Rodrigo Ximénez de Rada, gran señor feudal y hombre de negocios en la Castille." *CHE* 55–56 (1972): 1–302.
Graus, Frantisek. "Au bas Moyen Age: pauvres des villes et pauvres de campagnes." *Annales Economies Societés Civilisations* 16 (1961): 1053–1065.
Grayzel, Solomon. *The Church and the Jews in the XIIIth Century: A Study of Their Relations During the Years 1198–1254, Based on the Papal Letters and the Conciliar Decrees of the Period.* Philadelphia, 1933.
Guichard, Pierre. *Les musulmans de Valence et la reconquête (XIᵉ–XIIIᵉ siècles).* 2 vols. Damascus, 1990–1991.
Guilleré, Christian. *Girona medieval. L'etapa d'apogeu, 1285–1360.* Gerona, 1991.
——. "La Peste Noire a Gérone (1348)." *Annals de l'Institut d'Estudis Gironins* 27 (1984): 87–161.
Guitert y Fontsere, Joaquin. *El real monasterio de Poblet.* Barcelona, 1929.
Gunzberg Moll, Jordi. "Las crisis de mortalidad en la Barcelona del siglo XIV." Boletín de la *Asociación de Demografía Histórica* 7 (1989): 9–35.
Gutton, Francis. *L'Ordre de Calatrava.* Paris, 1955.
Gutton, Jean Pierre. *La société et les pauvres en Europe (XVIᵉ–XVIIIᵉ siècles).* Paris, 1974.
Gyug, Richard Francis, ed. *The Diocese of Barcelona During the Black Death: The Register Notule Communium 15 (1348–1349).* Toronto, 1994.
——. "The Effects and Extent of the Black Death of 1348: New Evidence for Clerical Mortality in Barcelona." *Mediaeval Studies* 45 (1983): 385–98.
Halbertal, Moshe, and Avishai Margalit. *Idolatry.* Translated by Naomi Goldblum. Cambridge, MA, 1992.
Halphen, Louis, and René Poupardin. *Chroniques des Comtes d'Anjou.* Paris, 1913.
Henry of Huntingdon. *Henrici Archidiaconi Huntendunensis Historia Anglorum.* Vol. 74 of *RS.*
Hernández, Francisco. *Los cartularios de Toledo.* Madrid, 1985.
Herrin, Judith. "Women and the Faith in Icons in Early Christianity." In *Culture,*

Ideology and Politics, edited by Raphael Samuel and Gareth Steadman Jones (London, 1983), pp. 56–83.

Hexham, Richard of. *Church Historians of England*. Translated by Joseph Stevenson. London, 1856.

Hicks, Sandy Burton. "The Anglo-Papal Bargain of 1125: The Legatine Mission of John of Crema." *Albion* 8 (1976): 301–310.

———. "The Impact of William Clito Upon the Continental Policies of Henry I of England." *Viator* 10 (1979): 1–21.

Hill, Donald R. "Trebuchets." *Viator* 4 (1973): 99–115.

Hillgarth, Jocelyn Nigel, and Guilio Silan, eds. *The Register "Notule Communium" 14 of the Diocese of Barcelona (1345–1348): A Calendar of Selected Documents*. Toronto, 1983.

Himyari, Abu Abd Allah Muhammad ibn 'Abd Allah. *Kitab al-Rawd al-mi 'tar fi khabar al-aqtar*. Translated by María del Pilar Maestro González. Textos medievales. Valencia, 1963.

Historia Compostelana. Vol. 20 of *ES*, 1–598. Madrid.

The Historians of the Church of York and Its Archbishops. Vol. 71 of *RS*.

The History of the Church of York. Edited by Charles Johnson. Oxford, 1990.

Hollister, C. Warren. *Monarchy, Magnates and Institutions in the Anglo-Norman World*. London, 1986.

Hong, Yang, ed. *Weapons of Ancient China*. New York, 1992.

Huici Miranda, Ambrosio, ed. and trans. *"Al-Hulal al Mawsiyya": Crónica árabe de las dinastias Almoravide, Almohade y Benimerín*. Tetuan, 1951.

———. "Un nuevo manuscrito de 'al-Bayân al-Mugrib'." *Al-Andalus* 24 (1959): 63–84.

Huntington, Richard. *Celebration of Death: The Anthropology of Mortuary Rites*. Cambridge, 1979.

Huuri, Kalevero. "Zur Geschichte des mittelalterlichen Geschützwesens aus orientalischen Quellen." *Societas Orientalia Fennica, Studia Orientalia* 9/3 (Helsinki, 1941).

Idrīsī, Abū Allah al. *Description de l'Afrique et de l'Espagne*. Translated by Reinhart Dozy and M.J. De Goeje. Leiden, 1968 (1866).

Iglesias Fort, Josep. "El fogaje de 1365–1370. Contribución al conocimiento de la población de Cataluña en la segunda mitad del siglo XIV." *Memorias de la Real Academia de Ciencias y Artes de Barcelona* 34 (1962): 249–356.

Iglesias y Fort, Josep. *La reconquista a les valls de l'Anoia i el Gaia, Episodis de la historia*. Barcelona, 1963.

James I. *Llibre dels fets del rei En Jaume*. Edited by Jordi Bruguera. 2 vols. Barcelona, 1991.

Jatïb, Ibn al. *Libro del cuidado de la salud durante las estaciones del año o "libro de higiene"*. Edited and translated by María de la Concepción Vázquez de Benito. Salamanca, 1984.

Jedin, Hubert, and John Dolan, eds. *Handbook of Church History*. 10 vols. New York, 1968.

Jiménez de Rada, Rodrigo. *Historia de rebus hispanie sive historia gothica*. Vol. 72 of *Corpus Christianorum, Continuatio Medievalis*. Edited by Juan Fernández Valverde. Turnholt, 1987.

———. *Historia de los hechos de España*. Translated and with an introduction by Juan Fernández Valverde. Madrid, 1989.

Johnson, C., and H.A. Cronne, eds. *Regesta Regum Anglo Normannorum*. Vol. 2. Oxford, 1956.

Jordan, W.K. *Philanthropy in England 1480–1660. A Study of the Changing Pattern of English Social Aspirations*. New York, 1959.

Junyent, Eduard. *La ciutat de Vic i la seva història*. Barcelona, 1976.

Kagay, Donald J. "The Development of the Cortes in the Crown of Aragon, 1064–1327." Ph.D. Dissertation, Fordham University. 1981.

———. *The Usatges of Barcelona*. Philadelphia, 1994.

Kantorowicz, Ernst. "Mysteries of State. An Absolutist Concept and Its Late Medieval Origins." In *Selected Studies*, Locust Valley, NY, 1965.

——. "Pro Patria Mori in Medieval Political Thought." In *Selected Studies*, Locust Valley, NY, 1965.

Kārdabus, Abu Marwan Ibn al. *Historial del Andalus (España Musulmana)*. Translated by Margarita La-Chica Garrido. Universidad de Alicante 6. Alicante, 1984.

Katz, Jacob. *Exclusiveness and Tolerance: Studies in Jewish-Gentile Relations in Medieval and Modern Times*. Oxford, 1961; reprint ed., New York, n.d.

Kern, Hanspeter. "La peste negra y su influjo en la provisión de los beneficios eclesiásticos." In *VIII Congreso de Historia de la Corona de Aragón*. 2 vols. (Valencia, 1967), 2:71–83.

King, D.J.C. "The Trebuchet and other Siege-Engines." *Chateau Gaillard* 9–10 (1982): 457–469.

Köhler, Gustav. *Die Entwickelung des Kriegwesens und der Kriegführung in der Ritterzeit von Mitte des II. Jahrhunderts bis zu den Hussitenkriegen*. 5 vols. in 4. Breslau, 1886–1889.

Küchler, Winifred. "La influencia de la peste negra sobre la Hacienca Real." In *VIII Congreso de Historia de la Corona de Aragón*. 2 vols. (Valencia, 1967), 2:65–70.

Lacarra, José María. *Alfonso el Batallador*. Zaragoza, 1978.

Ladero Quesada, Miguel Angel. *Los primeros europeos en Canarias (Siglos XVI y XV)*. Las Palmas de Gran Canaria, 1979.

Lafuente, Vicente de. *Historia ecclesiastica de España*. 6 vols. Madrid, 1873–1875.

Laiou, Angeliki. *Consent and Coercion to Sex and Marriage in Ancient and Medieval Societies*. Washington, 1993.

Le Goff, Jacques. *The Birth of Purgatory*. Translated by Arthur Goldhammer. Chicago, 1984.

Lea, Henry Charles. *History of Sacerdotal Celibacy in the Christian Church*. New Hyde Park, NY, 1966.

LeClercq, Jean. "Un document sur les débuts des Templiers." *Revue d'Histoire Ecclesiastique* 52 (1957): 81–91.

Lerner, Robert E. "Literacy and Learning." In *One Thousand Years: Western Europe in the Middle Ages*, edited by Richard L. DeMolen (Boston, 1974), pp. 165–233.

Levi-Provençal, Évariste. *Histoire de l'Espagne musulmane, 711–1031*. 3 vols. Paris, 1950–1953.

——. *La peninsule iberique au Moyen Age*. Leiden, 1938 (1934).

Levine, Kenneth. *The Social Context of Literacy*. London, 1986.

Lewis, Archibald. *The Development of Southern French and Catalan Society, 718–1050*. Austin, 1965.

Libro de Apolonio. Madrid, 1982.

Linehan, Peter. *History and the Historians of Medieval Spain*. Oxford, 1993.

——. *The Spanish Church and the Papacy in the Thirteenth Century*. Cambridge, 1971.

Loaysa, Jofré de. *Crónica de los Reyes de Castilla, Fernando III, Alfonso X, Sancho IV y Fernando IV, 1284–1305*. Translated and edited by Antonio García Martínez. Murcia, 1982 (1961).

Lomax, Derek W. *Las ordenes militares en la peninsula iberica durante la edad media*. Salamanca, 1976.

——. *La Orden de Santiago (1170–1275)*. Madrid, 1965.

——. *The Reconquest of Spain*. New York, 1978.

Loperráez Corvalán, Juan. *Descripción histórica de obispado de Osma*. 3 vols. Madrid, 1781.

López Agurleta, José. *Vida del venerable fundador de la orden de Santiago, y de las primeras casas de redempción de cautivos*. Madrid, 1731.

López Alónso, Carmen. *La pobreza en la España medieval. Estudio histórico social*. Madrid, 1986.

———. *Los rostros, la realidad de la pobreza en la sociedad castellana medieval (siglos XIII–XV)*. Madrid, 1983.

López de Menese, Amada. "Documentos acerca de la peste negra en la Corona de Aragón." *Estudios de Edad Media de la Corona de Aragón* 6 (1956): 291–447.

———. "Una consecuencia de la peste negra en Cataluña: el 'pogrom' de 1348." *Sefarad* 19 (1959): 92–131.

———. "La peste negra en Cerdeña." In *Homenaje a Jaime Vicens Vives*, vol. 1, 533–542. Barcelona, 1967.

———. "La peste negra en Las Islas Baleares." In *VI Congreso de Historia de la Corona de Aragón*, 331–44. Madrid, 1959.

López, Emilio Molina. "La obra histórica de Ibn Játima de Almería y algunos datos más en su Tratado de Peste." *Al-Qantara* 10 (1989): 151–173.

Lourie, Elena. "A Society Organized for War: Medieval Spain." *Past and Present* 35 (1966): 54–76.

———. "The Will of Alfonso I 'El Batallador', King of Aragon and Navarre: A Reassessment." *Speculum* 50 (1975): 635–651.

Luchaire, Achille. *Louis VI Le Gros, Annales de sa vie et de son Régne (1081–1137)*. Paris, 1890.

Luttrell, Anthony. "Los hospitalarios en Aragón y la peste negra." *AEM* 3 (1966): 499–514.

MacKay, Angus. *Spain in the Middle Ages: From Frontier to Empire, 1000–1500*. London, 1977.

Mansi, J.D. *Sacrorum consiliorum nova et amplissima collectio*. 31 vols. Florence and Venice, 1759–1798.

Mansilla, Demetrio. *Iglesia castellano-leonesa y curia romano en los tiempos del rey San Fernando*. Madrid, 1945.

Marks, Geoffrey. *The Medieval Plague: The Black Death of the Middle Ages*. Garden City, NY, 1971.

Marongiu, Antonio. *Medieval Parliaments*. Translated by S.J. Woolf. London, 1968.

Martín, José Luis. *Orígenes de la orden militar de Santiago*. Barcelona, 1974.

Martínez García, Luis. *La asistencia a los pobres en Burgos en la baja edad media. El hospital de Santa María la Real, 1341–1500*. Burgos, 1981.

———. "La asistencia material en los hospitales de Burgos a fines de la Edad Media." In *Manger et boire au Moyen Age. Actes du colloque de Nice*, 2 vols. (Nice, 1984), 1:335–347.

Martínez Ortiz, José. "Una víctima de la peste, la reina doña Leonor." In *VIII Congreso de Historia de la Corona de Aragón*. 2 vols. (Valencia, 1967), 2:9–25.

Martz, Linda. *Poverty and Welfare in Habsburg Spain. The Example of Toledo*. Cambridge, 1983.

Maya Sánchez, Antonio, ed. *Chronica Adefonsi Imperatoris*. Vol. 71 of *Corpus Christianorum Continuatio Mediaevalis*. Turnholt, 1990.

McCrank, Lawrence J. "La anatomía fiscal del periodo de post-restauración de la iglesia de Tarragona: Una revisión de las rationes decimarum hispaniae (1279–1280)." *Hispania* 35 (1985): 245–298.

———. "The Cistercians of Poblet as Landlords: Protection, Litigation, and Violence on the Medieval Catalan Frontier." *Cîteaux: Commentari Cistercienses* 26 (1975): 255–283.

———. "Documenting Reconquest and Reform: The Growth of Archives in the Medieval Crown of Aragón." *The American Archivist* 56 (1993): 256–318.

———. "The Foundation of the Confraternity of Tarragona by Archbishop Oleguer Bonestruga." *Viator* 9 (1978): 157–177.

———. *Frontier History in Medieval Catalonia*. London, 1996.

———. "The Frontier of the Spanish Reconquest and the Land Acquisitions of Poblet, 1150–1276." *Analecta Cisterciensia* 29 (1973): 57–68.

———. "A Medieval 'Information Age': Documentation and Archives in the Crown of Aragón." *Primary Sources and Original Works* 2 (1993): 19–102.
———. "Monastic Inland Empires and the Mediterranean Coastal Reconquest in New Catalonia, 1050–1276." In *Spain and the Mediterranean*, edited by Benjamin F. Taggie, Richard W. Clement, and James E. Caraway (Kirksville, MO, 1992), pp. 21–34.
———. "Norman Intervention in the Catalan Reconquest: Robert Burdet and the Principality of Tarragona, 1129–1155." *Journal of Medieval History* 7 (1981): 67–82.
———. "La restauración eclesiastica y reconquista en la Cataluña del siglo XI: Ramon Berenguer I y la sede de Tarragona." *Analecta Sacra Tarraconensia* 80 (1980): 5–39.
———. *Restoration and Reconquest in Medieval Catalonia: The Church and Principality of Tarragona*. Ph.D. Dissertation, University of Virginia. 2 vols. 1974.
McKitterick, Rosamond. *The Carolingians and the Written Word*. Cambridge, 1989.
McLaughlin, Terence P., ed. *The Summa Parisiensis on the Decretum of Gratian*. Toronto, 1952.
McNeill, William Hardy. *Plagues and Peoples*. Garden City, NY, 1976.
McVaugh, Michael R. *Medicine Before the Plague: Practioners and Their Patients in the Crown of Aragon, 1285–1345*. Cambridge, 1993.
Melechen, Nina. "The Aljama of Tudela during the Navarrese Civil War." In *Medieval Iberia: Essays on the History and Literature of Medieval Spain*, edited by Donald J. Kagay and Joseph T. Snow (New York, 1997), pp. 189–200.
Mercer, John. *The Canary Islanders: Their Prehistory, Conquest, and Survival*. London, 1980.
Mesmin, Simone C. "Waleran, Count of Meulan and the Leper Hospital of S. Gilles de Pont-Audemer." *Annales de Normandie* 32 (1982): 3–19.
Millás Vallicrosa, J.M. "Epigrafia hebraico-española." *Sefarad* 5 (1945): 285–320.
Mitre Fernández, Emilio. "Algunas cuestiones demográficas en la Castilla de fines del siglo XIV." *AEM* 7 (1970–1971): 615–622.
Moeller, Charles. "Lazarus, Saint, Order Of." In *The Catholic Encyclopedia*, 9:96–97. New York, 1910.
Mollat, M. "Pauvres et assistés au moyen âge." In *A pobreza*, 1:26–27.
———. *Les pauvres au Moyen Age*. Paris, 1978.
Monfor y Sors, Diego. *Historia de los condes de Urgel*. Vols. 9–10 of *Colección de documentos inéditos del Archivo General de la Corona de Aragón*. Edited by Prospero Bofarull y Moscaró. Barcelona, 1850–1856.
Monserrat, M. Grau. "La peste negra en Morella." *Boletín de la Sociedad Castellonense de Cultura* 46 (1970): 148–160.
Monterde Albiac, Cristina. *Colección diplomática del monasterio de Fitero (1140–1210)*. Zaragoza, 1978.
Moreno Koch, Yolanda, ed. and trans. *Fontes iudaeorum regni Castellae*. Carlos Carrete Parrondo gen. ed. Vol. 5. *De iure hispano-hebraico. Las Taqqanot de Valladolid de 1432: un estatuto comunal renovador*. Salamanca, 1987.
Morera y Llaurado, Emilio. *Tarragona cristiana: Historia del arzobispado de Tarragona*, 2 vols. (Tarragona, 1899).
Müller, Marcus Joseph. "Ibnulkhatîbs Bericht über die Pest." *Sitzungsberichte der Königlich Bayerische Akademie der Wissenschaften* 2 (1863): 1–34.
Mundy, John H. "Charity and Social Work in Toulouse, 1100–1250." *Traditio* 22 (1966): 227–230.
Muntaner, Ramon. *The Chronicle of Muntaner*. Translated by Lady Henrietta Goodenough. 2 vols. Hakluyt Society Publications, Series 2, nos. 47, 50. London, 1920–1921.
Mutel, André. "Recherches sur l'ordre de Saint-Lazare de Jérusalem en Normandie." *Annales de Normandie* 33 (1983): 121–142.
Myers, A.R. *Parliaments and Estates in Europe to 1789*. New York, 1975.

Needham, Joseph. "China's Trebuchets, Manned and Counterweighted." In *On Pre-Modern Technology and Science: Studies in Honor of Lynn White, Jr.*, edited by Bert S. Hall and Delno C. West (Malibu, CA, 1976), pp. 107–145.

Needham, Joseph and Robin D.S. Yates. *Science and Civilisation in China*, vol. 5, *Chemistry and Chemical Technology*, pt. 6, *Military Technology: Missiles and Sieges*. Cambridge, 1994.

Nelson, Lynn H., trans. *The Chronicle of San Juan de la Peña: A Fourteenth-Century Official History of the Crown of Aragon*. Philadelphia, 1991.

Nicholas, David. *Medieval Flanders*. London, 1992.

Nicholl, Donald. *Thurstan, Archbishop of York (1114–1140)*. York, 1964.

Nieto Soria, José Manuel. *Las relaciónes monarquia-epsicopado castellano como sistema de poder 1252–1312*. 2 vols. Madrid, 1983.

Noonan, John T. "Power to Choose." *Viator* 4 (1973): 419–434.

Núñez de Villazan, Juan. *Crónica de don Alfonso el Onceno*. Edited by Francisco Cerda y Rico. Madrid, 1787.

O'Callaghan, Joseph F. "The Affiliation of the Order of Calatrava with the Order of Cîteaux." *Analecta Sacri Ordinis Cisterciensis* 15 (1959): 161–193; 16 (1960): 3–59, 255–292.

——. "Las cortes de Fernando IV: Cuadernos inéditos de Valladolid 1300 y Burgos 1308." *Historia, Instituciones, Documentos* 13 (1987): 315–328.

——. *The Cortes of Castile-León 1188–1350*. Philadelphia, 1989.

——. "The Ecclesiastical Estate in the Cortes of León-Castile, 1252–1350." *CHR* 67 (1981): 185–231.

——. *A History of Medieval Spain*. Ithaca, NY, 1975.

——. *The Learned King: The Reign of Alfonso X of Castile*. Philadelphia, 1993.

——. "The Mudejars of Castile and Portugal in the Twelfth and Thirteenth Centuries." In *Muslims Under Latin Rule, 1100–1300*, edited by James M. Powell (Princeton, NJ, 1990), pp. 11–56.

——. "The Order of Calatrava and the Archbishops of Toledo 1147–1242." In *The Spanish Military Order of Calatrava and Its Affiliates*. London, 1975.

Oderic Vitalis. *The Ecclesiastical History of Orderic Vitalis*. Edited and translated by Marjorie Chibnall. 6 vols. Oxford, 1969–1980.

Ong, Walter J. *Orality and Literacy: The Technologizing of the Word*. London, 1986.

Ortega y Cotes, Ignatio Josef de. *Bulario de la Orden Militar de Calatrava*. Facsimile edition. Barcelona, 1981 (Madrid, 1761).

Otto of Freising. *The Two Cities: A Chronicle of Universal History to the Year 1146 AD*. Edited and translated by Christopher Mierow. New York, 1966.

Ozment, Steven. *The Age of Reform 1250–1550*. New Haven, 1980.

Painter, Sidney. "Castle-Guard." *AHR* (1935): 450–459.

Palau y Dulcet, Antoni. *La conca de Barbera: Monografía histórica y descriptiva*. Barcelona, 1912.

Peguera, Lúis. *Practica, forma, y estila de celebrar corts generals en Catalunya*. Barcelona, 1701.

Pere III of Catalonia. *Chronicle*. Translated by M. Hillgarth and J.N. Hillgarth. 2 vols. Toronto, 1980.

Pereda Llarena, F. Javier. *Documentación de la catedral de Burgos (1254–1293)*. Burgos, 1984.

Pérez Bustamante, Rogelio, ed. *El registro notarial de Dueñas*. Palencia, 1985.

Pérez de Herrera, Cristobal. *Amparo de pobres*. With an introduction by Michael Cavillac. Madrid, 1975.

Pérez Embid, Florentino. *Los descubrimientos en el Atlántico y la rivalidad castellano-portuguesa hasta el Tratado de Tordesillas*. Seville, 1948.

Pérez Moreda, Vicente, and David S. Reher, eds. *Demografía histórica en España*. Madrid, 1988.

Pérez Santamaría, Aurora. "El hospital de Sant Lázaro o Casa dels Malats o

Maselles." In *La pobreza y la asistencia a los pobres en la Cataluña medieval*, edited by Manuel Riu (Barcelona, 1980–1982), 1:77–115.

Pérez Tudela y Velasco, María Isabel. *Infanzones y caballeros: su proyección en la esfera nobiliaria castellano-leonesa (s. IX–XIII)*. Madrid, 1979.

Piskorski, Wladimiro. *Las cortes de Castilla en el periodo de transito de la Edad Media a la moderna, 1188–1520*. Barcelona, 1977.

Pons d'Icart, Luis. *Libro de las grandozas y cosas memorables de la metropolitana, insigne y famosa ciudad de Tarragona*. Lerida, 1883 (1572).

Pons i Marques, J. *Cartulari de Poblet: Edicio del manuscrit de Tarragona*. Barcelona, 1938.

Porres Martín-Cleto, Julio. "Los barrios judíos de Toledo." In *Simposio "Toledo judaico" (Toledo 20–22 Abril 1972)*. Simposio Medieval, 2nd, Toledo, Spain, 1972, 1:45–76. (Toledo, [1973].)

Potter, K.R., ed. and trans. *Gesta Stephani*. Revised by R.H.C Davis. Oxford, 1976.

Powers, Joseph M. *Eucharistic Theology*. New York, 1967.

Procter, Evelyn S. *Curia and Cortes in León and Castile 1072–1295*. Cambridge, 1980.

———. "The Development of the Catalan Corts in the Thirteenth Century." *Estudis Universitaris Catalans* 22 (1936): 525–546.

Rades y Andrada, Francisco de. *Crónica de las tres Ordenes y Caballerías de Santiago, Calatrava y Alcántara*. Facsimilie edition. Barcelona, 1980 (Toledo, 1572).

Rassow, Peter. "La Cofradía de Belchite." *AHDE* 3 (1926): 200–226.

Rathgen, Bernhard. *Das Geschütz im Mittelalter*. Düsseldorf, 1987 (1928).

Rau, Virginia. "Para o estudo da peste negra em Portugal." In *Actas do Congresso Histórico de Portugal Medievo. Guia Oficial en Bracara Augusta 14–15* (Braga, 1963), pp. 210–239.

———. Sesmarias medievais portuguesas. Lisbon, 1982.

Real Academia de la Historia. *Cortes de los antiguos reinos de León y de Castilla*. 5 vols. Madrid, 1861–1903.

Recasens i Comes, Josep María. *La ciutat de Tarragona*. 2 vols. Barcelona, 1975.

Les registres de Nicholas III (1277–1280). Edited by Jules Gay. Paris, 1938.

Regularis concordia. Anglicae nationis monachorum sanctimonialiumque. Translated by Thomas Symons. London, 1953.

Reilly, Bernard F. *The Contest of Christian and Muslim Spain 1031–1157*. Oxford, 1992.

Richardson, H.G., and G.O. Sayles. *Parliaments and Great Councils in Medieval England*. London, 1961.

Rivera Garretas, Milagros. *La encomienda, el priorato y la villa de Uclés en la Edad Media*. Madrid, 1985.

Rivera Recio, Juan Francisco. *La iglesia de Toledo en el siglo XII*. 2 vols. Rome, 1976.

Robert of Torigny. *Chronicle*. Vol. 82 of *RS*.

Rödel, W.G. "San Lazzaro, di Gerusalemme." In *Dizionario degli istituti di perfezione*, 8:579. Rome, 1974–.

Rodríguez, Honorio Alonso. *Algo sobre la fundación de la Orden de Calatrava*. Barcelona, 1917.

Rogers, R. *Latin Siege Warfare in the Twelfth Century*. Oxford, 1992.

Romano, David. "Otros casamenteros judíos (Barcelona-Gerona 1357)." *Estudios Históricos y Documentos de los Archivos de Protocolos* 5 (1977): 299–301.

Rosenthal, Joel T. *The Purchase of Paradise. Gift Giving and the Aristocracy, 1307–1485*. London, 1972.

Roth, Norman. "New Light on the Jews of Mozarabic Toledo." *AJS Review* 11 (1986): 189–220.

Round, J.H. *Calendar of Documents Preserved in France Illustrative of the History of Great Britain and Ireland, Vol. I, 918–1206*. London, 1899.

Rubio Vela, Agustín. "La ciudad de Valencia en 1348: la peste negra." *Primer Congreso de Historia del País Valenciano* 3 (1980): 519–26.

Rucquoi, Adeline. *Valladolid en la edad media*. 2 vols. Valladolid, 1987.

Rufinus. *Summa decretorum*. Edited by Heinrich Singer. Aalen, 1963 (1902).

Ruiz, Juan. *Libro de buen amor*. 2nd ed. Valencia, 1960.

Ruiz, Teofilo F. *Crisis and Continuity. Land and Town in Late Medieval Castile*. Philadelphia, 1994.

——. "Expansion et changement: La conquête de Seville et la société castillane (1248–1350)." *Annales Economies Societés Civilisations* 3 (1979): 548–565.

——. "Une royaute sans sacre: La monarchie castillane du bas Moyen Age." *Annales Economies Societés Civilisations* 3 (1984): 429–453.

——. "The Transformation of the Castilian Municipalities: The Case of Burgos 1248–1350." *Past & Present* 77 (1977): 3–32.

Rumeu de Armas, Antonio. *España en el Africa atlántica*. 2 vols. Madrid, 1956.

——. *Historia de la previsión social en España. Cofradias, gremios, hermandades, montepíos*. Madrid, 1944.

Runcieman, Steven. *A History of the Crusades*. 3 vols. London, 1952.

Russell, Josiah Cox. "The Effect of Pestilence and Plague, 1315–1385." *Comparative Studies in Society & History* 8 (1966): 463–473.

Saenger, Paul. "Literacy, Western European." In *Dictionary of the Middle Ages*, edited by Joseph R. Strayer and et al. 13 vols. (New York, 1982–1989), 7:600–601.

——. *Concilios provinciales y Sinodos toledanos de los siglos XIV y XV: la religiosidad cristiana del clero y pueblo*. La Laguna, Tenerife, 1976.

Sánchez-Albornoz, Claudio. *Spain, a Historical Enigma*. Translated by Colette July Dees and David Sven Reher. 2 vols. Madrid, 1975.

Sandoval, Prudencio de. *Antigüedad de la ciudad y iglesia catedral de Túy*. Barcelona, 1974 (1610).

Santacana Tort, Jaime. *El monasterio de Poblet 1151–1181*. Barcelona, 1974.

Santamaría Arández, Alvaro. "Mallorca en el siglo XIV." *AEM* 7 (1970–1971): 165–238.

——. "Peste negra en Mallorca." In *VIII Congreso de Historia de la Corona de Aragón*. 2 vols. (Valencia, 1967), 2:103–130.

Sayles, George O. *The King's Parliament of England*. New York, 1974.

Schneider, Rudolf. *Die Artillerie des Mittelalters*. Berlin, 1910.

Serrano, Luciano, ed. *Fuentes para la historia de Castilla*. 3 vols. Valladolid, 1906–1910.

Shatzmiller, Joseph. *Shylock Reconsidered: Jews, Moneylending, and Medieval Society*. Berkeley, 1990.

Sheehan, Michael M. "Choice of Marriage Partner in the Middle Ages: Development and Mode of Application of a Theory of Marriage." *Studies in Medieval and Renaissance History* n.s. 1 (1978): 3–33.

Shirk, Melanie. "The Black Death in Aragon, 1348–1351." *Journal of Medieval History* 7 (1981): 357–367.

——. "Violence and the Plague in Aragon, 1348–1351." *Journal of the Rocky Mountain Medieval and Renaissance Association* 5 (1984): 31–39.

Skoljar, Sergej A. "L'Artillerie de jet a l'époque Sung." *Etudes Song*, series 1, *Histoire et institutions* (Paris, 1978), 119–142.

Silva, Victor Deodato da. *A legislaçao económica e social consecutiva á Peste Negra de 1348 e sua significaçao no contexto da depressao do fim da Idade Média*. Sao Paulo, 1976.

Simeon of Durham. *Historia Regum*. Vol. 75 of *RS*.

Smith, Robert Sidney. "Fourteenth-Century Population Records of Catalonia." *Speculum* 19 (1944): 494–501.

Sobrequés Callicó, Jaime. "La peste negra en la Península Ibérica." *AEM* 7 (1970–1971): 67–102.

Solano, Emma. *La Orden de Calatrava en el siglo xv: los señorios castellanos de la orden al fin de la edad media*. Seville, 1978.

Southern, Richard W. "Lanfranc of Bec and Berengar of Tours." In *Studies in Medieval History Presented to Frederick Maurice Powicke*, edited by R.W. Hunt, W.A. Pantin, and R.W. Southern (Oxford, 1948), pp. 27–48.

Stenton, Frank. *The First Century of English Feudalism, 1066–1166.* Oxford, 1961.

Stock, Brian. *The Implications of Literacy: Written Language and Models of Interpretation in the Eleventh and Twelfth Centuries.* Princeton, NJ, 1983.

Strayer, Joseph R. *On the Medieval Origins of the Modern State.* Princeton, NJ, 1970.

Suárez Fernández, Luis. "Evolutión histórica de hermandades castellanos." *CHE* 16 (1951): 5–78.

Suger. *De rebus in administratione sua gestis*, in *Oeuvres complétes de Suger.* Edited by A. Lecoy de la Marche. Paris, 1867.

——. *Vie de Louis VI Le Gros.* Edited and translated by Henry Waquet. Paris, 1964.

Tabuteau, Emily Z. "The Role of Law in the Succession to Normandy and England, 1087." *The Haskins Society Journal* 3 (1991): 155–169.

Tarragó i Valentines, Josep F. *Hospitales en Lérida durante los siglos XII al XVI.* Lérida, 1975.

Tejada y Ramiro, J. *Colección de canones y de todos los concilios de iglesia de España y de America.* 7 vols. Madrid, 1849–1862.

Thaner, Friedrich, ed. *De Summa Magistri Rolandi.* Innsbruck, 1874.

Thrupp, Sylvia. "Plague Effects in Medieval Europe." *Comparative Studies in Society and History* 8 (1966): 474–483.

Tierney, Brian. *The Crisis of Church and State 1050–1300.* Engelwood Cliffs, NJ, 1964.

Tilander, Gunnar. *Fueros aragoneses desconocidos promulgados a consecuencia de la gran peste de 1348.* Vol. 9 of *Leges hispanicae medii aevi.* Stockholm, 1959.

Tomich, Pere. *Històries e conquestes dels Reys d'Aragó e Comtes de Catalunya. Reprint. Textos Medievales.* Valencia (Barcelona), 1970 (1534).

Torres Balbás, Leopoldo. "Extensión y demografia de los ciudades hispanomusulmanas." *Studia Islamica* 3 (1955).

Torres Fontes, Juan. *De historia médica Murciana. I. Las Epidemias.* Murcia, 1981.

——. "El Obispado de Cartagena en el siglo XIII." *Hispania* 13 (1953): 339–401, 515–580.

——. "Tres epidemias de peste ne Murcia en el siglo XIV." *Anales de la Universidad de Murcia. Medicina* 1 (1977): 123–161.

Trenchs Odena, José. "La archidiócesis de Tarragona y la peste negra: los cargos de la catedral." In *VIII Congreso de Historia de la Corona de Aragón.* 2 vols. (Valencia, 1967), 2:45–64.

——. "La diócesis de Zaragoza y la peste de 1348." Instituto Jerónimo de Zurita. *Cuadernos de Historia* 25–26 (1973): 119–140.

——. "Documentos pontificios sobre la peste negra en la diócesis de Gerona." *Cuadernos de trabajos de la escuela española de historia y arqueología en Roma* 14 (1980): 183–230.

Twigg, Graham. *The Black Death: A Biological Reappraisal.* New York, 1985.

Ubieto Arteta, Antonio. *Colección diplomática de Cuéllar.* Segovia, 1961.

——. "La creación de la cofradía militar de Belchite." *Estudios de Edad Media de la Corona de Aragón* 5 (1952): 427–434.

——. "Cronología del desarrollo de la Pesta Negra en la peninsula ibérica." In *Estudios sobre el Reino de Valencia*, vol. 5 of *Cuadernos de Historia: Anexos de la Revista Hispania* (Madrid, 1975), pp. 47–66.

——. *Orígenes del reino de Valencia: cuestiones cronológicas sobre su conquista.* Valencia, 1979 (1977).

Udina Martorell, Federico. *Guia historica y descriptiva del Archivo de la Corona de Aragón.* Madrid, 1986.

Uhagón y Guardamino, Francisco de. "Indice de los documentos de la Orden Militar de Calatrava." *BRAH* 35 (1899): 5–167.

Vaca, Angel. "Una manifestación de la crisis castellana del siglo XIV: La caída de las rentas de los señores feudales." *Studia Historica. Historia Medieval Salamanca* 1 (1983): 157–166.

Valdeón Baruque, Julio. "La Peste Negra: La muerte negra en la península. El impacto de la peste." *Historia* 16 (1980): 60–71.

——. "Aspectos de la crisis castellana en el primera mitad del siglo XIV." *Hispania* 29 (1969): 5–24.

——. "Reflexiones sobre la crisis bajomedieval en Castilla." *En la España Medieval* 4 (1984): 1047–1066.

Vallespinosa, Juan, ed. *Collectio de manuscrits inedits de monjos del Real Monestir de Santa María de Poblet.* Edited by Joaquin Guitert i Fontsere. Barcelona, 1947–1948.

Vann, Theresa M. "Lay and Ecclesiastical Encounters in the Medieval Castilian Frontier." In *Iberia and the Mediterranean World of the Middle Ages: Essays in Honor of Robert I. Burns, S.J.*, vol. 2, edited by P.E. Chevedden, D.J. Kagay, and P.G. Padilla (Leiden, 1996), pp. 201–220.

Verlinden, Charles. "La grande peste de 1348 en Espagne: Contribution à la étude de ses conséquences économoques et sociales." *Revue Belge de Philologie et Histoire* 17 (1938): 103–146.

Villaró, Albert. "La Pesta Negra, el 1348, a la Seu d'Urgell." *Urgellia* 8 (1986–1987): 281–282.

Viollet-le-Duc, E.N.L. *Dictionnaire raisonné de l'architecture du XIe au XVIe siècles.* 10 vols. Paris, 1854–1868.

von Schulte, J.F., ed. *Die Summa des Paucapalea über das Decretum Gratiani.* Giessen, 1890.

Webster, Jill R. *Els Menorets: The Franciscans in the Realms of Aragon From St. Francis to the Black Death.* Toronto, 1993.

——. "La reina doña Constanza y los hospitales de Barcelona y Valencia." *Archivo Ibero-Americano* 51 (1991): 375–390.

Weigand, Rudolf. "Paucapalea und die frühe Kanonistik." *Archiv für katholisches Kirchenrecht* 150 (1981): 137–157.

Wieruskowski, Helene. "The Rise of the Catalan Language in the Thirteenth Century." In *Politics and Culture in Medieval Spain and Italy, Storia e Litteratura, Raccolta de Studi e Testi* (Rome, 1971 (1944)), pp. 107–118.

William of Malmesbury. *Gesta Regum Anglorum.* London, 1964.

——. *The Historia Novella by William of Malmesbury.* Edited and translated by K.R. Potter. London, 1955.

William of Newburgh. *The History of English Affairs, Book I.* Edited and translated by P.G. Walsh and M.J. Kennedy. Warminster, 1988.

Williman, Daniel, ed. *The Black Death: The Impact of the Fourteenth-Century Plague.* Binghamton, NY, 1982.

Yates, Robin D.S. "Siege Engines and Late Zhou Military Technology." In *Explorations in the History of Science and Technology in China*, edited by Li Guohao, Zhang Mehgwen, and Cao Tianqin (Shanghai, 1982), pp. 414–419.

Yule, Henry, ed. *The Book of Ser Marco Polo, the Venetian Concerning the Kingdoms and Marvels of the East.* 3rd edition, 3 vols. London, 1926.

Ziegler, Philip. *The Black Death.* New York, 1969.

Zuñiga, Giuseppe de. *Epitome historica dell'illustrissima religione et inclita cavalleria de Calatrava.* Lecce, 1669.

Zurita, Jerónimo. *Anales de la Corona de Aragón.* Edited by Angel Canellas López. 2 vols. Zaragoza, 1967 (1562).

INDEX

THE

MEDIEVAL MEDITERRANEAN

PEOPLES, ECONOMIES AND CULTURES, 400-1453

Editors: Michael Whitby (Warwick), Paul Magdalino, Hugh Kennedy (St. Andrews), David Abulafia (Cambridge), Benjamin Arbel (Tel Aviv), Mark Meyerson (Notre Dame).

This series provides a forum for the publication of scholarly work relating to the interactions of peoples and cultures in the Mediterranean basin and the Black Sea area and is intended for readers with interest in late antiquity, the Middle Ages (Italy, Spain, the Latin East), Byzantium, Islam, the Balkans and the Black Sea. Manuscripts (in English, German and French) should be 60,000 to 120,000 words in length and may include illustrations. The editors would be particularly interested to receive proposals for monograph studies; studies with texts; editions with parallel translations of texts or collections of documents; or translations provided with full annotation.

1. Shatzmiller, M. (ed.), *Crusaders and Muslims in Twelfth-Century Syria*. 1993. ISBN 90 04 09777 5
2. Tsougarakis, D., *The Life of Leontios, Patriarch of Jerusalem*. Text, Translation, Commentary. 1993. ISBN 90 04 09827 5
3. Takayama, H., *The Administration of the Norman Kingdom of Sicily*. 1993. ISBN 90 04 09865 8
4. Simon, L.J. (ed.), *Iberia and the Mediterranean World of the Middle Ages*. Studies in Honor of Robert I. Burns S.J. Vol. 1. Proceedings from Kalamazoo. 1995. ISBN 90 04 10168 3
5. Stöckly, D. *Le système de l'Incanto des galées du marché à Venise (fin XIIIe- milieu XVe siècle*. 1995. 90 04 10002 4.
6. Estow, C., *Pedro the Cruel of Castile, 1350-1369*. 1995. ISBN 90 04 10094 6
7. Stalls, W.C., *Possessing the Land*. Aragon's Expansion into Islam's Ebro Frontier under Alfonso the Battler, 1104-1134. 1995. ISBN 90 04 10367 8
8. Chevedden, P.E., D.J. Kagay & P.G. Padilla (eds.), *Iberia and the Mediterranean World of the Middle Ages*. Essays in Honor of Robert I. Burns S.J. Vol. 2. Proceedings from 'Spain and the Western Mediterranean', a Colloquium Sponsored by *The Center for Medieval and Renaissance Studies*, University of California, Los Angeles, October 26-27, 1992. 1996. ISBN 90 04 10573 5
9. Lev, Y. (ed.), *War and Society in the Eastern Mediterranean, 7th-15th Centuries*. 1997. ISBN 90 04 10032 6
10. Ciggaar, K.N., *Western Travellers to Constantinople*. The West and Byzantium, 962-1204: Cultural and Political Relations. 1996. ISBN 90 04 10637 5
11. Skinner, P., *Health and Medicine in Early Medieval Southern Italy*. 1997. ISBN 90 04 10394 5

12. Parry, K., *Depicting the Word*. Byzantine Iconophile Thought of the Eighth and Ninth Centuries. 1996. ISBN 90 04 10502 6
13. Crisafulli, V.S. & J.W. Nesbitt, *The Miracles of St. Artemios*. A Collection of Miracle Stories by an Anonymous Author of Seventh-Century Byzantium. 1997. ISBN 90 04 10574 3
14. Antonopoulou, T., *The Homilies of the Emperor Leo VI*. 1997. ISBN 90 04 10814 9
15. Tougher, S., *The Reign of Leo VI (886-912)*. Politics and People. 1997. ISBN 90 04 10811 4
16. O'Callaghan, J.F., *Alfonso X and the* Cantigas de Santa Maria. A Poetic Biography. 1998. ISBN 90 04 11023 2
17. Gilmour-Bryson, A., *The Trial of the Templars in Cyprus*. A Complete English Edition. 1998. ISBN 90 04 10080 6
18. Reyerson, K. & J. Drendel (eds.), *Urban and Rural Communities in Medieval France*. Provence and Languedoc, 1000-1500. 1998. ISBN 90 04 10850 5
19. Kagay, D.J. & T.M. Vann (eds.). *On the Social Origins of Medieval Institutions*. Essays in Honor of Joseph F. O'Callaghan. 1998. ISBN 90 04 11096 8